SEX DIFFERENCES IN COGNITIVE ABILITIES

2nd Edition

DIANE F. HALPERN
*California State University,
San Bernardino*

LAWRENCE ERLBAUM ASSOCIATES, PUBLISHERS
1992   Hillsdale, New Jersey   Hove and London

Lawrence Erlbaum Associates, Inc., Publishers
365 Broadway
Hillsdale, New Jersey 07642

Library of Congress Cataloging-in-Publication Data
Halpern, Diane F.
    Sex differences in cognitive abilities / Diane F. Halpern. — 2nd
ed.
        p.   .cm.
    Includes bibliographical references (p.   ) and indexes.
    ISBN 0-8058-0844-2. — ISBN 0-8058-0845-0 (pbk.)
    1. Cognition.   2. Sex differences (Psychology)   3. Sex role.
I. Title.
BF311.H295   1992
155.3'3—dc20
                                                                            91-30966
                                                                               CIP

Printed in the United States of America
10 9 8 7 6 5 4 3

Contents

This book is dedicated to the loving memory of

Aaron Jay Silverstein

Aaron's life was tragically cut short
soon after his 25th birthday
in an alcohol-related accident.

Preface to the Second Edition

It seems that everyone has strong opinions about the ways in which females and males do and don't differ. Television talk show hosts and guests regularly "debate" (read that try to out-shout each other), research findings dot the front pages of newspapers, and the rest of us talk, listen, and argue about the many questions about sex differences and similarities.

Yet, despite all the heated rhetoric, few people outside of academia are aware of the way in which psychologists, biologists, sociologists, and researchers from almost every other discipline have studied the questions about sex differences and similarities and the kinds of answers they have provided. In this book, I synthesize and summarize the enormous research literature that pertains to the ways males and females differ in their cognitive abilities. The intended audience for this book is anyone who wants to read a thoughtful analysis of the complex issues involved in asking and answering multifarious questions. A basic-level background in psychology, biology, and research methods will help readers with some of the more technical points, but readers without such a background can follow the main points. Upper division undergraduates and beginning graduate students should benefit the most from reading this book as they have already addressed some of the issues in their other courses.

I hope that every reader will take away something of value from this book—a new idea, a different way of conceptualizing the issues, a more open mind, an appreciation for the immense complexity of the issues involved, a more thoughtful approach to complicated problems, a framework for interpreting the quality of evidence, an understanding of the way societal values influence the way questions are posed and the type of answers we get, and the knowledge that there is a reciprocal relationship among psychological, biological, and societal influences that makes simple answers to complicated questions simply wrong. This is a long list of desired outcomes, but if most readers gain in at least one of these areas, then, I have successfully accomplished the goals that I set for myself when I began writing.

ACKNOWLEDGMENTS

This is my favorite part, the opportunity to thank the many wonderful colleagues who helped me with this book. I am grateful to Dr. Claire Etaugh at Bradley University and Dr. Nora Newcombe at Temple University for reading an earlier draft of the entire book. Their insightful comments have greatly improved the text. Dr. Neil Campbell from the University of California, Riverside, Dr. Michelle Paludi from Hunter college, Dr. Anne Petersen from Pennsylvania State University, and Dr. JoAnna Worthley from California State University, San Bernardino, all read selected chapters and generously shared their expertise with me. Of course, I would like to be able to attribute any errors that may exist in the text to them, but, unfortunately, I will have to assume this responsibility.

Many colleagues have written to me to share their research and to comment on the myriad of issues. I thank them and the many other researchers whose work I have cited. I also thank my wonderful family, my husband Sheldon and my children Joan and Evan, for "being there" and for acting as sounding boards as I read my way through a mountain of literature and asked them to consider the many questions pertaining to sex differences in cognitive abilities.

Preface to Volume 1

It seemed like a simple task when I started writing this book. All I had to do was provide a comprehensive synthesis of the theories and research concerning the causes, correlates, and consequences of cognitive sex differences and make some meaningful conclusions that were supported in the literature. My interest in the area grew naturally out of several years of teaching both cognitive psychology and psychology of women to college classes. The idea that women and men might actually think differently, that is have different preferred modes of thinking or different thinking abilities came up in both classes. At the time, it seemed clear to me that any between-sex differences in thinking abilities were due to socialization practices, artifacts and mistakes in the research, and bias and prejudice. After reviewing a pile of journal articles that stood several feet high and numerous books and book chapters that dwarfed the stack of journal articles, I changed my mind. The task I had undertaken certainly wasn't simple and the conclusions that I had expected to make had to be revised.

The literature on sex differences in cognitive abilities is filled with inconsistent findings, contradictory theories, and emotional claims that are unsupported by the research. Yet, despite all of the noise in the data, clear and consistent messages could be heard. There are real, and in some cases sizable, sex differences with respect to some cognitive abilities. Socialization practices are undoubtedly important, but there is also good evidence that biological sex differences play a role in establishing and maintaining cognitive sex differences, a conclusion that I wasn't prepared to make when I began reviewing the relevant literature.

The conclusions that I reached about cognitive sex differences are at odds with those of other authors (e.g., Caplan, MacPherson, & Tobin, 1985; Fairweather,

1976). There are probably several reasons why the conclusions in this review are different from the earlier ones. I believe that the data collected within the last few years provide a convincing case for the importance of biological variables, and that earlier reviews were, of course, unable to consider these findings. Other reviewers were sometimes quick to dismiss inconsistent theories and experimental results as symptomatic of a chaotic field of investigation. If they had reviewed the inconsistencies, they would have found that many of them are resolvable and that some of the theories and research could be eliminated because they had become outdated or had not received experimental support, thereby reducing the dissonance in the literature. Although there is still much that we don't know in this area, plausible conclusions based on the information that is currently available can be made.

This book was written with a broad audience in mind—bright undergraduates and graduates and their professors and general readers who are intrigued with the questions and answers about cognitive sex differences. It could serve as a supplemental book in many courses in psychology and other fields. The issues raised in this book are appropriately addressed in introductory psychology, sociology, education, philosophy, human development, and biology courses. It is also appropriate for advanced courses in sex roles, sex differences, human genetics, child and adult development, education theory and research, social psychology and physiological psychology because of the broad perspective needed in understanding cognitive sex differences.

The topics addressed vary in their complexity, with brain-behavior relationships more difficult to explain than psychosocial influences on the development of cognition. My goal was to make even the advanced topics in biology and statistics comprehensive without oversimplifying multifacted relationships or losing sight of the fact that the problems are complex. The topics addressed in this book go far beyond the usual "pop" coverage found in the popular press. I hope that despite my efforts to emphasize serious research and conceptual issues, I have been able to convey to readers some of my fascination with one of the most controversial and politically charged topics in modern psychology, the psychology of cognitive sex differences.

1 Introduction and Overview

Contents

1

A HOT ISSUE IN CONTEMPORARY PSYCHOLOGY

*The difference between male and female is something
that everybody knows and nobody knows.*
—Money (1987, p. 13)

"Congratulations, you're the parents of a beautiful baby _____." I don't believe that there are new parents anywhere who wouldn't hold their breath until the missing word was filled in. Anxious friends and relatives await the momentous news about the new young person—is it a girl or a boy? The critical importance that we attribute to a newborn's sex reflects more than a curiosity about the shape of its genitals; it reflects a fundamental belief that the life of the newborn will differ in essential ways depending on whether it's a girl or it's a boy. But what are those beliefs and what is the evidence that supports them?

The questions of sex differences have been a consuming interest of psychologists and other social scientists for many years. Virtually every journal in every area of specialization, including the popular press and stories in nonprint media, contains reports of research on differences between women and men. Over 10 years ago, one observer noted that "women have become the latest academic fad" (Westkott, 1979, p. 427). More recently, Jacklin (1989) described the study of sex differences as a "national preoccupation." But the topic of sex differences isn't just "hot" in the sense of fashionable, it is, in fact, inflammatory. The answers we provide to questions like, "Which is the smarter sex?" or "Do girls have less mathematical ability than boys?" have implications for present and future societies. The questions are important, and no one is taking the answers lightly.

The political climate with regard to the questions of sex differences and the appropriate roles for men and women has been combative in the approximately 25 years since the Women's Movement began shaking up American society. During the last 2½ decades, women have been entering traditional male occupations at an increasing rate and, to a lesser extent, men have assumed a greater role

1

in child care and homemaking (U.S. Bureau of the Census, 1989). On the other hand, the Equal Rights Amendment, an attempt to constitutionally mandate equality between the sexes, failed to obtain ratification. Apparently, Americans are either opposed to social changes in the roles played by men and women in contemporary society or believe that an amendment ensuring equal protection is unnecessary.

Political commentators, late-night talk show hosts, teachers, and the rest of us have wrestled with issues such as: whether women should be permitted to participate in combat (Are women too weak for the rigors of war?), whether women could be good vice presidents or presidents of the United States (Are they too emotional to make reasoned decisions?), whether men should be given equal consideration in child custody suits (Are men able to assume the primary role in parenting?), whether the number of women in the sciences is likely to increase (Are women less able to comprehend advanced scientific concepts?), and whether men are naturally too aggressive to be trusted with world peace (Would there be fewer wars if women ran the military?).

Few areas of study engender as much controversy and acrimony as the questions about sex differences. The way we answer these questions will have extensive influences on the way we live our lives and the way we govern society. It is my goal to change not only how you answer these questions, but how you ask them as well. Perhaps the way we pose questions about sex differences contributes to the controversy and acrimony. Instead of assuming the perspective of which sex is better for a particular task or which sex has more of some hypothetical ability, there is a less polarizing approach to the many questions that society asks about the nonreproductive differences between men and women. The focus of the sex differences questions needs to change from "who is better?" to "where and when are meaningful differences found?".

Despite my plea for a more rational approach to questions of sex differences, there are some harsh realities that always cause an emotional response. Consider these grim facts:

1. Women who worked full time in 1989 earned only 66¢ for every dollar that men earned. This wage differential represents a difference that has narrowed by less than a dime over the past two decades.
2. Among Fortune 500 companies, less than 2% of the top executives are female.
3. Corporate women at the vice presidential level earn 42% less than their male peers.
4. More than 60% of all adults living below the poverty line in the United States are women (Wallis, 1989). (Contrary to common stereotypes, the majority are White women.)
5. Eating disorders such as anorexia, bulimia, and obesity are much more

common in females than in males (American Psychiatric Association, 1987).

On the other hand, approximately 94% of all prisoners in the United States are male (U.S. Bureau of the Census, 1989), the ratio of males to females diagnosed with Attention Deficit Disorder/Hyperactivity is 10:1, mental retardation is twice as common in males as in females, and schizoid disorders, transient tic disorders, stuttering, pathological gambling, pyromania (fire setting), and Antisocial Personality Disorder are several times more common in males (American Psychiatric Association, 1987). Of the professional baseball, basketball, and soccer players at the major league level, 100% are male.

Data of this sort demonstrate that women and men in contemporary industrialized societies can expect to live qualitatively different lives based solely on whether they are male or female. What is it about femaleness and maleness that determines, among other things, how much money you are likely to earn, the type of job you are likely to have, the type of psychiatric disorder you are likely to manifest, and the type of sport you are likely to play?

In the midst of all this brouhaha, psychologists and other social scientists have amassed mountains of data about sex differences in the belief that the answers can be determined in a scientific manner. The purpose of this book is to review the data that pertain to sex differences in cognitive abilities and the theories that have guided the way the data were collected and interpreted. The goal is to provide an up-to-date synthesis and summary of this highly complex and controversial area of research.

Should We Study Sex Differences?

Scholarship on gender is all too often dismissed as politicized mythology.
—Eagly (1990, p. 560)

There are controversies in every area of research about the way the research is conducted, the interpretation of the findings, and the theoretical and practical significance of the results. But, unlike other areas, there is the issue of whether sex differences research *should be* conducted. Outspoken critics claim that all sex differences research is inherently sexist and that the results legitimize negative stereotypes of women. McHugh, Koeske, and Frieze (1986), for example, argued that sex differences should be reported only under limited circumstances. Baumeister (1988) maintained that researchers should cease reporting any between-sex comparisons. On the other hand, Eagly (1990) has urged that findings of sex differences should be reported in all research.

The argument for limited reporting is that spurious findings of sex differences (a concept that is explained more fully in the next chapter) will create an emphasis on the way women and men differ while slighting the multitude of similarities. One argument against studying sex differences is the claim that such studies are inherently sexist and fail to address the vast range of differences within each sex.

Not surprisingly (this being a book on sex differences), I find the reasons for studying sex differences most convincing. These reasons have been persuasively articulated by Eagly (1990). First, arguments against studying sex differences are often based on the implicit assumption that if the truth were known, women's deficiencies would be revealed. This is simply not true. Much of the research has documented areas in which women as a group excel. A point that is made in numerous places throughout this book is that differences are not deficiencies, and it is only through a careful study of differences that similarities can be revealed. Sex differences research is not inherently sexist—it is the only way that we can empirically determine if common beliefs and stereotypes about males and females have any basis in fact. The only alternative to knowledge is ignorance. And ignorance does not counter stereotypes or dispel myths. If there were no sex differences research, we would never know that females earn much less than males or that males are much more likely to be diagnosed with certain mental illnesses. High quality research is the only way that we can determine if and when females and males are likely to differ. It is the only way that we can reject false stereotypes and understand legitimate differences.

NATURE-NURTURE CONTROVERSY

> *Nature is a political strategy of those committed to maintaining the status quo of sex differences.*
> —Money (1987)

Even in an area as complex and replete with contradictory results as the questions of sex differences in cognitive or thinking abilities, there are a few facts that virtually everyone will agree on. These facts concern the sex-related differences in the daily activities of a majority of women and men in contemporary Western cultures. The majority of mathematics, science, and engineering majors in coed colleges are male, whereas the majority of elementary school teachers, nurses, and secretaries are female. When one parent assumes the job of primary home-maker, it is almost always the mother. The vast majority of professions and avocations are comprised of a clear majority of one sex. In fact, very few sex neutral occupations come to mind. The important questions for experimental psychology are: (a) whether these differences in activities reflect sex-related differences in cognitive abilities, and if so (b) are the cognitive differences due to factors that are inherent in the biology of maleness and femaleness or due to differential sex-related experiences and expectations?

The second question is a familiar one to psychologists: Does nature or nurture play the greater part in the differences under study? When applied to differences in cognitive abilities, the question becomes controversial and politically charged. Like all loaded questions, the answers sometimes backfire. The implications of the way psychologists answer this question are similar to those about racial differences in intelligence. Results could be, and have been, used to justify discrimination and/or affirmative action based on sex.

The nature–nurture dichotomy has guided much of the research in the area of sex differences. Proponents on each side of the issue stack up their data hoping to overwhelm the opposition with the sheer weight of their evidence. Arguments on the nature side of the question point to the folly of denying that the biological manifestations of manhood and womanhood influence how we think and act. The nurture side is quick to point out that individuals develop in a societal context that shapes and interprets thoughts and actions in stereotypical ways. Of course, few modern psychologists maintain a strict "either/or" position. The naturally gifted poet and author, for example, will never develop this gift if denied an education. The gift will never be recognized if publishers refuse to publish the creative work. Nature and nurture must operate jointly in the development of cognitive abilities.

Although most researchers agree that the better question is how much do nature and nurture contribute to the development of cognitive abilities, it is virtually impossible to devise measures that allow for a direct and independent comparison. Nature and nurture are like Siamese twins who share a common heart and nervous system. The technology has not yet been developed that will allow them to be separated. Thus, although researchers pay lip service to interactionist positions, the research is, in fact, focused on either biological (nature) variables or environmental (nurture) variables. The nature–nurture controversy has been debated for over 2,000 years without resolution because it is essentially unanswerable. Yet, it has served as a framework for much of the sex differences research.

Nature and nurture are inextricably entwined. Biology responds to the environment and people adjust and select their environment to make it compatible with their biological propensities. Consider the biological question of whether male and female brains tend to differ in their organization of functions. Brain differences develop in the context of a socialization process (Petersen & Hood, 1988). There is a large research literature documenting the effects of different environments on the morphology of the brain. Diamond (1988) found that when rats were reared in either enriched or impoverished environments, their brains manifested systematic differences in cortical thickness and weight, the branching of dendrites (parts of the neurons), number of glial cells (nourishing tissues), and cell size. Furthermore, even in old age, the brain was altered in response to changes in the environment. Thus, even if we were to conclude that there are structural differences in male and female brains, we could not know whether

Copyright Leo Callum (1985).

such differences were due to sex-related biological mechanisms or occurred as a response to a socially differentiated environment.

The turbid relationship between nature and nurture is muddied even further when we consider that the links between cognitive performance and its underlying biology are only loosely conceptualized (Petersen & Crockett, 1987). All behavior results from the interaction of biological, psychological, and social influences. Suppose, for example, an interactive process such that some biological characteristic of maleness (e.g., hormone concentrations) creates a slight advantage on spatial tasks, and that because of this slight advantage, males seek more spatially related activities, which society, in turn, encourages as sex role appropriate. This hypothetical sequence could create an even greater difference in the biological underpinnings of spatial ability because of the spatial nature of the activities in which males engage (e.g., playing with building blocks). In this way, biological, psychological, and societal factors could operate in concert to enhance an initially small between-sex difference (Geary, 1989).

One of the most eloquent commentaries about the nature–nurture controversy was made by Reinisch, Rosenblum, and Sanders (1987):

> Consider the hoary, always dying, but never dead, pseudoquestion of the role of nature and/or nurture in determining the most commonly observed masculine and feminine characteristics. . . . Culture may seek to diminish, exaggerate, ignore, or even reverse the impact of these biological factors. . . . Nevertheless, although the pathways from genes to behavior may be extremely complex in all organisms . . . , culture and experience act on a given constellation of capacities and propensities present at the start of the whole process, even when that interactive process is seen as beginning prior to conception. (pp. 5–6)

Sociobiology

The furor may be inevitable.
Gelman et al. (1981)

The nature–nurture controversy erupted into a full-scale war when E. O. Wilson "sought to establish sociobiology 'as the systematic study of the biological bases of all social behavior' " (Bleier, 1984, p.15). Sociobiology is a subdiscipline within biology that attempts to use evolutionary principles to explain the behavior of humans and other animals. According to this theory, a species is fit if it reproduces well. A major tenet of sociobiology is that there are genetically programmed universal traits that improve the probabilities of producing many viable offspring. Given the basic assumptions of sociobiology, women, for example, should have a genetically determined predisposition that makes them better at child care because they are the ones that gestate and nurse the young. Like the female members of other species, women purportedly possess a "maternal instinct" because such an instinct would be beneficial to the survival of the species. Men, on the other hand, inherit a genetic predisposition that makes them prone to infidelity because multiple sexual encounters is a good reproductive strategy for males.

There are several flaws in this line of reasoning:

1. Hormones and other between-sex biological differences become decreasingly important as determinants of behavior as we ascend the phylogenetic scale.

2. Explaining male infidelity by analogy to the animal kingdom ignores the many species that form monogamous mateships; it is not the natural state of all males across species to have multiple sexual partners.

3. It ignores societal influences on complex behaviors such as child care and mating choices.

4. Even if it were true, it ignores many critical advances of modern society such as the availability of dependable methods of contraceptives (Ruse, 1987). A woman no longer has to consider every sex partner as a potential (genetic) father of her child (presumably the basis of female fidelity); thus, the advent of birth control renders this dubious line of reasoning meaningless.

The Hunter–Gatherer Hypothesis

Generalizations to human behavior from our closest relatives ignore 5 million years of exuberant evolutionary development of the human brain.
—Bleier (1978, p. 161)

Sex differences with respect to cognitive abilities are also explained by the adherents of basic principles of sociobiology. Consider, for example, a sociobiological argument to explain differences in spatial ability. Proponents of sociobiology maintain that because men were the hunters in primitive hunter–gatherer societies, they needed better spatial skills than the women, who performed the gathering tasks; therefore, men are genetically superior in spatial ability.

Numerous thoughtful critiques of sociobiology have been offered (Bleier, 1984; Janson-Smith, 1980). The possibility that there are genes that determine specific social behaviors (e.g., child-care arrangements, infidelity) and cognitive abilities is extremely remote. In addition, adherents of sociobiology ignore data that are not consistent with the theory. Spatial skills, for example, were also needed for gatherers, who often had to travel long distances to gather food. In addition, there were many hunter–gatherer societies in which women hunted (e.g., the Pygmies of the Zaire rain forest and the Tiwi of the Bathurst Islands) (O'Kelly, 1980). Women in these earlier societies had to weave the baskets needed for efficient gathering (a complex spatial skill). Pontius (1989) described the daily activities of women in a 20th-century hunter–gatherer society (nonmissionized nomadic Auca Indians of the Amazon) as heavily reliant on the use of spatial skills:

> The women, with amazing skill, fold a whole howler monkey to fit into a relatively small pot or two turkey-like birds into a pot which seems just large enough for only one bird. This skill implies accurate visualization of the body size of the animals in relation to one another and to the pot. Such spatial visualization is also used to a lesser degree in the knotting of hammocks from lianas. (p. 57)

Sociobiologists rely heavily on dubious analogies from other animal species to make their point. As Weisstein (1972) noted, this is the same as concluding "that it is quite useless to teach human infants to speak since it has been tried with chimpanzees and does not work" (p. 218).

Unfortunately, difficult questions like whether certain behaviors have a genetic link are rarely answered with a simple "yes" or "no." More recent sociobiological research has focused on differences among species that vary as a function of the types of tasks in which each specie engages. For example, Gaulin and his colleagues (Gaulin & Fitzgerald, 1989; Gaulin, Fitzgerald, & Wartell, 1990; Gaulin & Wartell, 1990) have studied sex differences in spatial abilities in two species of voles (rodents), one of which is monogamous and one of which is not. They found that only the nonmonogamous species show sex differences in spatial abilities. Gaulin argued that this is related to the larger home ranges found with nonmonogamous male rodents, which they have in service of finding mates. Although much more research is needed to determine if sex differences in other animal species depend on whether the males have a large or small home range, it is still a long leap to extrapolate findings of this sort to the complex environment of humans. Sociobiology provides neither an explanation of nor a justification for sex differences. (See Doyle & Paludi, 1990, for a contemporary review of the way sociobiological explanations have been applied to research on sex differences.)

THE NOTION OF COGNITIVE ABILITIES

Cognitive psychology is the branch of psychology concerned with how people think, learn, and remember. The ability to think, learn, and remember is, in turn, related to the concept of intelligence. Although intelligence has been defined in many ways (see Halpern, 1984a, 1989b), it is used in this context as the raw material or "stuff" of thought. It is frequently conceptualized as a limited quantity within each individual that is developed more or less fully depending on environment. Intelligence is not a unitary concept. It is comprised of several intellectual abilities that are related to each other, but yet somewhat different. The number and nature of these component abilities are frequently identified with a mathematical procedure known as factor analysis. Factor analysis is a useful descriptive technique that allows researchers to discover clusters of correlated variables. These clusters of variables, known as factors, can be thought of as the "underlying dimensions" of intelligence. Intelligence was one of the first interests of early psychologists, and there is probably more written about intelligence than any other topic in psychology. In a classical factor-analytic study of intelligence, Thurstone and Thurstone (1941) administered 60 different ability tests (e.g., arithmetic, spelling) to eighth-grade students. They found that scores on these tests formed three sets of clusters or factors, which they called verbal, number (quantitative), and perception (visual–spatial) factors. Modern psychologists concerned with cognitive sex differences still refer to these same three factors. In the years since 1941, several other models of intelligence have been proposed, but the notion of multiple intelligence is still widely supported (e.g., Cattell, 1963; Guilford, 1967; Sternberg, 1985).

Frames of Mind

One of the most recent and influential conceptions of intelligence was posited by Gardner (1983). In his seminal book, *Frames of Mind,* Gardner proposed seven different intelligences: linguistic, logical–mathematical, spatial, musical, body-kinesthetic, interpersonal, and intrapersonal. Gardner relied on multiple sources of evidence that these are seven distinct components of intelligence, or, as he called them, "frames of mind." Each of these seven abilities responds selectively to localized brain damage (suggesting localization of brain function). There are autistic savants who excel in only one of these areas and are dysfunctional in the other areas, and exceptional prodigies with extraordinary ability in only one of these areas. These abilities are differentially valued in different societies, and they conform to commonly held intuitive notions about the way people differ.

Gardner's seven intelligences are a good starting point for a discussion of sex differences in cognitive abilities. Much of this book reviews the literature pertaining to his first three intelligences: linguistic (or language), logical–mathematical (or quantitative), and spatial. Sex differences in musical abilities are considered only briefly because of the paucity of high quality research on this ability. There undoubtedly are sex differences in body-kinesthetic ability, but, like the other "intelligences," the nature of these differences must depend on the way body-kinesthetic ability is measured. If we were to consider the complex graceful movements of ballet dancers, we would find that although there are numerous outstanding male ballet dancers, the vast majority of accomplished ballet dancers are female. On the other hand, if body-kinesthetic ability is assessed as running speed or ability to "pass" a football, then males would appear more talented. There are also some areas of body-kinesthetic ability in which males and females have similar levels of performance, such as long distance swimming. Thus, it seems that females and males may excel at different types of body-kinesthetic performance depending on an interaction of physiological capacity and the opportunities provided by society for fully developing one's potential. Body-kinesthetic ability is a good example of two points that I emphasize repeatedly throughout this book—the evidence available suggests that there are sex differences, but (a) there is considerable variability within each sex, and (b) it would be foolish to try to decide which sex is "better" at tasks that require body-kinesthetic ability. The fact that differences probably exist does not mean that one sex is the "winner" and the other is the "loser." Differences do not require a value judgment.

Interpersonal intelligence is defined as the ability to determine the moods of other. By contrast, *intrapersonal intelligence* is knowledge of one's own feelings. It seems reasonable to conclude that there are sex differences in these areas as well. In a recent review of the literature on nonverbal communication (one measure of understanding the moods of others), Hall (1985) concluded that women, on the average, are better at decoding nonverbal communication. Intrapersonal intelligence is more difficult to assess because only each individual knows her or his own feelings. Common stereotypes reveal the belief that women are "more in touch with their own feelings than men are with their own feelings," but there is very little research on this topic. (See the excellent articles in Richardson & Taylor, 1989, for several different views of sex role stereotypes.)

In this book, I focus on the first three of Gardner's categories of intellectual abilities because linguistic, quantitative, and spatial are the three ability factors in which sex differences are most frequently reported. They are the only areas in which the literature is large enough and the research rigorous enough to permit a detailed review with conclusions.

Assessment of Cognitive Abilities

Underlying abilities are abstract constructs. They are what psychologists believe they are measuring when they administer certain tests. But not all tests measure abilities. In fact, it is very difficult to devise a test of ability that is not also measuring achievement. An achievement test measures what an individual knows at the time of the test. For example, if I wanted to know how much mathematics you know, I would give you a mathematics achievement test. If you had very few mathematics courses in high school, then I would expect that you would not know much about the type of mathematics taught in the high school courses you did not take. You would not be able to solve trigonometry or calculus problems, for example. This does not mean that you could not solve these problems with appropriate instruction, nor does it necessarily mean that you would have difficulty learning these mathematical concepts. A low score on this test would mean only that you cannot solve the mathematical problems at the time of the test.

Ability tests attempt to assess the likelihood of your being able to succeed at certain tasks in the future if you received proper instruction and if you were motivated to learn and demonstrate the skills needed to perform the task. A low score on a mathematical ability test, for example, is meant to imply that you are less able to learn certain advanced concepts such as calculus or other higher mathematics than someone obtaining a higher score. It can be loosely thought of as the ability to benefit from instruction in a certain area.

There are, however, several important "ifs" in ability testing. Suppose, for example, a young man who believes that language fluency is a "sissy trait" is tested in the area of verbal ability. He certainly would not be motivated to perform well on this test, leading the researcher to conclude that he had little verbal ability. Consider some of the other assumptions implicit in ability testing. We test mathematical ability by presenting individuals with mathematical problems to solve. Wouldn't someone who had taken more or better mathematical courses be expected to answer more questions correctly than someone with a poorer mathematical education background? In other words, aren't we also measuring achievement? To some extent, we are always measuring achievement whenever we try to measure ability. This is a troublesome problem for psychologists who want to understand possible sex differences in ability. In American and other Western societies, girls typically take fewer advanced mathematics courses and receive less encouragement to excel in mathematics than boys do. Females may take fewer advanced mathematics courses because they have less mathematical ability, or they believe they have less mathematical ability, or they get fewer rewards for studying advanced topics in mathematics. How can we ever be certain that what we are labeling sex differences in ability are not really sex differences in achievement? We can't. The blurry distinction between ability and achievement means that we have to be very careful about the conclusions that we draw from tests that show sex differences.

A pure measure of cognitive ability would separate what each of the sexes in fact do (achievement) from what each of the sexes can do (ability). This is not yet possible. Instead, we must rely on the only available data that we have. But, we also need to be careful about the kinds of extrapolations we make from it. Just because tests given in the 1980s or 1990s show sex differences does not mean that tests in the year 2000 will. The term *cognitive abilities* is used throughout this book because it is the term that is commonly used in the literature, but readers should not hesitate to question whether ability or achievement is actually being measured.

Tests of cognitive abilities, like all tests, contain a "margin of error." That is, they are not perfectly accurate in the kinds of predictions that they make. A good test of mathematical ability, for example, should predict fairly well an individual's ability to acquire mathematical concepts. Ideally, it should be validated by actually comparing scores on the test with achievement in future mathematics courses. Unfortunately, this is rarely done. More often, these tests are validated by comparing scores on one mathematical ability test with scores on another mathematical ability test. If, in general, the scores are in accord, we can probably conclude that they are measuring the same construct, but we still cannot say much about the predictive value of either test or the meaningfulness of the construct we have just measured. The construction of valid and reliable tests is a complex statistical endeavor. Some of the tests cited in the cognitive sex differences literature have poor or unknown psychometric properties (reliabilities and validities). These tests should be considered only as ancillary evidence for or against a particular position and not as primary evidence because of the questionable nature of their construction.

In all psychological measurement, there is always a gap between the test result and what it signifies. Test results are interpretable only to the extent that a plausible theory can link them to meaningful constructs. Although mountains of data exist that address the questions of cognitive sex differences, there are few good theories that can synthesize and interpret the empirical results. Thus, although we can talk about sex differences on various tests, we can't always interpret what these differences mean.

Cognitive abilities are theoretical constructs that represent the underlying components of intelligence. The quality of a construct in the sex differences literature can be assessed by how well it passes three tests:

1. If sex differences are found consistently on several different tests that tend to cluster or load onto a single factor, then we have reason to believe that, in general, the sexes perform differently on whatever these tests are measuring. This first step provides converging evidence from several tests that sex differences exist with respect to the construct being measured.

2. If, in addition, we can use these tests to predict performance on a task that requires the skills we believe that the tests are measuring, then the construct is useful.

3. If an empirically supported theory or theories have been devised to explain why sex differences exist in the ability being measured, then the construct and the theory that incorporates it have explanatory power.

The ability to explain phenomena is a major goal of research. The third requirement is needed to make the construct theoretically meaningful, and is the most controversial and difficult of the tests to satisfy.

VALUES AND SCIENCE

The Myth of Objectivity

> *All knowledge is constructed and the knower is an*
> *intimate part of the known.*
> —Belenky, Clinchy, Goldberger, and Tarule (1986, p. 137)

When most of us first learned about the scientific method, somewhere back in junior high school, we were told about the disinterested researcher who objectively and methodically goes about the business of collecting data with the goal of revealing truth. For those of us involved in research, the imagery that this description brings to mind is somewhat humorous. Although it is true that researchers collect data, very little of what most of us do could be considered "disinterested." Whatever the topic, few researchers who invest their energies in an experiment are neutral with respect to the type of outcome they expect or want. This is especially true in an area like cognitive sex differences, where there is so much at stake and where the potential for misinterpretation and misuse of experimental outcomes is so great.

There are numerous ways in which personal beliefs and values can influence the experimental procedure. Researchers make many decisions in the course of conducting an experiment and the way the decisions are made can deliberately or unwittingly bias the results. Although this topic is covered more extensively in chapter 2, let's think about a few of these decisions now: the way subjects are selected (e.g., retarded as well as normal subjects); the type of measurement employed (e.g., continuous or discrete); the kinds of items used on tests; how to analyze the data (e.g., multivariate or univariate, parametric or nonparametric tests); the number of subjects to include in the study; and whether to focus the discussion on significance levels or effect sizes. If I were interested, for example, in showing that there are no sex differences in mathematical ability, then I would want a sample in which women with high mathematical ability were included because I would want an overall high score for the women. I could opt for discrete measurement; the test items that I would select would have to include examples drawn from typical female experiences; I could use nonparametric tests which are typically less powerful (less likely to reveal group differences); and I would want to use a small number of subjects. Decisions concerning what to focus on in the discussion could be made post hoc depending on whether they would support or detract from my favored view. None of this is dishonest (although the use of a less powerful or inappropriate statistical test is very close to dishonest), nor are all of the decisions devious, especially if all of the relevant information is provided in the write up of the experiment. In fact, the decision to include test items from typical experiences of girls would make it a fairer test than including examples exclusively from typical boy activities. This discussion is not intended to show that research or researchers are "bad." An experiment is the most objective method for providing answers to questions. It is important to keep in mind, however, that even the most objective method can be slanted in ways that support the researcher's favored outcome.

In a discussion about the relationship between values and science, Wittig (1985) stated: "Knowledge about behavior is constructed, not merely deduced. Such constructions are affected by the historical, personal, social, and cultural context. Judgments of the meaning, validity, and usefulness of a particular analysis of human behavior are themselves socially influenced" (p. 803). It is important to remember that research is conducted in a social environment. The kinds of questions that we ask and the kinds of evidence we are willing to accept depend on its compatibility with the prevailing social view and each researcher's personal views on the topic.

Modern researchers can laugh at the evidence Broca provided in 1861 to support his contention that Blacks and women are intellectually inferior. According to Gould (1978), Broca won an epochal debate on this topic by citing the following evidence: "In general, the brain is larger in mature adults than in the elderly, in men than in women, in eminent men than in men of mediocre talent, in superior races than in inferior races" (p. 44). Broca failed to consider the relationship between body size and brain size, and had no data at all on his "inferior race–superior race" distinction. Yet, many 19th-century academics and physicians willingly accepted his "data" as support for the view that they favored on this issue. We can only imagine 21st-century researchers laughing at our own naivete in the way we sought to understand cognitive sex differences. In Shields' (1980) cogent discussion of the subservience of science to social values, she explained that the 19th-century belief that women were intellectually inferior to men because they had smaller frontal lobes in their brains was replaced later in the century with the belief that the parietal lobes were the true seat of intellectual prowess. Not surprisingly, the following report was published soon after the discovery of the importance of the parietal lobes: ". . . the frontal region is not, as has been supposed, smaller in women. . . . But the parietal lobe is somewhat smaller, a preponderance of the frontal region does not imply intellectual superiority . . . the parietal region is really the more important" (Patrick, 1895, cited in Shields, 1980, p. 741).

Feminist Scholarship

> *We do not have to ask for the head circumference*
> *of women of genius—they do not exist.*
> —Bayerthal (1911, cited in Janowsky, 1989, p. 257)

In recognition of the fact "that science played handmaiden to social values" (Shields, 1975), several psychologists have suggested that sex differences researchers adopt a "feminist scholarship" approach. One of the goals of feminist scholarship is the recognition and elimination of the "androcentric bias in both content and method" in traditional research (Lott, 1985, p. 156). Men and women who ascribe to the philosophy of feminist research are careful to consider the importance of context or situational variables as potent influences on the results they obtain from research. Sex is not only a subject variable, it is also a stimulus variable, when viewed from this perspective. Women and men may respond differently in certain situations because the other people in that situation are responding to them in a sex-differentiated manner. In other words, women may perform differently from men on a certain type of task because the other people in the setting are giving them more or less encouragement to perform that task than they are giving to the men.

Feminist research is based on the belief that the world is determined by the categories that we use to define it (Unger, 1989). The beliefs of the researcher influence the way abilities and traits are interpreted (Valentine & Brodsky, 1989). For example, if you believe that women are more likely to gossip than men, then you will interpret objectively identical behavior by a man or woman differently—the man's behavior is less likely to be labeled as "gossip" than the woman's behavior. In this case, any sex differences in the task performance should be attributed to sex as a stimulus variable rather than to sex as a subject variable.

Advocates of feminist scholarship utilize nontraditional methods in addition to traditional mainstream methods to examine qualitative differences in the psychology of maleness and femaleness. They will sometimes prefer lengthy individual interviews in attempting to understand a phenomenon or to suggest new areas of research. Feminist scholars of both sexes are concerned with similarities as well as sex differences. In a recent survey of feminist psychologists, Ricketts (1989) found that they tend to prefer external or social determinants of human behavior rather than internal or biological determinants. A feminist epistemology also contains a conscious awareness of the way sexist assumptions and other stereotypic beliefs guide the kinds of research questions that are investigated and the varieties of evidence researchers are willing to accept. Like all good researchers, feminists examine the quality of the data that are collected and the logic that links the data to a conclusion. Of course, they are no freer from their own personal biases than researchers with other epistemological beliefs, but hopefully they are more aware of them—an important fact in itself.

POLITICAL AND SOCIAL RAMIFICATIONS

As an area of research, sex and gender is fraught with dilemmas and decision points.
—Deaux (1985)

There are many commonly held stereotypes about differences between women and men. Women, for example, are usually perceived as being less intelligent than men (Broverman, Vogel, Broverman, Clarkson, & Rosenkrantz, 1972). Many people also believe that women should be less intelligent than men. In a survey of school teachers, Ernest (1976) found that both men and women teachers believed that boys are superior to girls in mathematical ability. We know that teachers act in ways that convey these beliefs to the children in their classrooms (Sadker & Sadker, 1985). Suppose that after a careful review of the literature, these stereotypes were found to be true! Teachers would knowingly or unknowingly increase the way they encourage and discourage different areas of intellectual development in their students depending on the student's sex. Advocates of sexual prejudice and discrimination could justify their beliefs and actions by an appeal to scientific findings. The social and political ramifications of such conclusions cannot be ignored.

The Bugaboo of Biological Explanations

It is frightening, and perhaps even un-American, to consider the possibility that even a small portion of the sex differences in cognitive abilities may be attributable to biological factors. This is probably because many people confuse biological contributions with the idea of an immutable or unavoidable destiny. Suppose, for example, that after reviewing the literature I conclude that males really are superior in mathematics and that sex-differentiated hormones or brain organizations are implicated in these differences. This does not necessarily reduce the importance of psychosocial variables, nor does it imply that the differences are large or that the differences could not be reduced or eliminated with appropriate instruction. What such a conclusion does do, however, is create the potential for misquotation, misuse, and misinterpretation, in an attempt to justify discrimination based on sex. Perhaps the very publication of such research results create a considerable risk.

Censorship in Science

There is perhaps no field aspiring to be scientific where flagrant personal bias, logic martyred in the cause of supporting a prejudice, unfounded assertions, and even sentimental rot and drivel, have run riot to such an extent as here.
—Helen Thompson Wooley (1910, cited in Russett, 1989, p. 155)

The question that is being raised is whether there should be censorship in science, even self-imposed censorship, when results are likely to be misused. However, the danger inherent in censorship is far greater than the danger in publishing results that could be used for undesirable purposes. The answers provided in this book to the questions of sex differences are complex and contain many qualifiers. Readers who read only the chapters on biological hypotheses or only the chapters on psychosocial hypotheses without reading the final chapter that integrates both approaches will come away with different erroneous conclusions about the area. Quotations taken out of context can be used to support virtually any position, because all sides of the issues have been considered and because it is possible to find research results to support almost any theory. The misrepresentation of biologically based explanations contributes to the chilly academic climate that women face in advanced courses in mathematics and that men face in "nurturing" fields like nursing and social work. Keep in mind that results obtained from groups of males and females do not justify discrimination against individuals. Nor can we afford to confuse what has been with what could or should be. Sex differences that exist in 20th-century American society do not necessarily exist in other societies or in the American society of the future.

Sex Differences—Good and Bad

Beliefs about the desirability or utility of sex differences research often depend on the topic being investigated. For example, research that showed that women's risk of heart attack rises after menopause or that women metabolize alcohol differently than men is usually hailed as beneficial. Similarly, Gilligan's (1982) book on sex-related differences in modes of thinking and reasoning about moral issues and the association of these modes with male and female "voices," has been embraced as a best seller. On the other hand, carefully executed research on sex-related differences in mathematical reasoning ability (e.g., Benbow, 1988) has generated hundreds of pages of vitriolic criticism (e.g., most of an entire issue of the journal *Behavioral and Brain Sciences,* Benbow, 1988; Fausto-Sterling, 1985). Why are differences in moral reasoning that are based on minimal support hailed as beneficial and differences in mathematical reasoning dismissed and belittled as sexist (Tiger, 1988)?

In an eloquent discussion of this question, Kenrick (1988) explained: "Advocates of this ideological approach have often used a two-front denial strategy. The first line is to deny that there are any substantial gender differences in behavior. This failing, the second line is to assume, a priori, that any differences that are demonstrated do not have a biological basis" (p. 199). It is important that each reader attempt to keep an open mind in considering the research and the way in which it is interpreted. To do anything less is self-deceptive.

TERMINOLOGY

The terms we use to convey ideas reflect our own biases about the topic being discussed. I have argued elsewhere that different images and meanings are evoked depending on the choice of words that are selected to convey our thoughts (Halpern, 1989b). Consider, for example, differences among the terms *senior citizen, old man,* and *golden ager.* Although, in some sense, these three terms can be considered synonyms, each conveys a somewhat different meaning. There is a reciprocal relationship between thought and language. The words that are used in the sex differences literature also influence how we think about the issues and the research results; therefore, I have decided to explain why I selected certain controversial terms.

Sex and Gender

Some psychologists prefer to use the term *sex* only when they are referring to biological distinctions between males and females, while reserving the term *gender* to refer to the psychological features or attributes associated with the biological categories (e.g., Deaux, 1985; Unger, 1979, 1989). Gender used in this way refers to societal definitions of female and male traits and abilities (Goodnow, 1985). Levy (1989) articulated this distinction as follows: "The term *sex* is used to refer to the grouping of people into the two distinct biologically defined groups of female and male. Gender, in turn, refers to the social categorizing of individuals based on social standards and ascriptions" (p. 306). I have decided to use the term *sex* to refer to both biological and psychosocial aspects of the differences between males and females because these two aspects of human existence are so closely coupled in our society. It is frequently difficult to decide if the differences that are found between females and males are due to biological (*sex*) differences or the psychosocial concomitants (*gender*) of biological sex.

The use of the term *sex* is not meant to imply that biological variables are more important than psychosocial ones or that the results being discussed are caused by differences in genes, hormones, sex glands, or genitals. The point that biological manifestations of sex are confounded with psychosocial variables is made repeatedly throughout this book. The use of different terms to label these two types of contributions to human existence seemed inappropriate in light of the interactionist position that I have taken in several places throughout this book.

Language purists probably will agree with my choice of the word *sex* instead of *gender*. *Gender* was originally a grammatical term used in languages that make a distinction between feminine and masculine nouns. It is not related to maleness or femaleness even in these languages. Gender is also sometimes used as a euphemism for the word *sex* because of the possible physical overtones implied by sex. Thus, for several reasons, gender seems to be an inappropriate label for the differences between females and males.

Sex and Sex-Related

Other psychologists have urged that the term *sex-related* differences be used instead of *sex* differences in order to emphasize the fact that many of the differences that are reported are correlates of the biological distinctions between females and males and not necessarily due to biological differences (i.e., sex differences in cognitive abilities are not *caused* by the differences in female and male genitals) (Sherman, 1978). Once again, the objective of this distinction is to separate biological and psychosocial determinants of between-sex differences. Although I am aware of the consciousness-raising aspect of this distinction, I have decided to use the shorter term *sex differences* in recognition of the close relationship between biological and psychosocial variables, using the term *sex-related* only occasionally for emphasis. The preference for the term *sex differences* is not meant to imply a preference for biological explanations.

Abilities, Skills, and Performance

Because there is considerable disagreement about how well various theories can explain sex differences and whether sex differences could be eliminated with appropriate instruction, other researchers have suggested that the term *abilities* should be replaced with other more neutral terms like *skills* or *performance* (Sherman, 1977). Once again, this distinction is based on the notion that the word *abilities* is suggestive of biological or immutable differences, whereas the terms *skills* or *performance* are not. These three terms are used interchangeably throughout this book. The use of the term *abilities* is not meant to imply that the trait under discussion is either biologically determined or genetically linked.

Pronouns

Traditional English usage has required that the masculine pronoun "he" be used whenever the sex of the referent is unknown. The male bias in our language and particularly the use of the male pronoun to refer to either females or males is discussed more fully in chapter 6. Psycholinguistic research has shown that listeners tend to think of males when the male pronoun is used (Hamilton, 1988; MacKay, 1983). For this reason and because of a personal dislike for this convention, I have rejected the exclusive use of the masculine pronoun and have alternated the use of female and male pronouns throughout this book whenever the sex of the referent is unknown. Sex neutral plural constructions (they) have also been used when they did not interfere with the topic being discussed.

SELECTIVE NATURE OF ALL REVIEWS

The purpose of this book is to provide a comprehensive review and synthesis of the research and theories that pertain to the questions of cognitive sex differences. Thousands, maybe even tens of thousands, of journal articles and books have been written that address this topic. Different experimental methods have sometimes been used to answer the same questions, and the answers do not always agree. Different results have frequently been obtained with the same tests, and similar results have been interpreted in different ways by different experimenters. Decisions had to be made continually as to which research is important and good. In an area as large as this one, only a subset of all of the available information can be presented. In addition, new knowledge is accumulating at an unprecedented rate. Thus, this review, like all reviews of the sex differences literature, is necessarily selective.

I would like to take this opportunity to apologize to the many researchers who have published in this field, but whose research has not been cited. In deciding which research to include in this review, I followed a few basic guidelines. I decided to include research that is representative of many experiments, when several similar investigations were reported on the same topic (e.g., many researchers have found that spatial skills can be learned), to include pivotal or "important" research that helped to clarify a theoretical position or to choose between two or more alternative interpretations of research, and to devote more space to the controversies than to the areas in which a consensus has been reached. I have also attempted to maintain a balanced view in this highly controversial area of psychology. This means that I probably manage to offend almost every reader as I explore alternative explanations of research findings and the theories that guide the research. I also believe that the answers we accept as true today will probably seem outdated and will sometimes be proven wrong in several years. There are no final answers, only the questions will endure.

ABOUT THIS BOOK

This introductory chapter is designed to set the stage for an examination of sex differences in cognitive abilities. Research methods and philosophies that determine how we answer the questions of cognitive sex differences are discussed in chapter 2. It is unusual to include a research methods chapter in a book on cognitive sex differences. It is included here in the belief that readers need to understand how the research questions were answered in order to understand the answers. Readers with a good background in experimental methods and statistics can skip or skim this chapter before going on in the book. Chapter 3 examines the question of whether or not sex differences in cognitive abilities exist, and, if so, are they large enough to be theoretically or practically important? Chapters 4 and 5 consider biological hypotheses devised to explain cognitive sex differences, and chapters 6 and 7 consider the psychosocial hypotheses. Competing and complimentary research and theories are integrated in chapter 8, along with suggestions for further research.

2 Searching for Sex Differences in Cognitive Abilities

Contents

2

THE NEED FOR RESEARCH

This study may generate more heat than light.
—Gunter and Gunter (1990, p. 367; conclusion from an experimental study on the domestic division of labor)

The first step in our quest to understand if, where, and when sex differences in cognitive abilities exist is an examination of the experimental and statistical procedures used to provide the answers. The kinds of questions we can ask about sex differences and the answers we get depend on the experimental and statistical methods used in research. The goal of this chapter is to consider the research issues that are important in evaluating the proliferating literature in the area of sex differences. Some of the issues are relevant to evaluating research claims in any area; others are unique to research about sex differences. The issues range from the basic assumptions underlying hypothesis testing to methods of integrating results across multiple studies. Readers with little or no background in statistical and research methods may have difficulty grasping some of the more technical explanations in this chapter; however, the general principles should be easily understandable to all readers. Reports of the actual research on sex differences are presented in chapter 3, and research and theories designed to explain why differences exist are presented in chapters 4 through 7. As you see in these chapters, not all of the research has employed the techniques that are identified as desirable or necessary. The validity of the conclusions rests on the quality of the research from which they were generated.

Consider, for example, the following conclusion about men and women made in a research report by Landauer (1981): "This may well indicate that women have greater cognitive abilities" (p. 90). It is unlikely that you would simply nod your head and accept these results as the *truth*. You would want to know which subjects were used, how cognitive abilities were measured, what the relevant values were for each group, and how the investigator reached this conclusion. (Landauer's dubious and overstated conclusion resulted from the finding that within a certain experimental paradigm, women made decisions faster than men.) In fact, the experimental and statistical methods used may be more important in determining the answers obtained than the underlying phenomenon being investigated.

A number of years ago, I had a conversation about the nature of sex differences with a member of an Eastern fundamentalist religion. There were no unresolved questions for him. One of the tenets of his religion was that women are best suited for home and child care, whereas men are best suited for the intellectual work needed to support a family. For him, any research on this question would have been superfluous, as the answers were God given. Of course, not everyone shares his religious beliefs. I later learned that some members of his religious sect doubt his interpretation of the religious principles. For most of us, the many questions pertaining to sex differences require an empirical test. An empirical test requires collecting information in as unbiased a manner as possible and then carefully scrutinizing it in accord with the rules of evidence to determine what, if any, conclusions can be drawn. Research methods provide the tools for understanding the relationships among variables, in this case, among sex and the cognitive or intellectual abilities. The experimental method is a potentially objective method that allows researchers to confirm or disconfirm their hypotheses or beliefs. I have described the experimental method as potentially objective because it is impossible for research ever to be totally objective. The very questions in which researchers are interested and the way in which they construct hypotheses and decide what variables to measure are contaminated by their beliefs, prejudices and societal values. The hostile and politically charged climate surrounding sex differences research has called into question the possibility of ever obtaining bias-free research. Although many people are distrustful of research results and, as discussed in chapter 1, research is not value-free, the scientific method is still the most objective, unbiased, and systematic approach available for finding answers to questions.

There are several different ways of conducting research, each of which has advantages and disadvantages. Let's consider how various research methods can influence the type of information they yield.

TYPES OF RESEARCH INVESTIGATIONS

Anecdotal Evidence and Surveys

Most people have strong beliefs about sex differences. Stop and ask almost anyone about sex differences with regard to a specific ability, math for example, and you are likely to get an answer like this one: "Of course, boys are better than girls in math. Both my sons did well in math, but my daughter just hated it." (Notice that this answer switched from performance in mathematics to attitudes toward mathematics.) Or, you might get an answer like this one: "Personally, I think that women are better at math than men. My husband always depends on me to balance the checkbook." There is a tendency for people to rely on and to prefer personal anecdotal answers to questions instead of general ones derived from large samples. This preference reflects a well-documented bias in favor of using one's own experiences in understanding human behavior (Holland, Holyoak, Nisbett, & Thagard, 1986). Many people find a single anecdotal example more persuasive than a series of well documented research findings. If you doubt the powerful influence of single examples, try this miniexperiment:

> Tell several people that the recent winner of a prestigious mathematics contest (make up a serious sounding name for the competition, like the Mathematics Scholars Program) was a 10th grade girl. Tell them also that numerous researchers have found that high school boys outscore high school girls on tests of mathematical ability. Now, ask them if the fact that a female won a prestigious contest in mathematics weakens the conclusions from the research studies. You'll find that many people, especially those who are not familiar with the research method, are willing to discount the results from numerous studies because of a single example that is contrary to the research results.

There are many problems with anecdotal answers or conclusions that are based on a single example. First, our own experiences and those of our friends and family may not be typical of people in general. We may be generalizing to all or most males and females from atypical observations. Second, they are biased in predictable ways. Our memories are fallible and may be influenced by our beliefs and expectations. There is a wealth of evidence in the social psychological literature that shows that stereotypes are difficult to disconfirm because we select and remember information from our environment that is consistent with our beliefs (e.g., Halpern, 1985). Third, anecdotal evidence lacks precision. You might remember that your brother got higher grades in mathematics than you did, but you might not remember how much higher. Most importantly, such evidence can rarely be used to determine cause. Did your sister perform poorly because she lacked ability or was she discouraged from performing well? Despite the typical reliance on personal experience to formulate general laws of human behavior, only systematic investigations of large samples of data that are representative of the population we want to know about (in this case, all men and all women) can provide answers to questions relating to sex differences.

Carefully controlled research is also needed because of the human tendency to reject results that are not in accord with our belief biases. Consider a recent letter to the editor that appeared in *The Chronicle of Higher Education:* The letter was written by an assistant professor of physics in response to an article about sex differences in spatial skills. Asaro (1990, p. B4) wrote that the notion that men have better spatial skills than women is "another of the erroneous stereotypes." You should be wondering "What is the strength and nature of the evidence that supports Asaro's conclusion?" The only evidence given by Asaro was that she observed no sex-related discrepancies in spatial abilities in her personal experience. An "alarm" should go off in your head every time someone offers a conclusion about all women and men based solely on his or her personal experience.

Another weak type of evidence for understanding the nature of sex differences comes from survey data. Surveys can take many forms. Sometimes, surveys ask what skilled activities you perform well or poorly. If more women than men were to report that they write poetry well, would you be willing to consider this finding as support for the notion that women have better poetry or language skills than men? I hope not, because differences in self-reports may not reflect differences in actual abilities. The unreliability of self-report data is well established across many fields of study. It is possible that more women report that they write poetry well because it is a more socially acceptable trait for women. It is possible that comparable numbers of men also write poetry equally well, but they are unwilling to admit it.

Sometimes, surveys involve simple head counts of the number of women and men in a selected category. For example, virtually every such survey finds that there are many more men than women in math-related occupations such as accounting, mathematics, and physics. Head count surveys may provide interesting information about "how many" and "how much," but they can never tell us *why* each sex has disproportionate representation in certain occupations. Are there more male mathematicians because men have greater mathematical ability or only because it is more difficult in our society for women to gain access to these occupations? Although anecdotes and surveys may seem intuitively appealing, they are limited in the type of research question for which they can provide answers.

On the other hand, one advantage of surveys is that the results can be used to suggest topics for future research. Fennema and Sherman (1977, 1978), for example, have conducted extensive surveys on attitudes towards mathematics among high school girls and boys. They found that girls perceive mathematics to be less useful than boys do and, in general, maintain less favorable attitudes toward the study of advanced mathematics. Sherman (1980) used these results as a springboard for further studies. She found that among equally able girls, perceived usefulness of mathematics and confidence in learning mathematics were significant factors in determining their enrollment in mathematics courses.

Correlational Approaches with Nonrandom Assignment of Subjects

In a correlational approach, the relationship between changes in two or more variables is examined. Consider, for example, an article on the relationship between marijuana use and scholastic aptitude that was recently published in a national newspaper. It argued that marijuana has a deleterious effect on scholastic aptitude, based on the finding that Scholastic Aptitude Test (SAT) scores declined during the years that marijuana was in heaviest use, and SAT scores increased when marijuana use declined. This argument is based on the negative relationship between SAT scores and marijuana use; when marijuana use increased, SAT scores declined, and when marijuana use decreased, SAT scores increased. Let's suppose that the data in support of this claim are correct. Can you find anything wrong with this line of reasoning? What is missing is the *causal link*. It is incorrect to infer that marijuana use was responsible for the rise and fall in SAT scores. It is possible that a third factor, for example, changes in the economy, was responsible for the increase in marijuana use and the decrease in SAT scores. (Perhaps when the economy is tight, students take school more seriously and have less money to spend on drugs, with the reverse occurring in a booming economy.) It is also possible that changes in SAT scores caused the changes in marijuana use. Maybe when students perform poorly on the SAT, they smoke more marijuana, and as their scores improve, they smoke less marijuana.

The problem being raised here is commonly known as "causal arrow ambiguity." The coincidence of changes in two variables does not provide support for the notion that one variable is responsible for the concomitant changes in the second variable. In order to determine if marijuana smoking *caused* changes in SAT scores, students would have to be assigned at random either to smoke or not to smoke marijuana for a predetermined period of time. If we found that the group who smoked marijuana scored, on the average, significantly lower on the SAT than the group that didn't smoke marijuana, then we could conclude that marijuana smoking is deleterious to SAT performance. Unless subjects are randomly assigned to conditions, it is likely that students who voluntarily smoke marijuana differ in many ways from those who don't (e.g., differences in socioeconomic status, attitudes toward illegal drugs, etc.). It is possible that any or all of the other differences are responsible for the decline and subsequent increase in SAT scores.

Most of the research on sex differences does not employ the random assignment of subjects to conditions because it usually is not possible to intervene in people's lives and change their life experiences. Sex differences research often involves studying males and females "the way they are," that is, without experimental manipulations. For example, suppose an investigator reports that the ability to visualize objects in space is positively correlated with the amount of male hormones present during prenatal development. Such a result constitutes only weak evidence for the hypothesis that the prenatal concentration of male hormones causes good visual spatial ability because of the problem of causal arrow ambiguity. It is possible that many children with high levels of prenatal male hormones also had different home environments or different socioeconomic backgrounds than children with low levels of prenatal male hormones. Or, more likely, males not only have prenatal "male" hormones, but also have life experiences that encourage the development of spatial skills. How can we determine if it is the life experiences or the prenatal hormones or both that are responsible for the good spatial ability? Alternative explanations are possible whenever subjects are not randomly assigned to experimental conditions. All research based on naturally occurring events without experimental manipulations are necessarily confounded (i.e., more than one variable changes at the same time, in this case, the biological determinants of an individual's sex vary along with sex-related life experiences) and cannot provide causal information.

Correlational data with nonrandom assignment can provide a stronger case for causation if the results are in accord with a highly plausible theory. Suppose, for example, there is reason to believe that if male hormones are high during fetal development, then the neurons in the area of the brain specialized for vision show a more complex pattern of dendritic growth with more interconnections with other neurons. If this theory were true, then the finding that high concentrations of prenatal male hormones are positively correlated with the ability to visualize spatial objects would provide corroborative evidence that these hormones underlie spatial visualization abilities. This is a totally fictitious theory that I devised to make the point that research conducted with nonrandom assignment of subjects in conjunction with a strong theory provides better evidence for causation than the research alone. In this case, data involving nonrandom assignment of subjects would serve to corroborate other empirical sources of support for the theory. In fact, any report of sex differences without a theoretical underpinning to explain why the sex differences occurred should be viewed with skepticism. Like survey results, serendipitous findings can be valuable if they are used as an impetus for additional research and if they can be incorporated in a testable theory.

All research results are necessarily probabilistic, which means that sometimes sex differences will occur in experiments by chance. If all of the human research conducted included a test for sex differences, many spurious reports of sex differences would clutter the literature. It is prudent to consider any atheoretical reports of sex differences as chance findings until they are replicated and cast in a theoretical framework.

If correlational data can be used to support a "highly plausible theory," the problem remains of determining what makes a theory "highly plausible." The mere existence of a theory is not sufficient. A theory needs to be supported empirically with research conducted in multiple settings, using different samples of subjects and different measurement techniques, before it gains the status of *highly plausible*. It also needs to fit within an existing framework of facts and beliefs. There are many theories about sex differences in male and female brains, for example. Yet, these theories are surprisingly mute on the mechanisms that underlie these differences. Like the proverbial chain, a theoretical network is only as strong as its weakest link. A strong theory can explain and predict the causes, correlates, and consequences of cognitive sex differences.

Observational Techniques

With observational techniques, researchers literally "look" at behaviors, usually in "real-world" situations. Suppose that you were interested in knowing if young girls really differ from young boys with respect to aggression. You could observe the playground behavior of young children, keeping a tally of the number of aggressive acts committed by boys and girls. One of the advantages of this technique is that you would be actually observing *real* behavior rather than relying on some secondary technique like asking girls and boys about how aggressive they are. However, this technique has many of the same problems associated with it as noted in previous sections. Even if you found that boys (or girls) committed more aggressive acts, observation can never provide an answer as to why these sex differences occur. There are also other drawbacks to this technique. Observations are never really objective because we tend to see what we expect to see. If a girl pushes a child on the playground, it may appear less aggressive to an experimenter than when the same push is done by a boy. It is also likely that children will behave differently if they know that they are being observed. Thus, by observing the behavior, the researcher may actually have changed it. The choice of where to observe behavior also becomes important. A researcher may find sex differences on the playground, but not in the classroom or on the soccer field.

True Experiments and Quasi-Experiments

Most researchers consider the experiment as the method of choice for determining cause. In a "true" experiment, the researcher has greater control over the variables because subjects are assigned at random to experimental and control groups. Consider the hypothetical example (cited earlier) of the relationship between prenatal hormones and spatial visualization ability. In a true experiment, the researcher would select the subjects, in this case female and male fetuses, assign them at random to either high-hormone or low-hormone conditions by administering drugs to their mothers, and measure their spatial visualization abilities later in life. The underlying assumption is that large groups of subjects selected at random will be more or less equivalent with respect to the variable of interest, in this case spatial visualization ability. If we systematically vary only one aspect of their lives (prenatal hormones) so that overall the two or more groups differ only in this way, we can attribute any major differences between groups to this "treatment." Presumably, there would be rich and poor, smart and dull, tall and short children of each sex in each group, but the only consistent between-group difference would be the nature of the variable the researcher has manipulated.

The major difference between a true experiment and the correlational approach discussed earlier is the random assignment of subjects to manipulated conditions. Random assignment allows the experimenter to control the variable of interest so that any systematic differences between the groups are attributable to the manipulated variable. The underlying rationale is that people differ from each other in many ways. If we assign people to different treatment groups at random, then preexisting group differences would be unlikely because people of all sorts should be found in each of the groups. It then becomes more likely that any difference between the groups is due to the treatment. Thus, only a true experiment that randomly assigns subjects to conditions allows the experimenter to infer cause.

Very few "true" experiments are ever conducted in the area of sex differences. Obviously, we cannot vary the concentration of selected hormones that certain fetuses will be exposed to before birth. Such interventions would be unethical and unconscionable. Instead, we must take people "as they come" and lose the control that is needed to understanding causal links. A paradox in sex differences research is that the major variable of interest—being female or male—is never assigned at random. If we find that women perform a task, on the average better or worse than men, we still can't answer the question, "Why?" There are many variables that covary (or go along) with biological indicators of sex in our society, such as hormone concentrations, social expectations, power, status, childbirth experiences, and learning histories, to name a few. Given that so many variables are confounded with sex, and sex is never randomly assigned, causal attributions for any between-sex difference will be difficult to support. This is an important point because *all sex differences research is basically correlational in nature*. Researchers can never be certain if any between-sex differences are due to the biological aspects of sex, psychosocial concomitants of sex, the interaction between them, or some unidentified factor.

Because subjects can never be assigned at random in sex differences research, a somewhat less stringent procedure for examining cause is sometimes used. Quasi-experiments, like true experiments, involve some sort of experimental manipulation, but do not randomly assign subjects to groups. An example of a quasi-experiment might be to provide an educational or counseling program to a group of females who score poorly on mathematics tests in order to reduce "math anxiety." In interpreting the results, the experimenters would determine if the girls scored significantly higher on the test of mathematics ability after they received counseling to reduce their math anxiety. Research of this sort must also include a control group, in this case a group of females who score low in mathematics but do not receive the counseling, so that meaningful comparisons can be made. An experimental design of this sort involves a manipulation (the counseling to reduce math anxiety), but the subjects were already identified as females who score low on tests of mathematics. This experimental design allows the researcher to examine causality (math anxiety possibly caused the low mathematics scores), but does not permit strong causal statements.

The fact that biological sex creates very different environments for males and females from the moment of birth means that differences in biological sex are always associated with different environmental experiences. Distinguishing between nature or nurture as the more probable cause of sex differences is so difficult because of the confounding of nature and nurture. This is particularly germane to the controversies surrounding cognitive abilities. I return to this theme in several places throughout this book because it is critical in understanding the etiology of sex differences.

Comparisons of Research Methods.   Hendricks, Marvel, and Barrington (1990) suggested a "methodological cube" for summarizing the differences among research designs. Their cube is shown in Fig. 2.1. As you can see in this figure, descriptive, correlational, quasi-experimental, and true experimental designs differ in the kind of information they provide. Research designs also vary as a function of setting (laboratory or field) and the way the data are collected (observation or self report). These three dimensions form the axes or edges of the cube. As you read about the research that is described in the following chapters,

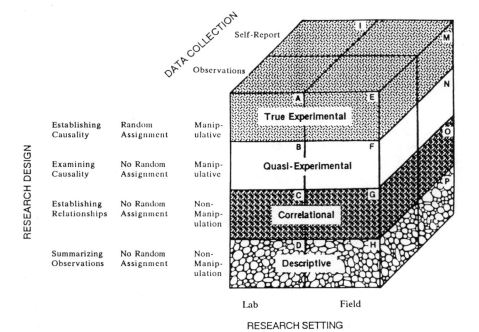

FIG. 2.1 Methodological cube of group research methods. From Hendricks, Marvel, and Barrington (1990). The dimensions of Psychological research. *Teaching of psychology, 17,* 76–82. Reprinted with permission from Lawrence Erlbaum Associates, Publishers.

keep these variables in mind because they determine the kinds of inferences that we can make from the data.

Factor Analytic Approaches

Traditionally, a common method of studying human cognitive or intellectual abilities has been the factor analytic approach (e.g., Thurstone & Thurstone, 1941). The underlying rationale for this approach is that cognition is not a single homogeneous concept. Most psychologists believe that there are several cognitive abilities and that individuals can be skilled or unskilled in one, some, or all of them. One of the most common theoretical distinctions is between verbal and spatial abilities. One way to test this hypothesis is to give a large number of women and men several tests of verbal abilities (e.g., vocabulary comprehension, verbal analogies) and spatial abilities (e.g., using maps, solving jigsaw puzzles). If these four tests are really measures of two different abilities, then through the statistical technique known as factor analysis, two factors or underlying dimensions will result from the data analysis. The first factor, which we believe represents verbal ability, will be created from the vocabulary comprehension and verbal analogies test scores, and the second factor, which we believe represents spatial ability, will be created from the using maps and solving jigsaw puzzles test scores. (The actual mathematical principles and procedures involved are not germane to the purpose of this discussion and therefore, are not described. The interested reader is referred to Kerlinger, 1979, for a lucid discussion.) If we obtained the same two factors for both our sample of women and our sample of men, then we would conclude that women's and men's cognitive abilities have similar factor-analytic structures. Suppose, by contrast, that we found that only one factor emerged for our sample of women. This would mean that these four tests had a single underlying dimension for women. (Another way of thinking about this hypothetical result is that the four tests were all measuring the same unitary construct.) If our sample of men yielded two factors from these tests, and our sample of women yielded only one factor, then we would conclude that there are sex differences in cognitive structures.

Only a handful of studies have actually used factor analytic techniques to compare the cognitive structures of men and women. This is an important approach because it poses the more fundamental question of sex differences in the organization and structure of cognitive abilities as opposed to asking which sex is better at a given ability. For this reason, it is a good technique for examining differences.

UNDERSTANDING RESEARCH RESULTS

The Logic of Hypothesis Testing

A researcher searching for sex differences is really considering two mutually exclusive hypotheses. The first hypothesis is that there are no differences between males and females with respect to the variable being studied and, therefore, any differences found between the two groups are due to random error or chance differences in the samples selected. This hypothesis is called the *null hypothesis*. The competing or alternative hypothesis is that there really are differences between women and men and these differences are reflected in the sample of males and females. The researcher uses statistical tests to decide if any between-group differences are likely to have occurred by chance. If the tests show that the differences between the samples of women and men probably were not due to chance factors, then the experimenter can reject the null hypothesis and accept the alternative hypothesis. Thus, we formulate conclusions in a somewhat backward fashion. We conclude that the alternative hypothesis is probably true by deciding that the null hypothesis is probably false. In hypothesis testing, demonstrations of sex differences rely on a clear-cut set of procedures that involve deciding that the null hypothesis (the one that states that there are no sex differences) is probably wrong, and therefore the competing hypothesis that sex differences exist is probably right.

The Problem of Null Results

What about failures to reject the null hypothesis? Any serious researcher in the field of sex differences is also concerned about sex similarities. How can she or he conclude that there are no sex differences? This is a much more difficult problem and one that is particularly troublesome for research in the area of sex differences. Unfortunately, we can never accept the null hypothesis. The best we can do is fail to reject it. The strongest statement that can be made from failures to reject the null hypothesis is that the data do not support the notion that sex differences exist. We cannot conclude that differences do not exist. There are two reasons why failures to find differences cannot lead to the conclusion that there are no differences: statistical (the alternative hypothesis is not precise enough to permit the computation of the probabilities needed to reject it), and logical. (A more detailed explanation of the statistical reasons is beyond the scope of this book. Readers who have not had a course in statistics or experimental methods will have to take it on faith that there are mathematical reasons why claims of no sex differences can't be accepted statistically. Interested readers are referred to Cohen & Cohen, 1983, and Howell, 1987.)

Consider a simple example that should help to clarify this point. Suppose you formulate the null hypothesis that no one has more or less than one head. You could collect a large sample of people, count the number of heads per person, and presumably find that each has only one. However, you have not *proved* the null hypothesis, because only one exception, that is only one person with more or less than one head, can disprove it, and it is possible that you failed to include this person in your sample. Similarly, even large amounts of negative evidence cannot be used to prove that sex differences do not exist.

It may seem that studies that do not show sex differences should "cancel" studies that show sex differences. Assuming the studies were well conducted, those that find sex differences (positive studies) carry more weight than those that don't (negative studies) because it is always possible that the negative studies were not sensitive enough to detect a difference. Too few subjects, a poor test, plain old sloppy research, or numerous other problems can lead to false negatives. Thus, in the logic of hypothesis testing, we can never directly prove a null hypothesis. We can only disprove or reject the null hypothesis (the one that states that there are no sex differences), which, in turn, allows us to accept a mutually exclusive alternative hypothesis (the one that states that there are sex differences). (See Rozeboom, 1960, for a classic discussion about the failure to reject the null hypothesis.)

Most sex differences researchers are as interested in discovering similarities between females and males as they are in differences, yet it is axiomatic that they can never conclude that differences don't exist. Consider an experiment conducted by Seth-Smith, Ashton, and McFarland (1989) in which they reported that there are no sex-related differences in brain organization for verbal functioning. Although their study was well designed, they used only 10 college males and 10 college females. Their sample size was too small and too restrictive (college students only) to conclude that there are no sex differences in brain organization. The strongest statement that can be made from studies like this one is that the researchers failed to find differences with the specific sample and experimental procedures that they used. We cannot use these results to conclude that there are no differences. The logic of hypothesis testing is the backbone of the experimental method, and it does not permit a similarities conclusion.

Rosenthal and Rubin (1985) have distinguished between the use of the experimental method to establish facts versus its use to summarize research. They argue that it is virtually impossible to establish facts with any single study. In their view, a research report is publishable "if it contributes important evidence on an important scientific question" (p. 527). I believe that their point is especially relevant to research into the nature of sex differences. Although it may not be possible to *prove* that sex differences in a particular area don't exist, because of the strict logic of hypothesis testing, it is important to know if large numbers of researchers fail to find sex differences. If, for example, we knew that 95 out of every 100 investigations of mathematical sex differences failed to find differences, this information would certainly cause us to alter our conclusions about this area.

What about the studies that report differences? If half of them find that females are superior and half find that males are superior, it seems likely that experiments that report differences are "statistical errors." That is, they may have occurred "just by chance." On the other hand, suppose that all of the studies that report differences find that one sex is consistently scoring higher on mathematical tests. This sort of evidence would suggest that the positive results are not occurring by chance and that differences may be specific to one type of test—for example, geometry—or to one subpopulation—for example, children.

There are some experimental and data analytic techniques that allow researchers to investigate similarities. Murphy (1990) suggested that if the focus of a research program is similarities, the researcher could specify a range of outcomes that would be consistent with the hypothesis that there are no differences. For example, if I wanted to show that there are no sex differences in intelligence, I could give a large sample of women and men an intelligence test. I would have to specify a priori (before the data are collected) that if the average difference between the sample of females and males is less than two points, this result would be consistent with the hypothesis that there are no sex differences. It is also important to consider the *size* of the difference, a topic that is discussed in more detail in a later section in this chapter. There are also measures of concordance or similarity that can be used to provide evidence of similarity (e.g., correlations, Cronbach alphas, and factor loadings).

Sampling Issues

There are several sampling pitfalls that are exacerbated in or unique to sex differences research. Five of these issues are considered here: comparable between-sex samples, sample size, inappropriate generalizations, age by sex interactions, and replication samples.

Comparable Between-Sex Samples.   Sex differences research is concerned with ways in which women and men, on the average, differ. Although we may want to know about all women and men in North America or in the world, we can only collect data from a sample or subset of the population in which we are interested. The people we actually use in our study must be representative of the population we want to know about if our generalizations are to be accurate. Consider the issue of mathematical ability. One common approach to the question of whether males or females exceed in mathematical ability is to administer mathematical aptitude tests to males and females who have attained a given level of mathematical training. For example, a researcher might give an aptitude test to all students in a high school calculus course and then compare the scores obtained by the girls and boys. The major problem with this sample is that there may already have been considerable self-selection of subjects before entry into the calculus class. If mathematical ability is possessed by more boys than girls, then the attrition rate in mathematics courses should be higher for girls than boys, with the result that fewer girls persist in mathematics courses. A study of high school calculus students would then be sampling only an extreme group of mathematically gifted or persistent girls (e.g., perhaps the top 10% of all girls) and a less extreme group of boys (e.g., perhaps the top 25% of all boys). As noted earlier, studies like this one will not permit any causal statements because the subjects are not assigned at random to math classes. It is impossible to know why sex differences that might emerge from this study exist. They could be due to some factor or factors inherent in the biology of maleness or femaleness, due to societal expectations, or due to a host of other possibilities.

There is no single satisfactory way to resolve the problem of how to sample the sexes so that bias is eliminated. The logical alternative to sampling girls and boys with an equivalent number of mathematics courses is to sample the sexes without regard to the number or type of mathematics courses they have taken in school. The obvious disadvantage to this plan is that any differences that might be found are most likely attributable to the differences in mathematics education.

Similar sampling issues arise with other cognitive abilities as well. One partial solution is to utilize statistical control in the form of partial correlations and analysis of covariance procedures. These techniques allow the experimenter to *hold constant* the effect of a variable, like the number of mathematics courses taken by each subject. These procedures statistically allow the researcher to ask a question like, "If boys and girls had taken the same number of mathematics courses, would we still find differences in mathematical ability?" Although these statistical approaches represent an improvement in the way we find answers to sex differences questions, they also are flawed. The use of analysis of covariance, for example, requires certain mathematical properties that are rarely true of any data set (e.g., linear effects across all groups, covariate unaffected by the treatment, homogeneity of between and within groups regression. Readers with an advanced background in statistics are referred to Evans & Anastasio, 1968, and Harris, Bisbee, & Evans, 1971, for a discussion of the use and misuse of analysis of covariance.)

Statistical techniques that control for sampling differences do provide some useful information. They could, for example, show that sex differences in mathematical ability tests can be explained on the basis of course taking alone. Despite these advantages, research that utilizes statistical control procedures still begs the basic question of why there are differences in mathematical achievement tests and in the number of mathematics courses taken by boys and girls. It's like asking if poor people would vote like rich people if they weren't poor. Even if the researcher found that they would, this result would be of little immediate value because the poor people are still poor and therefore will continue to vote for issues that concern the poor, despite the statistical control we've gained over our data with this technique.

Becker and Hedges (1984) focused on the importance of sampling issues in their review of the inconsistencies in the results obtained from research on cognitive sex differences. They concluded that "essentially all of the variability in the sex differences reported can be explained as a function of the publication date and the selectivity of the sampling plan used in the studies" (p. 583). Quite simply, the results you obtain from your study depend on whom you select as subjects. It is important to keep this in mind when interpreting research results.

In sex differences research there is no easy answer to the dilemma of sampling. If you were interested in determining whether cognitive abilities vary over the menstrual cycle, who is the appropriate comparison group? Is it women who are not menstruating (either because they have reached menopause or because of a hysterectomy or medications that suppress the cyclical change in hormone concentrations) or is it a group of men? Studies that have investigated the possibility that women become more aggressive during the premenstrual phase of the menstrual cycle seem to ignore the fact that men commit many more acts of aggression every day of the month.

Sample Size.   A second sampling problem in sex differences concerns sample size or the number of subjects we need to include in an experiment. In general, large samples yield good estimates of population parameters (true values in the population). One of the major factors concerning sample size is the amount of variability in the population from which the sample is drawn. If the population has little variability (i.e., there is very little spread among the scores) then a small sample will provide a good estimate of the population parameters, whereas a population with considerable variability (i.e., scores are spread out and do not cluster tightly around a mean value) will require a larger sample size in order to obtain stable estimates of its parameters. One theory in the sex differences literature is that male performance is more variable than female performance. (This hypothesis is discussed in more detail in chapter 3.) If this hypothesis were true, then we would have to sample more males than females in order to obtain the same level of confidence in our statistics. This is virtually never done in practice, nor have I ever seen it addressed as a sampling issue.

The number of subjects selected for a study has important implications for the conclusions we can draw. Although large samples are desirable because they yield good estimates of population parameters, they also virtually insure that statistically significant sex differences will be found. For mathematical reasons, small samples are less likely to provide evidence of sex differences than large ones. Many of the studies that fail to find differences use a small number of subjects. The experimenter who is honestly seeking answers to sex differences questions will have to be concerned with sample size. Far too frequently, the issue of sample size is ignored or resolved on the basis of hunch or intuition. Ideally, all sex differences research (and other research) should begin with an estimate of the size of the sex difference effect that would be important to detect. For example, a researcher studying sex differences in intelligence might decide that a sex difference of less than two IQ points would not be important in understanding differences in cognition. The two point difference would then be converted into an "effect size" (discussed in more detail later in this chapter). It is then a simple procedure to solve a mathematical equation for determining how many subjects should be included in the experiment. Details of this procedure are presented in Cohen and Cohen's (1983) statistical text. Unfortunately, this method of determining sample size is rarely used.

Inappropriate Generalizations.   A third issue in sampling concerns the use of atypical populations. Very frequently, researchers sample from abnormal populations to formulate conclusions about normal women and men. This approach is most commonly used in research that examines the effect of chromosomes and hormones on the cognitive abilities of normal women and men. The reasoning behind this approach is that by examining what happens when something goes wrong (e.g., extremely high concentrations of male hormones on developing fetuses), we can understand the role of the variable being investigated under normal circumstances (e.g., the effect of normal levels of male hormones on developing fetuses). There is an obvious flaw in this approach. First, abnormal populations differ from normals in many ways. An infant exposed to abnormal concentrations of prenatal hormones may develop a masculine body type or may receive specialized medical care or unusual treatment by family members. The secondary effects of the hormone anomaly may affect the variable under investigation and these effects could be mistakenly attributed to the hormone rather than the experiential factor. Thus, it is not possible to isolate the influence of hormones per se. In addition, abnormal hormone levels (or chromosome patterns or any other variable that is atypical) may have effects that are unrelated to the effect of normal hormone levels (or chromosome patterns). Research with abnormal populations can provide supporting or confirming evidence for a hypothesis, but cannot be used as the primary support of a hypothesis.

Often, researchers concerned about understanding human sex differences conduct their research with other animal species. The major difficulty is generalizing from rats or monkeys to humans. We know that hormones, for example, play a greater role in the behavior of nonhuman species than they do in humans, whereas cognitive and social variables are more important in determining human behavior. Generalizing from animal research to humans is also difficult because contradictory results are obtained with different species and different breeds within a specie. Thus, although animal research can provide information that is interesting in its own right, extreme caution is urged when extrapolating the results to humans. For example, Janowsky (1989) studied the brain mechanisms that underlie song behavior in canaries. Male canaries, but not females, exhibit a complex learned song behavior. When researchers administer testosterone (a male hormone) to female canaries, female canaries will develop the song behavior of male canaries. Research of this sort suggests that testosterone plays an important role in the development of canary song behavior. We cannot use this sort of data to conclude that testosterone is important in human verbal behavior because there are too many differences between human and bird brains and between canary songs and human verbal behavior. Nevertheless, this research is not "useless." It does suggest that, at least for some animals, testosterone plays a role in vocalization. Like research with abnormal human populations, research with nonhuman animals can provide supplemental support for relevant hypotheses, but cannot support a hypothesis without more relevant evidence.

Age by Sex Interactions.   Another issue in selecting subjects is age. It is likely that some sex differences change over the life span and in different ways for each sex. A difference may be nonexistent in childhood, emerge during puberty, and disappear again in old age. Some abilities decline at different rates for elderly men and women. The answers we find to sex differences questions are age dependent. Research that utilizes only young adults in college (the favorite subject pool of academics) will undoubtedly fail to capture the age dependent nature of any differences that exist.

One of the main criticisms of Maccoby and Jacklin's (1974) major review of the sex differences literature was their extensive use of research utilizing young children to formulate general conclusions about sex differences. In general, researchers have tended to ignore the developmental nature of adult age differences in cognition. Because our cognitive abilities do not remain static throughout the life span, generalizations about sex differences that may be true at adolescence may be false for mid-life or older adults. The elderly remain one of the most understudied populations for cognitive sex differences, despite the fact that understanding sex-related developmental differences is crucial in an aging society.

Replication Samples. Because all research is necessarily probabilistic, sometimes spurious reports of sex differences will be found in the literature. The ultimate test of whether a report of a sex difference is real is whether it is replicated (i.e., does it reliably appear) in other experiments. Good researchers are aware of this test and plan replications of their own work before they publish sex differences results. A replication sample is a second or third sample of subjects who are similar to those used in an original study. These subjects receive essentially the same treatment (if there is one) and have the same measurements taken as those in the original sample. If sex differences are also found in the second or third sample, then we can accept the results with greater confidence than if they were found in only one sample. Although replication samples are always a good idea, they are especially important in research that doesn't employ the random assignment of subjects to conditions, because research of this sort provides weaker evidence than true experiments. Unfortunately, few reports of sex differences are based on research with replication samples. Later in this book, I describe in detail a research report by Harshman, Hampson, and Berenbaum (1983) that I consider to be pivotal in determining the involvement of biological variables. One of the strengths of this study is the use of three separate samples, which means that we can be more confident that the results are not due to chance factors than we would be if only one sample had been used.

Measurement

Measurement is defined as the assignment of numbers according to rules. The way we measure or assign numbers directly influences the kinds of results we obtain. One of the major measurement issues with which sex differences researchers need to be concerned is how sex should be measured. This may seem

like a surprising question if you are not familiar with the problem. Usually, sex is measured as a dichotomous (two choice) variable with every subject being either male or female. However, there are many times when it is desirable to measure the degree of maleness or femaleness. For most of us, the usual indicators of sex are in agreement. Our chromosomes, hormones, genitals, gonads, sex of rearing, and self-definitions all agree that we are either male or female. However, this is not always true. Consider the anomalous case in which chromosomes may indicate maleness, but genitals and sex of rearing are female. Is this person somehow "less male" and "less female" than the typical male or female?

Part of the measurement problem is that it is not always clear what researchers mean by *sex*. Although I have decided not to make this distinction, sometimes sex is used to refer to biological differences with the term *gender* used for referring to the social construction of sex. The components of biological sex are usually, but now always, consistent, but gender identity, sexual preference, and gender role are often inconsistent with each other and with biological sex. These variations of sex make it difficult to think of sex as a single variable.

A more common dilemma with regard to dichotomous versus continuous measurement concerns sex-role orientation. This concept refers to the extent to which an individual's behavior conforms to the female or male sex role as defined in a given society. That is, does one conform to sex-typed expectations or stereotypes? The question of whether sex-role orientation should be dichotomous (i.e., men and women could be either masculine or feminine in sex-role orientation) or discrete with three or four possibilities (masculine or feminine or androgynous or undifferentiated) or continuous (more or less masculine or feminine) has been the subject of heated debate. Humphreys (1978) has argued that masculinity/femininity requires continuous measurement and Baucom and Welsh (1978) argue that a dichotomous (extreme groups) level of measurement is appropriate. Continuous measurement generally provides more information and may be preferred when measuring other variables like handedness, in which one can be more or less right or left handed instead of dichotomously right or left handed. However, both levels of measurement are useful in assessing sex differences. It may be that the extremely masculine individual is qualitatively, not just quantitatively, different from a feminine individual. It seems that both dichotomous and continuous measurement can be used depending on the nature of the question being asked. (For a lucid discussion of this topic, see Matlin, 1987.)

Date of Publication and Sex of Researcher

You may be wondering what the date of publication or sex of researcher has to do with understanding the results of research. The effects of these extraneous variables are indirect. Several experimenters have investigated the possibility that sex differences are diminishing over time. One way to do this is to find if results that were published in the 1940s showed larger sex differences than those published in the 1950s and so on. While it is logical to assume that researchers would report smaller and smaller sex differences over time if the size of the difference is diminishing, there is a major problem with this line of reasoning. There are many changes that occur with time. For example, if we were to measure reading ability among college freshmen over the last 50 years, we would have to consider the fact that the nature of college freshmen has changed in numerous ways. Fifty years ago, it was fairly unusual for females to enroll in college; those that made it into college more likely were from wealthy homes or were exceptionally intelligent or persistent. This is not true today. Over half of all college first-year students are female, so the group of females who are in college today are different in many ways from female college students 50 years ago. Research that has used date of publication to argue that sex differences are decreasing or increasing is considered in detail in chapter 3.

Sex of researcher is an even more subtle variable than date of publication. The reason that some people think that the sex of the researcher is important in understanding results is because there are numerous ways, both deliberate and unintentional, in which investigators bias the outcomes of their research. If we were to assume that more women are feminists than men, then we might expect that women researchers are more likely to provide results that are consistent with feminist philosophies than men who conduct similar research. We all interpret the world in terms of our own backgrounds and experiences. This does not mean that all research is biased or that we cannot keep an open mind and evaluate findings in a fair manner, only that we need to consider the ways in which personal beliefs can bias the outcomes of research. Hyde and Linn (1988), for example, found that female researchers were more likely to find evidence of female superiority in verbal abilities than male researchers. In an ideal world, sex of researcher would be an irrelevant variable.

Situational Variables

We are all social creatures. The way we respond in any situation depends much more on environmental factors than individual factors. If you are sitting in a college classroom, shopping in a supermarket, or getting up in the morning, I can predict what you are doing, without knowing anything about you. Situational variables are extremely potent in determining behaviors. Researchers frequently study sex differences by controlling all factors other than sex of the subject. Suppose you wanted to study nurturing behavior to decide if females are more nurturant than males. Eagly (1987) pointed out that research conducted in carefully controlled laboratory settings often finds that there are no sex differences in nurturance. But, if the same researchers were to investigate nurturing behavior in more natural settings (caring for sick children, assisting the elderly), they would find that women occupy more of the nurturing roles in society. Thus, setting is a salient part of any research report.

It is important to keep in mind that all behavior occurs in a context. Most everyone will agree that people often respond in different ways in different situations. This may be especially true of sex-related differences. Suppose, for example, that you are interested in sex differences in assertive behavior. Furthermore, you are aware that results obtained in laboratory settings may not generalize to the real world. So, you decide to examine assertiveness in a public place. Suppose, further, that you choose to study sex differences in assertiveness at the movies. You carefully note that in mixed sex dyads (pairs in which one member is female and the other member is male) the male usually drives to the movies, purchases the movie tickets, hands them to the ticket taker, and yes, even makes the important popcorn decisions (buttered or unbuttered). Based on this naturalistic observation, you would conclude that males are more assertive than females. However, you would have failed to study other situations in which women tend to be assertive, such as dealing with a child's angry teacher, returning defective merchandise, handling an emergency at the office, or negotiating the sale of a residence as a real estate broker. You probably recognize each of these scenarios as stereotypically female, yet, you may never have realized that each requires assertiveness, a stereotypically male trait.

Experiments conducted in laboratory settings often involve artificial situations. Because so much of our behavior is situation dependent, it is important to consider ways in which the experimental situation may have biased the results. This is an important point in understanding sex-related cognitive differences. Men, for example, may not perform as well on tasks that are viewed in our society as feminine (e.g., embroidery) when they are being observed as they do when performing the same tasks in private. Sex of experimenter is an important situational variable which is often overlooked. Subjects sometimes respond differently to same-sex and other-sex experimenters.

It is easy to see how situational variables can influence the results we get. In Eagly's (1987) review of sex differences in helping behavior, she noted that most of the literature is limited to the extent to which subjects helped strangers in potentially dangerous situations. Most of women's helping behavior occurs within the family or in the context of a long-term relationship. Not surprisingly, the research shows that men are more likely to offer help than women. Eagly concluded that this is not a valid conclusion because of the artificial and limited number of situations in most of the research.

Multivariate Indicators

An examination of sex-related differences in cognitive abilities requires that both sex and cognitive abilities be measured. In most research with normal populations, sex is measured by self-report. Virtually all people define themselves as either male or female. The measurement of cognitive abilities is more problematic. If you want to investigate spatial ability, for example, how can you measure it in a meaningful way? A clear definition of what constitutes spatial ability is needed. There is often disagreement among researchers, each of whom tends to work with a somewhat different definition (Caplan, MacPherson, & Tobin, 1985). There are literally hundreds of tests that can be used to measure spatial ability, and, as you can imagine, they do not all yield the same results. Some of the tests commonly employed include the performance section of the Weschler Adult Intelligence Scale (WAIS), finding simple figures that are embedded in larger ones, imagining how a figure will look if it is rotated in the depth plane, figuring out how the surfaces of a cube would fit together if a flat diagram were assembled, tracing a route on a real or imaginary map, and assembling a model from written instructions.

The problem for the researcher is to decide which of these tests will yield a *true* measure of spatial ability. It is usually possible to eliminate some tests on an a priori basis because they fail to meet certain criteria. Some of these tests may actually rely heavily on verbal skills or be inconsistent with working definitions of spatial abilities. There is probably no single ideal test. If a researcher wants to explore sex differences in spatial ability, then several tests of spatial abilities should be employed in the same experiment.

Multiple indicators of cognitive abilities are desirable for several reasons. If sex differences in the same direction are consistently found on four different tests of spatial ability, then a more convincing claim that differences exist can be made than if differences are found on one test. Second, if sex differences are found on some tests of spatial ability, but not others, the experimenter can examine ways in which these two types of tests differ, yielding a more fine-grained analysis of the nature of sex differences. A hypothetical example of the way several tests could be used to isolate the nature of the sex difference is the finding that the sexes differ on tests that require short-term memory of spatial information, but not on other tests of spatial ability. These results would suggest that the locus of spatial ability differences is in spatial memory and not the ability to utilize spatial information per se.

Sometimes researchers use multiple indicators and then inappropriately use univariate data analytic techniques. For example, a researcher might use ten different tests of spatial ability, then analyze each test separately to determine if sex differences exist. The use of multiple univariate analyses increases the probability that a researcher will find sex differences that are due to chance sampling differences. Multivariate statistical techniques (e.g., MANOVA) are usually needed when multiple indicators are used.

STATISTICAL AND PRACTICAL SIGNIFICANCE

In order to understand research results, the reader must consider both the statistical and practical significance of any mean difference between males and females. Let's begin with an example to clarify this point.

Suppose that a researcher wants to know if boys or girls watch more television. He carefully samples children within a given age range, socioeconomic status, etc., and then tallies the number of hours of television watched by each child in a week. He then computes the mean (average) number of hours of television watched by the boys and girls in the sample. Suppose that he finds that boys watch an average of 25 hours of television a week and girls watch an average of 25.4 hours a week. Obviously he cannot simply look at these two mean values and conclude that the sexes differ with respect to average amount of television viewing. These differences could be due to chance factors (sampling error). Conclusions based on simply *eyeballing* the data are humorously called "binocular tests of significance." All serious researchers require a statistical test of significance.

Because research in sex differences always involves samples of people and because people are variable, there is always some chance or probability that conclusions based on the research are incorrect. There is very little in life, and especially in sex differences research, that is known with absolute certainty. It is important to keep in mind the probabilistic nature of research results. Suppose that 100 studies are conducted comparing the number of hours of television watched by boys and girls. If we set $p < .05$, then by chance alone, even if boys and girls watch television the same number of hours each week, 5 of these studies would find sex differences. Furthermore, if only studies finding sex differences appear in the published literature, then it is easy to see how incorrect conclusions are reached. There is no simple remedy for the fact that sometimes researchers will find sex differences "just by chance." Tests of statistical significance constitute the backbone of research. They are essential in interpreting research results; however, they should be considered as a first step in making sense of the results.

When research results are statistically significant, it is correct to conclude that there probably are differences between the sexes, especially if the results can be interpreted in a theoretical framework and have been replicated with different samples. Given these results, a second question should be, "Is the difference large enough to have any practical significance?" In other words, are the results meaningful or useful? Considering the current example, the researcher and reader need to ask if the finding that girls watch, on the average, .4 of an hour more television each week than boys has any practical significance. Clearly it would be incorrect to construe this difference as implying that girls are glued to television sets while boys are off doing other things. The obtained mean difference translates into an additional 24 minutes a week or 3.4 minutes a day! Even if such a result is statistically significant, it tells us very little of any practical importance about boy/girl differences in television watching.

Variability and Shapes of Distributions

In order to understand if a sex difference exists with respect to a particular variable, the investigator needs to be concerned with the distribution of scores for women and men because the relative number of each sex that obtains a particular score on a test has important implications for the way we interpret the data. There are many ways distributions can differ. Consider the six hypothetical distributions of scores in Fig. 2.2.

The hypothetical distributions in Fig. 2.2 depict some possible outcomes for men and women on a test of musical ability. Figure 2.2A represents the case in which men and women obtain an identical distribution of scores, with most subjects obtaining a score of 50 on this test (the mean or average), and a few obtaining scores as extreme as 0 or 100. The finding that both sexes have the same distribution of musical ability is seen by the overlapping identical curves. Both curves show the same peak (corresponding to the mean of the distribution in normal distributions) and the same bell-shaped curve (indicating that they have the same variability or "spread-outness" of scores).

Figure 2.2B shows a somewhat different distribution of female and male scores. In this case, the sexes have the same mean score (the *average* for both women and men is 50), but the sexes differ in variability. The male scores are more closely clustered around the mean, indicating less variability for men than for women. Thus, any man selected at random would be expected to be near the mean value in musical ability while any women selected at random would be expected to be farther from the mean (either lower or higher) than her male counterpart.

Figures 2.2C, D, and E all depict situations in which the means between the

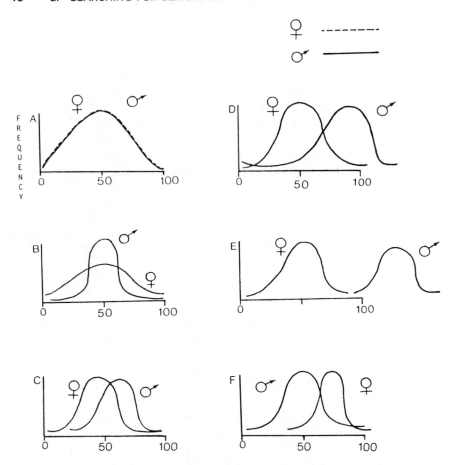

FIG. 2.2.   Six hypothetical distributions of male and female scores on a test of musical ability.

sexes differ (in this case with males, on the average, outperforming females), but the variability remains the same. There is much overlap between the sexes in Fig. 2.2C, an intermediate amount of overlap in Fig. 2.2D, and virtually no overlap in Fig. 2.2E. Although each of these scenarios represents a case in which a researcher could legitimately conclude that males scored higher in musical ability than females, each figure tells a different story about the distribution of musical ability by sex. If Fig. 2.2E depicted the true results for males and females, then we would expect the most tone deaf males to have more musical ability than the most musically talented females. On the other hand, if Fig. 2.2C represented the true distribution, then we might expect only slight differences in the percentage of women and men at every level of musical ability.

Figure 2.2F represents another possibility. In this figure the female and male distributions have both different means and different variances. In this hypothetical example, females scored higher than males and showed less variability. If Fig. 2.2F were a true representation of these distributions, then we could expect more females to score well on this test and to score close to the female mean, whereas men would be more variable with some obtaining low scores and others high scores. It is important to consider the shape of the distribution of scores when exploring sex differences. Research reports of sex differences that don't provide information about the relative shapes and amount of overlap between distributions provide only a small part of the information needed to understand the data.

Most of the research on sex differences reports mean group differences between women and men. Very few consider sex differences in the shape of the distribution of scores for the variable being measured and the extent to which they overlap. Percentiles of males and females at every ability level should also be provided. A report that women excel at verbal reasoning tasks is less meaningful than one that also indicates, for example, that 75% of women and 70% of men scored at or beyond a given score on the test. The additional information presents a clearer picture of the distribution of this ability between the sexes and allows a more meaningful comparison.

A related issue is the way researchers report measures of central tendency. Most report group means (averages) as a single number summary of the scores obtained by each sex. Although this is useful, and probably essential, in understanding what the data represent, mean values should also be reported along with confidence intervals, which are a range of scores that probably contains the true population mean. It would be more meaningful to know that the population mean for women in a hypothetical aptitude test is probably between 85 and 115, whereas the comparable confidence interval for men is 87 to 117 than it is to know that the sample mean for women is 100 and the sample mean for men is 102. (In a more statistical vein, confidence intervals are computed for selected confidence levels, such as 95%, and can be interpreted as meaning that if the experiment were repeated 100 times, 95% of the intervals computed would contain the true population mean.)

Meta-Analysis

The literature on sex differences is enormous. How can anyone sift through thousands, perhaps even tens of thousands, of research reports to determine which of the reported differences is *real?* No single experiment can ever provide the answer to sex differences questions. In an area as complex as this, researchers need to consider the preponderance of results before stating a conclusion. One of the best known attempts to synthesize the literature on sex differences was undertaken over 15 years ago by Maccoby and Jacklin (1974). They tallied all of the studies investigating sex differences that had been published in American journals during the 10-year period prior to 1974. They set a criterion that sex differences existed only when a large number of studies found sex differences in the same direction for a given variable. Although this was the first major attempt to synthesize the sex differences literature, their procedure has been criticized as the "voting method." (See Block, 1976, for a criticism of their methodology.)

A more sophisticated technique of integrating research findings is meta-analysis, which, as its name implies, is the analysis of analyses, or an analysis of many individual research results. It provides a measure of the strength or importance of a relationship between two variables. The need for meta-analysis is obvious in a research area in which the size of the literature can be measured in linear feet or pounds of paper generated. Meaningful integrations of research findings are the best way to interpret the voluminous literature. The purpose of meta-analysis is not only to determine how many studies obtained sex differences results in the predicted direction, but also how large the differences between women and men were.

The File Drawer Problem. Meta-analysis allows us to take a broad overview in summarizing research results (Hyde & Linn, 1986). It is important that the individual studies that are analyzed with meta-analytic techniques be representative of the research in the field. A major problem is finding representative research. The most logical place to find research is the journals and books found in libraries; however, due to publication practices, there is a bias to publish only studies that have found evidence of sex differences. Suppose that 100 researchers investigated sex differences in cognitive styles and that 90 of them found no differences. Suppose further that of the 10 that found differences, 2 found differences that favored men and 8 found differences that favored women. Given the current publication practices, it is more likely that the 10 studies that found sex differences would get published than the studies that found no differences. Suppose further that a researcher who is eager to understand the nature of sex differences in this area attempts to perform a meta-analysis. She would most likely use only the published studies in her analysis. After all, how would she even know about the unpublished studies that could have been conducted in universities and other settings around the world? If the 8 studies supporting female superiority found even moderately large sex differences, meta-analysis statistics would support the conclusion that females have better cognitive styles than males, a conclusion that may be unwarranted in light of the 90 studies that found no sex differences.

Fortunately, there are a few sources that allow access to unpublished research reports. Doctoral dissertations are usually available through *Dissertation Abstracts*. Education related research that appeared as paper presentations at conferences or other unpublished presentations are available in ERIC (an educational information retrieval service). Anyone who is contemplating a meta-analytic review of an area should be sure to search these sources for research so that unpublished experiments are included. Although inclusion of these sources of data will help to ameliorate some of the bias associated with publication practices, it is also true that papers that report significant group differences are more likely to be accepted for presentation at a conference than research reports that fail to find differences. Doctoral dissertations presumably reflect a concerted effort to obtain statistically significant results. Thus, there is probably no truly unbiased data source.

Meta-analysis has been criticized for its use of unpublished research on the grounds that unpublished research tends to be poorer in quality than published research that has undergone the peer review process. As explained earlier in this chapter, there are many ways to obtain null results, including shoddy research. If the peer review process has any merit at all, then those studies that are published should, on the average, be of a higher quality than those that are rejected for publication. Thus, a major criticism of meta-analysis is that it weighs good and poor research equally instead of somehow adjusting for the quality of the experiment.

The tendency to publish primarily statistically significant results has been declining in recent years, with more journal editors judging the quality of research apart from its results. It is, however, very difficult to judge the quality of research when the results are not statistically significant. Null results are almost impossible to make sense out of because it is not easy to determine why the researcher failed to find differences. Certainly, one possibility is that there are no differences between females and males with respect to the variable being studied. Although a single finding of null results does not mean much, numerous carefully conducted studies with large sample sizes, conducted by many different investigators at different laboratories, certainly does provide evidence that if there are any sex differences, the differences are exceedingly small.

How can anyone summarize a large body of research when the studies that are available for scrutiny are biased toward those that report statistically significant differences? This question has come to be known as the "file drawer problem." The term *file drawer problem* refers to all of the studies that found null results and were never published. The results of these studies are languishing in file drawers in various laboratories. We can never know how many studies that are unavailable did not show evidence of sex differences. One way to handle this problem is to examine all of the available studies, and if the researcher concludes that there are sex differences with regard to some variable, then she would also calculate the number of null results that would be needed to change her conclusion. For example, suppose a researcher summarized 35 different studies on sex differences in cognitive styles and concluded that females have a more introspective cognitive style than males. (This is a fictitious example.) The researcher would then compute the number of studies with null results that would be needed to change her conclusion to "no sex differences." The actual number of null results that would change the conclusion depends on several variables including the size of the difference, a topic that is discussed in detail later in this chapter. She would then add to her summary the finding that 20 (or whatever number is calculated) studies that found no between-sex differences would be needed to alter her conclusion. In this way, researchers can acknowledge the possibility that there are unpublished null results.

Effect Size Statistics

Three statistics that are used to determine the importance or size of the experimental effect are ω^2 (omega squared), d and Binomial Effect Size Display. Each has a somewhat different meaning and use, although all three are used in understanding how much the sexes differ with respect to a given variable. Each of these measures is described separately below and then compared so that readers can meaningfully grapple with the question, "When does an effect size become important?"

ω^2 *(Omega Squared).*   In order to understand the meaning of ω^2, we need to reconsider variance, the measure of the variability in a set of data. As previously described, variance is a measure of how dispersed or spread out the individual scores in a data set are. If the scores are very spread out, variance will be large; if the scores are closely clustered, variance will be small. If everyone in a study had exactly the same score, there would be no variability, and variance would be equal to zero. ω^2 is a measure of the proportion of total variance in a data set that can be explained by a particular variable, in this case, sex of subject (Hays, 1981).

Consider the following hypothetical example. If we asked a sample of young and old women and young and old men to respond as quickly as possible to a set of stimuli, we would usually find that the older subjects took longer to respond than the younger ones. We might also find sex differences, depending on the type of stimuli we employed. Suppose that in this hypothetical study we also found that men responded more quickly overall than women. The first test of the data would be to determine if the differences between age groups and sexes are likely to have occurred by chance. If we found that the results we obtained would have occurred by chance alone less than 5 times in 100, then we would conclude that the results were unlikely to be due to chance; therefore, real differences probably exist between the age groups and sexes. This type of test is a test of statistical significance. Virtually every research report includes a test of significance. Finding statistically significant results should constitute the first step, not the final step, in data analysis.

In the hypothetical example being considered, some of the variability is due to the fact that two age groups of subjects were used. If the differences in the age groups accounts for most of the variability in the data, then the proportion of total variability due to age will be large. Conversely, if there are large differences in the scores obtained by women and men, then ω^2 will be large for the sex variable. If ω^2 for sex is large, then if we know an individual's sex we can use this knowledge to predict his or her ability to perform the task. If ω^2 for sex is small, then knowing an individual's sex will yield poor predictions about her or his ability on the task. When two or more variables are investigated in the same experiment, the ω^2 associated with each variable can be compared to determine, for example, whether sex or age is more important with respect to the ability being investigated.

In a meta-analysis, ω^2 is computed for each of several experiments investigating the same ability. An average (median) ω^2 is computed from the values obtained in each of the studies. In this way, research results from many experiments on the same topic can be summarized with a single measure of the average effect size.

Despite the fact that effect size statistics have been available in the literature for decades (e.g., Hays, 1963), it is still unusual to find them reported. In an unpublished review of the use of effect size statistics, Riefer (1990) surveyed five leading journals in psychology. He found that only 2% of the research articles published in 1986 reported any measure of effect size. This failure to report effect size statistics is probably because they are often small, indicating that the variable being investigated was not an important determinant of the ability being measured. Effect size statistics are extremely important in understanding the extent to which sex plays a role in cognitive abilities.

A major limitation in interpreting ω^2 or any proportion of explained variance statistic is that the value obtained depends on the other variables investigated in the experiment. ω^2 for sex in an experiment that investigated sex and age variables is not comparable to the ω^2 for sex in an experiment that investigated sex and socioeconomic variables. Because ω^2 depends on the other variables in the experiment, across-experiment comparisons can only be made when the same set of variables are investigated in different studies.

d.   Another statistic used in meta-analysis is *d*. It is a measure of the magnitude of the difference between two groups. *d* is a standard unitless mode of expressing the difference between two group means. It is computed by calculating the difference between means on a given variable for men and women and then dividing by the standard deviation. (A *standard deviation* is a measure of variability. It is equal to the square root of the variance.) Mathematically,

$$d = \frac{M\ males\ -\ M\ females}{\text{Standard Deviation}}$$

One problem in using *d* is that the standard deviations for women and men are assumed to be equal when computing its value. As discussed earlier, equal variability cannot always be assumed, thus the actual value of *d* may be somewhat off, although this is not likely to be a major concern.

The value of *d* will be large when the difference between means is large and the variability within each group is small; it will be small when the difference between means is small and variability within each group is large. Unlike ω^2 d provides a measure of the direction of an effect. Thus, if we compare d from several different studies, a positive value will indicate that males scored higher than females and a negative value will indicate that females scored higher than males as long as the female mean is always subtracted from the male mean. Both ω^2 and d allow for comparisons of results across studies. In general, large values indicate large sex differences, and small values indicate small sex differences. For a more advanced discussion of meta-analysis, see Orwin and Cordray (1985) and Hyde and Linn (1986).

Meta-analysis also allows tests of homogeneity of effect sizes from several studies. If, for example, half of the studies in a particular area showed large effect sizes favoring males (positive values for d) and half showed large effect sizes favoring females (negative values for d), it would not be logical to conclude that, on the average, there are no sex differences with regard to the variable being studied. When a homogeneity of effect size test shows that the results are not homogeneous, then the reviewer is not sampling from a single population. In other words, moderator variables are causing the differences, and the studies should be subdivided into homogeneous subcategories. To clarify this concept, let's consider another example. Hyde (1986) conducted a meta-analytic review of sex differences in aggression. Because her test for homogeneity showed that aggression is not a homogeneous (uniform) concept, she subdivided the studies into meaningful categories. Hyde used "age of subject" as one of her subdivisions and found that "gender differences are larger with younger subjects" (p. 63). (In case you're wondering, she found that there are "no types or measures of aggression on which females are more aggressive than males" [p. 63]). I return to the concept of homogeneous types of studies in the next chapter when I examine the empirical evidence for sex differences in cognition.

Binomial Effect Size Display.   Because both ω^2 and d are somewhat advanced statistical concepts, Rosenthal and Rubin (1982) suggested that the size of a difference between any two groups is best understood with a *Binomial Effect Size Display* (BESD). The BESD is the percentage of each sex that is above the average response in the combined group of females and males. These values are readily comprehensible and do not require any statistical training to be understood. Unfortunately, very few researchers have employed this statistic in the reports of their research.

When is an Effect Size Large?   Even if a researcher computes the value of ω^2 and d, the reader is still left with the task of deciding if the value reflects a "large" or a "small" effect. This is not an easy decision to make because it involves a value judgment about how large an effect (difference between groups) has to be in order to be considered meaningful or important. The answer to this question is the same answer that I give to all difficult questions in life: "It all depends." The trick is deciding what it depends on. In medical research, an extremely small effect size can have enormous importance. If someone were to discover a drug that allows a small percentage of people with AIDS to recover from this dread disease, everyone would agree that is was an extremely important drug. If you were one of the people who recovered from AIDS, you would not care if the effect size were extremely small.

It is interesting to note that effect size is rarely considered in most other areas of psychological research. In Riefer's (1990) review of five different prestigious psychology journals for three different years, he found that only 1.67% of the articles reported any effect size statistic. Of these, 58% were below $d = .20$. As is seen in the next chapter, many effect sizes for cognitive abilities are considerably larger than this value. Thus, the effect sizes for sex differences in cognitive abilities are often larger than those obtained in most psychological research.

Comparing Effect Size Indicators.   In order to decide if an effect size is large enough to be meaningful, you have to understand what the numbers mean. Unfortunately, these values are not intuitive. In the next chapter, I give the values obtained by females and males on the Scholastic Aptitude Tests. These are numbers that are readily meaningful to most college students because they were required to take these tests. Other numbers, like average differences in reaction tests (which are given in milliseconds or thousandths of a second) or number correct on a finger tapping task (this will be explained later) are much more abstract. When you read about research, you have to consider if the results were statistically significant, whether the effect size is large enough to be theoretically important, and even if both of these conditions are met, whether the effect is large enough to be practically important.

Eagly (1987) has compared effect size indicators for several differences in social behavior. Let's consider differences in aggressive behavior. She reported that sex differences account for only 2% of the variance in aggressive behavior. (This is the ω^2.) This certainly sounds like a very small effect. The corresponding $d = .29$, or slightly less than one third of a standard deviation. This is conceptually a "small" effect. However, when we examine the BESD, the effect size seems much larger—43% of the females and 57% of the males scored above average on the measures of aggression. These three indicators of effect size all apply to the same set of data. The value of ω^2 seems quite small, while the BESD seems quite large.

Eagly also computed three different effect size indicators for Hall's (1985) report of sex differences in social smiling. Sex of subject accounted for 9% of the variability in social smiling. The corresponding value for d is .63. By comparison, the BESD showed that 63% of the females and 35% of the males scored above the average for social smiling. The point that I want to make by comparing these three different indicators of effect size is that even when sex differences account for a small percentage of the variability in the data, the BESD can be quite large.

A study of sex differences in activity level provides another example for comparing effect size indicators. Eaton and Enns (1986) concluded that males have a higher activity level than females. The size of the sex difference in standard deviation units is $d = .49$ (almost one half of a standard deviation). This difference accounted for approximately 5% of the variability in activity level. Eaton and Enns calculated that there would have to be thousands of unpublished studies showing null results (the file drawer problem) to render this result nonsignificant.

According to Rosenthal and Rubin (1982), an effect that accounts for only 4% of the variance is associated with a difference of 60% versus 40% of a group's performance above average. If there were a test such that an individual would have to score at least average in order to qualify for employment, then 60% of one group and 40% of the other group would qualify. When considered this way, it is easy to see how 4% of the variance can translate into huge between-sex differences that are of practical importance. Try to keep this in mind when evaluating research results.

The Interaction of Variables

One of the main themes of this book is that finding answers to sex differences questions will not be easy, nor will the answers be simple. The cognitive abilities women and men develop depend on many variables. It seems likely that our abilities are influenced by age, birth order, cultural background, socioeconomic status, sex role orientation, learning histories, and so forth, in addition to the simple fact that we were born either female or male. In reality, these variables work together in their effect on cognitive abilities. It is possible, for example, that wealthy females who are firstborn tend to develop excellent verbal ability, whereas lower middle class females who are second or third born do not tend to develop these same excellent abilities (perhaps because the first born wealthy female is talked to and read to more often). In this example, the influence of sex depends on the levels of other variables. A host of sociodemographic (e.g., age, place of residence), psychological (e.g., motivation), biological (e.g., health status), and life history (e.g., level of education) variables operate in conjunction with sex to determine the level of each cognitive ability that an individual obtains. The term *interaction* is used to denote the fact that the effect of sex differs depending on the value of other variables (e.g., low, middle, or high socioeconomic status).

It is important to consider any research on sex differences in light of the other variables that could be influencing the results. Understanding the manner in which sex interacts with other variables will provide a richer and more meaningful interpretation of the way maleness and femaleness influence cognitive development than merely considering the main effect of sex alone.

DEVELOPMENTAL ISSUES

Cognitive abilities, like physical abilities, do not remain static across the life span. Different activities follow their own developmental course, reflecting the influences of age-dependent biological and sociological changes. Sex differences may appear and disappear depending on the age of the subject. The welter of contradictory evidence in the literature makes it clear that there can be no useful answer about sex differences in any cognitive ability without reference to the ages of the subjects.

Cross-Sectional Versus Longitudinal Studies

If cognitive abilities wax and wane across the life span, developmental studies are needed to understand the phenomena involved. Developmental studies are usually either *cross-sectional* (sampling at random from different subjects in several age groups) or *longitudinal* (repeatedly measuring the same individuals at several ages as they mature). Sometimes combinations of these techniques are employed when, for example, several age groups are measured repeatedly over 5- or more-year periods.

A major problem with cross-sectional studies is the cohort or peer group effect. The cohort effect refers to the fact that people who are the same age also have had similar age-dependent experiences. Consider, for example, the following problem: A researcher wants to know about age-dependent changes in the ability to read maps (a spatial skill). Using cross-sectional samples, she tests men and women in their early 20s, mid-40s, and late 60s. Suppose she finds that there are no sex differences in the young group, small differences favoring males in the middle-aged group, and large differences favoring males in the oldest group. Could she conclude that sex differences favoring males develop throughout the adult years? She could not make this conclusion because experiences with reading maps of the oldest women are probably different from those of the middle-aged women, who in turn had different experiences than the young women. It seems likely that the oldest women have fewer years of driving experience—an activity that often requires map reading—while many of the middle-aged women and virtually all of the young women drive on a regular basis. By contrast, virtually all of the men in all three age groups drive regularly, thus having similar experiences with maps. The age-dependent sex difference in map reading is more likely due to cohort or generational experiences than it is to life-span changes in abilities. It may be that the young women will maintain their map reading skills into old age so that when they are in their late 60s they will perform in a manner comparable to their male counterparts.

Cohort effects, which are always possible in cross-sectional developmental research, are especially likely to contaminate developmental data in sex differences. Women's roles are changing rapidly, and it is therefore difficult to control experiential factors across generations. Generational differences in the experiences of women and men will make any determination of why the differences exist very difficult.

Longitudinal research also has drawbacks associated with it. When subjects are measured repeatedly throughout their life span, it is always possible that earlier testing experiences influence later ones. There is also the problem of subject loss due to death, moving out of the area, refusal to continue, and other reasons. It is likely that the lost subjects differ from those who continue in subtle ways (e.g., they may be less able). Finally, longitudinal research will take years to provide answers. If you want to study changes that occur from birth into old age, your children or grandchildren will have to collect the last of the data because the study would extend beyond a single lifetime.

SELF-FULFILLING PROPHECIES

It would be naive to believe that researchers approach their work without any bias or prejudice about the expected outcome. Researchers are committed, in varying degrees, to either proving or disproving the notion that females and males have comparable cognitive abilities.

A large body of literature exists to document the finding that experimenter expectancies often influence research results. One of the pioneers in this area was Robert Rosenthal who is famous for his work in the area of self-fulfilling prophecies. This term refers to the concept that experimenters and others often act in ways that influence results so that the outcome is in accord with their beliefs. In a classic study (Rosenthal, 1966), elementary school teachers were told that some of their pupils had obtained high scores on a special test designed to measure intellectual development. Intelligence tests given later in the school year showed that the "bloomers" had made greater gains in IQ points than the "non-bloomers." The teachers reported that the bloomers were more interested, more curious, and happier than the other children. What is remarkable about these results is the fact that the children identified as "bloomers" had been picked at random and, therefore, did not differ from the other children. Somehow, the teachers had communicated their expectations to the children, who in turn responded to these expectations.

Sex differences research is particularly vulnerable to experimenter and subject expectations. If an experimenter believes that females will outperform males on a particular test, he or she may unknowingly act friendlier toward the females, provide them with a little more encouragement, or allow them a little extra time to complete the test. Subject expectations also influence results. If, for example, girls believe that mathematical ability is unfeminine, it is likely that they will reflect this belief in their performance. The girls could give up easily on the more difficult problems because they do not believe that they could solve them, or even deliberately select wrong answers in order to maintain a feminine self-concept.

In reading research reports, it is difficult to detect ways that either experimenter or subject expectancies biased the results. One way to circumvent this problem is by having the data collected by researchers who are "blind" to or uninformed about the hypothesis being investigated. Subjects should also be unaware of the fact that sex differences are being examined. Experiments in which the sex of the subject is unknown to the experimenter also eliminate the effects of sex-related experimenter expectancies. This is possible, however, only in research with young children and research that does not require face-to-face interaction between the researcher and subject. (Young children could dress in standard smocks or jeans that don't provide the experimenter with clues as to the child's sex.)

Research in the area of sex differences is particularly vulnerable to self-fulfilling prophecies. In Fausto-Sterling's (1985) discussion of the way beliefs can bias research, she asked that every researcher understand that, by definition, no one can see her or his own blind spots. For this reason, every research report should provide enough information so that readers can identify possible biases in the research.

It is not necessarily true that simply because someone maintains a philosophical position (e.g., feminist, misogynist, defender of status quo), he or she is unable to conduct research or formulate conclusions in a fair manner. Readers, regardless of their personal beliefs about the issues discussed in the following chapters, are asked to maintain an open mind and to consider the evidence on all sides of the issues.

EVALUATING RESEARCH CLAIMS

The purpose of this chapter has been to raise issues that are important in evaluating research claims about sex differences. In evaluating conflicting claims or strong statements, keep in mind the following issues:

1. Who were the subjects and how were they selected? Is the sample size appropriate for the question being examined (keeping in mind that large samples virtually insure significant differences and small samples yield unstable estimates of population parameters)? Are results from abnormal populations or other species being generalized to all women and men?

2. Are studies that employed neither random assignment of subjects to conditions nor manipulation of any variables inferring causal information?

3. Is the measurement appropriate? Have multiple indicators of abilities been used, and if so, were the data analyzed with multivariate statistical techniques?

4. Are the results both statistically significant and practically significant? How large is the effect size? Do the results fit into an established theoretical framework? If not, why not?

5. Has detailed information about the distribution of scores within each sex been provided? Are the results logical and understandable?

6. Has the way sex interacts with other variables in determining the results been investigated? What alternative explanations are plausible?

7. How might the results vary across the life span? Have cohort effects been included as a possible explanation of the results?

8. Are the results reported consistent with the prior literature and/or theory of sex differences? If not, why not?

9. How could the results have been influenced by experimenter and subject expectations?

The literature on sex differences has been proliferating in recent years. Although much of it is thoughtful and high in quality, some of it is not. The goal of finding answers to the broad, complex, and socially and politically sensitive question of sex differences is of profound importance. The informed reader will have to evaluate the research with an open mind and an awareness of what constitutes good research.

3 Empirical Evidence for Cognitive Sex Differences

Contents

3

INTELLIGENCE

The first question most people ask about sex-related cognitive differences is which is the smarter sex, males or females? It might seem that a logical way to answer this question would be to obtain large random samples of women and men, give them a psychometrically sound intelligence test (one with good mathematical properties), and compare the scores for women and men. The sex with the higher average score would be the smarter sex. Although this may seem like a logical, straightforward approach to answering the question of sex differences in intelligence, it will not work. Intelligence tests are carefully written so that there will be no average overall difference between men and women. During the construction of intelligence tests, any question that tends to be answered differently by males and females is either thrown out or balanced with a question that favors the other sex. Therefore, average scores on intelligence tests cannot provide an answer to the sex differences question because of the way the tests are constructed.

A second way to decide whether men or women are, on the average, smarter might be to look at who performs the more intelligent jobs in society. Of course, one would have to decide which jobs require greater intelligence. Suppose that we could agree in principle that jobs like government leader, architect, lawyer, physician, professor, mathematician, physicist, and engineer all require a high degree of intelligence. An examination of who performs these jobs reveals that the overwhelming majority of these jobs are held by men. Does this mean that men are, in general, more intelligent? Looking at the types of jobs typically performed by women and men in society can't provide an answer to the intelligence question because of differential sex roles for women and men. Many professions were formally or informally closed to women until recent years. Similarly, there are few male nurses, secretaries, and child care workers because of the constraints imposed by the male sex role. There are still considerable differences between the sexes in background experiences, types of encouragement, amount and type of education, and social expectations for success. We do not know if the differences in the numbers of men and women in the various job classifications are related to overall intelligence differences, to differential socialization practices, or to some combination of the two. This issue is discussed in greater depth in the chapters on psychosocial hypotheses (chapters 6 and 7).

A third way of answering the intelligence question is to look at school achievement. Which sex, on the average, gets better grades in school? It seems clear that females get better grades than males in school (Johnson & Gormly, 1972). Paradoxically, girls get better grades than boys even in "traditionally male" content areas, such as mathematics, in which boys score higher on ability tests (Hyde, 1985; Kimball, 1989; Wentzel, 1988). Once again, however, this does not prove that there is a smarter sex because alternative explanations are possible. Being a good student is more consistent with the female sex role than it is with the male sex role. Our schools tend to reward quiet, neat students who do as they are told. These are characteristics that are seen as more appropriate for girls than for boys in our society. Thus, school achievement cannot be used to decide if males or females are smarter. In fact, we have not yet discovered a satisfactory way to answer this question.

The problem with questions like, "Which is the smarter sex?" is that they contain the assumption that there is a "smarter sex." The research reviewed in this book suggests several areas in which sex differences are consistently found, but in no way does this mean that one sex is the "winner" and the other the "loser." The real question is when and where are cognitive sex differences found. Modern society is complex and diverse. There is no single best set of intellectual abilities for all of society's tasks. It is important that we come to think of differences apart from value judgments about who and what is better. If society consistently values the abilities that are more frequently associated with one sex, then the problem lies in the way differences are valued, not in the fact that they exist.

A more fruitful approach to the cognitive sex differences question is to examine specific abilities, especially in light of the fact that intelligence is not a unitary concept. It is theoretically more useful to think of multiple "intelligences" than to consider intelligence as a single homogeneous mental ability. The question then becomes, "What are the sex differences in cognitive abilities?" Although intelligence tests are constructed so that there will be no overall sex difference in intelligence, the tests do differ in the pattern of intellectual abilities for the two sexes. Surprisingly, in an area as controversial as this one, there is little disagreement about which of the cognitive abilities differ by sex. As you will see, the most heated debates revolve around whether the differences are large enough to be important and why these differences exist.

THE WHEN, WHERE, WHO, AND HOW
OF DIFFERENCES

Why is it that researchers have been unable to reach a consensus regarding the nature of cognitive sex differences? To the extent that there are any sex-related cognitive differences, these differences are found consistently only under certain conditions. Let's consider an example from an area outside of cognition. Virtually all social scientists believe that males, on the average, are more aggressive than females. What does a conclusion like this really mean? No one believes that the meekest male is more aggressive than the brashest female. There must be considerable overlap between the female and male distributions for aggression. As is seen in this example, the kind of conclusion we draw depends on the portion of the distribution we study. Let's consider the extremes of aggression, that is people who are exceptionally high and exceptionally low on aggression.

Tales of Distributions

If we considered only the most aggressive individuals in society, we would have to conclude that there are huge sex differences with respect to aggression. The overwhelming majority of violent crimes (sadistic murders, rapes, mutilations, serial killings, slasher crimes) are committed by males (U.S. Bureau of the Census, 1989). Thus, by sampling the upper end or upper "tail" of the aggression distribution, we would conclude that sex differences are enormous. Similarly, we could consider the lower end of the aggression distribution and see if substantially more females are found among those who are classified as low on aggression. I do not know of any study that has actually examined the low end of the aggressive distribution (in fact, I am not sure what it would mean), but if we found that there were significantly more females among those who are least aggressive, this finding would support the conclusion that males are more aggressive than females.

What about the vast majority of people who fall in the middle portion of the distribution? Between-sex differences for the middle portions of distributions are much smaller than those found in the tails. Thus, there is much less difference in female and male aggression for "average" people than there is for criminals. The kind of answer we are likely to get depends on the portion of the distribution from which the researcher samples.

Developmental Perspectives

Conclusions about cognitive sex differences also depend on the age of the subject. I use aggression again as an example. Developmental psychologists have identified adolescence as a time of great change. If a researcher looked at adolescent delinquency rates to assess sex differences in aggression, she would find that sex ratios for adolescents who are arrested are approximately 4:1, with the higher value obviously representing the male rate (Kimmel & Weiner, 1985). If we examined sex ratios for those adults in United States prisons, the figure is closer to 8 or 9:1 (U. S. Bureau of the Census, 1989). Suppose, instead, the focus of the research was senior citizens sampled from a home for the elderly. Very few, if any, sex-related differences in aggression would be found among seniors (in part because there are so few men in the oldest age groups). It is easy to see how the age of the sample will influence the data we get and the conclusions we can make based on the data.

Type of Test

How can we best measure an amorphous concept like aggression? This is a difficult question to answer. The way I choose to measure it will also affect my results. Hyde (1986) found that studies in naturalistic environments (e.g., playgrounds) yielded larger sex differences in aggression than those conducted in laboratories and that differences were somewhat larger with measures of physical aggression than with measures of verbal aggression. Thus, the way we measure aggression will also determine the results we get. As is seen later in this chapter, measurement is an important determinant of cognitive sex differences as well.

PERCEPTION AND ATTENTION

All of our information about the world around us comes from our sensory systems. The cognitive or thinking process begins with the ability to sense changes in the environment and to make meaning out of the bewildering array of sensory stimuli constantly impinging on us. The first steps in the cognitive process are perception and attention. Sex differences in perception and attention are of particular interest for two reasons: (1) if there are sex differences at the earliest stages of information processing, this would provide a theoretical basis for positing sex-related differences in later stages; and (2) perception and attention are two areas in which there are no sex role stereotypes because we have little conscious awareness of the way the sensory and attentional systems function.

Baker (1987) has summarized sex-related differences in perception and attention; interested readers are referred to her excellent book on this topic. She discussed numerous sex differences in each of the sensory systems. In hearing, for example, females are better at detecting pure tones (tones of one frequency) during childhood and most of adulthood. There are also sexually distinct patterns of hearing loss in middle-age, with males beginning to lose the ability to detect high tones at about age 32 and females beginning to lose this ability at about age 37. These results are confirmed by Rebok (1987) and Schaie (1987).

Vision is a critically important sensory system for humans. In general, males under the age of 40 have better dynamic visual acuity (ability to detect small movements in the visual field) than females. Age-related loss of far vision occurs earlier for females (between ages 35 and 44) than for males (between ages 45 and 54). Baker also documents sex differences in taste (e.g., females have lower thresholds for detecting sweet, sour, salty, and bitter substances) and in touch (e.g., females are more sensitive to touch on 19 out of 20 tested body parts—the only exception was a touch on the nose). She documents a wide array of sex differences in perception ranging from binaural beats (a somewhat abstruse auditory phenomen) to visual acuity (the need for eye glasses). It is unlikely that differences of this sort can be attributed to sex-differentiated socialization practices.

The ability to attend to stimuli and to switch attention is both a precursor to and a result of the thinking process. There are huge sex discrepancies in attention disorders. Sex ratios for Attention Deficit Disorder (a psychiatric diagnostic category that often includes hyperactivity) range from 3:1 to 9:1 with the larger value corresponding to the proportion of males (Rebok, 1987). Thus, sex differences are found in both perception and attention—the earliest stages of information processing.

Even though there is considerable evidence for some sex differences in perception and attention, it is difficult to translate findings like differential touch sensitivity and hearing thresholds into predictions about cognitive performance. A conservative conclusion is that while there seem to be perceptual and attentional differences between women and men, we can only speculate about their influence on cognitive abilities.

A COGNITIVE ABILITIES APPROACH

As stated earlier, there are no overall differences in the scores obtained by males and females on intelligence tests. Sex differences are, however, often reported for some of the subscores on intelligence tests. Intelligence tests are comprised of several subscores, each presumably reflecting a separate cognitive component. One of the most widely used intelligence tests was devised by David Weschler. The adult version is known as the Weschler Adult Intelligence Scale (WAIS), and the child's version is the Weschler Intelligence Scale for Children (WISC). The newest version of these tests carries the letter "R" To indicate that it has been revised (e.g., WAIS-R).

The WISC and WAIS yield three scores of intelligence: an overall IQ score which does not show sex differences, a verbal subscore comprised of scores on verbal subtests, and a performance subscore comprised of scores on performance or spatial subtests. In a recent administration of the WISC-R to 1,100 normal girls and 1,099 normal boys, Lawson, Inglis, and Tittemore (1987) found that the girls were "reliably superior" to boys in the verbal factor, with the reverse true for the performance factor. (They found no sex differences in a group of learning disabled children.) These results are typical of numerous studies that have investigated sex differences as a function of specific abilities.

In 1974, Maccoby and Jacklin published a text that has become a classic in psychology. In their text, they reviewed over a thousand research reports on sex differences that had been published prior to 1974. Although their synthesis and review of the literature is now over 15 years old and has been severely criticized on methodological grounds, it has provided a foundation for much of the research that has followed. They identified three cognitive abilities and one personality variable in which sex differences are "fairly well established" (p. 351). The sex differences literature has burgeoned in the years since 1974 and has, in general, confirmed their conclusions. The three cognitive abilities that have been identified as the loci of sex differences are verbal, quantitative, and visual–spatial ability. Each of these abilities is discussed in turn below. Aggression was identified as the personality variable that differs by sex. The possibility that aggression mediates or influences cognitive abilities is discussed in the next two chapters. It is important to keep in mind that although the preponderance of the data support these conclusions, there is also conflicting evidence in each of these areas, and no single sex difference is unanimously supported in the literature.

VERBAL ABILITIES

Evidence from a variety of sources supports the finding that, on the average, females have better verbal abilities than males. The term *verbal abilities* is not a unitary concept. It applies to all components of language usage: word fluency, which is the ability to generate words (both in isolation and in a meaningful context), grammar, spelling, reading, verbal analogies, vocabulary, and oral comprehension. The size and reliability of the sex difference depends on which of these aspects of language usage is being assessed. Consider the various verbal questions that are shown in Fig. 3.1. As you can see, they draw on related, but somewhat different abilities. Much of the confusion in the literature comes from the failure to distinguish among language tasks, some of which show no sex differences, whereas others do.

TESTS OF VERBAL ABILITIES

1. Name as many words as you can that start with the letter "k."

2. Select the word that is most nearly the same in meaning:

VIVACIOUS   (A) HONEST
                             (B) MEDIOCRE
                             (C) LIVELY
                             (D) BRAT

3. IGLOO : INDIAN :: TEPEE :

(A) ICE   (B) CANVAS   (C) ESKIMO   (D) HOME

4. Answer the questions based on the information provided in this passage.

The literature with regard to sex differences in verbal abilities has been mixed
with some researchers reporting large differences and others reporting no
statistically significant differences. It seems that the controversy can be
resolved by looking at the types of verbal tasks in which differences are
found and determining how they differ from tasks in which differences are
not found. It may be that tasks like solving verbal analogies are more
similar to mathematical problem solving than to some of the other verbal tasks.

(a) What is the "controversy" that is referred to in the second sentence?

(b) Why does the author suggest that verbal analogies are similar to mathematical
problems?

5. Which is correct?

(a) Give the money to Bob and I.

(b) Give the money to Bob and me.

FIG. 3.1.   Tests of verbal abilities. Each of these tests may be tapping a
qualitatively different type of verbal ability.

There are numerous indicators of sex differences in verbal abilities when we
consider the low end of the verbal abilities distribution. Stuttering, a disability in
the production of fluent speech, is overwhelmingly a male problem. Approximately 4% to 5% of the population are considered stutterers. Of this large
number, there are 3 to 4 times more male stutterers than female stutterers (Skinner & Shelton, 1985). Dyslexia, a severe reading disability found in individuals
whose other cognitive abilities are within normal ranges, is also predominantly a
male problem (Vandenberg, 1987). Although approximately 2% of the school
population is dyslexic, mild dyslexia is 5 times more likely to occur in males than
in females, and severe dyslexia is 10 times more likely to appear in males than in
females (Bannatyne, 1976; Gordon, 1980; Sutaria, 1985). Even young boys who
do not fall into the extreme low ability end of the distribution are more likely to
stutter when producing speech and more likely to have difficulty in learning to
read (Corballis & Beale, 1983); however, it is important to note that differences

are much smaller when we consider the majority of the population that fall within the "normal" range of verbal abilities.

There are also sex differences in the ability to regain language following strokes and brain surgery, with males suffering more language impairment and recovering language ability more slowly than females (Witelson, 1976). The research evidence from a variety of sources favors female superiority on verbal tasks. Despite the finding that females score higher on most tests of verbal ability, the overwhelming majority of critically acclaimed writers are male. There are several possible reasons for this discrepancy. It is possible that women are not using their talents as frequently as men, or the tests are not measuring high-level creative ability, or differential criteria are being used to judge women's and men's writing. Another likely reason for the lack of critically acclaimed female writers is the fact that until recently women were not educated and, even when educated, had little time to write. It is interesting to note that several outstanding women writers such as Dickinson and the Brontes were single women with other means of support. If ability is only a small part of eminence, then the lack of eminent female writers is not surprising.

Age Trends in Verbal Abilities

Of all the cognitive sex differences, differences in verbal ability are probably the first to appear developmentally. Females aged 1 to 5 years are more proficient in language skills than their male counterparts (McGuiness, 1976; Smolak, 1986). There is also some evidence that girls may talk at an earlier age and produce longer utterances than boys (e.g., Moore, 1967; Shucard, Shucard, & Thomas, 1987), although this finding has not always been replicated in recent investigations. In one of the most detailed investigations of language development among children aged 2½ to 4 years, Horgan (1975) examined the mean length of utterances (MLU) for girls and boys. She argued that MLU is a good indicator of linguistic maturity for preschool children who are learning their first language. Horgan reported that prior to MLUs of four words, boys and girls perform equally well; however, sex differences favoring girls occur beyond MLUs of four words (i.e., girls use longer utterances at younger ages than boys). Horgan also analyzed other indicators of linguistic maturity including: use of the passive voice (e.g., "the lamp was broken"); truncated passive (e.g., "the window's broken"); and use of participles (verbs used as adjectives—e.g., "the moving truck crashed"). Girls spontaneously generated all of these advanced linguistic forms at an earlier age than males; furthermore, they made fewer errors in language usage overall. Horgan concluded the following: "Girls produce longer utterances at younger ages, they produce more varied constructions, and they make fewer errors" (p. 48). A recent review of language development concluded that girls have larger vocabularies at earlier ages than boys (Shucard, Shucard, & Thomas, 1987). Of course, not every study shows exactly the same findings. Wolf and Gow (1985–1986) for example, found that among 5- and 6-year-olds, girls were better in language and reading processes, but boys showed an advantage in vocabulary knowledge. In general, the majority of the evidence tends to support the idea that females are more verbally precocious than males.

There is also evidence that girls maintain their superiority in verbal skills through elementary school (e.g., Butler, 1984). Martin and Hoover (1987) conducted a large-scale longitudinal study in which they examined children's scores on the Iowa Test of Basic Skills in each grade from third to eighth for 4,875 girls and 4,497 boys. They reported that girls scored higher on tests of spelling, capitalization, punctuation, language usage, reference materials, and reading comprehension. Although I discuss effect sizes later in this chapter, it is probably important to note here that the between-sex differences were quite large. In Grade 8, for example, two-thirds of the highest scoring students on the language tests were females.

Female superiority on verbal tasks may seem reminiscent of the stereotype that females talk more than males, but it is important to keep in mind that it is the quality of the speech produced and the ability to comprehend or decode language that is being assessed, not merely the quantity. Studies in naturalistic mixed-sex settings show that males talk more and interrupt more than females (Bilous & Krauss, 1988).

In an extensive meta-analytic review of the literature on sex differences in verbal ability, Hyde and Linn (1988) divided experiments based on the age of the subjects and type of verbal ability assessed—all tests, vocabulary tests, and tests of reading comprehension. Differences were found in the "all tests" category for children 5 years and younger ($d = .13$) and for adults over the age of 26 ($d = .20$), both favoring females and both fairly small in size. There were no notable differences as a function of sex for ages 6 through 25. The developmental pattern of vocabulary proficiency is difficult to comprehend. They reported a male advantage in the 6- to 10-year-old age range ($d = -.26$) and a female advantage in the 19- to 25-year-old age range ($d = .23$), with essentially no differences in the other age categories. The largest differences were in reading comprehension for children 5 years of age and younger, with females reading more proficiently than males ($d = .31$). The use of meta-analyses to make valid conclusions is discussed in the section on "magnitude of effect sizes" later in this chapter.

VISUAL-SPATIAL ABILITIES

Spatial ability *generally refers to skill in representing, transforming, generating, and recalling symbolic, nonlinguistic information.*
—Linn and Petersen (1985, p. 1482)

The term *visual-spatial abilities* may not convey much meaning to people who are not cognitive psychologists. In fact, it is not an easy term to define because it is not a unitary concept. Generally, it refers to the ability to imagine what an irregular figure would look like if it were rotated in space or the ability to discern the relationship among shapes and objects. The ability to utilize spatial relationships is an important aspect of human thought. Visual-spatial skills are used extensively in engineering, architecture, chemistry, the building trades, and air crew selection (Lohman, 1988). Tests of visual-spatial ability have been used to predict success in first-year engineering courses (Poole & Stanley, 1972).

Early factor-analytic studies that sought to delineate the structure of intelligence found that verbal tests and visual-spatial ability tests formed two distinct factors. The distinction between verbal and visual-spatial abilities as separate components of intelligence has been replicated many times. In their extensive review of the spatial abilities literature, Morrow and Ratcliff (1988) concluded that there is "ample evidence that spatial knowledge is a separate component of human intelligence, distinct from verbal and analytic aspects" (p. 85).

Part of the difficulty in understanding the literature on visual-spatial ability is due to the fact that it is not a unitary concept. In 1983, Nyborg summarized the literature to date by noting that males usually score higher than females on numerous tests of spatial ability including: Porteus Mazes, Money's Road Map Test, Piaget's Perspectives, Water-Level Tasks, Geometric Forms, House Plans Task, Rod and Frame Test, Embedded Figures Test, Tilting Room/Tilting Chair, Mental Rotation, and WAIS Analytic Triad. More recently, tests of visual-spatial abilities have been analyzed, and three separate factors have emerged (Linn & Petersen, 1986). It seems that visual-spatial abilities are comprised of the following factors:

1. *Spatial Perception,* which requires subjects to locate the horizontal or the vertical while ignoring distracting information. Examples are the rod and frame task, which requires subjects to position a rod within a tilted frame so that it is either vertical or horizontal and the Piaget Water Level Task, which requires subjects to draw in the water level of a tilted glass to show it half filled with water.

2. *Mental Rotation,* which includes the ability to imagine how objects will appear when they are rotated or how a flat object will appear if it is folded or how a solid object will appear if it is unfolded. There are timed and untimed versions of these tests.

3. *Spatial Visualization,* which refers to complex analytic multistep processing of spatial information. Tests that tap spatial visualization are the embedded figures test, paper folding, hidden figures and spatial relations test.

Figure 3.2 depicts test items similar to the kinds used to measure spatial perception, mental rotation, and spatial visualization abilities.

A fourth category of spatial ability that was not identified in Linn and Petersen's (1986) extensive review is *Spatiotemporal Ability,* which involves judg-

TESTS OF SPATIAL ABILITIES

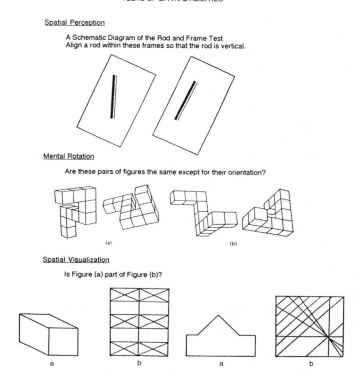

Spatial Perception

A Schematic Diagram of the Rod and Frame Test
Align a rod within these frames so that the rod is vertical.

Mental Rotation

Are these pairs of figures the same except for their orientation?

(a)   (b)

Spatial Visualization

Is Figure (a) part of Figure (b)?

a   b   a   b

FIG. 3.2.   Examples of tests used to measure spatial perception, mental rotation, and spatial visualization. In the Rod and Frame Test subjects are required to position a rod to the vertical position within a tilted rectangular frame. The rod is incorrectly positioned in the right-hand figure.

ments about and responses to dynamic (i.e., moving) visual displays. There are several different tasks that involve information that is moving, such as having subjects press a key when a target is coincident with a stationary line (Smith & McPhee, 1987) and making "time of arrival" judgments about a moving object (Schiff & Oldak, 1990). Investigators have concluded that the ability to reason about dynamic visual displays is correlated with, but different from, the abilities used in reasoning about static displays (Hunt, Pellegrino, Frick, Farr, & Alderton, 1988). Although it is difficult to isolate any single factor that might be responsible for these results, judgments concerning dynamic visual displays must involve time estimation (i.e., when will the moving object reach a destination). Recent research by Rammsayer and Lustnauer (1989) found sex differences in time perception with females overestimating time intervals more than males suggesting that some portion of the sex-related differences found with dynamic displays may be due to differences in time perception.

Given the large variety of tests that have been used to measure visual-spatial ability, it is not surprising that sex differences seem to depend on the type of test used. Not coincidentally, this is an area replete with contradictory findings because of the multidimensional complexity of visual-spatial abilities.

Caplan, MacPherson, and Tobin (1985) questioned the legitimacy of the assumption that the construct "spatial abilities" exists. They believe that the entire notion suffers from a "definitional dilemma." As noted in a response to Caplan, MacPherson, and Tobin (Halpern, 1986), much of the confusion in this area is attributable to the types of spatial ability tests used. Although some researchers have failed to find sex differences (e.g., Fennema & Sherman, 1978, using the Spatial Relations Test), sex differences that favor males are consistently found with two of the three factors that entail static displays—spatial perception and mental rotation tasks (Linn & Petersen, 1986)—and with spatiotemporal tasks (Schiff & Oldak, 1990; Smith & McPhee, 1987). McGee's (1979) summary of the literature is apparently still valid: "male superiority on tasks requiring these abilities is among the most persistent of individual differences in all the abilities literature" (p. 41). This conclusion was echoed more recently by Schiff and Oldak (1990): "There is strong converging evidence for gender-related differences in accuracy of judging time of arrival" (p. 315). In fact, this conclusion is supported by research with other species. Even male rats excel in maze learning, a spatial task (research cited in Newcombe & Baenninger, 1989).

Caplan, MacPherson, and Tobin (1985) noted that the types of tasks that are used to assess spatial ability are fairly abstract and that a much more valid test would involve finding one's way in a real-world environment. This is certainly a sensible suggestion, even though spatial ability tests that are conducted outside of the laboratory are more difficult to administer. There is always the problem that some subjects will have greater knowledge of a given geographical area. Furthermore, subjects could rely quite well on verbal strategies when they have to maneuver through a real-world space (e.g., turn at the green house). The few studies that have investigated route knowledge and "way finding" are mixed in the results that they provide. Holding and Holding (1989) found that when college students made judgments about traveled distances (with route information provided on slides), the male students were much more accurate than the female students. In contrast, Pearson and Ferguson (1989) found the usual male advantage on a mental rotation task, but did not obtain sex differences on a map test. There is not enough research at this time to conclude that there are any differences in how males and females find their way around in the world. (This may be the most practically significant spatial task.) Nor are there any data to support the notion that females are less able drivers than males. In fact, all of the data suggest that the opposite is true—women have far fewer automobile accidents and auto citations than men, who are involved in 63% of all reported auto accidents (Time, 1990). (Of course, it is possible that the female superiority in driving—fewer accidents and citations—is due to personality and/or sex-role variables and not spatial ability.)

One curious problem with sex differences in visual-spatial abilities concerns the variability of test scores. Most major reviews of the literature have concluded that males are more variable in their visual-spatial performance than females (e.g., Maccoby & Jacklin, 1974); however, some researchers report opposite results. Kail, Carter, & Pellegrino (1979), for example, concluded that "it appears that the important difference is not the average level of ability, but in the variability within each sex" (p. 186). They found that female performance was more variable than male performance. One of the most interesting reports of sex differences in variability in spatial tests was reported by Burnett, Lane, and Dratt (1979), who found that with the same sample of college students the men were significantly more variable on one spatial test (Guilford-Zimmerman Spatial Visualization Test) and the women were significantly more variable on another test (Identical Blocks Test).

One of the implications of group differences in variability is that predicting any individual's performance becomes more difficult. Differences in variability also support the notion that there may be differences in the way men and women perform spatial tasks. Suppose, for example, that the women in the group sampled use different strategies. Perhaps some try to visualize an answer and others try to use verbal labels. These different approaches could result in increasing the variability in the women's scores. If men, on the other hand, tended to use a similar strategy, visualization for example, then their group might be expected to show less variability. It is difficult to say at this time why there are variability differences (with men's performance more variable in some studies and women's performance more variable in others), but the differences are probably not due to chance and suggest some differences in the way females and males solve visual-spatial problems. One possible explanation of the inconsistent and contradictory findings with respect to sex differences in variability on visual-spatial tests is that the differences among the results can be attributed to the nature of the tests. It is possible that women are more variable on certain visual-spatial tasks, and men are more variable on other types of visual-spatial tasks. Understanding the inconsistent and contradictory findings in variability on tests of visual-spatial ability is a fruitful area for further research.

Age Trends in Visual-Spatial Abilities

In their meta-analysis of static spatial abilities tasks, Linn and Petersen (1986) concluded that sex differences in mental rotation tasks appear as soon as they can be measured reliably (around age 10 or 11). The developmental pattern for spatial perception tasks is more complicated. In general, differences favoring males can first be detected around age 7, they accelerate to adult levels around age 11, but only reach statistical significance by age 18. The developmental question was also examined in a large-scale study of 1,800 students in grades kindergarten through 12 (Johnson & Meade, 1987). The authors of this study compared performance on seven spatial tests by sex at each grade level. They concluded that a male advantage in spatial ability exists at least as early as fourth grade (age 10) over a wide range of paper-and-pencil measures with no differences between African-American and White students.

The developmental pattern of sex differences in spatiotemporal ability (e.g., time of arrival judgments about a moving display) is unknown at this time, although sex differences in spatiotemporal ability are generally found in college populations.

In addition to sex differences, there are also age-related differences in verbal and visual-spatial abilities. It is well established that both males and females maintain their verbal abilities into old age, whereas visual-spatial abilities (especially when measured with speeded performance tests) begin to decline considerably earlier. The decline in old age of visual-spatial abilities is so well established that it is often referred to as "the classic aging pattern" (Winograd & Simon, 1980). In applied research on this question, Halpern (1984b) found that older drivers took significantly longer to respond to common symbolic or pictograph traffic signs (e.g., a red slash through an arrow pointing to the right) than to their verbal analogues (e.g., the words "No Right Turn"), whereas young adult drivers were equally fast at responding to both types of traffic signs. Furthermore, there is some evidence of a sex and age interaction with the finding that visual-spatial abilities may decline more rapidly in older women than in older men (Elias & Kinsbourne, 1974), although there is insufficient evidence to provide strong support for this contention.

A common experimental paradigm for assessing visual-spatial abilities is the mental rotation task devised by Shepard and Metzler (1971). In this paradigm, subjects are required to make a comparison between a rotated figure and its standard form and to decide whether the rotated figure is the same as its standard or the mirror image. An experiment by Clarkson-Smith and Halpern (1983) found that both the time to respond and number of errors in a mental rotation task increased as a function of age; however, when their subjects, all of whom were women, were encouraged to use verbal strategies in this task, errors decreased significantly for the oldest group. It seems that verbal mediation strategies can attenuate the sex- and age-related deficits in visual-spatial abilities.

Although some tests of visual-spatial ability do not reveal sex differences, others yield reliable differences. One test that is sensitive to sex differences is the "Water Level Test," originally devised by Piaget and Inhelder (1956). In one version of this test, the subject is shown a bottle partially filled with water and is told to notice the way the water fills the bottle. The subject is then asked to predict where the water will be when the bottle is tipped. Piaget and Inhelder believed that the knowledge that water level remains horizontal would be attained at an average age of 12 years. It seems that girls demonstrate this principle at a later age than boys. In fact, it has been estimated that 50% of college women do not know the principle that water level remains horizontal. This is a surprising result that has been replicated many times (Thomas, Jamison, & Hummel, 1973; Wittig & Allen, 1984). Robert and Chaperon (1989), for example, reported that 32% of college women and 15% of college men failed the water level task. Although there is a paucity of cross-cultural research with regard to any of the cognitive abilities, at least one experimenter using subjects in Bombay, India, confirmed that males outperform females on the water level task (De Lisi, Parameswaran, & McGillicuddy-De Lisi, 1989). It is difficult to understand why this should be such a formidable task for college women. (See Harris, 1978, and Robert & Tanquay, in press, for an extensive discussion of the research in this area.) One possible version of the Water Level Test is shown in Fig. 3.3.

Results from the Water Level Test are strange. Why should women (in many samples college women were used as subjects) perform less well on a test of whether water remains horizontal in a tilted glass? As discussed in chapter 6, at least part of the sex differences we find with spatial tasks can be attributed to differential learning experiences, with boys typically engaging in more spatial activities. Sex differences in the Water Level Test are not amenable to this sort of explanation as no one believes that boys have more experiences than girls with glasses of water. Kalichman (1989) investigated the possibility that the results reflect some idiosyncracy of the test rather than sex differences in either the knowledge that water remains horizontal or the ability to draw an approximately horizontal line. Kalichman devised a more "ecologically valid" (i.e., more like the real world) test in which the tilted glass was held in a human hand. An example of his stimuli is shown in Fig. 3.4.

Kalichman found that significantly fewer college women than college men draw an approximately horizontal line to indicate the water level in both the standard test format and in the human context format. He concluded that "sex differences on the water-level task remain robust regardless of task context" (p. 138). Furthermore, sex differences on this task are found throughout the adult age span and into old age (Robert & Tanquay, in press) and among college students in all academic disciplines (Robert, 1989).

FIG. 3.3. One version of the Water Level Test. Assume that these glasses are half filled with water. Draw a line across each glass to indicate the top of the water line.

FIG. 3.4.   The Water Level Test embedded in an ecologically valid (i.e. real world) context. This glass is half filled with water. Draw a line across the glass to indicate the top of the water line. Reprinted by permission from Kalichman (1989).

Cognitive Styles

There has been considerable interest in recent years in the notion that males and females may have different cognitive styles. The term *cognitive styles* does not have an intuitive meaning. In general, it refers to individual differences in modes of perceiving, remembering, and thinking (Kogan, 1973). It is used by some psychologists in conjunction with the concept of psychological differentiation (Witkin, Dyk, Faterson, Goodenough, & Karp, 1962). An individual who is highly differentiated can separate herself or himself from the environment and can separate items from each other in the environment. According to the theory of psychological differentiation, we all differ in terms of how well we can separate items in the environment. There are several dimensions or aspects of psychological differentiation. One dimension along which the sexes are said to differ is in *field articulation* or *field dependence and independence*. These terms were coined by Witkin and have been used to characterize the degree to which subjects are influenced by objects in their visual field.

One way of assessing field dependence and independence is with the "Rod and Frame Test." In this test, subjects are seated in a darkened room and are presented with a luminous rectangle (the frame) that has a luminous rod posi-

tioned inside of it. The rectangle is rotated to different orientations by the experimenter. The task for the subject is to position the rod so that it is vertical. Figure
3.2 shows a schematic drawing of some rod and frame combinations that subjects
could be presented with. Some subjects' judgments of true vertical for the rod are
influenced by the tilt of the frame surrounding the rod. They are labeled *field
dependent.* Other subjects' judgments of true vertical for the rod are not influenced by the tilt of the frame surrounding the rod. They are labeled *field independent.* In general, sex and age differences are found with the Rod and Frame Test
(although differences are not unanimously reported). The usual findings are that
children are more field dependent than adults, and females are more field dependent than males.

Measures of field dependence and independence obtained with the Rod and
Frame Test are highly correlated with measures obtained with a test known as the
Embedded Figures Test. In the Embedded Figures Test, subjects are shown a
simple geometric form and then must maintain it in memory and pick it out from
a more complex form. Sample items similar to those found in Embedded Figures
Test were shown in Fig. 3.2.

Both the Embedded Figures Test and Rod and Frame Test require the subject
to segregate a geometric form from its context, and in both tests females are more
influenced by the context than males. Field dependence has been hypothesized to
reflect personalities that are conforming, submissive to authority, into comfortable ruts, and passive (Elliot, 1961). Women's field dependence has been described as "accepting the field more passively than men" (Sherman, 1967, p.
290). On the basis of these test results, women's cognitive style has been described as "global," "conforming," and "child-like." According to Witkin, it is
similar to the undifferentiated thought processes found in "primitive" cultures.
The field independence associated with male performance has been described, by
contrast, as reflecting a cognitive style that is "analytic" and "self-reliant." (The
value-laden bias in these descriptive terms is too obvious to require comment.)
Witkin et al. (1962) believe that because women are unable to maintain a "sense
of separate identity" (p. 218), they are less skilled at certain types of problem
solving, more likely to conform to group pressure, and more concerned with the
facial expressions of others. Thus, different cognitive styles have been ascribed
to men and women on the basis of their performance on these two tests. Pur-
ported differences in men's and women's cognitive styles was recently suggested
to explain the low participation rate of women in the physical sciences (Bar-Haim
& Wilkes, 1989).

Several researchers have argued that sex differences in field independence are
an artifact of sex differences in visual-spatial ability because both the Rod and
Frame Test and the Embedded Figures Test have a strong spatial component
(Sherman, 1967). What about other measures of field dependence and independence that do not rely on spatial abilities? None of the nonspatial tests (e.g., tests
that require subjects to match the brightness of a rotating disk to some standard

level of brightness) that measure field dependence and independence yield sex differences. In a test of the hypothesis that sex differences in the Rod and Frame Test and Embedded Figures Test merely reflect differences in visual-spatial ability, Hyde, Geiringer, and Yen (1975) administered a series of tests to a sample of college women and men. The tests included the Rod and Frame Test, the Embedded Figures Test, a spatial ability test, an arithmetic test, a vocabulary test, and a word fluency test. All between-sex results were in the predicted direction, with males performing better on the test of spatial ability, Rod and Frame Test, Embedded Figures Test, and arithmetic test, and females performing better on the vocabulary test and word fluency test. When they reanalyzed their data statistically controlling for differences in spatial ability, the results changed dramatically. Sex differences in the Rod and Frame Test, Embedded Figures Test, and arithmetic test became nonsignificant. A similar analysis in which they statistically controlled for differences in vocabulary ability had little effect on the two tests of field independence. It would appear that the two spatial tests of field dependence and independence are not indicative of cognitive styles; that is, they are unrelated to passivity or submissiveness, notwithstanding the claims of Witkin and others (Witkin, 1950; Witkin et al., 1954), but merely reflect sex differences in visual-spatial abilities.

Developmental data support the notion that sex differences in field independence are really reflections of sex differences in visual-spatial abilities. Several investigators have found that field independence declines in old age, so that older people of both sexes are generally more field dependent than comparable samples of younger adults (e.g., Crosson, 1984). As already stated, visual-spatial abilities also show a parallel decline in old age. This finding needs to be interpreted with caution because almost all of the research has employed cross-sectional sampling techniques, and results may represent generational effects rather than actual declines within individuals.

Chess and Music

If there are sex differences in visual-spatial abilities, then they should be found in the everyday tasks and activities that utilize spatial skills. Two highly skilled activities that seem to have spatial components are chess and music. Is there any evidence of sex differences in these activities? This is not an easy question to answer, and research has not provided us with useful conclusions. Clearly, the vast majority of chess masters and master musicians are men, but, as discussed earlier, this does not mean that women have less ability.

In a careful study of chess masters, de Groot (1966) found that the ability to reproduce the positions of the pieces on the chess board after only a brief glimpse of a legitimate game in progress is what distinguished master players from novices. The masters could quickly code and utilize information from actual "plays," but were no better than the novices when the pieces were placed randomly on the board. This finding suggests that the master players have a highly developed visual memory for the spatial array of meaningful chess boards, but not for other visual-spatial arrays. These results support the conclusion that an extraordinary memory for a visual-spatial array is not a distinguishing characteristic of chess masters. The special ability of chess masters seems to lie in their knowledge of the rules of chess and their ability to organize the displays in terms of the rules. If these inferences from the research are correct, then superior visual-spatial ability is not needed for success in chess, and the most likely reason that women are underrepresented in high level chess tournaments is psychosocial. This is a difficult hypothesis to test experimentally. Although we know that fewer women participate in chess tournaments, we don't know if this is due to actual ability differences or societal pressures to eschew tasks that are typically considered to be "masculine."

Music is another ability that is, at least partially, spatial in nature. High and low notes are placed in different spatial locations on the staff, and melodies and tunes have a definable shape or contour. In addition, the right hemisphere of the brain which is specialized for visual-spatial tasks also underlies musical ability (Springer & Deutsch, 1989). If sex differences in visual-spatial abilities are real, then you would expect similar differences in musical ability. For a variety of reasons, these have been under-studied areas. If reliable sex differences favoring males were found, then we would have convergent validity for sex difference in visual-spatial ability. In one of the few longitudinal studies of the development of musical talent, Hassler, Birbaumer, and Feil (1987) found a positive relationship between musical talent and spatial abilities. This single correlational study shows how little we know about the cognitive abilities that underlie musical talent. The only reliable finding of sex differences in musical ability is that females exceed males on tests of dynamic interpretations, which includes the ability to distinguish subtle changes in volume and musical "phrasing" (McGuiness, 1976). Music, like chess, is a very complex activity which probably involves both verbal and spatial components. Karma (1979, 1980, cited in Shuter-Dyson & Gabriel, 1982) hypothesized that musical ability is more highly associated with spatial ability than with verbal ability, and that females might process musical stimuli verbally while males might process it spatially. Although his earlier research tended to support his hypothesis, he later concluded that the essential difference in how people process musical stimuli is the amount of experience with music one has and not the sex of the subject. Thus, in music, as in chess, at least part of the ability that is associated with skilled performance develops with practice (Glaser, in press).

In Shuter-Dyson and Gabriel's (1982) review of the psychology of music, they concluded that sex differences in most tests of musical ability are small enough to disregard. Currently, there is no good reason to believe that there are sex differences in musical ability, despite the tremendous disparity in sex ratios among society's most accomplished and recognized musicians. A recent literature search for experimental studies showed that this is an underinvestigated area. Given the paucity of research in this area and findings that are sometimes opposite to those predicted, this is another area ripe for additional research. It is hoped that future researchers will include tests of chess and musical abilities in their investigations of sex differences because information about these areas of ability will help to advance our understanding of the interrelationship among several visual-spatial variables.

QUANTITATIVE ABILITIES

Plake, Loyd, and Hoover (1981) summarized findings of sex-related differences in quantitative (mathematical) ability this way: "There is little doubt that females score differently from males on mathematical tests" (p. 780). As you can probably guess, "differently" is a euphemism for poorer, but does this necessarily mean that males have more quantitative ability? It seems that quantitative ability, like spatial ability, is a heterogeneous concept. There are several different aspects of quantitative ability, and there is good evidence that sex differences are manifested in only some of them. Examples of the types of tasks that are used to assess quantitative ability are shown in Fig. 3.5.

Stones, Beckmann, and Stephens (1982) examined this question with students at 10 different colleges. The students, who obviously are not representative of all females and males because they had already met college admissions require-

---

SAMPLE QUESTIONS USED TO ASSESS QUANTITATIVE ABILITIES

(1)   276
        x 18

(2)   If Fred can paint the room in two hours and Sally can paint it in three hours, how long will it take them if they work together?

(3) $\int\int_s\int f = \int_0^{\pi/2} \int_{\pi/A}^{\arctan 2} \int_0^{\sqrt{6}} \frac{1}{\rho} \rho^2$

(4) $\hat\sigma = \sqrt{\dfrac{1}{n}\sum_{i=1}^{n} [y_i - (\hat\alpha + \hat\beta x_i]^2}$

FIG. 3.5.   Sample questions used to assess quantitative ability.

ments, were given tests in 10 different mathematical categories. No significant overall sex differences were found using multivariate procedures that allowed the experimenters to consider all 10 test scores at once. Sex differences were found, however, on the individual subtests. Females scored significantly higher than males on the tests of mathematical sentences and mathematical reasoning, perhaps reflecting the use of verbal strategies in solving these problems. Males scored significantly higher than females in geometry, measurement, probability and statistics, perhaps reflecting the use of visual-spatial strategies in these areas.

The finding of sex differences in some tests of quantitative or mathematical ability is robust. Consistent sex differences have been found in many large-scale studies. The largest differences favor males, who tend to outscore females on the quantitative portion of the Scholastic Aptitude Test (SAT-M). The male advantage on this highly standardized test, which is administered nationally to college bound high school seniors in the United States, is approximately 50 points (National Education Association, 1989).

Quantitative skills are a prerequisite for entry into jobs requiring scientific and technical skills. Sells (1980) has described mathematics as a "critical filter" which allows only some to pass into the higher paying prestigious jobs. One major problem with reports of sex differences in quantitative ability is the failure to take into account the fact that the sexes are disproportionately represented in advanced mathematics courses. The single best prediction of scores on tests of mathematics is the number of mathematics courses an individual has taken (Jones, 1984). Meece, Eccles-Parsons, Kaczala, Goff, and Futterman (1982) reported that when the data are adjusted to take into account the number of prior mathematics courses, sex differences are substantially reduced, but not eliminated. Thus, a major portion of the difference can be attributed to mathematical background, but not all of it.

Like all of the cognitive areas, results are highly dependent on the portion of the distribution that is being studied. Sex differences have been reported among mathematically gifted boys and girls. Johns Hopkins University has been involved in a nationwide talent search to identify boys and girls who are exceptionally talented in mathematics (Benbow, 1988; Benbow & Stanley, 1980, 1981, 1983). One finding was that there were substantial sex differences in the number of girls and boys identified as "mathematically precocious." They reported that among seventh- and eighth-grade youth identified as mathematically talented, the male to female ratio on the College Board's Scholastic Aptitude Test (SAT-M) were as follows: 2:1 at >500, 5:1 at >600, and 17:1 at >700 (Stanley & Benbow, 1982). Furthermore, Benbow (1988) reported that this ratio has remained stable over 15 years. This is a considerable sex difference that has generated heated controversy and has received extensive coverage in the popular press and nonprint media. The fact that these differences emerged from very large samples and have been replicated numerous times lends credibility to these results. Do these differences reflect actual ability differences or are they artifacts of the way the students were identified? Benbow and Stanley believe that students were selected in an unbiased manner and that the large sex differences are attributable, at least in part, to biological mechanisms, whereas their detractors argue that girls will always be underrepresented in fields that are defined by society as masculine (e.g., Halpern, 1988). These two possibilities are considered in the following chapters.

Stanley (1990) documented the absence of females from the highest levels of mathematical achievement with the following statistics: In the U.S.A. Mathematical Olympiad contest for high school students, there have been 144 winners since 1972. Of these, only 2 were female. Comparisons with the International Mathematical Olympiad show an equally unbalanced representation by sex. There have been no female participants from the United States since 1975. In the 1988 International Mathematical Olympiad (the only year with detailed data), there were only four female participants from 3 of the 49 countries that sent delegates. Interestingly, for the 4 years that China has competed in the International Mathematical Olympiad, there was a female on their team each time. These four Chinese females won three silver medals and one gold medal. What can we learn from these astounding statistics? First, females are seriously underrepresented from the highest achieving mathematical groups and, second, although their absence is also found in other countries, the extremely low participation rate of females is not universally true; the Chinese have managed to produce extremely high-achieving females in mathematics.

Rossi (1983) believes that even if these numbers reflect genuine sex differences at the upper end of ability, the way they are presented is misleading. He has argued that by reporting sex differences in terms of ratios instead of an effect size statistic such as d of ω^2, the actual group differences are exaggerated. (See chapter 2 for a discussion of these statistics). Only 5% of Stanley and Benbow's sample scored above 599 on the mathematics portion of the SAT. For the other 95%, the actual sex differences were only moderately large ($d = .44$). Although these distinctions may seem highly technical to a reader without an extensive background in statistics, they are important in understanding the size and nature of sex differences in mathematical ability. In summary, the differences seem large when considering only the most highly gifted youth and much smaller when considering moderately gifted youth.

Age Trends in Quantitative Ability

The developmental nature of quantitative sex differences was examined in a study of over 5,000 students aged 13 and 17. No sex differences were found for the 13-year-olds, whereas by age 17 the males were significantly outperforming the females, with an average of 5% more correct answers (Jones, 1984). There is also evidence that sex differences in quantitative abilities emerge earlier for boys and girls pursuing an academic curriculum than for students in a nonacademic course of study. A longitudinal study conducted by the Educational Testing Service found that sex differences emerged in 7th grade for a group of college bound students, but did not appear until 11th grade for their peers who were not college bound (Hilton & Berglund, 1974).

In a recent meta-analytic review of 100 studies, Hyde, Fennema, and Lamon (1990) found that there was a slight female superiority in the elementary and middle-school years, a moderate male superiority in high school ($d = .29$), and larger male advantages in college ($d = .41$) and later adulthood ($d = .59$). However, these age trends were modified by type of task, with female superiority in computation in elementary and middle school and no difference with respect to computation in later years. There were essentially no sex differences in understanding mathematical concepts at any age. The most dramatic age trends were found on tests of mathematical problem solving favoring females slightly in elementary and middle school with a moderate effect favoring males in high school and college. Hyde, Fenemma, and Lamon's conclusions are the most reliable because of the large number of studies in their meta-analysis and the care they used to divide the data into homogeneous categories. Aiken (1986–1987), in his review of the area, also concluded that the largest differences occur in mathematical problem solving, with males answering more questions correctly than females. Marshall and Smith (1987) confirmed these results with their study showing that third-grade girls surpass boys in computation, an advantage that they retain through sixth grade; whereas, boys show superiority in solving word problems and on geometry and measurement problems.

RELATIONSHIP BETWEEN VISUAL-SPATIAL ABILITIES AND QUANTITATIVE ABILITIES

Several researchers have suggested that sex differences in quantitative abilities, like those in field dependence and independence, are a secondary consequence of differences in visual-spatial ability. There are a number of logical and empirical reasons to support this causal link. If you think for a minute about the nature of advanced topics in mathematics—geometry, topology, trigonometry, and calculus—you will realize that they all require spatial skills. In addition, a National Science Foundation study of women mathematicians found that they were more likely to select algebra and statistics as an area of specialization than other mathematics specialties in which spatial perception is central (Luchins, 1979). Empirical evidence for this relationship comes from a variety of studies. In Anderson's (1990) review of cognitive abilities, he concluded that "Psychometrically, measures of mathematical ability tend to be strongly correlated with spatial ability" (p. 449).

Fennema and Sherman (1977) found a significant positive relationship between scores on a spatial relations test and achievement in mathematics ($r = .50$)

(although they did not find this relationship in later studies). Hills (1957) found that scores on tests of spatial visualization and spatial orientation are correlated with performance in college mathematics courses ($r = .23$ and $r = .22$, respectively) Additionally, when spatial ability was statistically controlled, sex differences in quantitative ability became nonsignificant (Burnett, Lane, & Dratt, 1979; Hyde, Geiringer, & Yen, 1975). Because of the concerted research efforts of Benbow and her colleagues (Benbow, 1988; Benbow, Stanley, Zonderman, & Kirk, 1983), we know more about extremely gifted adolescents than almost any other group. Benbow found that the mathematically gifted youth in her studies also tended to have very high spatial abilities. Maccoby and Jacklin's (1974) conclusion that the magnitude of sex differences in quantitative abilities is probably not as large as in spatial abilities is also in accord with the hypothesis that much of the difference in quantitative abilities is attributable to sex differences in visual-spatial abilities.

A recent factor-analytic study of skills conducted with college undergraduates also supports the relationship between visual-spatial and mathematical skills. Hunt (1985) found that three distinct ability factors or dimensions emerged when his subjects were given a variety of cognitive tests. The first factor was a verbal ability factor comprised of reading comprehension, grammar, and vocabulary tests. The second factor was a quantitative/spatial factor comprised of tests of visual-spatial ability and mathematics tests. The third factor was identified as "mechanical reasoning." The fact that quantitative and spatial skills loaded on one factor suggests that there is a single underlying dimension that is responsible for performance on both types of tasks.

Like almost every other hypothesis concerning ability differences, data relating spatial ability to mathematical ability have been mixed. It seems most likely that there is a spatial component to some, but not all, mathematical tasks. For example, computation is not a spatial task, and females excel in computation during the early grades. Fennema and Tartre (1985) found that spatial ability relates to the use of spatial processes in mathematical problem solving. Thus, it seems that the use of spatial skills in solving mathematical problems is task specific.

MAGNITUDE OF THE DIFFERENCES

Although the preponderance of the experimental evidence points to some sex differences in verbal, visual-spatial, and quantitative ability, the question of the size or magnitude of these differences has not been easy to resolve. Are the differences trivial and of no practical significance or do they represent meaningful ability differences between the sexes? Even if we were to conclude that there are large between-sex differences with respect to a cognitive ability, it is very important to remember that most research analyzes group-average results that cannot be applied to any individual.

All of the cognitive sex differences have been replicated numerous times and are statistically significant, which means that they are unlikely to have occurred by chance, but are they of any practical significance? Can they be used to explain why we have so few female mathematicians or engineers? Can they help us predict a male's or female's ability to perform a task? Can they be used to justify discrimination? Are they merely curiosities whose only value is to keep psychologists (and publishers) busy? Answers to these questions are hotly debated and have important implications for modern society.

On an intuitive level, effect size is a quantification of the size of the average between-sex difference on a particular test or set of tests. Unfortunately, the numbers we use to express effect size are not intuitive. Differences like the finding that men tend to outscore women an average of 50 points on the quantitative portion of the SATs have an immediate meaning to anyone who is familiar with the scoring system for the SATs. Unfortunately, sex differences in abilities are measured with many different tests, and a common measure of the average difference is needed to make comparisons across many studies. The effect size statistic is used to convey the size of the differences when many different tests are used. (Readers for whom this is a new concept are referred back to chapter 2 where statistical concepts are discussed in more depth. It is also possible to follow the gist of the following discussion without understanding the fine points of some of the statistical concepts that are discussed.)

There are few guidelines for determining if the size of a sex difference with respect to a cognitive ability is large enough to be important. Cohen (1969) provided an arbitrary statistical definition of small, medium, and large effect sizes using standard deviation units (.20 s.d. is small, .50 s.d. is medium, and .80 s.d. is large). There is however, no good reason to accept his effect size markers except for the fact that they provide a common ruler for comparing differences. As noted in chapter 2, the majority of the research published in psychology (in fields other than sex differences) reveals an effect size less than .20 (Riefer, 1990). Thus, if we accept .20 as a "small effect," we are, in effect, deciding that most psychological research deals with very small effects. It is also important to realize that effect size should not be confused with importance. A small effect could still be important, depending on how importance is defined and who defines it. Percentage of explained variance statistics (e.g., omega-squared, R^2, eta squared) are useful in this regard, but they still leave us with the question of how much explained variance is large enough to be important. If sex explained 5% of the variance in the data, is this a large or small number? In another context, like medicine, 5% of explained variance attributable to a treatment could mean many lives would be saved. Thus, the question of whether 1% or 5% or 50% of explained variance is important depends on both the context and value judgments. Value judgments never lend themselves to statistical analysis, and thus, precise answers to the question of how large does a difference have to be to be important will remain debatable.

Williams (1983) and others (Gelman et al., 1981; Hyde, 1981) have concluded that looking at the ways large numbers of women and men differ, on the *average,* is misleading because the magnitude of the differences is quite small. "This means that when we look at measures of such behavior we invariably find that differences within a sex category, for example, differences *among* women, are greater than differences *between* women and men" (Williams, 1983, p. 115). Although this statement focuses on the finding that there is considerable variability among women, it does not necessarily imply that the between-sex differences are small or unimportant. Readers are asked to keep all of these admonitions in mind when considering whether the effects are large enough to be meaningful.

Effect Size for Verbal Abilities

The magnitude of the sex difference for verbal ability is probably the smallest among the cognitive sex differences. In their review of the literature published before 1974, Maccoby and Jacklin (1974) found that the female advantage on verbal tests ranged from .1 to .5 standard deviation units, with the usual difference approximately .25 standard deviation units. In other words,the mean of the female distribution of scores was one fourth of a standard deviation above the mean of the male distribution. (Reiterating a point raised earlier, differences need to be reported in terms of standard deviation units because the way verbal abilities are measured varies among the studies.) Using Cohen's heuristic for judging effect size, this is a small effect.

More recent analyses of the verbal ability effect size have yielded a more differentiated picture of the nature of sex differences in verbal abilities. In an extensive meta-analytic review, Hyde and Linn (1988) have provided a detailed quantitative summary of 165 studies that reported data on sex differences in verbal ability.

Out of the 56 studies that found statistically significant differences, 78% (44) found that females performed better than males. However, the majority of the studies (66%) did not find statistically significant sex differences in verbal abilities. Although most people would tend to interpret the large number of null results as indicating that there are no differences, if you have already read chapter 2, you will recall that the interpretation of null results is not this straightforward. Studies that fail to reject the null hypothesis cannot "cancel" studies that report differences because there are so many ways to obtain null results. The probability of finding significant differences (in any study) depends on the number of subjects in the study. Any researcher can virtually assure that there will be no significant differences by using a small number of subjects in a study, and, conversely, a large number of subjects will virtually assure statistically significant results. Research that uses a large number of subjects offers a better estimate of the actual differences in the population, and for this reason, large sample studies are better than small sample studies. Thus, large sample studies are generally preferred, and these are the studies that will more likely report significant differences. Effect sizes computed from studies that have found statistically significant differences may be the most reliable indicator of the "true" difference in the population because they are usually based on a larger sample size than studies in which the null hypothesis (the one that states that there are no differences between groups) *cannot* be rejected. (Recall that a study can yield statistically significant differences and also reveal a small effect size.)

The conclusions that we make about sex differences in verbal abilities depends on whether we decide to include studies that found null results or focus only on those studies that report statistically significant differences. Meta-analyses always include studies that report no differences and therefore will always yield smaller estimates of differences than data summary techniques that only include studies that were statistically significant.

Hyde and Linn's meta-analysis established the following: virtually no sex differences in vocabulary ($d = .02$), reading comprehension ($d = .03$), essay writing ($d = .09$), and SAT-V ($d = -.03$, with the negative value indicating that males tend to score higher); small sex differences in anagrams ($d = .22$), and general/mixed verbal abilities ($d = .20$), and in analogies ($d = -.16$, indicating male advantage), with the largest differences ($d = .33$) in speech production. When the mean of all of the effect sizes are computed, the overall value is $d = .11$. They conclude from these results that "gender differences in verbal ability no longer exist" (p. 53). I don't believe that this conclusion is supported by their own data. The 165 studies that they reviewed showed no sex differences for some verbal abilities, small differences for others (with some results favoring males), and moderate differences for at least one component of verbal ability. To conclude from this mixed pattern of results that overall there is no difference is like telling a person who has his feet in the oven and head in the freezer that, on the average, he is really quite comfortable.

The size of the sex differences effect in verbal abilities would be much larger if the experiments that were included in the meta-analysis had involved more subjects from the low end of the abilities distribution. As already noted, the largest effects are found in areas of stuttering (which suggests that the moderate size effect for speech production is much larger than Hyde and Linn reported) and in dyslexia and other extreme forms of reading disabilities. If more of the studies included in the meta-analysis had contained samples from the low end of the distribution, the overall effect size favoring females would have been much larger.

We also get a very different picture of the results when we examine only those studies that report significant differences. This approach is justified on the grounds that if there really are no (or extremely small) differences, then about half of the studies would show results favoring males and half would show results favoring females with similar distributions of effect sizes. This is clearly not the case. Of the 19 statistically significant studies published after 1974 that favor females, the median effect size is $d = .44$. The comparable figure for the 7 studies that favor males is $d = -.22$. Among the 15 studies published prior to 1974 that reported statistically significant results favoring females the median effect size was $d = .34$. (Only four studies published prior to 1974 showed results favoring males, so a pre-1974 median effect size for verbal tasks in which males outperform females is not meaningful.)

As psychologists learn more about the nature of verbal abilities, new tests have been devised that show very large sex differences. Hines (1990) recently found very large differences on tests of associational fluency (which is a fancy term for generating synonyms). Her results show a huge female advantage with $d = 1.2$! Similarly, high values have recently been reported on a consonant–vowel matching test, with a female advantage of $d = 1.3$ (Block, Arnott, Quigley, & Lynch, 1989). These are enormous effect sizes—so large that tests of statistical significance are not even needed.

What can we conclude from all of these numbers? Most readers want a simple answer. Unfortunately, simple answers are not possible. The best conclusion that we can make to date is that many types of verbal abilities show no sex differences, but there are some consistent sex differences. Females outperform males in fluent speech production, anagrams, and general and mixed tests of verbal abilties; males outperform females on solving analogies, with a small advantage on the verbal portion of the SATs. Most literature reviews underestimate the female advantage in verbal ability because there are so few studies of populations with extremely low verbal abilities—a group that is comprised mainly of males. The SAT results are considered again later in this chapter because they produce anomolous results and because of their tremendous importance in determining eligibility for higher education.

Effect Size for Visual-Spatial Abilities

As stated earlier, findings of sex differences in visual-spatial ability are the most robust (found consistently) of the cognitive sex differences. It also appears that the largest sex differences are found here.

Although Hyde (1981) reported that the difference between the means on tests of visual-spatial abilities for females and males was "only" .45 standard deviation units, accounting for only 4.3% of the variance, data from other researchers suggest that these values underestimate the population effect size. A substantial effect size was reported by Sanders, Soares, and D'Aquila (1982). They gave 672 college women and 359 men two tests of visual-spatial ability and got very different results for each test. Although the men scored, on the average, higher on both tests, the magnitude of the difference varied substantially between the tests. For one test, a card rotations test, the means were .29 standard deviation units apart, with sex accounting for a mere 2% of the variance. The other test, however, was a mental rotation test with group means .83 standard deviation units apart and 16% of the variance accounted for by sex. In Cohen's (1965) cogent discussion of effect size, he describes effects that are of this magnitude as being so large that no statistical analysis is needed to document the between-sex difference. In order to make the magnitude of this difference understandable, Sanders, Soares, and D'Aquila claim that it is as large as the difference in IQ scores between PhDs and typical college freshmen or as large as the difference in heights between 13- and 18-year-old girls.

Other tests that require the mental rotation of objects in space yield similar effect sizes. Petersen and Crockett (1985), for example, found a sex effect of one standard deviation on a three-dimensional mental rotation test, whereas the effect size on another spatial ability test (Primary Mental Abilities Space Subtest) and other two-dimensional rotation tests was only one third of a standard deviation. The magnitude of the sex effect seems to depend on the test used to measure spatial ability. In their extensive meta-analytic review, Linn and Petersen (1986) reported that the effect size for spatial perception is $d = .64$ for adults and $d = .37$ for younger ages. Mental rotation effect sizes were divided by type of test. The Vandenberg Mental Rotation Test showed an effect size of $d = .94$. This value is almost identical to the effect size of $d = .91$ with males scoring higher on paper and pencil rotation tasks reported by Block, Arnott, Quigley, and Lynch (1989). The other mental rotation tests yielded $d = .26$. Spatial visualization had the lowest effect size with $d = .13$.

The finding that the magnitude of the sex difference in visual-spatial ability depends on the type of visual-spatial test used helps to explain some of the discrepancies in the literature. This result is consistent with the notion that visual-spatial ability is not a homogeneous construct and sex differences depend on which component of visual-spatial ability is being measured. Sanders, Soares, and D'Aquila (1982) suggest that the female advantage with verbal tasks might be as large as the male advantage with visual-spatial tasks, if we found the right test to tap into the sex-related verbal difference. It may be that Hines' (1990) test of associational fluency will prove to be such a test.

Another way of understanding the size of the sex-related differences is to compare the percentage of females and males exceeding a given score on a test. This is the Binomial Effect Size Display that was discussed in chapter 2. To underscore the size of the sex difference on a mental rotation test, Bouchard and McGee (1977) reported that only 20% of the females in the 200 families they tested scored above the median (50%) for males. A number of other researchers found similar male–female disparities (Harris, 1978). In fact, the Differential Aptitude Tests are separately normed for each sex because of these differences. At Grade 12, for example, a girl who scores at the 80th percentile has a test score that is equal to that of a boy at the 70th percentile.

Effect Size for Quantitative Abilities

The magnitude of the effect size for sex differences in quantitative ability is medium, placing it somewhere between the small effect associated with verbal ability and the large effect associated with some visual-spatial abilities. Hyde (1981) reviewed 16 studies that examined sex differences in quantitative ability and found that the median between-sex difference was .45 standard deviation units, with approximately 1% of the variance accounted for by sex. This means that 99% of the variance was due to sampling error and/or variables that were not investigated in the study. In general, when effect sizes are presented as "proportion of explained variance," we find that only a small proportion can be explained by sex of subject. However, as explained in chapter 2, the corresponding value of d makes these differences seem larger, and the corresponding Binomial Effect Size Display can make the same between-group differences seem even larger.

When we examine quantitative sex differences among mathematically gifted preteens and teenagers, the sex effects appear to be much larger. In Benbow and Stanley's (1980, 1981; Benbow, 1988) highly publicized report of the Johns Hopkins talent search for mathematically precocious youth, they reported several indices of sex differences. They identified seventh graders in the top second, third, and fifth percentile in the United States in a test of mathematical reasoning ability. The male/female ratio over several years of testing remained stable at 57 boys for every 43 girls. The mean between-sex difference on the mathematics portion of the Scholastic Aptitude Test (SAT-M) was 32 points for the gifted students. Among the highest scoring students, the differences were magnified to an even greater proportion. Boys outnumbered girls 2:1 among students who scored above 500. When they examined scores over 700, 23 boys and no girls were found in this extreme range. In effect size units, the boys' mean was .50 standard deviation above the girls' mean on the SAT-M.

It may seem strange that a medium effect size (.50 standard deviation units) is associated with such large sex differences in this mathematically gifted sample. In fact, small mean (average) differences often create large differences at the tails or extreme ends of distributions. To demonstrate this point, Hyde (1981) considered a hypothetical example in which group means were .40 standard deviation units apart. If we considered only the top 5% of scores we'd find that 7.35% of males and 3.22% of females would exceed this cut point. This is a 2:1 ratio, similar to that reported by Benbow and Stanley for students scoring above 500 on the SAT-M. Thus, if we are concerned with extremely gifted individuals, small average sex differences can create large sex differences in this highly elite group, and small or medium effect sizes become important.

Effect Size for Cognitive Abilities Overall

Some researchers assumed a broader view and studied the effect size for several cognitive abilities in the same study. Backman (1979), for example, studied the relationship among ethnicity, socioeconomic status (SES), and sex, and their joint influence on mental abilities. She administered tests of verbal knowledge,

English language, grammar, mathematics, reasoning with spatial forms, perceptual speech, and memory to over 2,000 Grade 12 students. She accounted for over 90% of the total variance with the main effects and interactions of her variables, but the relative importance of these variables was surprising. "Differences between the patterns of mental abilities of males and females were more marked than were differences among the patterns of ethnic or SES groups. Sex accounted for 69% of the total variance, ethnicity 9% and SES 1%" (p. 264). It is difficult to know how to interpret the extremely large effect of sex in this study, given that it accounted for a very much smaller percentage of explained variance in the other studies of individual abilities. It seems that sex was a very important determinant of how well the students performed on these tests. It also seems that sex as a variable can explain a much greater proportion of the total variance when several sex-related cognitive abilities are considered simultaneously in a single experiment than when individual abilities are being studied.

In one of the most lucid analyses to date, Rosenthal and Rubin (1982) attempted to shed light on the question of how large an effect size must be in order to be of practical importance. Using a statistical test known as the Binomial Effect Size Display (BESD), they calculated that when sex explains only 4% of the variance in test scores, this translates into distributions in which 60% of the higher scoring sex is above the median and only 40% of the lower scoring sex is above the median. They argue that outcome rates of 60% versus 40% are important because they can be used to predict performance on ability tests in these areas. They also looked at the consistencies among effect sizes across 12 studies of verbal ability, 7 studies of visual-spatial ability, 7 studies of quantitative ability, and 14 studies of field articulation (field independence and dependence). They concluded that effect sizes differed from study to study, supporting the idea that the magnitude of the sex difference in any area depends on the type of test used.

UNDERLYING COGNITIVE PROCESSES

Examining sex differences for cognitive abilities is only one way of conceptualizing how females and males may differ in their intellectual processes. The division of abilities into verbal, visual-spatial, and quantitative has been useful, and as discussed in the next two chapters, each of these abilities has distinct biological correlates. But there are other ways of investigating the thinking process. One such way is to consider what the subject does when he or she is engaged in a particular task. This alternate approach can be thought of as examining the underlying cognitive processes.

Look carefully at Table 3.1. I have listed the types of tasks on which females tend to excel and the types of tasks on which males tend to excel. One approach is to consider these two types of tasks as representing different underlying cog-

TABLE 3.1
Possible Sex Differences in Underlying Cognitive Processes

Tasks at which females excel:

-Generating Synonyms (Associational Fluency)
-Language Production and Word Fluency
-Computation
-Anagrams

Underlying Cognitive Processes: Rapid Access to and Retrieval of Information in Memory

Tasks at which males excel:

-Verbal Analogies
-Mathematical Problem Solving
-Mental Rotation and Spatial Perception
-Spatiotemporal Tasks (dynamic visual displays)

Underlying Cognitive Processes: Maintaining and Manipulating a Mental Representation

nitive processes. The tasks at which females excel include language production, generating synonyms, word fluency, anagrams, and computation. Skilled performance in all of these tasks requires rapid access to and retrieval of information that is stored in memory. On the other hand, consider those tasks at which males tend to excel—mathematical problem solving, verbal analogies, mental rotation, spatial perception, and using information in dynamic visual displays (spatiotemporal tasks). These sorts of tasks require the ability to maintain and manipulate mental representations. Thus, it may prove meaningful to differentiate cognitive tasks on the basis of the type of cognitive process that each requires. When we adopt this framework, we can account for sex differences that do not divide neatly under the tripart cognitive abilities rubric (verbal, mathematical, and visual-spatial) such as female superiority on some verbal tasks and computation.

ARE SEX DIFFERENCES DECREASING?

The next four chapters describe theories that have been proposed to explain why sex differences are sometimes found. If these differences were created by sex-differentiated psychosocial variables like sex roles and different rewards for males and females, then we would expect to see some decline in the magnitude of the differences as the impact of sex roles diminishes. Thus, the question of whether sex differences in cognitive abilities are decreasing is important. Unfortunately, this is not an easy question to answer. There is some evidence that suggests that differences are decreasing and other evidence that they are not.

In order to conclude that sex differences are decreasing, we need to have comparable samples of subjects that have taken the same cognitive abilities tests in different time periods. We do not have any samples that meet these stringent requirements.

Several experimenters have examined effect sizes as a function of the date that the study was published. The underlying rational for investigating results as a function of their date of publication is that more recent studies should, in general, show smaller sex differences than studies published many years ago, if sex differences really have been decreasing. The problem with this approach is that a great many other variables have also changed during the intervening years. In response to concerns that publication practices tend to be biased toward studies that report significant differences, many more journals and paper presentations now report nonsignificant results, thus, changing the nature of the studies that can be included in meta-analyses. (In other words, a study that fails to find significant differences is more likely to be published than in the past.) The more recent tendency to publish nonsignificant results would cause effect sizes to decrease as a function of publication date.

The nature of samples has also changed with time. Two to three decades ago, college enrollments were overwhelmingly male. Now, women make up more than 50% of college enrollments in the United States (U.S. Bureau of the Census, 1989). Because a larger percentage of all females are now attending college than the percentage of males, a more select group of college men is probably being sampled than college women. The nature of many of the tests has also changed (Halpern, 1989a). The Educational Testing Service, which authors the SATs, has come under severe criticism for the disparities in female and male scores. Accordingly, they have responded in the last few years by scrutinizing every test question for sex-related bias in content or use of pronouns. The Educational Testing Service now trains all of its test committees on ways to avoid bias in the questions that are used on their examinations. Many of the other tests that show the greatest sex differences have been developed within the last few years (e.g., paper-and-pencil mental rotation tests, word fluency, and consonant vowel matching tests) and therefore cannot be compared with comparable older studies to see if the effect sizes are diminishing.

Hyde and Linn (1988) reported that for studies published before 1974 the effect size for verbal abilities was $d = .23$ and for those after 1974 $d = .10$. While this difference suggests that sex differences are decreasing (and are presently so small as to be considered nonexistent), a very different conclusion emerges if we exclude nonsignificant results from the summary analysis. Based on studies that show statistically significant results, the pre-1974 median effect size is $d = .32$; the post-1974 median effect size is $d = .33$ (favoring females). These results don't support the idea that effect sizes in verbal ability are decreasing. Instead, they support the idea that more studies with nonsignificant results have been published since 1974.

Hyde, Fennema, and Lamon (1990) also concluded that sex differences in mathematics are decreasing. They found that $d = .31$ for studies published prior to 1974 and $d = .14$ for those studies after 1974 (favoring males). Unfortunately they did not present their data in a way that allows the separation of statistically significant and nonsignificant studies. Although these values suggest that sex differences may be declining, the decline in effect size could be caused by changes in publication practices, the composition of the samples of subjects, types of test used, or numerous other confounding factors.

Meta-analyses on spatial abilities have not examined the question of whether effect sizes are decreasing. Feingold (1988) argued that sex differences in spatial abilities are decreasing, but his conclusion was based on scores on the Space Relations subtest on the Differential Aptitude Test. As described in the section on visual-spatial abilities, this test assesses spatial visualization—the only visual-spatial ability that does not show reliable sex differences. Thus, we can make no conclusion about whether sex differences in visual-spatial abilities are changing at this time.

The SATs

Sex differences in verbal ability are commonly found in the American College Tests (ACTs) and Scholastic Aptitude Tests (SATs) used for college admissions, but the differences are not easy to interpret. Male and female scores on the Scholastic Aptitude Test-Verbal (SAT-V) are shown in Fig. 3.6. SAT-V data are difficult to interpret because it appears that the female advantage that was found in the late 1960s and early 1970s has turned into a sizeable male advantage. I do not believe that females have somehow "lost" verbal ability relative to males, especially in light of the fact that females still continue to score higher than males on the English subtest of the ACTs (Dodge, 1989). It seems more likely that the population of students who take college entrance examinations has changed radically over the past 25 years and the test itself has also undergone numerous revisions that may have implications for the way females and males score. These data are particularly difficult to interpret because females outscore males on the writing achievement test that can be taken with the SAT (Cordes, 1986). Thus, while females excel on two college entrance tests of verbal ability (the English subtest of the ACTs and the writing sample portion of the SATs), males are presently outscoring females on the verbal portion of the SATs.

The correlation between the difference in female and male SAT-V scores and year of test is $r = .93$, $p < .001$. This extremely high correlation shows how closely related the size of the sex difference is in SAT-V scores and year of the test. The difference favoring males has been steadily increasing over time.

SAT-V data provide a different picture of sex differences in verbal ability than many of the other studies. We can only speculate as to why they are so discrepant. Possible reasons include: (a) low ability males do not take the SATs

SCHOLASTIC APTITUDE TEST--VERBAL

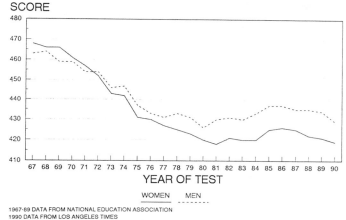

FIG. 3.6. Scholastic Aptitude Test Scores—Verbal for College-Bound Seniors: 1967–1990.

because they have a significantly higher dropout rate from high school (Halpern, 1989a); (b) SAT-V items are biased in some way, perhaps drawing more vocabulary terms and more reading examples from scientific or other male-biased domains; (c) the males who take the SATs are more advantaged in terms of socioeconomic status (Ramist & Arbeiter, 1986); (d) the verbal areas that show the largest female advantage are not included on the SAT-V (e.g., word fluency); (e) the low ability end of the verbal distribution (e.g., dyslexics, retarded) do not take the SATs, and therefore the verbal advantage of females is underestimated; and (f) the only verbal ability in which males exceed females in other verbal ability measures is in solving analogies. The SAT-V is heavily weighted with analogies, thus giving undue weight to the one verbal ability area in which males outscore females. It seems likely that the abilities used in solving verbal analogies are similar to those used in mathematical problem solving, which also shows a large male advantage. Future research is needed to determine which, if any, of these possibilities is responsible for the anomalous results with the SAT-V.

SAT-M (mathematics) scores do not reveal much in the way of time trends. The correlation between size of the sex difference (in SAT-M points) and year of publication is not statistically significant. As shown in Fig. 3.7, the female and male curve appear almost parallel. The mean (average) point difference in 1967 was 47. In 1989 the mean point difference was 46 points.

Further evidence that there has been no change in the magnitude of sex differences in mathematics was provided for the intellectually precocious youth

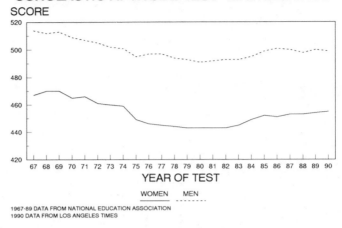

FIG. 3.7.   Scholastic Aptitude Test Scores—Mathematics for College-Bound Seniors: 1967–1990.

studied by Benbow (1988). She reported that the ratio of high scoring boys to girls as well as the magnitude of the difference has remained relatively constant over the last 15 years.

SEX DIFFERENCES IN FACTOR STRUCTURES

Terms like *verbal, visual-spatial,* and *quantitative ability* are hypothetical constructs that represent underlying unobservable variables that help to explain test results that presumably measure them. Terms like these have been called *convenient fictions* invented by psychologists who want to understand human intellect. One way to confirm or disconfirm our belief that tests of vocabulary, reading, and verbal analogies are all tapping the hypothetical entity we've labeled *verbal ability* is to subject scores on these tests from many individuals to a statistical procedure known as factor analysis. Kerlinger (1979) described factor analysis as a way of explaining phenomena by describing the way variables are related to each other. If the vocabulary, reading, and verbal analogies tests are all tapping the same ability, then they will be highly related to each other, and a single factor will emerge from the factor analysis. By examining the number of factors and the extent to which each test is associated with each factor, we can assess the structure or architecture of the human intellect.

A few researchers have attempted to address the question of sex differences in the factor structure of these abilities. With a factor analytic approach, the experimental question is no longer whether there are sex differences on any particular test (there is already ample evidence that reliable sex differences will emerge on certain tests), but whether both sexes use similar abilities in how they solve different problems. The scanty evidence we have to date suggests that there are few, if any, major differences between the sexes in the factor structure of their cognitive abilities.

In an attempt to examine the possibility that there are qualitative differences in cognitive abilities, Hertzog and Carter (1982) administered 10 different cognitive ability tests (e.g., vocabulary, spatial reasoning, arithmetic) to two generations of women and men. They compared the way the 10 tests were related to Spatial Abilities and Verbal Abilities factors for each sex and generation group using a sophisticated statistical technique known as *structural equation modeling.* Hertzog and Carter concluded that women and men in both generations had similar intellectual factor structures. In other words, cognitive abilities are organized in similar ways for both sexes in both generation groups. Thus, although there are quantitative differences (males better in mental rotation tasks and females better in certain aspects of verbal ability), there do not appear to be any qualitative between-sex differences in the structure or organization of cognitive abilities.

In a similar investigation, Hyde, Geiringer, and Yen (1975) gave nine different tests to male and female college students: spatial ability; Rod and Frame Test; Embedded Figures Test; mental arithmetic; vocabulary; word fluency; alternate uses (creativity); femininity; and achievement motivation. These tests were chosen to allow them to investigate the relationship among spatial ability, two tests of field articulation (Rod and Frame and Embedded Figures) and arithmetic for each sex separately and for the entire sample as a whole. One hypothesis that was considered earlier in this chapter was that sex differences in field articulation and mathematics are really artifacts of sex differences in spatial ability. If this hypothesis is correct, then these four tests should emerge on a single factor while the verbal tests should emerge on a separate factor. (The reasoning behind the inclusion of tests of creativity, femininity, and achievement motivation is not considered at this time.) They found typical sex differences in each of these tests verifying the well known sex differences in these abilities (males outscoring females in spatial ability and arithmetic and appearing more field independent on the Rod and Frame Test and Embedded Figures Test, and females outscoring males on the vocabulary and word fluency tests). In general, factor structures were similar for both sexes; however, spatial ability seemed less related to the factor composed of the Rod and Frame Test, Embedded Figures Test, and mental arithmetic for the women than for the men. Thus, it is possible that women use different approaches in solving spatial problems than men. One possibility, for example, is that women rely on verbal strategies whereas men tend to use spatial ones to solve the same problems. Additional support for this claim comes from the finding reported earlier of male and female differences in variability on spatial tests.

SIMILARITIES

Although the focus of this chapter has been the identification of cognitive abilities that show sex differences, the flip side of this issue is at least as important— those areas of cognition in which similarities are found. I have focused on differences because the logic of hypothesis testing only allows conclusions about differences. Despite this limitation, it is important to note that the number of areas in which sex differences are even moderate in size is small. Males and females are overwhelming alike in their cognitive abilities. It is important not to lose sight of this fact as we consider theories that have been posited to explain the differences and similarities in cognitive sex differences. Also, please keep in mind that even in the relatively few areas in which differences are found, these conclusions are based on data gathered from a large number of subjects. They can't be applied to any single individual because the within-sex variability is so large.

CHAPTER SUMMARY

Although sex differences have not been found in general intelligence, there are some types of cognitive abilities that vary, on the average, as a function of sex. There are some sex-related differences in the earliest stages of information processing—perception and attention, but the effect of these early stage differences on later cognitive processes is unknown. Males comprise a disproportionate share of the extremely low ability end of the verbal abilities distribution, with males overwhelmingly categorized as stutterers, dyslexics, and retardates. The only type of verbal ability that shows a male advantage is solving verbal analogies. By contrast, females excel at anagrams, general and mixed verbal ability tests, speech production, and associational fluency. The female advantage is largest during the preschool and adult years. Females excel in computation during elementary school, with males showing superiority in mathematical problem solving. The highest ability end of the mathematical ability distribution is disproportionately male. There are four types of visual-spatial ability that have been identified: visual perception, mental rotation, spatial visualization, and spatiotemporal ability. Sex differences favoring males are found on all of them except spatial visualization. The effect size for mental rotation is among the largest found in the literature and can be found developmentally by the mid to late elementary school years. SAT-V data show a steady decrease over the last two decades in the female scores relative to male scores, with males now outscoring females by an average of 13 points. Numerous reasons for this alarming decline in female SAT-V performance were suggested. An analysis of the underlying cognitive processes was proposed, with males performing especially well on tasks that involve maintaining and manipulating mental representations and females performing especially well on tasks that require rapid access to and retrieval of information. It is important to keep in mind that the list of cognitive differences is relatively small and that cognitive similarities between the sexes are greater than the differences.

4 Biological Hypotheses Part I: Genes and Hormones

Contents

4

After sexism is stripped away, there will still be something different—
something grounded in biology.
—Konner (1988, p. 35)

Perhaps this chapter and the next should come with a warning similar to the ones found on cigarette advertisements:

> **WARNING: Some of the research and theories described in this chapter may be disturbing to your basic belief systems.**

I have taught this material many times, and there have always been students who find the possibility that even a small portion of the sex differences in cognitive abilities may be attributable to biological factors profoundly disturbing. When reading this chapter and chapter 5 (devoted to sex-related brain differences), it is important to keep in mind that even if we were to conclude that biological variables are partial determinants of sex differences in cognitive abilities, the importance of psychosocial factors is not necessarily diminished. Biological and psychosocial variables interact in their influence on the development of individuals, and although biological and psychosocial hypotheses are presented in separate chapters, this organization is not meant to imply that they are diametrically opposed or that they are independent concepts. These two positions are brought together in the section on biopsychosocial hypotheses in the final chapter in this book.

THE NOTION OF BIOLOGICAL DETERMINATION

The concept of *biological determination* can take a strong or weak form. A proponent of the strong form was Sigmund Freud who is well known for his often quoted aphorism, "Biology is destiny." This quote represents the strong form of biological determination or determinism because it implies that, for each of us, our destiny is unavoidably preplanned by biological forces beyond our control. A proponent of the weaker form of biological determinism would maintain that although biology may underlie some tendencies or make certain experiences more probable, we are not inevitably the products of the biological systems that comprise our bodies. Biology imposes certain limitations on our abilities, but environment determines the extent to which we develop our abilities. An analogy from health science may help to explain this point. Some people may be born with a biological tendency to become fat; however with proper exercise and diet they can avoid or postpone this destiny. Similarly, a weak form of biological determinism allows for the possibility that females and males may, by self determination or some other means, overcome or avoid sex-related biologically based predilections or tendencies to develop certain cognitive abilities; the weak form of biological determinism considers the impact of environmental influences on male and female human existence.

Of course, there are numerous and obvious biological differences between women and men, but these differences are much less pronounced in humans than in any other vertebrates. If we were concerned with sex differences in reproduction instead of cognition, there would be little or no controversy. The different roles that men and women play in reproduction are incontrovertible. But, when the issue is cognition, the questions and answers become more difficult. Are the sex-related differences in cognitive ability inherent in the biology of femaleness and maleness? Or are the biological factors that make you male or female unrelated to the types of cognitive abilities that you develop?

Are Biological Theories Sexist?

> *Woman is a pair of ovaries with a human being attached, whereas man is*
> *a human being furnished with a pair of testes.*
> —Rudolph Virchow, M.D. (cited in Fausto-Sterling, 1985, p. 90)

There are numerous sex-related inequalities in contemporary society. As noted in the first chapter, women earn much less than men, spend more time on housework, and comprise the majority of persons living in poverty. Men, on the other hand, often find it difficult to obtain custody of their children following divorce and have been effectively closed out of female-dominated professions such as secretarial work and nursing. Suppose researchers conclude that there are biologically determined sex differences in cognition. Could this conclusion be used to justify the social inequality that exists between women and men?

The possibility that biological theories could be used to justify discrimination is chilling. One tacit assumption that is inherent in this line of reasoning is that, if the truth were known, females would be found to be "less"—less smart, less able, less strong, or less of whatever society values. There is no support for this fear. As is seen from the data reported here, the results of biological research do not favor either sex. Although differences are reported, they are exactly that. A point that is made in several places throughout this book is that differences are not deficiencies. If we find that society values the traits and skills that are associated with being male and devalues the traits and skills that are associated with being female (or vice-versa), then it is time to rethink societal values instead of denying the existence of biologically based male–female differences.

Benbow was recently criticized for publishing her findings about mathematically precocious youth. She responded by asking, "Do we really help females by ignoring these facts?" (Benbow, 1990, p. 988). I believe that this is an apt response to critics who claim that psychologists should not study cognitive sex differences. The study of cognitive sex differences is not predicated on the belief that one sex is superior to the other. It should be an open and honest attempt to understand the multiplicity of factors that create and/or mitigate differences. It is important for readers to "keep an open mind" when considering the information that is presented in the following chapters.

As you read about biological research into cognitive sex differences, keep in mind the distinction between research results and the interpretation of research results. As Reinisch, Rosenblum, and Sanders (1987) noted, correlations between biological and behavioral differences may be bidirectional, imperfect within and between people, and inconsistent across species. Even if we find biologically based differences, we are a long way from understanding how they are manifested in an environmental context that provides different rewards for its females and males.

Researchers have identified three biological systems that could be responsible for cognitive sex differences: (1) chromosomal or genetic determinants of sex; (2) differences in the sex hormones secreted from the endocrine glands; and (3) neuroanatomical differences in the structure, organization, and/or function of the brain. Theory and research on the biological determinants of sex-related cognitive differences have centered on these three biological systems. Like any division in biology, these are not separate systems; genes and hormones presumably operate on behavior via some neurological mechanism, and differences in sex hormones are dependent on genetically coded information.

One of the major difficulties in understanding the contribution of each of these biological systems is that in normal individuals they are confounded. Chromosomes determine the type of sex hormones that are secreted, and these hormones influence brain development. Sex hormones also direct the development of the internal reproductive organs and external genitals. Thus, for most people, all of the biological indications of sex are congruent and interdependent. Although these three systems exert influences on each other, one way to comprehend these intricately enmeshed biological systems is by examining each system separately and then putting them back together to understand how they work in concert.

Possible genetic and hormonal influences are presented in this chapter. Brain mechanisms and links among these three systems are presented in chapter 5. The question for research psychologists is whether any or all of these biological sex differences underlie cognitive sex differences.

GENETIC THEORIES

Adoption data show that resemblance among nonadoptive family members for IQ is due in nearly equal portions to heredity and environmental factors.
—Plomin (1990, p. 68)

Fetal development proceeds under the direction of the genetic information coded on the genes. Whether you were born male or female with black or white skin and blue or brown eyes was determined by the chromosomes and genes that are responsible for your very existence. Every trait that you have inherited from your ancestors was transmitted via your genes. Genetic information constitutes the *genotype* of an individual, whereas traits that are expressed are called the *phenotype*. Phenotype depends on the interaction of genes with environmental influences. The term *gene–environment transaction* is sometimes used to emphasize the fact that most behavioral traits that are expressed depend on the mutual effect of genetic and environmental influences.

Researchers use observable characteristics (phenotypes) to infer genetic information (genotypes). There are four research strategies commonly used to study the influence of genetic information on cognition (Eliot & Fralley, 1976):

1. Examine a large number of people to determine, for example, the proportion of women and men who exhibit good spatial or verbal abilities.

2. Look at the heritability pattern of abilities across generations to determine the "pedigree" of cognitive abilities. Researchers utilizing this approach might examine siblings or parents and children to ascertain whether good mathematical or verbal ability tends to run in families.

3. Utilize individuals with genetic abnormalities to infer the effect of genetic information in normal individuals. An example of this approach would be to discover if individuals who are genetically male, but appear female, show typical "male" patterns of cognitive abilities.

4. Examine monozygotic ("identical") and dizygotic ("fraternal") twins to determine the extent to which cognitive abilities are under genetic control. If monozygotic twins are more similar than dizygotic twins, then these results would provide some support for genetic influences on cognitive abilities. (This is especially true when researchers are able to compare

cognitive abilities for identical twins who were reared apart. In this case, the twins share a common heredity, but have experienced a different environment.)

All of these strategies have been used to understand the role of sex-related genetic factors in the development of cognitive abilities.

An example of arguing from twin data is seen in the study of reaction time measures of intelligence. One controversial measure of intelligence is "speed of processing." The underlying idea in measuring speed of processing is that differences in intelligence can best be understood by determining the time that it takes to complete simple cognitive tasks. Such measures are called "reaction times," and they are commonly used in cognitive research.

Sex differences are more likely to be found with timed than untimed tasks. For example, the large sex differences in mental rotation are often based on the time that it takes to "mentally rotate" a complex figure in order to determine if it is identical to another figure. According to this view, a fast speed of processing is indicative of a high level of spatial ability. Vernon (1987) presented evidence that reaction time measures and other measures of intelligence are "highly correlated" (p. 2). In his review of this area of research, Vernon concluded that sex differences in mental abilities—specifically in verbal, spatial, and quantitative—may be related to differences in the speed with which women and men perform specific cognitive operations. In support of his conclusion that speed of processing is an inherited trait, he cites studies that report that there is greater similarity among monozygotic (identical) twins than among dizygotic (fraternal) twins. Vernon made a case for using reaction time data as an index of the "hardware" or underlying neural structure of intelligence and suggested that sex differences in reaction times can be viewed as part of one's genetic inheritance.

Sex-Linked Versus Sex-Limited

Nature is a political strategy of those committed to the status quo of sex differences.
—Money (1987, p. 14)

One of the major differences between males and females is the pair of sex chromosomes that differ markedly from each other in size and shape. Females have two X chromosomes—one is contributed by the biological father and the other by the biological mother during fertilization. The male sex chromosome pair is designated XY. The X is contributed by the biological mother and the Y is contributed by the biological father. The Y chromosome is very small and contains little genetic information except for determining sex (Carter, 1972). In contrast, the X chromosome is relatively large and contains a great deal of genetic information. Characteristics (like whether an individual develops ovaries or testes and certain types of red-green color blindness) that are determined by genes on the sex chromosomes are called *sex-linked characteristics*. Such characteristics are inextricably tied to the fact that we are born either male or female because they are carried on the chromosomes that determine sex.

In addition to the pair of sex chromosomes, humans have 22 pairs of other chromosomes known as autosomes. Sometimes a characteristic that is coded on an autosome appears predominantly in one sex or the other. Such characteristics are called *sex-limited,* and appear predominantly in one sex because of a multiplicity of genetic influences. Pattern baldness, for example, occurs primarily in men and is inherited through genetic information on an autosomal pair of chromosomes. Such characteristics are less intimately tied to genetic determinants of sex than sex-linked characteristics.

Studies have shown that males are more biologically vulnerable from the moment of conception. Researchers estimated that at conception there are 140 males conceived (called "46, XY" to denote the fact that there are 46 chromosomes with the sex chromosome pair XY) to every 100 females conceived (46, XX). The ratio of male:female live births is 105 males born for every 100 females. By age 65, the male:female ratio is 70:100 (Money, 1986). These numbers reflect the fact that fewer male embryos ever make it to birth and, after birth, males die an average of approximately 6 to 7 years earlier than females (Coren & Halpern, 1991; Halpern & Coren, 1988, 1990).

Genetic research is progressing at a rapid rate as biomedical sleuths unravel the mystery of the DNA molecule. Recent research (Braun, reported in Angier, 1990) has located the gene that acts as a switch for maleness, "transforming a growing human fetus that otherwise would become a girl into a boy." The gene for maleness is located on the Y chromosome. It becomes operative during the seventh week of pregnancy "setting off a complex biological cascade that turns the fetus's immature sex organs into testes" (p. 3). If this gene is missing (as it is in normal females), the developing organism will be a female. This fact has lead some researchers to note that the basic human blueprint is female, although it is probably more accurate to think of female and male genitals as two variations of a common theme. During embryonic development, the internal and external structures go through an "indifferent" stage from which either male or female versions develop.

Heritability of Spatial Skills

More behavioral genetic data have been obtained for measures of intelligence than for any other trait (Plomin, 1990). The whole question of the extent to which intelligence is inherited has been hotly debated throughout the history of psychology and seems no closer to being resolved today than it was over a century ago.

Despite the lack of agreement on the question of how much intelligence is inherited, even staunch environmentalists will agree that it is, at least, partially inherited. In Plomin's (1989) review of the literature, he concluded that sibling correlations for the cognitive abilities that comprise intelligence are approximately .40.

There has been considerable interest in the hypothesis that spatial ability is inherited. Vandenberg (1969), for example, administered a test of spatial abilities to a sample of twins, reasoning that the greater the percentage of genes shared by two people, the greater the similarity you would expect in their ability scores if the ability is inherited. The test included measures of the ability to visualize and mentally rotate figures in space. High correlations between twin pairs led Vandenberg to conclude that these abilities are partially determined by heredity factors. However, simply knowing that some cognitive abilities may be inherited does not explain sex differences in these abilities.

Sex-Linked Recessive Gene Theory

Any genetic explanation of sex differences in visual-spatial ability would need to posit an inheritance mechanism that is differentiated by sex. A major genetic theory of cognitive sex differences is based on the assumption that high spatial ability is a sex-linked recessive trait that is carried on the X chromosome. (A recessive trait is one that will be expressed, that is, it will appear in a person's phenotype, only if the corresponding gene on the other member of the chromosome pair also carries the recessive trait.) If this theory were correct, then females would have a double dose of the genes that determine spatial ability because they have two X chromosomes; whereas, males have only one dose and that one always comes from the mother, who contributes the X chromosome in her son. For males, the other member of the sex chromosome pair is the very small Y chromosome which does not carry any genetic information about spatial ability. According to this theory, the high spatial ability gene is recessive; therefore, this trait will occur more frequently in males than in females because males have no other gene to mask the effects of the recessive gene. Given that females would have to have the genetic information on both X chromosomes and males only need to have it on one, males are therefore more likely to demonstrate good spatial ability. Table 4.1 depicts which individuals would be predicted to demonstrate good spatial ability as a function of their genotype if the sex-linked recessive theory were true.

The beauty of this theory is the explicit quantitative nature of the predictions derived from it. One of the predictions generated from the sex-linked recessive gene theory concerns the total proportion of men and women who would be expected to show good spatial ability. Bock and Kolakowski (1973) estimated that a recessive spatial ability gene should appear among American Caucasians

TABLE 4.1
Predictions Derived from the X-Linked Recesive Gene Theory of Spatial Ability

---

Good spatial ability would be found in:

1. Hemizygous recessive males
   (Gene for good spatial ability is carried on the X chromosome)   ♂ X^r Y

2. Homozygous recessive females
   (Gene for good spatial ability is carried on both X chromosomes)   ♀ X^r X^r

Good spatial ability would <u>not</u> be found in:

1. Hemizygous dominant males
   (Gene for poor spatial ability is carried on the X chromosome)   ♂ X^D Y

2. Heterozygous females
   (Gene for poor spatial ability is carried on one X chromosome,   ♀ X^D X^r
   gene for good spatial ability is carried on the other X chromosome)   or
   ♀ X^r X^D

3. Homozygous dominant females
   (gene for poor spatial ability is carried on both X chromosomes)   ♀ X^D X^D

Note. r = recessive, D = dominant.

with a frequency of approximately 50%. (Estimates for other racial groups were not given.) If this were true, then approximately 50% of all Caucasian men and approximately 25% of all Caucasian women would be expected to show this trait phenotypically. This prediction can be seen in the male genetic configurations shown in Table 4.1. There are two equally likely male genetic patterns, one of which would be associated with good spatial ability. The 25% prediction for females can also be seen in Table 4.1. There are four equally probable female configurations, only one of which would be associated with good spatial ability. The data, however, do not conform to these proportions. The prediction that half of all males and one-fourth of all females would show this trait phenotypically has not been supported (DeFries, Vandenberg, & McClearn, 1976).

Another prediction derived from the sex-linked theory of spatial ability is an explicit pattern of relationships among parents, children, and siblings (Boles, 1980). One of the hypothesized relationships is that sons' spatial abilities should resemble their mothers' more than their fathers'. The reasoning behind this hypothesis is that males have a single X chromosome that they inherit from their mothers. If a spatial ability gene is carried on this chromosome, then, on the average, a son should be more similar to his mother in spatial ability than he would be to his father. Daughters, on the other hand, should tend to be more similar to their fathers in terms of their spatial ability than they would be to their mothers. The reasoning behind this relationship is somewhat more complex.

Mother–daughter pairs have a total of four X chromosomes, two each from the mother and daughter. Two of these four are held in "common" because the daughter receives one of her X chromosomes from her mother. Daughter–father pairs have a total of three X chromosomes, two of which are jointly held because daughters receive one of their X chromosomes from their fathers. According to this logic, daughters share a larger proportion of their total daughter–parent X chromosome pool with their fathers than with their mothers. The prediction that sons' spatial abilities should resemble their mothers' more than their fathers' and that daughters should resemble their fathers' more than their mothers' is opposite from any predictions made from psychosocial theories which would posit some sort of same-sex modeling. Thus, if this pattern of relationships were empirically supported, this would constitute strong support for genetic determination.

Early studies with small samples provided weak support for this hypothesis. Stafford (1961, 1963) found the pattern of relationships among daughters and fathers, daughters and mothers, sons and mothers, and sons and fathers in the order predicted by this theory, but only for 1 of the 10 tests he used to measure spatial abilities, and even that one failed to obtain statistical significance. Later studies with larger samples failed to replicate this pattern (Bouchard & McGee, 1977; Loehlin, Sharan & Jacoby, 1978).

Additional fine-grained predictions are also derivable from this theory. For example, if a father does not have the gene responsible for good spatial ability, then none of his daughters will have this trait, but his sons could have it if they received the trait from their mother. If a father does have the gene for good spatial ability, then his sons and daughters could show this ability, depending on whether their mother is heterozygous (one X chromosome carries the gene and the other one doesn't) or homozygous (both X chromosomes carry the gene).

Despite early support for the sex-linked recessive hypothesis, it now seems clear that its validity is unfounded. Thomas (1983) has suggested that the basic assumptions of this model were wrong, and all of the studies that reported correlation orderings as evidence for this model were using incorrect assumptions about the mathematical properties of inheritance. Perhaps one of the biggest problems is with the notion that a complex multidimensional variable like visual-spatial ability would have a single genetic determinant. As described in chapter 3, spatial ability is comprised of at least four distinct components (mental rotation, spatial perception, visualization, and spatiotemporal). These components are not necessarily related. Genetic theories that fail to make distinctions among these components of spatial ability will never be able to adequately describe the phenomenon. All of the sex differentiated cognitive abilities are composed of multiple components, and it is unlikely that there is a single gene that controls the expression of any of these abilities. In addition, visual-spatial ability is a characteristic that we all exhibit to some degree, a fact that cannot be explained with a single gene.

Heritability of Verbal Skills

There is very little support for the notion that verbal skills are highly heritable. In Vandenberg's (1968) study of the verbal and spatial abilities of twins, he came to two conclusions: (1) both abilities have heritability components, and (2) verbal abilities are more influenced by environmental events than spatial abilities. Vandenberg's conclusions were based on the similarity between twins on verbal tests. Monozygotic or identical twins who share 100% of their genetic make-up were more similar than dizygotic or fraternal twins. Nontwin siblings showed the least similarity. A major problem in inferring the heritability of any cognitive ability from twin data results from the fact that twins are also more likely to be similar to each other than other pairs of nontwin siblings in terms of their social and learning histories. It is just as likely that the similarity in environmental factors could be responsible for the similarity in their scores as the hypothesis that the degree of genetic information that they shared is responsible.

An X-linked recessive trait theory for verbal ability, similar to that proposed for visual-spatial ability, was proposed by Lehrke (1974). Lehrke's hypothesis was based on the inheritance pattern or pedigree of certain mental deficiencies involving verbal abilities. Although it remains possible that some mental deficiencies are transmitted via X-linked recessive genes, there is no evidence for an X-linked gene for verbal ability among individuals within the normal range of intelligence.

Heritability of Mathematical Skills

Stafford (1972) offered a pattern of family intercorrelational data in support of the notion that mathematical skills are inherited via the now familiar X-linked recessive gene. Sherman (1978) provided a cogent criticism of these data, which not only failed to fit the proposed model, but were substantially divergent from those predicted by the model. There is no support for a sex-differentiated mode for the inheritance of mathematical skills.

Arguing from Abnormalities

In normal individuals, genetic information and concentrations of sex hormones are confounded. Individuals whose sex chromosomes are XX also appear female, are raised as females, and secrete sex hormones associated with being female. The reverse is, of course, true for males with XY sex chromosome pairs. The problem is isolating the effect of any one of these variables on the cognitive abilities that are differentiated by sex. In order to decide if the finding that men and women tend to excel in different types of intellectual tasks is due to genetic programming, the influence of genetic information needs to be disentangled from that of hormones and other life experiences that vary with sex. One way of examining genetic effects is to study people with genetic abnormalities such that the sex hormones and/or external genitals are not consistent with genetic sex.

There have been several studies of people with genetic abnormalities on their sex chromosomes. Rovet and Netley (1979) for example, studied five females with a genetic anomaly known as Turner's Syndrome. Instead of the usual pair of X chromosomes, females with Turner's Syndrome have a single X chromosome. This syndrome is designated as 45XO to indicate the fact that they have 45 chromosomes instead of the usual 46 and only one X chromosome. The second X chromosome is missing. Individuals with Turner's Syndrome are clearly female in appearance. Perhaps their major distinguishing feature is that they tend to be short and will usually require treatment with female hormones in order to exhibit the female secondary sex characteristics at puberty. According to the X-linked recessive gene theory, Turner's Women, as they are sometimes called, should display the male pattern of cognitive abilities, that is, on the average, they should score higher on visual-spatial performance tests than verbal ones. The reasoning behind this prediction is straightforward. Like men, they have a single X chromosome, and thus should be more likely to show a recessive X-linked characteristic because there is no other gene to carry the dominant trait. Rovet and Netley found results opposite to those predicted from this theory. All five of the females they tested had higher verbal scores than visual-spatial performance scores.

In the same study, Rovet and Netley (1979) also tested three individuals who were phenotypically male (appeared to be male), with a 46XX genotype (female gene pattern). If the sex-linked recessive gene pattern were correct, then these males should show a "female pattern of cognitive abilities," with higher verbal skills than visual-spatial skills. The reasoning behind this prediction is that if the sex chromosomes are important determinants of cognitive ability, then any group of individuals with female sex chromosomes should, on the average, tend to show the pattern of abilities associated with being female. Again this theory was not confirmed. Contrary to predictions, all three of the phenotypical males scored higher on the visual-spatial performance tests than on the verbal tests. Although this study used only a small number of subjects, these results are compelling and have been confirmed by other researchers (Money & Ehrhardt, 1972). It seems clear from these studies that cognitive abilities conform to phenotypic rather than genotypic sex. Currently, there is little support for the notion that sex differences in cognitive abilities are due to inherent differences in male and female genetic make-up per se.

The reason that I added "per se" to the last sentence is that genes underlie the development of every living organism. Later in this chapter, I return to the finding that Turner's Women are similar to control females in their verbal abilities, but seriously deficient in spatial ability and show how this lopsided pattern of cognitive development has provided support for the hypothesis that prenatal hormones (which are under the direction of genes) affect brain development in sexually differentiated ways.

SEX HORMONES

All of the sex hormones are human hormones.
—Money (1986)

Mention sex differences with respect to almost any ability and someone is sure to say, "It's all in the hormones." Clearly, one of the major biological differences between females and males is the relative concentration of the "female" sex hormones, estrogen and progesterone, and "male" sex hormones or androgens, most notably testosterone. Sex hormones are powerful chemical messengers secreted by the ovaries in women, testes in men, and adrenal glands in both sexes. Because they circulate freely throughout the blood stream, sex hormones are able to affect distant target organs, including the brain and sensory organs.

Despite common misconceptions, it is not true that women have only female hormones and men have only male hormones. Both sexes have measurable quantities of estrogen, progesterone, and testosterone. The relative concentrations of each of these hormones vary by sex and throughout the life cycle. Hormonal actions on the human brain are exceedingly complex. Not only do all normal humans have measurable amounts of all of the hormones that we tend to think of as "female" or "male" hormones, but the body converts these hormones from one chemical configuration to another. According to Money (1986), before the cells of the brain can use testosterone, the body converts it into estradiol, a form of estrogen, which is chiefly a hormonal secretion of the ovaries. Thus, it is very difficult to discern the effects of what we typically think of as female or male hormones because these two types of hormones can be chemically transmuted from one to the other.

Because of dramatic age-dependent fluctuations in hormone levels, it seems likely that the influence of these hormones would also vary with age. The age-dependent nature of hormone effects will be examined in separate sections for each developmental stage beginning with prenatal influences and ending with adulthood and old age.

Prenatal Hormones

Research on the importance of experience during prenatal life has documented the ability of fetuses to respond to changes in the intrauterine environment, to learn by association of stimuli, and to retain prenatal experiences into postnatal life.
—Smotherman and Robinson (1990, p. 97)

Prenatal hormones are critically important determinants of whether a developing fetus will grow into a male or female infant. The genetic configuration of the sex chromosomes (XX for female, XY for male) determines whether the undifferentiated developing gonads (sex glands) will become ovaries or testes. If they are developing according to a male program, they will begin to differentiate approximately seven weeks after conception. The newly formed testes will secrete male hormones (primarily testosterone), which, in turn, directs the development of the internal male reproductive organs and external genitals. If, on the other hand, the genetic program is XX, the gonads will develop into ovaries and, in the absence of male hormones, internal female reproductive organs and external female genitals will develop. It is important to note that it is the absence of male hormones, not the presence of female hormones, that directs the growth of female organs because in the absence of hormones, or usable hormones, the sexual differentiation of the fetus will be female. As Newcombe and Baenninger (1989) noted, without testosterone during gestation, a male is not a male. A schematic diagram of prenatal development is presented in Fig. 4.1. It charts the development of females and males from conception until birth. If you read the first edition of this book you will note that this figure differs from a similar one that appeared in the first edition. Data presented in the following chapter now shows that "female" prenatal hormones play a role in the differentiation of the brain, but not in the differentiation of the genitals. It was formerly believed that these hormones were not important during prenatal development.

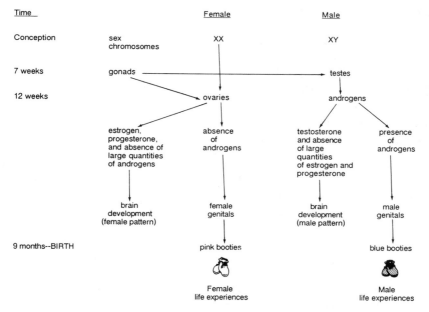

FIG. 4.1. Schematic diagram of sex differentiation during prenatal development.

There is good evidence that the presence or absence of particular sex hormones during critical stages of prenatal development also plays a role in the sexual differentiation of the developing brain. Thus, the hormones that are secreted by the newly formed testes in males or the absence of these hormones in females, affect the appearance of the genitals *and* the development of neural pathways in the newly formed brain. Recent research suggests that prenatal hormones secreted from the female's ovaries also play a role in brain development, although our knowledge of the effect of prenatal ovarian hormones on the developing neural system is extremely limited at this time (e.g., Berrebi et al., 1988; Diamond, Johnson & Ehlert, 1979).

Approximately 7 weeks after conception, which is when the testes begin secreting male hormones, the first fully developed neurons (basic brain cells) begin to form a rudimentary brain. At 28 weeks after conception, "interneurons" form, which are essential to the higher level cognitive activities that we consider distinctly human. Brain development continues after birth, and perhaps for the entire life span (Patlak, 1990).

Much of the experimental research in this area has been performed on nonhuman mammals, especially rats. Although there are numerous biological similarities between nonhuman mammals and humans, one of the major differences is the extent to which hormones direct and control behavior. Hormones are less important in determining behavior for humans than for nonhuman mammals. Thus, although results obtained with rats or other mammals may be suggestive of possible relationships for humans, they are not directly applicable. Extrapolation from animal data to humans can lead to erroneous conclusions and, for this reason, must be made very carefully.

For most people, the configuration of their sex chromosomes, prenatal and postnatal sex hormones, reproductive organs, genitals, sex role pressures, and sex of identification are the same. In order to understand the role that hormones play in shaping the other biological and psychological indices of sex, it is necessary to isolate experimentally and manipulate sex hormones independent of the other covariates of sex. Two general approaches are used to understand the effect of sex hormones. The quantity and type of sex hormone are manipulated in nonhuman mammals under careful laboratory conditions, and naturally occurring or drug induced abnormalities in humans are studied. There are strengths and weaknesses associated with each of these approaches.

Laboratory Investigations With Nonhuman Mammals.   The majority of the work in this area has been conducted with rats, although other mammals and primates have been used. Prenatal hormones are manipulated by either castrating the developing male, thereby depriving him of the testosterone secreted by the testes, removing the ovaries of a developing female rat, thereby depriving her of the hormones secreted by her ovaries, administering androgens ("male hormones") to developing females and/or administering ovarian hormones to developing males, or administering any hormone of interest to the pregnant mother who will pass the hormone onto the developing fetus. Timing of these manipulations is important because there appears to be a critical developmental period for brain differentiation. Research with rodents using these techniques has mapped hormone sensitive cells in the brain that respond differentially to prenatal sex hormones (McEwen, 1981). In their review of the literature, MacLusky and Naftolin (1981) cited a number of sex differences in brain morphology that depend on prenatal hormone exposure, including volume differences in certain cell groups and differences in synaptic and dendrite organization. Diamond (cited in Kimura, 1985) found that testosterone can have asymmetrical effects on the developing brains of prenatal female and male rats. When additional testosterone was supplied, male rats showed increases in the thickness of their right hemisphere; whereas, female rats showed increases in the thickness of their left hemispheres. I return to the possibility that female and male humans differ in the way their hemispheres are specialized for different tasks in the next chapter, in which I discuss sex differences in brain structure and function. Although these results are of scientific interest and suggest that neurons in the brain respond to sex hormones, it is not possible to relate this finding directly to human brains or any aspect of human functioning.

One well-established effect of prenatal hormones is in the function and development of a tiny brain structure known as the hypothalamus. The hypothalamus influences reproductive behavior and controls the release of reproductive hormones from the pituitary gland. There is no reason to believe that the hypothalamus and pituitary are involved in the higher level cognitive abilities that vary by sex; however, other brain structure may also be affected by prenatal hormones. Clear cut findings in lower mammals have led researchers to conclude that prenatal hormones influence sexual behavior, aggression, activity in open fields, and maze learning (a spatial activity). In general, if "male hormones" are administered, typical male behavior results, and if "male hormones" are removed, typical female behavior results. (As explained earlier, we know much less about the role of prenatal ovarian hormones than we know about the role of prenatal hormones secreted by the testes.) Male rodent behaviors include male sexual posturing (mounting), increased open field activity, increased aggression, and faster maze learning. Female rodent behaviors include female sexual posturing (lordosis), decreased open field activity, decreased aggression, and slower maze learning.

One area of the brain that figures prominently in theories about female–male differences in the brain is the corpus callosum. The corpus callosum is a thick band of neural fibers that connects the two halves of the brain. Again, we know more about the corpus callosum of the rat brain than the human brain because scientists are able to conduct research with rats that would be unethical with humans. The rat's corpus callosum is "sexually dimorphic." This means that there are two different forms that vary as a function of sex. For rats, the male's corpus callosum is larger than the female's even after adjusting for brain size and body weight. In recent research, Denenberg and his colleagues (Berrebi et al., 1988; Denenberg, Berrebi, & Fitch, 1988) have administered testosterone to newborn female rats and have castrated newborn male rats. (Yes, I know what you're thinking. The quest for knowledge can lead to bizarre experiments.) The administration of testosterone masculinized the corpus callosum of the female rats, but castration had only a minor effect on the size of the corpus callosum of the male rats. They also found that prenatal "female" hormones affected the size of the corpus callosum, debunking the long held myth that prenatal ovarian hormones do not influence brain development. This set of experiments provides strong evidence that sex differences in the corpus callosum are created by prenatal and perinatal (around the time of birth) sex hormones.

The finding that sex differences in rodent and primate brains and sexual and aggressive behaviors are mediated by prenatal and postnatal hormones is interesting in its own right, but there is ample reason to believe that for humans, sexual and aggressive behavior is shaped, to a greater extent, by social learning and other life experiences. (Evidence in support of this claim is presented in chapters 6 and 7). Thus, human applications of these results are highly speculative and await replication in humans. Of course, such manipulations are unethical for human subjects. The closest we can come to examining hormone effects in humans is to examine "human accidents" or hormone abnormalities.

Prenatal Sex Hormone Abnormalities

Fetal Androgenization. What are the effects of high levels of male hormones on a developing fetus? This question has been answered with two different groups of subjects who were exposed to abnormally high levels of androgens during fetal development.

Since the early 1950s, millions of pregnant women have been treated with synthetic sex hormones to prevent miscarriage. Although a variety of hormones has been used in varying doses depending on the individual situation and current medical practice, all have some androgenic or masculinizing effect. Research with nonhuman mammals has shown that aggressive behavior is hormonally mediated. Reinisch (1981) reasoned that if prenatal hormones have similar effects in humans, then individuals who had been exposed to high levels of masculine hormones before birth should also demonstrate an increased potential for aggressive behavior. She studied 17 female and 8 male subjects who had been exposed to synthetic hormones before birth. The measurement of aggression in humans poses a research problem because most people demonstrate aggressive impulses only under limited and threatening circumstances. For this reason, Reinisch utilized a paper-and-pencil measure of aggression (fantasies about aggression). She used same-sex unexposed siblings as the control group in the belief that siblings offer a control for environmental and genetic influences. Both her subjects and their siblings had a mean age of 11 years at the time of testing.

As expected from all of the sex differences literature, Reinisch found that males had higher aggression scores than females. Reinisch also found that her subjects who had been exposed to synthetic hormones before birth reported higher physical aggression than their unexposed same-sex siblings. She interpreted these results as providing strong support for prenatal hormone mediation of human aggressive behavior. The implication of this research is that because, under normal conditions, males are exposed to more androgens before birth than females, sex differences in aggression are due to sex differences in prenatal hormonal milieu. Other researchers have provided corroborative evidence that prenatal hormones contribute to aggression and/or general energy level (Ehrhardt & Meyer-Bahlburg, 1979). Although it is reasonable to conclude that, at least under abnormally high concentrations, prenatal hormones affect human aggressive potential, what about their role in sex differentiated human cognitive abilities?

In a direct test of the role of prenatal sex hormones on cognitive abilities, Dalton (1976) studied English children whose mothers had been given extremely high doses of sex hormones during pregnancy. Dalton reported that these children had significantly better "number ability," a result that would be predicted if these hormones also influenced quantitative ability. However, Dalton's studies have been criticized on a number of statistical and methodological grounds, including her failure to utilize a control group when evaluating number ability, thus considerably weakening the impact of these findings. Meyer-Bahlburg and Ehrhardt (1977) attempted to replicate these results using better controls and more rigorous research methods. They did not find any relationship between prenatal hormone exposure and number ability, although the synthetic hormones taken by Meyer-Bahlburg and Ehrhardt's subjects' mothers were less potent than the one investigated by Dalton.

Congenital Adrenal Hyperplasia.   A second condition that exposes developing fetuses to extremely high levels of androgens is Congenital Adrenal Hyperplasia (CAH, also known as Androgenital Syndrome or AGS). CAH is a genetic recessive disorder in which the adrenal glands produce abnormally high amounts of androgens beginning in the third month of fetal life (Nyborg, 1983). When the genetic pattern for the developing organism is female (XX), she is exposed to abnormally high levels of prenatal androgen; when the genetic pattern is male (XY), he is exposed to above normal levels of prenatal androgen (Newcombe & Baenninger, 1989).

Do high levels of androgens during fetal life influence the cognitive abilities of the developing organisms? In an attempt to answer this question, researchers examined 17 females and 8 males with CAH (Resnick, Berenbaum, Gottesman, & Bouchard, 1986). The CAH girls scored significantly higher than their unaffected relatives on three different tests of spatial ability (out of five), thus providing evidence that, for females, prenatal androgen is associated with higher spatial ability. The researchers also found that the CAH girls were more likely to engage in "aggressive play," which provides more evidence for a causal link between prenatal hormones and behavior in later life (at least for females exposed to very high levels of prenatal androgen). It is interesting to note that the CAH boys did not differ from their unaffected relatives on any of the cognitive and behavioral measures.

Androgen Insensitivity and Turner's Syndrome.   All of the studies discussed in the previous section examined the effect of high levels of prenatal masculinizing hormones. Another experimental approach is to examine the effect of extremely low levels of masculinizing hormones. Will such individuals develop cognitive abilities and personality traits usually associated with being female?

Androgen insensitivity is the term used to describe genetic males whose bodies are unable to respond to male hormones. (This disorder is also known as testicular feminization.) During fetal development their testes produce the appropriate male hormones, but for reasons not fully understood, their tissues are insensitive to these hormones and development proceeds as though no male hormones were present (Christiansen & Knussmann, 1987). These genetic males develop female genitals and are usually raised as girls. Ehrhardt and Meyer-Bahlburg (1979) reported "a significant, but modest, tendency toward verbal rather than space-form abilities" among genetic males with androgen insensitivity (p. 422). Even if these subjects were much better at verbal tasks than spatial ones, we would not know if this pattern of results was due to prenatal hormone effects, postnatal hormone effects, or the fact that the subjects were identified and raised as girls. Thus, these results cannot be used to understand hormone effects on cognition.

Turner's Women.   Another possible population for investigating prenatal hormone effects is women with Turner's syndrome. Recall that these women have a genetic abnormality such that their second sex chromosome is missing. They are genetically denoted as 45XO to signify that they have 45 chromosomes and only a single X sex chromosome. They usually have underdeveloped ovaries and very low levels of both female and male hormones. Hines (1982) found that although Turner's women have normal range IQs and verbal abilities, they tend to have specific deficits in visuospatial functioning. Could these specific deficiencies be due to extremely low levels of male hormones? McCauley, Kay, Ito, and Treder (1987) think so. These researchers were interested in understanding why Turner's women also tend to have social problems. They hypothesized that specific cognitive deficits were, in part, responsible for the social problems. To test this possibility, they had Turner's syndrome girls, aged 9 to 17 years old, judge the emotions being expressed in pictures of several faces. They found that the Turner's syndrome girls were less accurate at judging emotions than matched control subjects. (The control subjects were similar to the Turner's syndrome girls with respect to height, socioeconomic status, age, and verbal intelligence scores.) The researchers believe that Turner's syndrome females have social difficulties because they are poor at interpreting facial expressions. Extracting information from a face is, in part, a spatial task. The researchers found that these same subjects were also poorer than the controls on tests of arithmetic, digit span (a short-term memory task), picture completion, and object assembly. It seems likely that there is a mutual relationship between cognitive and social skills. The relatedness between cognition and socialization makes it difficult to ever determine whether the poor spatial skills caused poor social skills or vice versa.

Turner's women also have certain physical characteristics that could be mediating these results. They tend to be short with a relatively unfeminine body type (small breasts, thick necks). If they respond to these external manifestations of their genotype, it is possible that they exaggerate female tendencies, including poorer visual-spatial abilities. Thus, what appears to be a physiological response in Turner's women to low levels of hormones, may in part be due to a social response to their appearance.

Taken together, research on the influence of prenatal sex hormones on cognitive abilities suggests that the prenatal environment is important in determining the development of one's cognitive potential, although the data do not yet permit any definitive conclusions. In general, high levels of androgens during prenatal development are associated with higher than average levels of spatial ability for girls, but not for boys, and low levels of androgens (or an inability to respond to androgen) are associated with poorer than average spatial ability. But remember, even in those instances in which positive effects have been reported, it is very difficult to tease out the contributions of genetic influences, postnatal hormones, and life experiences. Furthermore, abnormal hormone levels could produce results that are not associated with normal levels of the same hormones.

Prenatal Hormone Effects on Normal Development

> *Hormones do not exert their actions simultaneously or directly, but rather they exert their influence in concert with many other biological events in a variety of different systems. There appears to be a running conversation in the CNS among hormones, neurotransmitters, neuromodulators, and probably other, as yet unknown, elements of CNS function.*
> —Brush and Levine (1989, p. xiii)

You may be wondering whether concentrations of prenatal hormones that are within "normal levels" affect cognitive development. An influential theory proposed by Geschwind and his colleagues is based on the belief that prenatal hormones have a pervasive effect on cognition (e.g., Geschwind, 1983, 1984;

Geschwind & Galaburda, 1987). Geschwind and Galaburda's (1987) theory is based on the assumption that the prenatal sex hormones that both direct and reflect the sexual differentiation of the fetus also exert powerful influences on the central nervous system of developing organisms. In humans, the right hemisphere (half) of the brain normally develops at a faster rate than the left. Because of this differential rate of development, the left hemisphere is at risk for a longer period of time than the right, and therefore is more likely to be affected by an adverse intrauterine environment. Proponents of this theory assert that high levels of testosterone slow the growth of neurons in the left hemisphere. The result is right hemisphere dominance, which means that the right hemisphere has greater control than the left hemisphere.

One index of which hemisphere is dominant is handedness, that is whether an individual is right or left handed. Because the right hemisphere coordinates movement for the left half of the body and the left hemisphere coordinates movement for the right half of the body, a right-hander is (usually) left-hemisphere dominant and a left-hander is (often) right-hemisphere dominant. (People with mixed hand use, performing some tasks with the right and others with the left, are usually considered as left-handers.) If high levels of prenatal androgen slow neuronal growth in the left hemisphere, as proposed, the result would be right hemisphere dominance which is manifested in left-handedness. (For an extensive review of the literature on left-handedness, see Coren, 1990.)

There are two sources of prenatal testosterone; maternally produced testosterone which comes from the maternal ovaries, adrenals, and other structures such as fat and, for male fetuses, testosterone produced by their own developing testes. Thus, normal males are exposed to higher levels of prenatal testosterone than normal females. As would be predicted by this theory, numerous studies have found a higher proportion of left-handedness in males than in females (Bryden, 1977; Hardyck, Goldman, & Petrinovich, 1975; Porac & Coren, 1981). Although other animals do not show a population preference for one side (unlike humans, approximately 50% use their right paw and 50% use their left paw), there is ample evidence that intrauterine sex hormones affect brain structures and functions in other mammalian species as well as in humans. In Gorski's (1985) review of the experimental literature, he concluded that "The existence of functional and structural sex differences in the rat brain is firmly established, as is the dependence of these sex differences on the hormonal environment during development" (p. 590).

An important corollary of sex hormone hypothesis is that other susceptible organs in the developing fetus are also affected by high testosterone levels. One such organ is the thymus gland which is an essential component of the developing immune system. The simultaneous effect of testosterone on the development of the left hemisphere and the thymus and other organs results in the prediction that there would be a greater incidence of immune disorders among left handed individuals. The first evidence for this relationship came from Geschwind and

Behan (1982, 1984). They showed that autoimmune diseases (especially those involving the intestinal tract and the thyroid gland) and atopic diseases (allergies, asthma, eczema and hay fever) are 2.5 times as frequent in strong left-handers as in strong right-handers. These results have been essentially confirmed in several subsequent studies (e.g., Pennington, Smith, Kimberling, Green, & Haith, 1987; Smith, 1987).

If, as this theory predicts, left-handedness is sometimes the result of exposure to higher than average amounts of prenatal testosterone, then we would expect a positive association among being male, being left-handed, immune disorders, and patterns of cognitive abilities that are known to be lateralized (or specialized) in the right or left hemisphere. There are at least two possibilities:

1. overall poorer performance by males on cognitive tasks that are usually associated with the left hemisphere, and/or
2. exceptionally high performance on cognitive tasks that are believed to be primarily under right hemisphere control.

As you know from the last chapter, males tend to excel at some spatial tasks and some mathematical reasoning tasks, most notably the mathematics section of the SATs. These are both associated with right hemisphere functioning. Males also have a majority of the language production and reading problems. Thus, confirming, in a general way, some of the theoretical predictions. Geschwind and Galaburda's theory is summarized in Table 4.2.

More direct evidence for the effect of prenatal sex hormones on normal cognitive development was found by Jacklin (1989). Jacklin obtained blood samples taken from the umbilical cords of newborn babies. The concentration of androgens found in these samples is a direct measure of the level of androgens that were present in the prenatal environment. Jacklin correlated prenatal an-

TABLE 4.2
Summary of Geschwind and Galaburda's Theory

RELATIONSHIP AMONG:	sex, handedness, immune disorders, and cognitive abilities
THEORY:	High levels of prenatal testosterone slow neuronal growth in the left hemisphere and diminish the size of the developing thymus gland
PREDICTIONS:	Positive Associations Among
	Being Male Being left-handed Immune disorders (e. g., allergies) Anomalous right hemisphere cognitive abilities (e. g., mathematical giftedness, some types of retardation)

drogen levels with spatial ability displayed by normal girls 6 years after birth (Jacklin, Wilcox, & Maccoby, 1988). In general, girls with higher levels of testosterone in their blood at birth had lower scores on tests of spatial ability at age 6. Three facts are clear from these findings: (a) prenatal sex hormones affect cognitive development later in life; (b) the effects are not simple. At least for this sample of normal girls, higher amounts of androgens were associated with poorer spatial ability; (c) much more research is needed before we can understand how, when, and why prenatal hormones exert their influence.

Childhood and Puberty

Throughout infancy and childhood, both girls and boys have very low levels of all sex hormones. In fact, in those instances where, for some medical reason, sex reassignment surgery is needed (e.g., ambiguous or deformed genitals), there is usually no need to begin hormone therapy until adolescence. The body shapes of young boys and girls are so similar that it is difficult to tell girls and boys apart unless they wear sex-typed clothing or hair styles. Sex hormones, however, become extremely important at puberty because they are necessary for the development of secondary sex characteristics in both sexes and the timing of menarche (first menstruation) in girls. Several researchers have investigated the possibility that hormone events at puberty are also implicated in the development of cognitive sex differences.

Maturation Rate Hypotheses

Two different theories of cognitive sex differences are based on the well established fact that girls physically mature at a faster rate than boys. At birth, girls are more mature physiologically and they continue to mature more quickly than boys through puberty (Smolak, 1986). One of these theories is concerned with general rate of maturation; the other is specific to maturation processes at puberty. Each of these theories is reviewed here.

Do Early Maturers Have an Intelligence Advantage?   In the 1960s, Tanner (1962) suggested the possibility that growth spurts in physical height are associated with spurts in mental ability. If this were true, then there would be an intelligence advantage for children who mature at a young age because they would have enhanced intellectual capabilities at a younger age than their peers. Newcombe and Dubas (1987) conducted a meta-analytic review of the literature that pertained to this question. They found a small but reliable advantage in IQ for early maturers before, during, and after puberty. The extended line of reasoning is that because girls mature earlier than boys, girls have a "maturation advantage" that could explain the finding that girls outperform boys in early language-related skills. The major problem with this hypothesis is that the underlying cognitive mechanisms that vary as a function of maturation are unspecified,

Calvin and Hobbes

by Bill Watterson

making this a weak theory. It also requires two assumptions: (a) verbal abilities rely on different biological mechanisms than spatial abilities, and; (b) that it is verbal abilities that primarily benefit from early maturation.

Age at Puberty. A second hypothesis that links sex-related cognitive patterns to rate of maturation posits that sex-differentiated cognitive patterns are a by-product of sex differences in maturation rate at puberty. Waber (1976, 1977), a proponent of this theory, found that later maturing adolescents, regardless of sex, exhibited better spatial skills than earlier maturing adolescents of the same age. (Waber measured maturation by the development of secondary sex characteristics during a well child physical examination conducted in a nurse's office. There are numerous problems with such a subjective measure.) Thus, in general, late maturers have higher spatial skills than verbal skills and early maturers have higher verbal skills than spatial skills. The fact that girls generally attain physical maturation earlier than boys could explain cognitive sex differences. Thus, according to this view, the same hormonal events that are responsible for the timing of puberty are also responsible for sex differentiated patterns of cognitive differences. The idea that cognition could be predicted by the age at which an individual experiences puberty was appealing for several reasons. Most importantly, Waber linked this theory to developmental differences in brain organization (a topic discussed in the next chapter), which gave this theory a solid grounding in biology. In support of this theory, Herbst and Petersen (1980) also found that late maturing adolescents were better than their early maturing peers on the Embedded Figures Test.

Sanders and Soares (1986) investigated the age at puberty hypothesis with a sample of college students. The students responded to a series of questions about the timing of puberty events. The students used a 5-point scale in which they indicated, relative to others of the same sex, when they experienced several milestones of puberty such as menstruation (for females), nocturnal emission (for males), underarm hair growth, and so forth. They found that college students' scores on a mental rotation test were significantly related to their reports of when they reached puberty. As predicted by Waber's "Age at Puberty" hypothesis, late maturers of both sexes had higher scores on a mental rotation test than early maturers.

Despite its appeal and early support, more recent research has shown that age at puberty has limited validity in our quest to explicate the biological bases of cognitive sex differences. Two different literature reviews (Newcombe & Dubas, 1987; Signorella & Jamison, 1986) concluded that the association between spatial ability and age at puberty is small, and another two research reports (Dubas, Crockett, & Petersen, in press; Geary, 1988) concluded that there is *no* association between sex differences in spatial ability and timing of puberty. As is discussed in chapter 6, there are good reasons to believe that psychosocial events that occur at puberty (such as choice of preteen activities) play a more important role in the development of spatial skills. Furthermore, it is difficult to tease apart hormonal and genetic influences. The timing of puberty is under genetic control. It begins as a brain event with the release of a hormone (gonadotrophin-releasing hormone) from the hypothalamus. Thus, genes, hormones, and brain activity work in concert to make each of us the unique beings that we are.

In a meta-analytic review of the development of spatial abilities, Linn and Petersen (1986) found that sex differences for mental rotation can be found in middle childhood, probably as early as it can be measured. Similarly, sex differences in spatial perception do not change in magnitude at puberty. Thus, it seems that the normal maturational processes that occur at puberty are not directly tied to the development of spatial abilities.

Two other theories have been proposed to explain the relationship between sex hormones and cognitive abilities. Like Waber's theory, these other two also point to puberty as a critically important time in one's life for the development of these abilities.

Hier and Crowley (1982) have proposed that the amount of androgens available at puberty can be a determinant of visual spatial ability. They studied 19 men with androgen deficiencies at puberty. Compared to normal male adolescents, the androgen deficient males showed impaired spatial abilities. There were no differences between the groups with regard to verbal ability. Furthermore, they found a direct relationship between the severity of the androgen deficiency and the severity of the spatial impairment. That is, the men with the lowest amounts of androgen were also the poorest at spatial tasks and those whose androgen levels were closer to normal showed the least impairment. Hier and Crowley believe that puberty is a critical period for the development of spatial skills, and once spatial skills are established via sufficient levels of androgens at puberty, these skills are viable for a lifetime, even if androgen levels fall later in life. Conversely, if spatial abilities fail to develop in puberty because of low levels of androgens, this disability cannot be corrected later in life. They support their argument by noting that both Turner's women and genetic males with androgen insensitivity have poor spatial ability, and both groups have abnormally low levels of androgen (or, in the case of androgen insensitivity, usable androgen) at puberty.

Hier and Crowley admitted that they do not understand the mechanism by which male hormones mediate the development of spatial ability. They hypothesize that testosterone, the major male hormone, influences the central nervous system. Their own conclusion was, "Our results suggest that androgenization (presumably mediated by testosterone or one of its metabolites) is essential to the full development of spatial ability" (p. 1204).

It is important to keep in mind the fact that Hier and Crowley used a small sample of abnormal males to arrive at their conclusion. Even if it were true that a minimal level of male hormones is needed for the development of spatial ability, we have no idea what that minimal level is. Females have measurable quantities of male hormones in their bloodstreams, most of it produced by their adrenal glands, with a smaller quantity produced by their ovaries (Bleier, 1984). Although males have more of these hormones, it has not been demonstrated that unusually high levels of androgens are correlated with exceptionally good spatial ability. (As is seen later, the reverse may be true; that is, good spatial abilities in males may be related to relatively low levels of androgens.) Logical follow-ups to this study would examine: (a) males administered androgens during puberty, (b) the spatial abilities of females with malfunctioning adrenal glands, and (c) both males and females with high levels of male and female hormones during puberty.

A third theory about the relationship between the sex hormones available at puberty and the development of spatial skills is based on the idea that it is not the absolute quantity of androgens that is important; rather, it is the relative amounts of female and male hormones that determine spatial ability. In a test of this hypothesis, Petersen (1976) inferred the quantity of sex hormones available from the development of secondary sex characteristics in a sample of normal females and males at 13, 16, and 18 years. She found that for males, high levels of male hormones were associated with low spatial ability, while the reverse was true for females. For females, high levels of male hormones were associated with high spatial ability. In other words, superior spatial ability was associated with more male hormones for females and less male hormones for males. Taken together, these sex differentiated results point to an optimal balance of female and male hormones. Support for this position was provided by Maccoby (1966) who reported that boys with high spatial ability test scores were rated as less masculine by their peers than boys with low spatial ability test scores. Using the theoretical framework provided by Petersen's theory, Maccoby's results can be understood by reasoning that the boys who appeared less masculine probably had lower levels of androgens, a condition that Petersen believes is correlated with high spatial ability in males.

A major criticism of Petersen's study concerned the method she used to infer sex hormone levels (McGee, 1979). She rated photos of her subjects on the extent to which they had developed secondary sex characteristics. There is considerable room for inaccuracies with this measurement technique. Petersen's results need to be replicated with the more precise measurement of hormone levels that is possible with hormone assays (blood samples) collected from large samples of adolescents.

Another hypothesis that also posits an optimal amount of hormones for the development of spatial ability was proposed by Nyborg (1984, 1988, 1990). Nyborg's model is called the "General Trait Covariance—Androgen/Estrogen Balance Model." (Quite a mouthful! I don't know why they can't give these models simple names like "Fred.") Nyborg's model is based on two important assumptions. The first is that spatial ability is inversely related to certain verbal abilities. To support this assumption, Nyborg cites a study by Lynn (1987) which showed a negative correlation between spatial ability and verbal ability (after controlling for general level of intelligence). The second assumption is that there is a range of hormone levels that yields optimal expression of spatial ability. Unlike some of the other hormone-based theories, Nyborg targets estradiol as the critical hormone. Recall that androgens are chemically converted (the correct term for this is "aromitized") to other hormones for use by the brain. One of these other forms is estradiol, a hormone that is secreted by the ovaries. According to Nyborg, it is estradiol, a hormone that is usually thought of as a "female" hormone, that is consequential in the expression of spatial abilities. (I know this is confusing because we can't separate hormones into "female" and "male" categories.) Nyborg's model is depicted in Fig. 4.2.

Look carefully at Fig. 4.2. As you can see, the central portion of the inverted U-shaped curve represents the optimal concentration of estradiol for spatial ability. In general, females will have greater amounts of estradiol (more than the optimal amount) and males will tend to have smaller amounts of estradiol (less than the optimal amount). According to this theory, males who are more "feminized" and females who are more "masculinized" will have better spatial skills. In a recent test of this hypothesis, Shute and her co-workers (cited in Kimura, 1989) found that men with lower levels of androgens were better at spatial tasks than men with higher levels of androgens. Recall that Turner's women have extremely low levels of sex hormones and very poor spatial skills. When they are treated with estradiol (usually to begin menstruation), these women show dramatic increases in spatial ability (Nyborg, 1983). If you look closely at Fig. 4.2, you will see that the left hand portion of the curves represents low levels of estradiol. When the concentration of estradiol is raised in Turner's women, they move closer to the middle portion of the curve—the part that represents good spatial ability. Thus, Nyborg cited research with Turner's women in support of his hypothesis.

According to Nyborg, prenatal hormones determine each individual's sen-

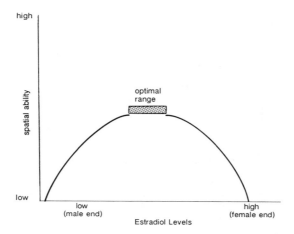

FIG. 4.2.   Graphic depiction of Nyborg's model (1990) that posits that there is an optimal range of estradiol that is needed for the expression of spatial abilities. Note that most males are relatively low on estradiol and most females are relatively high on estradiol. According to this theory, increasing estradiol for most males and decreasing estradiol for most females will improve their spatial abilities.

sitivity to the sex hormones that are secreted at puberty. Prenatal hormones permanently alter the body's sensitivity to puberty sex hormones. Nyborg's theory targets both prenatal and pubertal hormones as important determinants of spatial ability. However, this theory also allows for learning and environmental effects on the development of spatial ability.

In summary, four theories have been proposed to explain the effect of sex hormones available during puberty on the development of cognitive abilities. I have summarized these theories in Table 4.3 for review and ease of comparison.

When considering the role of sex hormones in the development of cognition, it is important to remember the social and environmental effects that come into play at every stage of development. Although there is some evidence that adolescence is the time in the life cycle when sex-related cognitive differences most clearly emerge, as well as the time when dramatic changes in sex hormone levels begin, the coincidence of these two events may be secondary to other salient life changes that occur at the same time, such as the adoption of adult sex role and different expectations of adolescents with mature bodies. This topic is considered more extensively in chapter 6.

One problem with the theories that focus on the biology of adolescence is that they cannot explain the sex differences that are found in childhood. Although cognitive differences are found more reliably at adolescence, there are reports in the literature of differences emerging earlier, most notably for verbal skills and selected tests of spatial ability (mental rotation and the Water Level Test). The

TABLE 4.3
Summary of Theories Designed to Explain the Effect of Sex Hormones at Puberty on
Cognitive Abilities

---

1. RATE OF PHYSICAL MATURATION:

Early physical maturation is associated with enhanced verbal abilities—girls, in general, mature earlier than boys.
Current Status: Some support for this theory, although the effect is probably small.

2. AGE AT PUBERTY:

A later age at puberty is associated with enhanced spatial skills (because of the effect of sex hormones on the organization of the brain)—boys, in general, experience puberty 2 years later than girls.
Current Status: Little or no support for idea that the timing of the biological events that occur at puberty influence spatial abilities (although social events may be important).

3. ANDROGENS AT PUBERTY:

A minimal concentration of androgens is needed at puberty for spatial ability to develop; puberty is a critical period for the development of spatial skills.
Current Status: Only confirmed with abnormal populations.

4. OPTIMAL HORMONE CONCENTRATION:

There is an optimal concentration of some hormones (possibly estradiol) which is needed for expression of spatial ability.
Current Status: Recent research shows some support that more "feminine" men and more "masculine" women have better spatial skills, but much more research is needed.

---

nature and validity of cognitive sex differences in childhood is likely to be an active area of research during the next several years. If future researchers can document childhood and toddler differences, then theories that focus on adolescence as the critical period for the development of these cognitive abilities will have to be revised.

Adulthood and Old Age

Sex hormones throughout adulthood and old age follow very different patterns for women and men. For women, the female hormones follow a monthly (approximately) cycle in which they ebb and flow while the concentrations of male hormones remain relatively constant. At menopause, the amount of the female hormones diminishes substantially with little change in the levels of male hormones. For men, the concentrations of sex hormones remain fairly constant throughout the adult years, with a gradual decline into old age. In recent years, there has been considerable interest in the notion that male hormones fluctuate in a cyclic fashion throughout the month, but there has been too little research on this topic to warrant a conclusion (Doering, Brodie, Fraemer, Becker, & Hamburg, 1974).

A hormone-based theory devised to explain cognitive sex differences was proposed by Broverman, Klaiber, Kobayashi, and Vogel (1968). They began with the premise that sex hormones activate the central nervous system in a manner that facilitates the performance of simple, overlearned, repetitive tasks and interferes with tasks that require inhibition of an initial response. Their second supposition was that female hormones are more "powerful" than male hormones, with the result that women are superior on "simple, overlearned, perceptual motor tasks" such as those found on "clerical aptitude tests." Males, on the other hand, are naturally better at "more complex tasks requiring inhibition of immediate responses." Broverman et al.'s theory has been criticized on a number of grounds (Singer & Montgomery, 1969). One major problem concerns the way they classified their tasks. Verbal skills, including language comprehension and usage, are neither simple nor overlearned, yet these are the tasks at which females usually excel. Their initial assumptions about the effects of estrogens and androgens on the central nervous system are incorrect on physiological grounds. There is little supporting evidence and considerable contradictory evidence for the hypothesis of Broverman et al. that neural processes respond in the ways they propose.

Do Cognitive Abilities Vary Over the Menstrual Cycle?

Monthly fluctuations in sex hormones affect women's cognitive skills.
—Kimura (1989, p. 83)

Tests to study sex differences don't relate to anything in real life.
—Benderly (1989, p. 68)

Given that the major female hormones vary in a cyclical fashion throughout the month in adult women, it would seem that cognitive abilities should also vary in a similar cycle if these hormones mediate cognitive processes. For most healthy adult women, both estrogen and progesterone, the major female hormones, are available only in small quantities during the premenstrual, menstrual, and immediately postmenstrual portion of their cycle. Both hormones increase to a peak quantity at approximately midcycle (estrogen peaks slightly before midcycle, and progesterone peaks soon after midcycle) and then decline to premenstrual levels. Monthly variations in progesterone and estrogen are shown in Fig. 4.3.

Is there any evidence that women's cognitive or intellectual abilities vary during the menstrual cycle? In response to this question, Tiger (1970) wrote:

An American girl writing her Graduate Record Examinations over a two-day period or a week-long set of finals during the premenstruum begins with a disadvantage

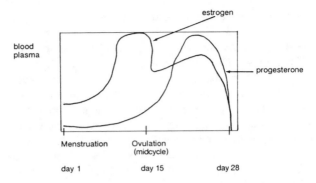

FIG. 4.3. Ovarian hormone levels as they vary over the menstrual cycle. Note that both estrogen and progesterone are available in very low levels immediately prior to and during menstruation and at high levels midcycle.

which almost certainly condemns her to no higher than a second class grade. A whole career in the educational system can be unfairly jeopardized because of this phenomenon.

In the first edition of this book, which was published in 1986, I wrote "Research on this question has clearly shown that Tiger is wrong" (p. 101). More recent research has shown that some cognitive abilities may vary over the menstrual cycle; however, Tiger is still wrong. Before I consider the research that has addressed this controversial question, think about Tiger's comments. Even if we had solid evidence (which we do not) that monthly hormone fluctuations affect cognition, it would not follow that women are inferior to men either at some portion or during the entire monthly cycle. The unstated assumption in Tiger's statement and those of many others is that women are (or will be shown to be) inferior to men intellectually, at least during some portions of their menstrual cycle. The finding that women and men differ does not imply that whatever traits are associated with being male are "better" than those associated with being female. Similarly, the mere fact that women's cognition may vary over the menstrual cycle doesn't mean that they are more or less intellectually able than men.

"The Women Have Less" Fallacy.   Before you read the following section, stop for a few minutes and think about the possibility that monthly hormone fluctuations affect the cognitive skills of women. Do you find this to be a repugnant idea? If so, why? Are you afraid that the results will be used to discriminate against women? If you answered "yes" to this question, then you are also demonstrating what I call "the women have less" fallacy. It is the fallacious (erroneous) belief that the biological bases of cognition will reveal that women

have less ability than men. Society decides which skills and abilities it values. If female skills and abilities are devalued, the fault lies in the society we have created, not in the biology that has created us.

Cognition and Monthly Hormones.   One of the first scientific investigations of whether there are differences in women's cognitive functioning over the menstrual cycle was conducted by Golub (1976). Her results with 13 different cognitive tests administered to 50 women aged 30 to 45 showed no significant menstrual cycle effect. Even though some women reported mood changes between the premenstrual and menstrual phases of their cycle, apparently these changes were not large enough to affect their ability to perform cognitive tasks.

However, more recent research suggests that there is evidence to support the notion that women's cognitive abilities fluctuate in a cyclical fashion. This research received a great deal of coverage in the popular press, with front page stories in the *Los Angeles Times* and the *New York Times* and articles in weekly news magazines (e.g., *Newsweek*). This research received such widespread coverage because it is an emotionally explosive issue. Unfortunately, the coverage tended to be more sensationalistic than scientific and may have created a false impression about the nature and findings of the research. Because it is "cutting edge" research and because so much has been written and said about it, I go into some detail about what was and wasn't found.

First, the idea that cognitive abilities may vary over the menstrual cycle is not viewed as heresy by anyone who has studied sensation and perception. As noted in the previous chapter, there are some differences between men and women in their ability to sense and perceive certain stimuli and in their attentional ability. It is well documented that for women, sensation and perception change at adolescence and also vary over the monthly cycle. Consider, for example, the ability to detect small concentrations of a chemical called "androstenone." Androstenone is a scent that is known to influence the sexual responsiveness of female pigs. (Odorants that impel behavior are called *pheromones.*) It is found in the urine, sweat, saliva, fatty tissues, and blood plasma of all human males. It is also present in much lower concentrations in females. Researchers found a decline in the ability to detect androstenone during adolescence with approximately 28% of males unable to detect the odor and 42% of females unable to detect the odor (Dorries, Schmidt, Beauchamp, & Wysocki, 1989). The experimenters believe that the sex hormones that flood the body during adolescence are responsible for the sex differences in the ability to detect this scent.

Monthly variations in sensation and perception are reviewed in a book by Coren and Ward (1989). They maintain that sex hormones can directly affect sensation and perception because they are carried in the blood that supplies the sensory receptors and higher cognitive mechanisms. Women become more or less sensitive to certain odors as a function of their menstrual cycle. Women's sense of smell is more acute than men's, but it also varies over the cycle with greatest sensitivity midcycle, when estrogen levels are highest. The role of monthly hormones in mediating this sensitivity was demonstrated in research with women who have inactive ovaries. (Therefore their blood hormone levels do not vary in a cyclical fashion.) These women had an impaired sense of smell that was remedied with the administration of estrogen. Other research reviewed by Coren and Ward showed that the administration of androgens could reduce smell sensitivity.

Research with rats has shown that when their ovaries are removed, their preference for sweet tastes is reduced. If they are later administered estrogen, the same rats show a renewed preference for sweet tasting substances. Research with human females has also shown a cyclical variation in the preference for sweet tastes. This has led some investigators to speculate that many women gain weight while taking oral contraceptives (which contain estrogen), in part, because they may overeat sweets.

The ability to perceive pain is another example of a sensory/perceptual system that shows periodic fluctuation. It has been shown that women are more sensitive to painful stimuli during the midcycle portion of the cycle (when hormone levels are highest) than at menstruation (Goolkasian, 1980, 1985). The change in sensitivity to painful stimuli was found only for menstruating women. Women who did not menstruate (e.g., had undergone surgical removal of ovaries) did not show the change in pain sensitivity. Goolkasian (1985) concluded from a carefully executed series of studies that "It is apparent that a woman's ability to discriminate the presence of painful stimuli varies as a function of menstrual phase" (p. 25). Other sensory/perceptual effects that are known to vary periodically are the ability to detect a pure tone and the ability to discriminate between two closely spaced touches (Baker, 1987b).

Although I have mentioned the differences in the concentrations of sex hormones across the menstrual cycle, it might be useful to consider exactly how much the hormones fluctuate. The level of estrogens in adults vary monthly from 3 times as much in women as in men after menstruation to 50 times as much at ovulation. Levels of progestins (e.g., progesterone) vary from equal to that in men following menstruation to 17 times as high. Conversely, men average about 17 times more androgens than women (Kimmel & Weiner, 1985). Thus, fluctuations of the sex hormones within women across the month and between the sexes are so large that it seems unlikely that they would have little or no effect on men and women.

Hampson and Kimura (Hampson, 1990a, 1990b; Hampson & Kimura, 1988) examined whether women's cognitive abilities would vary as a function of the monthly ebb and flow of estrogen and progesterone. One possibility is that midcycle, when both of these hormones are abundant, women would excel on those tasks that tend to favor women and show a detriment in those tasks that typically favor men. Conversely, at menstruation, when both of these hormones are at low levels, women would show improved performance on those tasks that favor men and decreased performance on those tasks that favor women. As you know from the last chapter, women tend to excel in speech articulation. There is also evidence that women are better, on the average, than men at fine muscle movements (such as those that would be needed in surgery, machine repair, and, yes, also typing and needlepoint). By contrast, men tend to score higher on some spatial tasks (e.g., mental rotation, rod and frame task). Hampson and Kimura selected those tasks that vary most dramatically as a function of sex and examined the way they vary over the menstrual cycle. They found that women performed significantly better on speech articulation (speed of reciting a tongue-twister), a test of manual dexterity, and verbal fluency in the high hormone or midleutal phase than during the menstruation portion when hormones are low. By contrast, performance on spatial tasks (e.g., size of errors on rod and frame test) was better during the low hormone phase of the cycle than the midleutal phase. Control groups included nonmenstruating women who were receiving hormone replacement therapy (they showed the same variations) and nonmenstruating women who were not receiving hormone replacement therapy (they did not show the variation). Heister, Landis, Regard, and Schroeder-Heister (1989) recently obtained results that confirm those of Hampson and Kimura. They found that women were faster and more accurate on nonverbal tasks during the midcycle phase than the menstrual phase. These authors believe that the periodic fluctuations seen in women's cognitive performance can explain the variability often found in experimental results. The theory of periodic fluctuations across the menstrual cycle is summarized in Table 4.4.

What do these results mean? It is easier to report research findings than it is to interpret them. Although I find this research fascinating, I do not believe that it has much immediate application. What are the implications of being able to say tongue twisters several seconds faster during one portion of the month? We have

TABLE 4.4
Do Women's Cognitive Abilities Vary Across the Menstrual Cycle?

Portion of Cycle	Estrogen	Progesterone	Prediction
Menstruation	low	low	better performances on maps, mazes, and spatial tasks (cognitive tasks on which males typically excel)
Midcycle	high	high	better performance on speech articulation, manual dexterity, and verbal fluency (tasks on which females typically excel)

no idea if this differential ability has more extensive consequences. The real finding is the *reciprocity* of spatial and verbal abilities such that when one is high, the other is low. These results tell us little about sex differences because only women menstruate, so they cannot be used for between-sex comparisons. Furthermore, monthly variability for women cannot explain differences between women and men.

Nyborg (1990) has used these results to support his theory that spatial ability depends on an optimal level of estradiol (which is secreted by the ovaries). Because women tend to have more estradiol than men, their spatial skills improve when estrogen levels are low around the time of menstruation (bringing them closer to the optimal range) and their spatial skills decrease when estrogen levels are high around midcycle (bringing them farther from the optimal range).

Research on nonhuman mammals also support these findings. Becker (cited in Kimura, 1989) found that female rats were better at walking on a narrow plank (a paw dexterity task or perhaps "paw-eye" coordination?) when estrogen and progesterone levels were high than when they were low. She also found that she could enhance performance on this task by directly implanting estradiol into the female rats' brains.

As you consider this line of research, keep in mind that fluctuations in hormone levels have very little effect on the day to day life of normal women. Speculating on how hormones affect performance, Sherwin (1988) suggested that estrogen may affect certain brain enzymes that in turn alter the way the body metabolizes (uses) the neurotransmitters that underlie these tasks. Much more research is needed before we can say with certainty whether the finding of monthly variations in women's cognitive performance is reliable and, if so, whether it has any discernable effect on the more complex and multifarious tasks of everyday life. Certainly, there is nothing in this research that could be used to support the notion that women or men are better fit for any type of job. Monthly fluctuations within menstruating women tell us nothing about their absolute level of ability, and so far have only been documented with very fine-grained tasks such as speed of reciting a tongue twister.

Old Age

Several researchers have sought to explain the cognitive sex differences that occur at the end of the life span. There is a well documented decline in the ability to utilize and retain spatial information relative to the ability to utilize and retain verbal information among the elderly (Clarkson-Smith & Halpern, 1983; Halpern, 1984b). Parallel to the decline in spatial abilities is a decline in both female and male sex hormones in both women and men. Although it is possible that there is a cause and effect relationship between these two events that occur at approximately the same time in the life cycle, there is little research to support the idea that they are directly linked. We have no satisfactory theory that can account for the age-related decline in spatial skills while verbal skills remain high in old age. Psychosocial and environmental explanations that are discussed in chapter 6 account for this finding much better than any of the sex hormone theories.

Sex Hormones, Sexual Orientation, and Cognition

Unless you are familiar with the theories in this area, you are probably surprised to learn that some theorists have suggested a link among sex hormones, sexual orientation (gay, lesbian, bisexual, heterosexual) and cognitive abilities. Research with nonhuman animals (rats, hamsters, ferrets, pigs, zebra finches, and dogs) has shown that prenatal sex hormones contribute to variations in sexual orientation. In Adkins-Regan's (1988) review of the literature relating the effect of prenatal sex hormones to sexual orientation, she concluded that early castration of males or early testosterone administration to females can change sexual orientation in nonhuman mammals.

Recall that Geschwind and Galaburda (1986) hypothesized that high levels of prenatal testosterone alter the innate human bias towards left cerebral hemisphere dominance by slowing its development in early life. As predicted by their theory, left handedness (a correlate of right hemisphere dominance) is more frequently found in males (who, of course, are exposed to higher levels of prenatal testosterone) than females (Halpern & Coren, 1991). Extrapolating from Geschwind and Galaburda's theory, it also seemed possible that the amount of prenatal testosterone available to a developing fetus will influence the sexual differentiation of the brain (a topic considered in more depth in the next chapter) as well as the sexual orientation of the developing fetus when it obtains maturity. Thus, there might be a link among hand preference (right handed, left handed, or mixed hand use, a correlate of cerebral dominance) sexual orientation, and cognition. Preliminary studies of gay males show some evidence that left handedness is more prevalent in homosexual males than in heterosexual males (e.g., Annett, 1988). Lindesay (1987) for example, found significantly more left handedness in a sample of gay males at a venerology clinic than in a sample of heterosexual males from the same clinic. He concluded that male sexual orientation is related to biological mechanisms that underlie the distribution of hand preference and cerebral dominance. (I should note that Rosenstein and Bigler, 1987, failed to find a relationship between hand preference and sexual orientation. Their study, however, used an extremely small number of subjects, which virtually insured that they would not detect group differences. This is a good example of why we cannot argue from null results.)

Sanders and Ross-Field (1986) reasoned that male homosexuality might be affected by the same prenatal hormones that are involved in cognitive sex differences. Using several different tests of spatial ability, they found that a sample of gay males demonstrated a level of spatial ability that was similar to that of a sample of females (whose sexual orientations were unknown). Both the gay males and the females scored significantly lower in visual-spatial ability than the male heterosexuals. Sanders and Ross-Field replicated this finding in three different experiments. They concluded that "the results are interpreted as support for a common biological determinant of cognitive ability and male sexual orientation" (p. 280). They maintain that there is a link among sexual orientation, cognitive abilities (specifically visual-spatial), brain organization and the level of prenatal testosterone. These results have been replicated by other researchers. In a carefully controlled study in which subjects were matched for age, education, and vocational interests, Gladue, Beatty, Larson, and Staton (1990) found that "male homosexuals performed more poorly than male heterosexuals on a version of the water jar test and on the Mental Rotation Test" (p. 101).

You may be wondering if there has been any similar research with lesbians. Gladue et al. (1990) recently found that lesbians performed more poorly than heterosexual women on the water jar test (aka water level test) of spatial ability. Given these results, Gladue et al. conclude that simple hypotheses like lesbians are cognitively more similar to males than to heterosexual females are certainly wrong. Furthermore, there is no indication that heterosexuals and homosexuals differ in the levels of sex hormones in their adolescent or adult life (Money, cited in Adler, 1990). It seems likely that sexual orientation is influenced by a host of factors which may include the effect of prenatal hormones on a developing nervous system. Thus far, researchers have not found any social or experiential variables that could predict sexual orientation. Of course, much more research is needed on this question before we can make any meaningful conclusions. If prenatal hormones are an important factor, then sexual orientation is just another one of the myriad of ways in which humans differ. This is all part of natural human variation and does not support any bias that one sexual orientation is "better" or "worse" than another.

It is presumed that both genes and hormones operate via their influence on the brain—that marvelous organ that is responsible for our every thought and action. The question of sex differences in the structure and function of the brain is discussed in the next chapter. General statements about the limitations of biological theories and the way biology interacts with psychosocial variables are also made in the next chapter. So, stay tuned for Biological Hypotheses: Part II—The Brain, playing soon in a textbook near you.

CHAPTER SUMMARY

Although many people are disturbed by biological theories that have been used to explain cognitive sex differences, such theories are not necessarily sexist. Biology always operates in an environmental context and it is the interaction of biology and environment that permits or prohibits the development and expression of cognition.

Genetic theories have been proposed to explain cognitive sex differences. The genetic theory that has received the most attention is the "sex-linked recessive gene theory." According to this theory, spatial ability is determined by a genetic code on the X chromosome. Predictions from this theory (such as the proportion of women and men that would be expected to show good spatial ability) have not been supported. There is no good evidence for a sex-differentiated link between heredity and cognition.

Sex hormones—estrogen, progesterone, and testosterone—have been identified as possible causes of sex differences in cognition. Research with abnormal populations (e.g., Turner's women, CAH) and nonhuman mammals suggests that prenatal hormones have a major influence on the development of intellectual abilities. There is limited support for the idea that females have an intellectual advantage (especially verbal) because they mature earlier than males. Two theories of spatial ability that have some support are (a) the need for a minimum amount of testosterone at puberty for good spatial ability (at least for males) and, (b) there exists an optimal range of estradiol for the expression of spatial ability. Recent research has shown that women's cognitive abilities vary in a reciprocal fashion over the menstrual cycle with verbal skills and manual dexterity best at midcycle when estrogen and progesterone levels are high and worse during menstruation when estrogen and progesterone levels are low. Spatial ability varies in an inverse fashion. Verbal abilities tend to remain high into old age while spatial skills decline at an earlier age. Several researchers have found a relationship among sex hormones, sexual orientation, and cognitive abilities. This area of research is still in its infancy and there is not enough known about this relationship to permit strong conclusions. Hormones most probably exert their influence via the brain, which is the topic of the next chapter.

5 Biological Hypotheses Part II: Brains and Brain-Behavior Interactions

Contents

5

It may be no benefit to society to assume that the two sexes are basically homogeneous with respect to cognition and that the only heterogeneity is that imposed by different experience. Zero variation is not a requirement of equal opportunity.
—Witelson (1988, p. 217)

A BRIEF INTRODUCTION TO THE BRAIN

Every thought you have ever had, every movement you have ever made, every emotion you have ever felt were brought to you by that amazing mass that sits within your skull. If you could examine your own brain, you would, no doubt, be surprised to find that it looks like a giant (approximately 3 pound) mushy walnut with the consistency of a soft-boiled egg. The brain and the spinal cord that it sits on top of make up the central nervous system.

Not surprisingly, researchers have considered the possibility that sex differences in cognitive abilities may, in part, reflect sex differences in the underlying neural structure or organization of the brain. All intellectual activity results from patterns of neural activation by large groups of neurons. I begin with a brief introduction to the brain so that you can follow the logic of the research that has investigated sex-related brain differences.

Look carefully at the picture of a human brain in Fig. 5.1. Like many other organs, the brain appears bilaterally symmetrical. Each half of the brain is called a hemisphere. The two hemispheres are connected by a thick band of neural fibers called the corpus callosum. There are spaces in the brain that are filled with cerebrospinal fluid—a fluid that serves two purposes. It helps to cushion the brain against injury and carries hormones and nutrients to different parts of the brain (Campbell, 1987).

The cerebral cortex is the outer portion of the brain. In humans, the cortex is the largest and most complex part of the brain. Its highly convoluted (wrinkled) appearance is the distinguishing feature between human brains and those of other animals. We know that different parts of the cortex are specialized for different

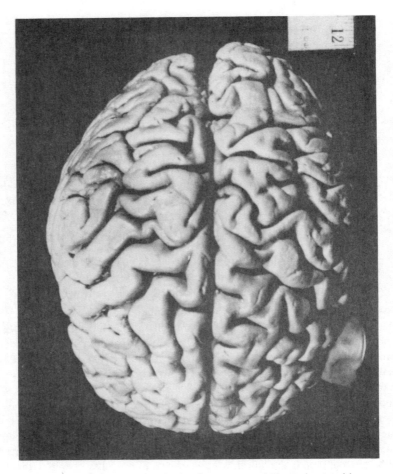

FIG. 5.1. A normal human brain. Can we ever fully understand how
all of human experience is processed and stored in this complex web
of neurons and chemical neurotransmitters?

functions and that different aspects of the same cognitive function can have
different locations in the brain. For example, one part of the brain that is known
as Wernicke's area is primarily responsible for the meaningful components of
speech; whereas, a different area known as Broca's area is primarily responsible
for the production of speech. Both of these verbal-related areas are typically
found in the left half of the brain. Similarly, there are different cortical areas for
recognizing *what* an object is and for knowing *where* an object is in space. These
two types of spatial processing are primarily accomplished in the central portion
of the cortex known as the parietal lobe. (For a review of this area of research,
see Morrow & Ratcliff, 1988.)

Although the brain appears symmetric, extensive research has shown that each side of the brain controls different functions. The left half of the cortex receives sensory information about the right half of the world and it controls the motor responses on the right side of the body. Sensory information and motor control for the left half of the world are under the control of the right hemisphere. Thus, brain mechanisms for sensory input and motor output are under contralateral (or opposite side) control.

You may have read or heard some "pop" psychology that makes a distinction between the "right brain" and "left brain." As you probably have guessed by now, the picture of brain functioning that is emerging is more complicated than a simple division of functions by right or left hemisphere. Because a major theory of sex differences in brain organization concerns the possibility that female and male brains differ in the way the two hemispheres are specialized for different tasks, this is a focal topic in sex differences research. The brain is divided into regions that are relatively more important for certain tasks and relatively less important for other tasks. In general, the language areas of the brain are found in the left hemisphere, which tends to be more involved in symbolic and analytic thought processes. For most people, the right hemisphere is involved more in perceptual and spatial processing. Research on the specialization of the two hemispheres (e.g., Gazzaniga, 1983) suggests that the difference between verbal (sequential) processing and spatial (analog) processing is a "fundamental dichotomy in human cognition" (Lohman, 1988, p. 182) with different brain regions involved in verbal and spatial information processing.

THE QUESTION OF SEX-RELATED BRAIN DIFFERENCES

Sex differences researchers have been concerned with the question of whether there are differences in male and female brains, and, if so, whether these differences can be used to explain sex-related cognitive differences. In an influential article on this topic, Kimura (1987, p. 133) asked, "Are men's and women's brains really different?" Her simple answer is "yes, of course," but the real questions is how and how much.

If we were to examine brains taken from females and males there would be no gross differences that could be used to identify the sex of their owner. Microscopic examinations of the structure of the nerve cells and nerve tissues that comprise the brain would show that the cells are morphologically identical except for visible X chromosomes (known as Barr bodies) in many of the nerve cells in women's brains and Y chromosomes in the men's nerve cells (Gersh & Gersh, 1981).

Although there are no gross anatomical differences in female and male brains, it is clear that there are some sex-related brain differences. Menstruation, for example, begins as a brain event with a hormone feedback loop involving the pituitary and hypothalamus, which are brain structures. Certain between-sex synapse differences are visible microscopically in the hypothalamus, presumably reflecting the role of the hypothalamus in menstruation. Thus, there are sex-related brain differences that reflect the fact that women menstruate and men don't.

The picture becomes somewhat more complicated when we also consider that there are cortical hormones that function as sex hormones, indicating some between-sex cortical hormone differences (Keeton, 1967). Despite these well-documented differences in female and male brains, the brain structures and systems involved in menstruation are not thought to be important in influencing intellectual abilities. There is no reason to believe that the portions of the brain that regulate menstruation in females and sexual behavior in males and females are also involved in the higher cognitive functions we have been considering.

Size, Weight, and Complexity

> *Just, therefore, as higher civilization is heralded, or at least evidenced, by increasing bulk of brain; . . . so we must naturally expect that man, surpassing woman in volume of brain, must surpass her in at least a proportionate degree in intellectual power.*
> —Popular Science Monthly (1878–1879, cited in Russett, 1989, p. 16)

Early reports of differences between female and male brains parallel findings of Black and White race differences. According to earlier theorizing, the supposedly inferior race and the supposedly inferior sex had similar brain deficiencies. Nineteenth-century physicians warned that the female nervous system was delicate and not well suited for intellectual work. According to Burnham (1977, p. 10), these physicians claimed that both women and Blacks had "smaller brains with less capacity." One of the arguments for denying women and African-Americans the right to vote was their purportedly inferior biology. Presumably, their smaller and less complex brains could not handle the complex decisions required of informed voters. The "theory" went even further in suggesting that intellectual endeavors would be bad for women's health because the increased blood flow to the brain would drain the blood normally needed for menstruation.

The fact is that women's brains are somewhat smaller than men's brains; male brains at birth are approximately 12% heavier and 2% larger in circumference than female brains (Janowsky, 1989). But this does not support the ludicrous position that females are inferior. Brain size and weight are positively correlated with body size, and relative to body size, there are no sex differences in brain weight. Because men, on the average, tend to be larger than women, they also tend to have larger brains. There is no evidence that larger brains are, in any way, better than smaller brains (within normal limits). If this hypothesis were true, then people with the largest hat sizes (reflecting greater brain sizes) would be the smartest, a "prediction" that is obviously untrue. (I have had students with large heads argue with me about this one.) Furthermore, there is no evidence that male or female brains differ in complexity. Similar earlier reports that Blacks have smaller brains than Whites are totally unfounded and merely reflect racism (Gould, 1978).

If there are no meaningful sex-related differences in the size, weight, and complexity of the human brain, where might we find the differences that underlie cognition? Several theorists have reasoned that the differences are due, in part, to differences in the way the brain is organized. The most prominent theory is that male and female brains differ, on the average, in the extent to which different tasks are specialized in each hemisphere. The possibility that there are female and male patterns of brain organization is discussed in the next section. Other theories that posit that the brain basis of sex differences is in the organization of cognitive functions within each hemisphere and/or in the structure of the corpus callosum are also discussed in following sections.

SEXUAL DIMORPHISM IN HEMISPHERIC SPECIALIZATION

All of the major theories of sex differences in cerebral organization began with a simple analogy. Given that the types of abilities that differ by hemisphere of specialization are the same ones that differ by sex, it seemed to many psychologists only a short leap to suggest that the sexes differ in the way their hemispheres specialize these abilities. The logic behind this reasoning is that since sex differences are primarily found with verbal and visual-spatial tasks and that hemispheric specialization differs with respect to these two abilities, then it is plausible that there are sex differences in cerebral lateralization. Recall from the last chapter that the term "sexually dimorphic" refers to two different structures that vary as a function of sex. The question being posed here is this: "Are female and male brains different in the way the hemispheres are lateralized (or specialized) for cognitive tasks?"

A large body of research has revealed that the two hemispheres or halves of the brain are, to some extent, lateralized or dominant for different cognitive functions. But, what does it mean to say that one hemisphere is dominant with respect to a cognitive ability? According to Geschwind (1974), "One hemisphere may be said to be dominant for a given function when it is more important for the performance of that function than the other hemisphere" (p. 9). Hemisphere dominance does not mean an either/or division of tasks. It means instead that one half of the brain is more or less specialized or proficient in its ability to process certain types of stimuli.

Laterality and Handedness Groups

Although this book is concerned with sex differences in cognition, there are other groups that show some consistent cognitive differences. People differ in many ways besides sex. One of the differences that has been of interest to psychologists is the difference between right and left handers. Hand differences are of particular interest when we consider brain organization because preferred hand use (right, left, or mixed) is an indirect index of lateralization of brain dominance. Recall that the right hemisphere controls the movements of the left side of the body and the left hemisphere controls the movement of the right side of the body. Thus, most right-handers have dominant motor control in their left hemisphere, and most left-handers have dominant motor control in their right hemisphere. (This has lead some left-handers to conclude that they are the only ones in their right mind.) Of course, many people are not consistently right or left handed; handedness is a continuous variable with each of us more or less right or left handed. However, in order to simplify the following discussion, I refer to right and left handedness as though there were just these two categories. (For many purposes, people who use their right hand for some tasks, such as writing, and their left hand for other tasks, such as throwing a ball or drawing, are classified along with the left-handers.)

We are not only right or left handed, we are also right or left footed (Which foot do you use to step on a bug?), right or left eared (Which ear do you use to listen to a faint conversation that is on the other side of a wall?), and right or left eyed (Which eye do you sight with when you shoot a rifle?). Preferred eye, ear, foot, and even nostril are also measures of laterality. Although these other measures can be useful, most research in laterality has used preferred hand, so we will think of hand group (right or left handed) as a measure of brain lateralization. In general, preferred hand and preferred foot are the same.

Although there had been social pressure placed on natural left-handers to write or eat with their right hand, research has shown that such pressures are usually not successful, or if they are, the change in hand use is limited only to writing or eating (Porac & Coren, 1981). There are no social pressures to change foot preference, and because foot preference is usually in agreement with hand preference, researchers believe that hand preference is a biologically determined index of cerebral organization. The functional asymmetry of the hemispheres (different cognitive functions specialized in different hemispheres) is present at birth, so it is not due to experience (Witelson, 1989). Additional evidence to support this view can be found in a comprehensive book edited by Coren (1990).

The research literature on handedness groups must be at least as large as the literature on sex differences. We know that there is a higher proportion of left-handers among architects, engineers, university mathematics teachers and mathematics students, artists, astronauts, chess masters, championship "Go" players, and performing musicians than in the general population (Deutsch, 1980; Mebert & Michel, 1980; O'Boyle & Benbow, 1990). Many researchers have concluded that left-handers (who are presumably right-hemisphere dominant) are superior on cognitive tasks that are mediated by the right hemisphere such as spatial abilities (Burnett, Lane, & Drott, 1982; Lewis & Harris, 1990). It also seems that left-handers are more likely to have some of their language functions specialized in their dominant right hemisphere (Harshman & Hampson, 1987; Hines, 1990).

Approximately 95% of all right-handed people maintain speech and language control in their left hemisphere. Actual percentage estimates vary somewhat for the proportion of left-handed people who maintain the same lateralization pattern as right-handed people. Levy and Reid (1978) have estimated that among the left-handed population 60% maintain language functions in the left hemisphere, with the remaining 40% having the reversed pattern. Springer and Deutsch (1989) have estimated that among left-handers 70% have speech and language control in their left hemisphere, with approximately 15% maintaining verbal control in their right hemisphere, and the remaining 15% with control in both hemispheres. Small variations in these estimates are of no practical concern for the purposes of this review; however, the fact that a much larger proportion of left-handers than right-handers have right hemisphere language specialization is important in understanding hypotheses about the relationship between sex and cerebral lateralization.

There is a large research literature documenting the finding that left-handers differ from right-handers on some cognitive abilities. For example, recent research has shown that left-handers are inferior to right handers on certain verbal tasks (Bradshaw & Bradshaw, 1988). If you are thinking that this result is the same as some of the findings in the sex differences literature, you are right. In fact, there are many parallels between the findings of researchers who study cognitive sex differences and researchers who study cognitive handedness differences.

Reading disabilities, stuttering, and some categories of mental retardation are more prevalent in males than in females and in left-handers than in right-handers. Similarly, precocious mathematical giftedness is more likely found in males than in females and in left-handers than in right-handers (Benbow, 1988). Precocious verbal ability (as measured on the SAT-V) is also associated with being male and left-handed (O'Boyle & Benbow, 1990). Although this result seems to run counter to the "typical" sex difference in verbal skills, recall from chapter 3 that males now outscore females on the SAT-V. I speculated earlier that this seemingly anomolous result may be due to the large number of analogies on the SAT-V. Analogies seem to be the one "verbal" skill at which males tend to score higher than females.

Given that the pattern of cognitive results is the same for males and left-handers and for females and right-handers, you may be wondering if more males are left-handed (and, by inference, more females right-handed). Estimates of the percentage of each sex that is left-handed vary considerably depending on how handedness is measured, the group that is selected as subjects, and the age of the subjects (Coren & Halpern, 1991). Virtually all studies find that a greater proportion of males are left-handed than females (e.g., Coren, 1990). Thus, because left-handedness is statistically associated with being male and right-handedness with being females, the similarity in cognitive patterns is not surprising.

Assessing Brain Laterality

Handedness provides only an indirect measure of brain laterality. There are numerous other methods of determining which hemisphere is more specialized for selected cognitive tasks. One such method is writing hand posture. Levy (1974) posited that left-handers who write with a "hooked" or inverted hand posture have language specialization in their left hemisphere; whereas, those who write with an "upright" hand posture have language specialization in their right hemisphere. Similarly, right-handers who write with a "hooked" posture have language specialization in their right hemisphere (very rare) and those who write in an "upright" posture have language specialization in their left-hemisphere. These different hand postures are shown in Fig. 5.2.

Laboratory tests have been conducted with both clinical and normal populations to determine the extent to which different cognitive abilities are lateralized.

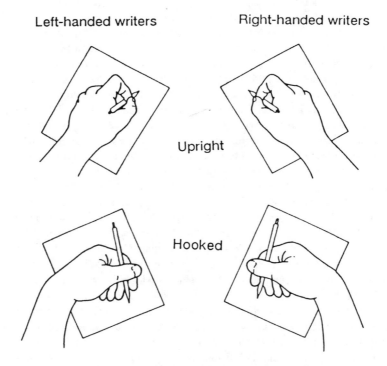

FIG. 5.2. Using writing hand posture to determine which hemisphere is lateralized for verbal abilities. According to Levy, a "hooked" hand posture indicates ipsilateral (same side) lateralization and an "upright" hand posture indicates opposite side lateralization for verbal abilities. Thus, a left-hander with a "hooked" posture is dominant for verbal abilities in her left hemisphere; whereas a left-hander with an "upright" posture is dominant for verbal abilities in her right hemisphere.

Clinical populations have included people who have had their corpus callosum (the thick bundle of nerve fibers that connects the two halves of the brain) split to alleviate the symptoms of epilepsy, individuals with damage to one area of the brain, post mortem examinations of corpses, and patients undergoing laboratory tests such as direct electrical stimulation of selected brain regions. Normal populations include people who have had EEG activity and evoked potentials recorded off their scalp (measures of the electrical activity in the brain), their blood flow monitored with radioactive isotopes, and CAT scans (a type of imaging that is frequently used in medical research) to identify brain anomalies. Both populations have shown a distinct distribution of abilities between the two hemispheres.

In an examination of the early development of lateralization, Shucard, Shucard, and Thomas (1987) took electrophysiological recordings off the right and left hemispheres of infants who were processing both speech and musical stimuli. They concluded that the right hemisphere is more active in processing both speech and music for infant males than for infant females. They also found that female infants shift to the more usual adult pattern at an earlier age than male infants. (The usual adult pattern is greater left-hemisphere response to verbal stimuli and greater right-hemisphere response to musical stimuli).

Molfese (1990) also found a different pattern of brain activity to known words for female and male infants. He was able to record different brain responses to known words than to unknown words in 16-month-old infants. Molfese found that different regions of the brain appear to be involved in female infants' comprehension of words than in male infants' comprehension of words.

Another way of assessing hemispheric involvement in a particular task is by having subjects perform some task with each hand (such as tapping rhythmically) while performing either a verbal or spatial task. Consider the rationale for looking at finger tapping. If you are tapping with your right hand, your left hemisphere is coordinating the movement. Suppose while you are tapping, I have you perform some verbal tasks (e.g., anagrams) and then some spatial tasks (e.g., mental rotation). If the verbal tasks interfered more with the right hand tapping than the spatial tasks did, I could conclude that you were primarily using your left hemisphere for the verbal tasks and not for the spatial tasks. The underlying idea is that two tasks interfere with each other more if they are performed by the same hemisphere than if they are performed by different hemispheres (Bowers & LaBarba, 1988; Kee & Cherry, 1990).

Dichotic Listening and Divided Visual Fields

Laboratory investigations of hemispheric dominance rely on the fact that most of the nerves from one side of the body connect to the contralateral (opposite) hemisphere. Consider audition (or hearing) for example. A majority of the nerves in the auditory track that connect to the right ear send their impulses to the left hemisphere, with the reverse innervation for the left ear. In a classic experimental paradigm, the researcher will present different stimuli to each ear simultaneously. The subject would be required to respond to the stimuli in some way such as classifying it as a letter or word or responding with a key press as quickly as possible to certain types of stimuli. The usual finding is that right-handed subjects respond more accurately to linguistic stimuli (letters or words) when they are presented to the right ear than when they are presented to the left ear (known as a right ear advantage or REA), suggesting that for right handers the left hemisphere is dominant or specialized for linguistic tasks. Stimuli that are difficult to verbalize (random sound sequences or noises that are not readily identifiable) are usually responded to better when they are presented to the left ear than the right, suggesting that the right hemisphere is specialized or dominant for nonlinguistic tasks for right-handed subjects (Bryden, 1986).

The presentation of different stimuli to each ear is called *dichotic listening*. You can get some idea of what this is like by having two friends stand next to you, one on each side, and having them read different passages at the same time. You will hear one message in your right ear and a different one in your left ear. In Bryden's (1988) review of sex differences in dichotic listening research, he concluded that although not all studies found significant handedness effects, virtually all have found at least a trend for left-handers to show a reduced laterality effect. This means that they showed less difference in how quickly or accurately they responded to stimuli presented to their right or left ear than the right handers did. In his extensive review, Bryden concluded that 82% of right-handers and 64% of left-handers show an REA in dichotic listening. When he examined the same studies as a function of sex, he found that 81% of males and only 74% of females showed an REA, with no studies showing a greater proportion of REA in females. He used these data to conclude that, in general, females have a more bilateral organization of cognitive abilities than males.

In a recent literature review, Hines (1990) agreed with Bryden's conclusion that the *degree* of left hemisphere dominance is greater in males than in females. Thus, according to this hypothesis, females have a more bilateral organization of brain function than males. A more bilateral organization means that the two hemispheres are more equal in the degree to which they underlie a specific type of cognitive task. The hypothesis that women's brains are more bilaterally organized (which also implies that males' brains are more laterally or one-sided organized) is hotly contested in the research literature.

Research similar to that described with hearing is also conducted with vision, although the pattern of innervation, or the way the neurons connect, is somewhat more complicated. Nerve fibers from the left half of each eye connect to the left hemisphere and nerve fibers from the right half of each eye connect to the right hemisphere. Researchers can determine which hemisphere is receiving visual information by presenting visual stimuli very briefly (a fraction of a second) to the right or left of a subject's fixation point. A fixation point is the point an individual is looking directly at when she or he is looking straight ahead. Any stimuli presented to the left of the fixation point, an area known as the left visual field, are, initially, represented in the right hemisphere. Similarly, any stimuli presented to the right of the fixation point, an area known as the right visual field, are, initially, represented in the left cerebral hemisphere (Kitterle & Kaye, 1985). A schematic diagram of this experimental paradigm is presented in Fig. 5.3. Results with visual stimuli support those found with audition: the right hemisphere is primarily important in visual-spatial skills (depth perception, detecting the orientation of a line, visual point location), and the left hemisphere is primarily important in verbal skills (naming concrete nouns and the recognition of words and digits) (Geschwind, 1974).

Research that displays stimuli to the right or left visual field is called divided visual field research. In order to conclude that mens' brains are more lateralized than women's, we would need to find that there is a greater difference in how

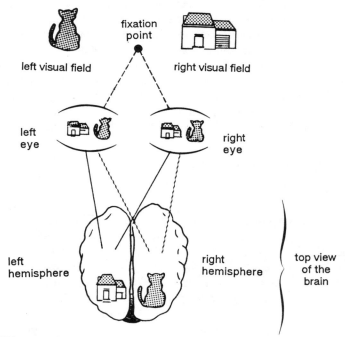

FIG. 5.3.   Schematic drawing of the images projected onto the right and left half of each eye when a subject is looking at a fixation point that is straight ahead. Notice that the cat in the left visual field is projected onto the right half of the left eye and the right half of the right eye. Both of these portions of each eye connect to the right hemisphere. The opposite pattern occurs for the house shown in the right visual field.

men respond to stimuli in their left and right visual fields than how women respond to stimuli in their left and right visual fields. For example, suppose a researcher presents words to the right or left visual field. The task for the subject is to say the word as quickly as possible. The dependent measure in this example is reaction time, or the time between presenting the stimulus and the subject saying the word. If we had a large sample of women and men, we could compute the average difference in reaction time for stimuli presented to the left visual field and stimuli presented to the right visual field for each sex. If this difference were significantly larger for men than for women, this would be evidence that men's brains are more lateralized or specialized than women's brains.

The literature using divided visual fields is not as clear cut as we would like it to be in order to reach a conclusion about sex differences in cerebral organization. Some researchers believe that we have good evidence that women's and men's brains have different patterns of lateralization (McGlone, 1980); whereas, other researchers strongly believe that cerebral lateralization does not differ as a function of sex (Denenberg, 1990). Healey, Waldstein, and Goodglass (1985) concluded that "females demonstrated consistently greater laterality differences" when the dependent measure is an oral report (e.g., naming the stimuli) and males show greater laterality differences when the dependent measure is a manual response (e.g., pressing a button). This is clearly a complicated area of research in which results seem to depend on the nature of the dependent measure as well as the type of stimuli that are presented.

Theories of sex differences in brain organization have relied on experimental research for their support. Let's consider some of the prominent theories.

Cognitive Crowding Hypothesis

Levy (1976; Levy-Agresti & Sperry, 1968; Levy & Nagylaki, 1972) hypothesized, at least in her earlier work, that spatial performance is optimized when spatial ability is strongly lateralized in one hemisphere. Thus, she begins with the assumption that lateralization is the best neural organization for spatial tasks. According to Levy (1976), when verbal and spatial processes are confined to single and separate sides of the brain, the underlying neural connections are optimal for each of these functions. However, if lateralization is incomplete or weak, then the two hemispheres will compete when an individual is performing a task. This aspect of her hypothesis has come to be known as the *Cognitive Crowding Hypothesis,* based on the reasoning that if two (or more) cognitive abilities are primarily controlled by the same hemisphere, there will not be enough "neural space" for each to be developed optimally. Task performance is impaired under these conditions. Levy goes on to suggest that because verbal skills are so important to the human species, spatial ability is more likely to suffer when verbal and spatial processes compete in the same hemisphere.

In explaining sex differences in cognitive abilities, she posits that females are less lateralized than males because of sex-related biological differences in the rate and pattern of development, and, therefore, they are more likely to have bilateral representation of verbal abilities. Bilateral representation of verbal abilities will be an advantage to verbal skills because more "cortical space" is devoted to language functions. On the other hand, bilateral representation of verbal skills impairs the ability to perform spatial tasks because there is less cortical space devoted to spatial function due to the "crowding out" of spatial representation by the bilateral cortical representation language. In other words, females are more likely to involve both hemispheres when solving spatial tasks than males. One implication of this brain organization is that females may use a verbal cognitive style when solving spatial problems, a point that I return to in the next chapter. According to this theory, bilateral representation is not an optimal neural organization for spatial tasks, and, therefore women show impaired performance on spatial tasks.

Levy has also suggested that women's patterns of cognitive abilities should be similar to that of left-handed males. Given that approximately 95% of all right-handed people maintain language control primarily in their left hemisphere and spatial control in their right hemisphere, and less than 70% of left-handed people have this pattern of neural organization, as a group, left-handers of both sexes are more likely to have bilateral representation of language functions. According to Levy's hypothesis, women, as a group, are also more likely to maintain bilateral representation. Thus, left-handed men and women in general should have bilateral representation of verbal skills, which is a cerebral pattern that is detrimental to spatial skills. Both groups would be expected to have better verbal skills than spatial skills, if this theory were true. Later in this chapter, I return to the theme that cognitive abilities depend on both sex and handedness. A schematic diagram of the Cognitive Crowding Hypothesis is shown in Fig. 5.4.

Support for the Cognitive Crowding Hypothesis comes from a variety of sources: In dichotic listening tasks there is a stronger right ear advantage for verbal stimuli for males than for females (Lake & Bryden, 1976); when stimuli are presented visually for brief periods to divided visual fields, males show greater right visual field superiority for verbal materials (Day, 1977; Voyer & Bryden, 1990), and greater left visual field superiority for spatial stimuli (Kimura, 1969; Kimura & Durnford, 1974); Dimond and Beaumont (1974) reported a consistent right hemisphere superiority for males with spatial tasks, but could only demonstrate this result with females under limited and specific conditions; males with high spatial ability showed EEG patterns of right hemisphere activity that were associated with successful spatial performance with an opposite hemisphere pattern for males with low spatial ability, whereas, no consistent hemispheric activity pattern was found for high and low spatial ability girls (Ray, Newcombe, Semon, & Cole, 1981); recordings of the electrical events in the brain with electroencephalograms (EEG's) show sex differences in the underlying neural activity. The patterns of electrical activity suggest that boys tend to use their right hemispheres when performing spatial tasks while girls use their left hemispheres for both spatial tasks and verbal tasks (Levy, 1976). Although these results support the idea that boys' brains are more lateralized than girls' brains, it is also possible that they reflect strategy differences between the

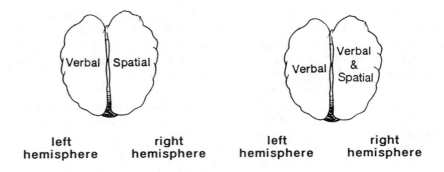

<table>
<tr><td>**Hand**:</td><td>Right handers</td><td>Left handers</td></tr>
<tr><td>**Sex**:</td><td>More male-typical</td><td>More female-typical</td></tr>
</table>

Predicted
Interactions: Left-handed males have cognitive patterns similar to that of
women (verbal skills better than spatial skills)

(Other sex by handedness interactions were not specified, but possibilities
include left-handed women are most likely to have higher verbal than spatial
skills and right-handed men are most likely to have higher spatial skills than
verbal skills)

> FIG. 5.4. A schematic representation of the Cognitive Crowding Hy-
> pothesis. According to this hypothesis, women (in general) and left-
> handers (especially males) have better verbal skills because language
> is bilaterally organized and poorer spatial skills because spatial ability
> is "crowded out" due to the fact that spatial abilities share the neural
> architecture in the right hemisphere with the neural substrate for ver-
> bal abilities.

sexes, with girls using verbal strategies to solve spatial problems. Clinical investigations of the recovery of cognitive functions following unilateral brain damage
also differ by sex such that males show more impairment on verbal tests following left hemisphere damage and more impairment on spatial tests following right
hemisphere damage than females (Inglis & Lawson, 1981).

Additional support for the hypothesis that there are sex differences in cerebral
lateralization was provided by Witelson (1976). Witelson used a tactile perception task in which 200 children ranging in age from 6 to 13 were required to
match a meaningless shape that they manipulated with either their right or left
hand to a visual display. (This experimental paradigm is called dichaptic presentation. It is the touch analogue to dichotic listening or the divided visual field
research.) She found that the boys performed this task more accurately when the
shapes were presented to their left hand than when they were presented to their
right hand, presumably reflecting a right hemisphere advantage in dealing with

spatial information. There were no significant hand differences for the girls. It is important to note, however, in interpreting these results that there were no overall sex differences in accuracy, so that while there were no hand (or hemisphere) differences for the girls, they were, on the average, as good at this task as the boys.

If the Cognitive Crowding Hypothesis is correct, and females rely more on both hemispheres in processing information than males, then we should expect a lower incidence of language disorders for females because they can rely on both hemispheres and would be less impaired by local brain injury or trauma. This is true. Females have fewer reading disabilities including dyslexia, fewer speech disorders including aphasia, dysphasia, and stuttering, and a lower incidence of autism (McGlone, 1980; Witelson, 1976).

Five reviews of the literature have also arrived at similar conclusions. Kimura (1983) said, "It is now widely agreed that males and females probably differ in brain organization for intellectual or problem solving behaviours" (p. 19). Springer and Deutsch (1989) concluded that "a variety of evidence suggests that males tend to be more lateralized for verbal and spatial abilities, whereas women show greater bilateral representation for both types of functions" (p. 222). McGlone (1980) stated, "There is an impressive accumulation of evidence suggesting that the male brain may be more asymmetrically organized than the female brain both for verbal and nonverbal functions" (p. 215). Further support for this conclusion was provided by Seward and Seward (1980), who stated, "Subject to future developments, the bulk of the evidence suggests that women's hemispheres are probably more symmetrical than men's" (p. 64). A more cautious conclusion along the same lines was made by Bryden (1989): "There seems to be at least reasonable evidence that women are somewhat less lateralized than men" (p. 11). It is important to keep in mind, however, that these quotes do not represent the unanimous opinion of researchers in the field. There are many researchers who failed to find experimental results that would support the idea that the female brain is more symmetrically organized than the male brain. What is most compelling is that when hemisphere differences are found, they are almost always in the same direction—females less lateralized than males. If these were spurious findings, then you would expect the results to go in either direction about equally often.

The Effect of Prenatal Sex Hormones on Lateralization

In the last chapter, I discussed an influential theory by Geschwind and Galaburda (1987) that posited that prenatal sex hormones play a critical role in brain development. As you recall (note my optimism), the underlying idea was that during prenatal development the left hemisphere is at greater risk than the right because the left hemisphere takes longer to develop than the right. According to this theory, high levels of prenatal testosterone slow neuronal growth in the left hemisphere. The result is right hemisphere dominance that is manifested in left-handedness. Because males are usually exposed to higher levels of testosterone during prenatal development (from their own developing testes that secrete testosterone, in addition to the lower amounts that are supplied by the mother), males are more likely to be right hemisphere dominant. Data presented in the last chapter showed that males are more likely to be left-handed (e.g., Vandenberg, 1987). But, is there any way to relate this theory to cognition?

As previously explained, this theory predicts that males would be either exceptionally adept at right hemisphere cognitive tasks (such as spatial ability) and/or exceptionally poor at left hemisphere cognitive tasks (such as some verbal tasks). Because this is a difficult theory to test in normal populations, we turn to extreme groups and abnormal populations to determine if specific findings support predictions derived from this theory. The substantial male advantage on mental rotation and other spatial tasks supports the superiority on spatial tasks part of the hypothesis; the high proportion of males among stutterers and dyslexics supports the poor performance on verbal tasks part of the hypothesis. Both males and left-handers are more likely to have severe language disorders, thus indicating the tendency for severe language disabilities to be associated with being male and being left-handed (Neils & Aram, 1986). Additionally, data from girls who were exposed to abnormally high male hormones conform to predictions from this theory.

Hines (1982) examined the relationship between prenatal sex hormones and cognitive abilities using 16 females whose mothers had taken DES (a hormone) during their pregnancies to prevent miscarriage. (DES has recently been in the news as a probable cause of a rare form of genital cancer among girls born from DES pregnancies.) DES, like the other synthetic prenatal hormones, has masculinizing effects on the developing fetus. If the synthetic hormones influence brain development in a masculine direction, then females would be expected to show a brain organization that is more similar to the masculine pattern than their unexposed sisters. Hines found that the DES females she tested were more strongly lateralized for verbal stimuli than their sibling control group. Recall from the previous section on sex differences in cerebral asymmetries that males may be, in general, more strongly lateralized than females, a result that has been linked to sex differences in verbal and spatial abilities. Hines' findings that DES-exposed females have strongly lateralized brain functions support the view that prenatal hormones are determinants of female and male brain organizations.

Another way to investigate the relationship between prenatal hormones and brain lateralization is to examine the extent to which Turner's women are lateralized for cognitive tasks. (Turner's women have particularly poor spatial skills.) When Hines (1982) investigated this relationship, she found that Turner's women had reduced laterality for cognitive tasks. Although this result is consistent with a brain organization that may be detrimental to spatial tasks, the cause of this organization is not entirely clear. Postnatal hormones could also be contributing these results.

Other research has suggested brain differences that are linked to differential hormone exposure. For example, McCardle and Wilson (1990) compared several groups of patients who had been exposed to abnormal hormone levels. They found that with regard to cognition, genetic sex was not important, but hormone exposure was: "In summary, the estrogen-exposed group appears to have greater strength in semantic-dependent tasks, while the androgen-exposed group performed better on timed tasks, more automatic syntactic functions, and memory dependent tasks" (p. 419). Although they were uncertain about the locus of the hormone effect in the brain, they suggested that it might be either at the corpus callosum, a theory we consider later in this chapter, or in the rate of axon differentiation, a fancy term for the growth (branching) of neural structures in different parts of the brain. Even individual rats show distinct lateral biases (pawedness?) on behavioral measures, many of which are sex dependent (LaHoste, Mormede, Rivet, & Le Moal, 1988).

Maturation Rate Hypothesis

It is widely documented that girls begin puberty earlier than boys. Girls in sixth and seventh grade not only tend to be taller than their male classmates, but also tend to exhibit secondary sex characteristics at an earlier age and develop reproductive capabilities earlier (Faust, 1977). One of the leading proponents of the maturation rate hypothesis is Waber (1976), who speculated that sex differences in lateralization were due to differences in maturation rate. As explained in chapter 4, Waber believes that early maturation will be beneficial to verbal abilities and detrimental to spatial abilities. To test her hypothesis, she compared early and late maturers of both sexes ranging in age from 10 to 16 years old. All subjects participated in a dichotic listening task to ascertain hemispheric specialization for speech perception and took three tests each of verbal and spatial skill. The results provided strong support for her theory.

Early maturers of both sexes were better at the verbal tests than the spatial ones; late maturers of both sexes showed the reverse pattern of results. This difference in performance, however, was almost entirely due to the considerable superiority of the late maturers on the spatial tests. Also, there were no statistically significant sex differences in the verbal and spatial tests when the sexes were equated for maturation rate. A final result was the finding that the dichotic listening task showed the strongest lateralization among the older subjects who were late maturers, regardless of sex. Taken together, these results suggest that late maturation is associated with good spatial skills and strong lateralization for both sexes, and early physical maturation is favorable to the development of good verbal abilities and weaker lateralization. Because, in general, girls mature earlier than boys, they would be expected to show less lateralization, better verbal ability, and poorer spatial ability.

Partial confirmation of Waber's maturation rate hypothesis was provided by Ray, Newcombe, Semon, and Cole (1981). They found a positive correlation between age at puberty and performance on the Guilford-Zimmerman test of spatial orientation, with later maturing individuals solving more problems correctly than those who experienced puberty at an earlier age. Herbst and Petersen (1980) also found a timing of puberty effect in their study of 135 post-pubertal adolescents. Late maturers outperformed early maturers on the Embedded Figures Test. However, a timing of puberty effect was not found with a mental rotation test—a test that usually shows large sex differences prior to adolescence. Thus, the notion that the biological substrates that are responsible for the onset of puberty also affect spatial ability has been replicated, but only with selected spatial ability tests.

.The notion that males develop right hemisphere specialization sooner than females was supported in a study that examined the ability of normal sighted children to learn how to read Braille. Braille is an alphabet system developed for the blind in which letters are presented as a pattern of raised points in a matrix. Rudel, Denckea, and Spalten (1973) found a left-hand (right hemisphere) advantage for 13- and 14-year-old boys, but not for girls on this task. They concluded that these results support the hypothesis that boys develop right hemisphere superiority for spatial tasks earlier and/or more completely than girls.

There are, however, several problems with any theory that ties cognitive abilities to rate of maturation at puberty. The most obvious one is that many of the sex differences are found in childhood (e.g., mental rotation), so puberty explanations come too late in development for these differences. Furthermore, the effect of timing of puberty on spatial ability is small. Newcombe and Dubas (1987) estimated d to be .21 that is about $\frac{1}{5}$ of a standard deviation. As is shown in the next chapter, which discusses psychosocial explanations of sex differences, the finding that a later age at puberty is correlated weakly with better spatial skills does not necessarily support any biological hypothesis. Early and later maturers could adopt different strategies for solving different sorts of problems and/or could be reacting to sex differentiated social pressures (e.g., Newcombe, Dubas, & Baenninger, 1989).

Sex, Lateralization, and Cognitive Abilities

Lateralization is a fundamental property of brain organization with widespread evolutionary significance.
—LaHoste, Mormede, Rivet, and Le Moal (1988)

It would probably be useful at this point to recapitulate the main points in the theories concerning the relationship among sex, lateralization, and cognitive abilities:

1. Women are more likely to have language functions represented in both hemispheres; this means that there is less "room" for spatial abilities to develop in their nondominant hemisphere. Conversely, men are more lateralized for

language; this means that their nondominant hemisphere is more specialized for spatial tasks. Because spatial abilities do not have to share neural space with verbal abilities, men, in general, excel at (some) spatial tasks.

2. Sex differences in cerebral specialization are caused by the effect of prenatal hormones on the development of each hemisphere (Geschwind & Galaburda, 1987) and/or differences in maturation rate at puberty (Waber, 1976).

Status. There is a large body of research that shows sex differences in cerebral lateralization, but we cannot yet specify the exact nature of the differences. When differences are found, women's brains are more bilaterally organized and men's brains are more laterally organized. This is a controversial area of research. Prenatal hormones do seem to play an important role in the development of brain organization; timing of puberty has a very small effect.

A critical, but weak link in the argument that sex differences in brain organization underlie cognitive sex differences is that strong lateralization (a "male" organization) be related to high spatial performance. The relationship between degree of lateralization and cognitive ability must be demonstrated before we can accept the hypothesis that cerebral lateralization is sexually dimorphic. The data in support of this relationship are not strong. Levy and Reid (1978) found partial support for this hypothesized relationship using spatial performance tests with a sample of male subjects, but they used an atypical sample of extremely high functioning subjects. Their experiment was weak for several reasons: (a) the males in their study surpassed the females in the verbal test, a result that would not be predicted from this theory, and (b) the verbal test results collected from their female subjects failed to confirm the predictions derived from their model. (The actual research results are quite complex, involving hand posture in writing as a variable. Readers interested in the details of this research are referred to Levy and Reid's report.) Thus, the prediction that strong lateralization would be related to good spatial ability and weak lateralization would be related to good verbal ability has received only weak confirmation.

Disconfirming Evidence

As you probably guessed, all of the research does not support the conclusions about sex differences in lateralization that were listed earlier. In an area as complex as understanding the human brain, there are inconsistent and contradictory data. The twin foundations of Levy's theory are that females are better in verbal skills because of their bilateral representation of language and males are better in spatial skills because they are more strongly lateralized.

Some brain researchers maintain that the differences in female and male brains cannot be described along a continuum from more or less lateralized. Denenberg (1990), a leading researcher in this area, wrote to me to protest the lateralization hypothesis: "I must say I strongly object to the conclusion that the human female's brain is less lateralized than the male's. I think it is accurate to say that the female's brain is organized differently from the male's" (p. 2). Thus, Denenberg believes that there are sex-related brain differences, but these differences are not found in degree of cerebral laterality. McKeever and Van Deventer (1977) also believe that there are no sex differences in hemispheric organization: "It is concluded that the hypothesis of verbal-spatial processing incompatibility within the same hemisphere is not supported" (p. 321). Thus, keep in mind that the notion that women's and men's brains differ in the extent to which they are lateralized is a hotly debated topic that can only be resolved when we amass enough evidence to support it or disprove it, or more likely, replace it with a different theory.

Although many of the research results support the notion of sex differences in cerebral asymmetries, it is difficult to understand why some researchers report contradictory results. Of course there are always differences in procedures, samples, and materials that could account for empirical differences. Berenbaum and Harshman (1980) have pointed out a number of methodological weaknesses that could be responsible for some of the negative findings in this area. It is also possible that females and males rely on different underlying processes and strategies to perform the same task. If, for example, women use verbal strategies in a spatial task, they could perform the task quite well by compensating for weaker spatial abilities with superior verbal abilities.

Another possible locus for the inconsistencies reported in the literature concerns the way laterality is measured. In the usual paradigm, verbal or spatial (nonverbal) information is initially presented to either cerebral hemisphere via different auditory presentations to the right and left ear (dichotic listening) or by presenting visual stimuli to the right or left visual field. Lateralization is then measured by analyzing for right or left ear or right or left visual field advantages. For example, if a subject reports significantly more verbal stimuli correctly when they are presented to the right ear (left hemisphere) than when they are presented to the left ear (right hemisphere), we would conclude that the subject has left hemisphere dominance for verbal information. Identical logic is used for determining cerebral dominance or lateralization for nonverbal stimuli or for visual field presentations. Group differences with respect to lateralization report percentage of subjects with a particular pattern of correct answers (e.g., 78% reported more verbal stimuli correctly when they were presented to the right ear) or the mean difference in correct responses between right and left ears (Richardson, 1976). Teng (1981) has expressed numerous concerns about the reliability and validity of these methods of measurement. Although Teng's reservations about the measurement of lateralization are too technical for review here, readers should be aware that measurement problems could be responsible for some of the inconsistencies reported in this area. It seems clear that there will be no simple answers to the many questions of cognitive sex differences, and additional unexplored variables including the technical aspects of measurement and method of stimulus presentation will need to be considered to resolve the inconsistencies.

Handedness, Reasoning Ability, and Other Moderator Variables

Perhaps one of the more controversial aspects of Levy's Cognitive Crowding Hypothesis is the notion that if an individual maintains a bilateral representation of verbal skills, then there will be less room left (or fewer neural structures) for spatial abilities in the right hemisphere, and therefore, spatial abilities will suffer. In addition, left-handers and women should, in general, have more bilateral representation of verbal ability and thus should have poorer spatial skills. Levy verified this prediction in her early work at California Institute of Technology, where she found that left-handed graduate students had lower performance subscales on a standardized intelligence test than their right-handed counterparts, with no difference between the groups on the verbal subscale (Levy, 1969). Despite Levy's own success in supporting her hypothesis, the majority of studies that have attempted to replicate this relationship have failed (e.g., Hardyck, Petrinovich, & Goldman, 1976; Sherman, 1979). Levy's earlier notion that left-handed men are similar to women in terms of their cognitive abilities has proven to be too simple. As is seen later in this chapter, specific combinations of sex and handedness need to be considered before ability predictions can be made.

Recent research on the relationship between handedness and sex may have provided some of the missing puzzle pieces while also suggesting a locus for some of the inconsistencies in the earlier literature. Harshman, Hampson, and Berenbaum (1983) have provided some of the most convincing evidence to date to support the hypothesis that sex and handedness differences in cognitive ability are, at least in part, neurological in origin. To ensure the generalizability of their results and to control for spurious findings (Type I errors—concluding that differences exist when the results were really due to chance), they employed three separate large scale samples and multiple measures of spatial ability, verbal ability, dichotic listening (to assess laterality), and reasoning. A test of reasoning was included in the belief that intellectual or reasoning ability could be mediating the sex and handedness effect on spatial ability.

Harshman, Hampson, and Berenbaum's results were clear-cut: Among subjects who scored high on the reasoning test, males outperformed females on 14 of the 15 spatial tests, as expected; however, the most interesting results were obtained with the sex by handedness interactions. Across all three samples and all 15 spatial tests, left-handed males performed worse than right-handed males, while on 12 of the 15 spatial tests left-handed females performed better than right-handed females. Among subjects who scored low on the reasoning test, males again outscored females on 14 of the 15 spatial tests, with a somewhat inconsistent pattern of sex by handedness interactions.

When reasoning ability is used as a mediator in verbal ability, the results are the mirror image of those found with spatial ability. Among subjects high in reasoning ability, left-handed males performed better than right-handed males, and left-handed females performed worse than right-handed females. Again, among the low reasoning ability subjects, the results were less consistent. These results are summarized in Table 5.1.

If, as these results suggest, sex and handedness differences in cognitive abilities depend on reasoning or intellectual ability, then contradictory and negative results would be expected if the researcher used either low ability subjects or mixed high and low ability subjects in a single experiment without controlling for ability level. The pattern of results for the "high reasoners" is in accord with predictions made by Levy and Gur (1980), that is, left-handed males had lower spatial ability than verbal ability. Harshman, Hampson, and Berenbaum (1983) also provided converging evidence to support their conclusion that these results reflect neurological organization. (Cognitive differences were associated with familial sinistrality [family history of left handedness], hand posture during writing, and ear of asymmetry in the dichotic listening task. Further discussion about this ancillary evidence is beyond the scope of this chapter, but interested readers are referred to their research report.)

You may be wondering why reasoning or intellectual ability should be important in mediating these results. Harshman, Hampson, and Berenbaum believe that certain brain organizations promote high reasoning ability and that by dividing their data into reasoning ability subsets, they have produced homogeneous subsets that allow them to investigate "how sex and handedness differences in brain organization impose various hardware trade-offs that produce better performance on one type of task, at the cost of reduced performance on a different type of task" (p. 182).

Numerous studies have reported sex by handedness interactions in cognition

TABLE 5.1
Summarization of Sex by Handedness by Reasoning Ability Interactions
(Harshman, Hampson, and Berenbaum, 1983)

Spatial Ability

Subjects with high reasoning ability
males > females
left-handed males < right-handed males
left-handed females > right-handed females
Subjects with low reasoning ability
males > females
no consistent sex by handedness effects

Verbal Ability

Subjects with high reasoning ability
females > males on selected tests
left-handed males > right-handed males
left-handed females < right-handed females
Subjects with low reasoning ability
no consistent sex by handedness effects

Note: > should read "better than"
< should read "worse than"

(e.g., Gottfried & Bathurst, 1983; McGhee, 1976; Yen, 1975). O'Boyle and Benbow (1990) reviewed the literature on sex and handedness effects on cognitive tasks. From a highly complex group of studies, they concluded that "In sum, differences in cognitive abilities are seemingly influenced by underlying patterns of cerebral lateralization, which may in turn be related to hand dominance . . . sex . . . and level of reasoning ability" (p. 356). Interested readers are referred to the excellent review of this area by O'Boyle and Benbow.

These results suggest that Levy was correct in her belief that sex and handedness (as an index of laterality) would be important determinants of the pattern of cognitive abilities; however, she underestimated the complexity of the relationship in her earlier work. It is reasonable to assume that the California Institute of Technology graduate students that she employed as subjects in her 1969 study were high in reasoning/intellectual ability and thus showed the pattern of cognitive results Harshman, Hampson, and Berenbaum found in their high ability group. Additional work by Levy (Levy & Gur, 1980) corroborate these results with "high reasoners."

Lewis and Harris (1990) recently tested the Cognitive Crowding Hypothesis with respect to spatial ability. For their sample of "high intelligence" subjects, they found that left-handed females performed significantly better on four different tests of spatial ability than right-handed females (confirming Harshman, Hampson, & Berenbaum), and that left-handed males performed significantly lower on two tests (out of four) of spatial ability than right-handed males (partially confirming Harshman, Hampson, & Berenbaum). The verbal part of the cognitive crowding hypothesis was indirectly confirmed by Benbow (1988). Recall that she has collected data on tens of thousands of extremely intelligent adolescents. The very highest incidence of left-handedness was among verbally gifted males, a result that conforms to predictions of sex by handedness interactions.

There have been numerous other studies that point to the importance of sex by handedness interactions in understanding the way cognitive abilities differ. Some studies have examined familial sinistrality or family history of left-handedness as an indicator of laterality and have found that sex by familial sinistrality or sex by familial sinistrality by handedness interactions are significant factors in cognitive ability (McKeever & Van Deventer, 1977; Piazza, 1980, for auditory tasks, but not for visual tasks; Tinkcom, Obrzut, & Poston, 1983, for nonverbal dichaptic tasks; Yeo & Cohen, 1983, for spatial tasks, but not verbal tasks). Two studies that addressed the relative importance of sex and handedness in predicting cognitive abilities concluded that handedness is the more important factor (Johnson & Harley, 1980; Nagae, 1985), although it is difficult to determine exactly what that means in a given context.

Although sex by handedness interactions are complicated, most of the time they follow the pattern shown in Table 5.1. Numerous investigators have reported that results need to be interpreted in light of both the sex of the subjects and her or his handedness (Corballis & Sergent, 1989; Gordon, 1980; Kee,

Gottfried, Bathurst, & Brown, 1987; McKeever, 1986; Neils & Aram, 1986; Nyborg, 1983; Voyer & Bryden, 1990). Results also seem to depend on intellectual (or reasoning) level. It seems that answers to all of the important questions in psychology require a qualifying "it depends" or "sometimes." At least among those who are high in intellectual ability, left-handed men seem to be poorer in spatial ability than right-handed men, and left-handed females higher in spatial ability than right-handed females; however, these results are still tentative and probably best considered as a "working hypothesis."

Are There Monthly Variations in Cerebral Lateralization?

In the last chapter I presented some recent research that showed small variations in manual dexterity and speech fluency that varied over the menstrual cycle. Some researchers have wondered if there are monthly variations in cerebral lateralization for menstruating women. Recall that during the menstrual phase of the cycle, estrogen and progesterone are available in very small amounts, and during midcycle, they are available in large amounts. Is there any evidence that during menstruation women's patterns of brain organization are more male-typical (larger differences between the hemispheres) than during midcycle?

As predicted from this theory, Heister, Landis, Regard, and Schroeder-Heister (1989) found the largest male-typical patterns of lateralization during menstruation when the female hormones are low. But this difference was only found for some tasks (large right hemisphere superiority during menstruation relative to a small left hemisphere superiority during the midcycle phase when the task was face perception, but not when the task was determining whether a string of letters formed a word). There is clearly not enough evidence to support any meaningful conclusion at this time. It is only within the last few years that any menstrually related cognitive differences have been reported. We still need much more confirmation of reports that cognitive abilities vary over the menstrual cycle before we can determine if monthly variations in cerebral lateralization are responsible for this effect. I am certain that there will be a flurry of research on this question over the next 5 to 10 years. Until then, the conclusion will have to be that there is no strong evidence to support this idea.

SEX DIFFERENCES
WITHIN EACH CEREBRAL HEMISPHERE

Brain researchers who are opposed to the notion that there are sex differences in cerebral lateralization posit other ways in which male and female brains differ that could explain cognitive sex differences. One concept that they all agree on is that sex differentiation of the brain is a more subtle and more complex process than sex differentiation of the genitals (Goy, Bercovitch, & McBrair, 1988).

Kimura (1987) has completed a fascinating set of studies over a 10 year time span that show sex differences within the hemispheres that she believes can explain some of the usual cognitive results. She examined a large sample of patients selected from individuals with brain damage to only one hemisphere. She looked at the kind of disability that resulted and the area of the brain that was damaged. (I am greatly simplifying her work. This is an engrossing article that I recommend to interested readers.) Kimura concluded that the language areas in the female brain are more focally organized in the left hemisphere (specifically the anterior or frontal region), whereas the language areas in the male brain are more diffusely organized, also in the left hemisphere. Kimura cited corroborating work by other investigators working in other laboratories. She also found even sharper sex differences when she examined the brain areas responsible for manual dexterity. Recall from chapter 3 that most studies report that females are better on many tasks of dexterity than males. Kimura found that the area of the brain that seems especially important in manual dexterity is also more focal (less spread out) than the corresponding area in males. She concluded that there is "no evidence in the clinical findings of a more . . . bilateral organization for speech and related praxic functions in women" (p. 140). (Praxia [or praxic] is the formal word for what I am calling manual dexterity.)

Kimura bolstered her argument by noting that the anterior regions of the left hemisphere are larger in female brains during the first two trimesters of prenatal development. Thus, she also ties her theory of sex differences within each hemisphere of the brain to prenatal development. Other researchers have identified the left central portion of the brain as critical in language. Recent research that has examined the brains of dyslexics using modern imaging methods (CAT scans and magnetic resonance) has shown that the brains of dyslexics are more symmetrical and smaller in these areas than the brains of normal readers (Hynd & Semrud-Clikeman, 1990). (For readers who have had a basic course in physiology or in the neurosciences, the areas involved are regions in the left planum temporale and parietooccipital cortex. These are the areas that are involved in phonological coding, language comprehension, and auditory perception. The names of the specific regions will have little meaning unless you have already studied these brain areas in other coursework.) Thus, this is a body of research that supports the concept that male and female brains differ in the way cognitive functions are represented within each hemisphere and not in differences between the hemispheres.

THE CORPUS CALLOSUM AS THE LOCUS
OF SEX-RELATED BRAIN DIFFERENCES

A third theory of sex differences in male and female brains targets the thick band of neural fibers that connect the two hemispheres as the most important sexually differentiated region. Most of the research that has adopted this position was conducted with experiments on nonhuman mammals and from brain measurements taken during autopsies. Investigators have found that if they administer testosterone to newly born female rats, the corpus callosum becomes larger—a typical male-rat brain finding—and when pregnant females rats are given an anti-androgen, the size of the corpus callosum of their male offspring becomes smaller—a typical female-rat brain finding (Denenberg, Berrebi, & Fitch, 1988; Fitch, Berrebi, Cowell, Schrott, & Denenberg, in press). It seems clear that for rats, the corpus callosum is larger in the male and that the size differences is caused by prenatal sex hormones. This research is particularly important because it is one of the first experimental demonstrations that ovarian hormones play an active role in organizing the fetal brain in a female direction. Virtually all of the earlier research has emphasized the importance of androgens in prenatal development. We now know that ovarian hormones also play an important role in prenatal brain development.

There has been much controversy over whether the corpus callosum is also sexually differentiated in humans. Researchers who have found sex differences in the corpus callosum report that they are largest in the posterior portions (Kimura, 1987) and that for humans, the corpus callosum is larger in females (Adler, 1989a; Kimura, 1987; Witelson, 1989). Furthermore, in a recent study by Hines (cited in Adler, 1989a), she found that among women, those with the larger splenium (the area involved) performed better on three separate tests of verbal fluency.

Some of the researchers related the finding that human females have a larger corpus callosum to the theory that females have a more bilateral brain organization. The corpus callosum is the main tract of neural fibers that connect the right and left cerebral hemispheres. Thus, this finding could be used to support the idea that female brains are less lateralized than male brains because the two hemispheres "communicate" more effectively over a larger corpus callosum. Other researchers believe that the important sex differences in the brain are found in the corpus callosum and that this is a separate theory, independent of the theory of sex-related lateralization patterns.

Researchers also report size differences in the corpus callosum for right- and left-handers. Witelson (1989) reported that left-handers had larger corpus callosum that right-handers. Thus, the left-hander's brain is similar to the female brain with respect to the size of the corpus callosum. In Hines' (1990) extensive review of 13 empirical studies pertaining to sex differences in the size of the corpus callosum, she concluded that most of the studies found that a particular region of the corpus callosum is larger (relative to brain weight) in female humans than in male humans. She believes that a larger corpus callosum is associated with better interhemispheric transfer of information, which contributes to verbal fluency. In other words, females, in general, are better than males, in general, in verbal fluency *because* females have a larger and more efficient corpus callosum.

I have summarized the three theories of cerebral sex differences in Table 5.2. It should be useful at this point to look over Table 5.2 and to consider how the theories differ.

TABLE 5.2
Summary of Theories of Sex Differences in the Organization and Structure of the Brain

Sex Differences in Lateralization

This is really a class of theories with the underlying premise that female brains are more symmetrically organized for cognitive functions (called a more bilateral organization) and male brains are more asymmetrically organized (called a more lateralized organization)

—Cogitive Crowding is one theory of how male and female brains differ in lateralization. According to this theory, female brains are more likely to have verbal ability represented in both hemispheres with visual ability sharing neural space with verbal abilities in the right hemisphere; male brains are more likely to have the left hemisphere devoted exclusively to verbal abilities and the right hemisphere devoted exclusively to spatial abilities.

—Prenatal hormones have been suggested as the cause of sex differences in lateralization. According to this hypothesis, high levels of male prenatal hormones slow neuronal growth in the left hemisphere. The result is a male-typical brain pattern with more right-hemisphere dominance among males than among females.

—Maturation rates at puberty have also been suggested as the cause of sex differences in lateralization with early maturers less lateralized than late maturers. (Girls tend to mature earlier than boys.) There is very little support for the maturation rate hypothesis.

—Brain researchers are divided about whether they believe that there are sex differences in lateralization. While there is some good evidence for this distinction, there is also a large body of research that does not conform to this hypothesis. If there are sex differences in lateralization, these differences will depend on a host of moderating variables including handedness and intellectual level.

Intrahemispheric Sex Differences

Sex differences in the organization of cognitive abilities within each hemisphere have also been proposed. There is some evidence that these functions are more focally organized in female brains and more diffusely organized in male brains. Much more research is needed to determine if this finding replicates well.

Size of the Corpus Callosum

The corpus callosum, the thick band of neural fibers that connect the right and left hemisphere, has also been suggested as the site of sex differences in brain structures. The usual finding is that the posterior portion of the corpus callosum is larger in human females than in human males. Much more research is needed to determine if this is a reliable brain difference, and if so, if it has any importance for cognitive functioning.

SOME TENTATIVE CONCLUSIONS
ABOUT SEX-RELATED BRAIN DIFFERENCES

Although current researchers have made obvious progress in unraveling the tangle of brain and sex variables, there are still many knotty issues that have to be resolved before a strong theory of sex-differentiated brain functioning is posited. A falsifiable theory that can account for the diverse nature of the experimental results is still needed. Numerous questions still remain to be answered. What are the principles of brain organization that can account for results that are only found among "high reasoning" subjects? Why are there so many glaring inconsistencies in the data? How does familial sinistrality fit into the cognitive sex differences literature? What is the role of genes in determining cerebral laterality? Can we meaningfully answer questions about the functioning of such a complex organ as the human brain by examining its structure and organization? A fundamental question that is addressed in the final chapter of this book is, "How and when does experience alter brain structure and organization?"

Three different theories with several variations on them have been proposed. Some conclusions about sex-related brain differences are in order at this point. Based on current data, there are some differences in brain organization and structure that, on the average, vary by sex. This conclusion is in no way meant to imply that men cannot write poetry or that women cannot be architects or mathematicians because their brains are not "wired" for these tasks. Obviously, there are outstanding male poets and female architects, and the number of women in the natural sciences and mathematics is increasing dramatically; these are facts that can't be explained on the basis of brain differences. Environmental and sex role influences on cognitive sex differences are discussed in the next two chapters, and their importance in directing how we develop our cognitive abilities cannot be overestimated.

Despite the importance of environmental influences, there is no reason to believe that sex role pressures or other environmental pressures are different for right- and left-handed individuals. The fact that cognitive ability results depended on both sex and handedness is difficult to explain with a strictly environmental theory. The only plausible explanation of the sex by handedness interactions found by Harshman, Hampson, and Berenbaum and others is that they are reflective of underlying neurological differences. This is obviously an incendiary topic, and the possibility that these conclusions will be misused poses a serious concern to anyone who is concerned with prejudice and discrimination. The practical effect of sex differences in cerebral lateralization needs to be interpreted in a societal context in which skills and abilities are prized and encouraged in a sex-differentiated manner.

It is important to note that not all reviewers agree with the conclusion that there are sex differences in brain organization and structure. For a dissenting view, the reader is referred to a commentary by Janowsky (1989) that she titled, "Dispelling the Myth of Sexual Dimorphism in the Human Brain." She argues that we do not know enough about the complex network of neural structures that underlie cognitive processes to conclude that these structures differ between males and females. It is also part of the popular *Zeitgeist* to dismiss the possibility that biological differences are involved in sex-related cognitive differences. Social psychologists are often averse to any biological explanations of behavior, and many recent texts on female and male differences and similarities devote very little space to biological theories (e.g., Matlin, 1987).

I believe that the research reviewed in this chapter provides strong evidence for the conclusion that there are sex differences in the human brain that underlie cognition, although we are a long way from understanding the organ that is responsible for all we know and do.

CRITIQUE OF BIOLOGICAL HYPOTHESES

Why are so many people opposed to any biological theory of cognitive sex differences? Benbow (1988, 1990) has been the object of vituperative criticism because she has documented a large sex difference in the SAT-M favoring males among highly gifted adolescents and because she suggested that both endogenous and exogenous factors are involved in creating this difference. Perhaps we can understand some of the intense emotions generated by biologically based theories by examining their weaknesses.

Biological and Environmental Interactions

It is likely that sex-related brain differences result from or are influenced by sex-differentiated patterns of socialization. Most of the biological theories discussed in this chapter have either failed to consider or have down played the fact that biology and the environment interact. For example, while it is possible that males are better at spatial skills because their cerebral organization is more lateralized than that of females, it might also be possible that *because* males excel at spatial skills or perform them more frequently, their hemispheres develop a more lateralized organization. Similarly, we know that young girls receive more verbal stimulation and are encouraged to read and speak correctly. (These data are described more fully in the next chapter.) Their early reliance on verbal skills could cause verbal skills to be developed at the expense of other types of abilities such as spatial skills. Although the possibility that life experiences influence biological processes such as brain lateralization must be considered, it is also clear that biology influences the types of experiences to which people are exposed. For example, if boys are better than girls at spatial tasks for biological reasons, parents could differentially encourage this ability by buying them spatial toys (e.g., puzzles, erector sets), which in turn provides them with more experience with spatial manipulations than their sisters would receive. Numerous other examples are possible.

As an example of how difficult it is to disentangle biological from environmental influences, consider the following problem that has come to be known as the "20th-century conundrum." Over the last two generations, girls have begun menstruating at an earlier age than their mothers, who experienced earlier menarche than their mothers (Frisch, 1983). Although no one is really sure why this has been happening, it is probably related to improved nutrition, sanitation, and change in work environments. According to Waber (1977), early menarche implies early physical maturation, which is related to bilateral cerebral organization. Taken to its logical conclusion, we would have to conclude that the improved living conditions of the 20th century have been detrimental to women's spatial ability! This is an unsatisfactory conclusion because it implies that conditions that are good for women's physical development are bad for their intellectual development. In addition, early menarche among 20th-century girls would also predict that the current generation of young women are less good at spatial skills than their mothers, who in turn are less good at spatial skills than their mothers. All of the evidence suggests the reverse: Today's young women are better at spatial tasks than previous generations of women. Women have been entering traditional academic fields that require these skills at increasing rates over the last 20 years. Almost all engineering and architecture schools report that the proportions of women have increased substantially since the Women's Movement began in the 1960s. Biological explanations cannot account for this phenomenon.

On the other hand, psychosocial variables cannot account for all of the data presented in this chapter. The strongest case for the importance of biological variables comes from the sex by handedness interactions described earlier in this chapter (Harshman, Hampson, & Berenbaum, 1983). In a large scale study with three separate samples, cognitive abilities for women and men differed as a function of whether they were right- or left-handed. These results are interpretable only if handedness is accepted as an index of hemisphere organization. There is no plausible reason to believe that sex roles or any other psychosocial variables differ for right- and left-handed individuals of either sex. It is more plausible to interpret these results as at least partly due to sex differences in cerebral lateralization. A strong theory of brain organization that can relate lateralization differences to sex and cognitive abilities is still needed.

Quantitative Abilities

You may have been wondering why I have not mentioned quantitative or mathematical abilities in this chapter. The reason is that there are no good theories of sex-related brain differences that can account for the finding that females excel at computation during early development and males score higher on some tests of mathematical reasoning abilities such as the SAT-M. Gardner (1983) has used the fact that there are idiot savants with exceptional mathematical skill as evidence that mathematics is a distinct, localizable intellectual ability, but mathematical ability is difficult to localize. Some mathematical problems are largely verbal in nature, such as some word problems, and others are clearly spatial in nature, such as some geometry problems. Mathematics educators believe that mental representations of math ideas are coded in a nonverbal form that is most probably spatial (Davis, 1986).

A severe mathematics disability called acalculia is usually found when there is left hemisphere damage, and dyscalculia, the mathematics analogue to dyslexia, frequently accompanies severe language disorders (Spiers, 1987). Damage to the right hemisphere frequently causes difficulties in developing spatial relations, a skill that is fundamental in mathematics. Thus, we can conclude that mathematics requires the use of both right and left hemispheres, so lateralization theories cannot be useful in understanding sex differences in mathematics. Mathematical abilities do not divide neatly into categories. For now, psychosocial explanations are much more plausible in explaining sex differences in mathematics. They are discussed in the next chapter.

The Notion of Optimal Cerebral Organization, Optimal Hormone Balance, and Optimal Genetic Configuration

All of the biological theories began with the notion that there is a single optimal organization of hemisphere specialization, or an optimal hormone balance, or even an optimal genetic pattern that is associated with cognitive excellence. None of these theories consider the multidimensional nature of verbal and spatial tasks. Why should a single biological configuration be ideal for spatial visualization and spatial orientation tasks or for spelling, verbal reasoning, and language comprehension?

It may even be that an optimal organization for males is not optimal for females. Perhaps bilateral organization is best when the hormone concentrations are female and lateralized cerebral organization is best when the hormone concentrations are male. The finding that males tend to be more lateralized and better at spatial tasks does not mean that they are better at spatial tasks *because* they are more lateralized. They could be better at spatial tasks for environmental reasons and more lateralized for unrelated biological reasons. It does not necessarily follow that lateralization is the optimal brain organization for spatial ability because it is found more frequently in the sex that tends to have better spatial ability.

Much of the research on identifying the "best" brain, or hormone, or genetic pattern has been conducted with people with abnormalities in these biological systems. For example, the hypothesis that a minimal level of androgens must be present at puberty in order for spatial ability to develop was supported solely on research with males with abnormally low levels of these hormones (Hier & Crowley, 1982). How can we justify extrapolating these results to normal males and especially to normal females? In short, the notion that there exists a single best biology for the development of cognitive abilities needs to be questioned.

Intervening Variables

It is also possible that biology affects the development of cognitive skills in indirect ways that are generally not considered by proponents of the biological theories. Evidence was provided in the last chapter for the position that aggressive behavior is, at least in part, under hormonal control. Research with lower animals has clearly shown a link between prenatal hormones and later aggressive behavior and energy levels. Although the research reviewed with humans is less clear, there is still good reason to believe that prenatal and possibly postnatal hormones play a role in human aggression and activity levels. Suppose that males tend to be more active because of higher levels of prenatal hormones. Individuals who are more active would be expected to develop better spatial skills because they move around the environment more often, roam farther at an earlier age, and interact with more objects. Thus, there could be biological reasons for sex differences in cognitive abilities, but they could be different from those being investigated.

A second intervening variable that could mediate between biology and environment is body type. Consider the notion that early maturing adolescents have poorer spatial skills than late-maturing adolescents (Waber, 1976, 1977). As Waber pointed out, early maturing adolescents may not only have different patterns of cerebral lateralization, they also have different social environments. Shapely seventh-grade girls and tall muscular seventh-grade boys are responded to differently than their less developed peers. This could cause them to consider their math and science classes less seriously and create or increase differences in these areas that correlate with maturation rate. Support for these hypotheses is examined in the following chapter.

Body type is also a likely intervening variable for individuals with genetic or hormonal abnormalities. Much of the research in this area has used Turner's women to support or refute biological arguments. As stated earlier, these women have unfeminine body types (small breasts, thick necks). Their body type could cause them, consciously or unconsciously, to exaggerate feminine traits including eschewing stereotypically masculine cognitive skills. Hier and Crowley's (1982) research on minimal androgen levels utilized males with underdeveloped testes. Although the finding that they are poorer on "masculine" tasks goes against the idea that they attempted to compensate for their feminine body type, it does seem likely that they sought certain experiences that would help them adjust to their body type. It is difficult to know how these special experiences affected their cognitive growth.

Differences and Deficiencies

Many people are concerned that if we concede that there are sex differences in the "underlying hardware" of human thought, then those who are anxious to keep women out of nontraditional occupations will use this finding to justify discrimination. Weisstein (1982) offered a stern and wise caveat when she said, "Biology has always been used as a curse against women" (p. 41). It is important to keep in mind that sex differences are not synonymous with sexism. The empirical research that has been reviewed in this chapter is not anti-female. It is neither misogynist nor antifeminist to report that, on the average, males have superior spatial ability and females have superior verbal ability and that some of these differences could be biologically based. It could even be argued that these results are more pro-female because verbal abilities are needed in every academic field and every endeavor in life, and it seems that females have a small advantage for some verbal abilities.

It is also important to keep in mind that although the major focus of this book and research in this area is on sex differences, similarities are more often the rule. In McGlone's (1980) review of the cerebral asymmetry literature, she concluded that "thus, one must not overlook perhaps the most basic conclusion, which is that basic patterns of male and female brain asymmetry seem to be more similar than they are different" (p. 226). Perhaps the most striking finding from all of the neuropsychological research is the overwhelming number of similarities between the sexes and the relatively few sex differences that have emerged.

We know that there are sex differences in cognitive abilities, sex hormone concentrations, and probably patterns of cerebral organization. There are also undisputable sex differences in the reproductive organs and genitals. No one would argue that either sex has the better reproductive organs or genitals. They are clearly different, but neither sex would be considered deficient in these biological organs. However, when cognitive differences are considered there is sometimes an implicit notion that one sex will be found better than the other. Is it better to be high in verbal skills or spatial skills? This is a moot question. The answer depends on the type of task that needs to be performed, the quantification of how much better, and individual predilection. To argue that female hormones are better than male hormones or that male brains are better than female brains is as silly as arguing which sex has the better genitals. It seems almost embarrassing and obvious to state that neither sex has the better biology for intellectual ability and that differences should not be confused with deficits.

Readers have probably noticed that a majority of the biological hypotheses have been concerned with sex differences in spatial ability. Only a few addressed the differences in verbal ability, a fact that some reviewers have seen as basically sexist (Sherman, 1979). The greater concern with spatial ability is probably due to two factors: (a) sex differences are greatest for spatial tasks, and (b) they appear more often in the biological investigations. (Males with low levels of androgens at puberty showed low levels of spatial ability with no impairment of verbal ability, for example.)

When it comes to biological explanations for cognitive processes, we still have more questions than answers. It remains the task of future scientists—both females and males—to ask questions and formulate answers about the mutual influences of biology and cognition.

CHAPTER SUMMARY

There are no sex differences in the size (adjusted for body weight), weight, or complexity of male and female brains. The theory that has generated the most research in this area posits sex differences in the way the hemispheres are lateralized or specialized for cognitive tasks. According to this theory, male brains are more lateralized and female brains are more symmetrical in terms of the areas that are responsible for cognition. The Cognitive Crowding Hypothesis specifies the way the brains are lateralized—males maintain verbal abilities in one hemisphere and spatial in the other. By contrast, females have neural space dedicated for verbal abilities in both hemispheres and spatial abilities in one hemisphere. This means that spatial abilities get "crowded out" for females. This theory goes on to associate the brain patterns of left-handers as more similar to the female brain pattern.

Some theorists have identified prenatal sex hormones as responsible for these sexually dimorphic patterns of lateralization. Specifically, high levels of prenatal testosterone slow neuronal growth in the left hemisphere, which results in an increased incidence of right hemisphere dominance among males. Other psychologists have suggested that maturation rate during adolescence was an important determinant of sex differences in lateralization, but this theory has not been borne out.

Other theories of sex-related brain differences suggest that there are important differences in the way cognitive abilities are organized within each hemisphere and that the size of the corpus callosum is the most important sex-related brain difference. It is also likely that basic biological influences are modified by environmental factors such that experience alters or enhances between-sex brain differences. Theorists are strongly divided over which of these theories they believe is most likely correct.

Our current knowledge of biological–cognitive influences remains sketchy and largely incomplete. Even those theories that have received empirical support remain open to criticism on methodological and logical grounds. Readers and researchers are urged to avoid interpreting sex differences as a cognitive deficiency for either sex.

6 Psychosocial Hypotheses Part I: Sex Role Stereotypes Through the Life Span

6

THE IMPORTANCE
OF PSYCHOSOCIAL VARIABLES

May you be the mother of a hundred sons.
—traditional Indian blessing (and title of a book by Bumiller, 1990, that
depicts the life of Indian women)

If you have been reading the chapters in order and just finished the preceding two chapters that examined biological hypotheses as possible explanations of the sex differences in cognitive abilities, you probably spent much of the time considering alternative hypotheses. Whenever I teach this material to college classes, I always find that there are students who simply cannot wait to point out the ways in which differing life experiences for males and females could be used to explain the data. Hypotheses that favor the nurture side of the nature—nurture controversy are considered in this and in the following chapter. These two approaches are synthesized, and conclusions about the relative merits of each are presented in the concluding chapter.

There is little doubt that environmental and social factors play a major role in the cognitive development of every member in our society. The crucial question for the purpose of understanding cognitive sex differences is, "How and how much do the socialization practices and other life experiences that differ for males and females influence the ability to perform intellectual tasks?" Of course, this question is based on the assumption that life experiences differ in systematic ways depending on biological sex. I have found that some people are willing to accept this assumption at face value, taking it as a statement of the obvious, and eager to consider the ramifications of these differences. Others, however, believe that sex differentiated socialization practices are a "thing of the past." These people believe the magazine and billboard ads that proclaim, "You've come a long way baby!" The underlying message is that contemporary women do the same sorts of things that men do, and sex-related differences in life experiences are either inconsequential or nonexistent. It is ironic to note the subtle influence of language as typified in this slogan that supposedly announces sexual equality.

If women had, in fact, "come a long way," then they would not be referred to as infants or children, just as Black men are no longer called "boy." (These ads, which you probably recognize, are designed to sell cigarettes. The incidence of lung cancer among women is now almost as high as that of men. The ad is correct with respect to lung cancer. Women have come a long way, but in this case, in the wrong direction.)

If anyone doubts that women and men still tend to live sex-segregated lives in contemporary American society, a casual visit to a PTA meeting, or the restaurant in a large department store midweek, or a trade union hall, or a corporate engineering department will attest to the fact that while changes in the societal roles of women and men are occurring, there are still considerable differences in men's and women's experiences. High school cheerleaders are still virtually all female while shop classes remain virtually all male. Few girls play in the now "coed" little league games (especially in the high school leagues), and few boys elect to take home economics classes. Despite all of the efforts of those associated with the "women's movement," de facto sex-related life differences are alive and well.

Implications of Psychosocial Explanations

If we can use psychological and social explanations to understand cognitive sex differences, then the possibility of reducing or eliminating these differences is quite real. On the other hand, if we find that we are unable to explain these differences with psychosocial explanations, then there is little hope of being able to alter them by changing learning environments, attitudes, or educational and employment opportunities. Thus, the primary importance of psychosocial hypotheses is not in their heuristic value or for the development of some abstract theoretical model, but in the promise they hold for changing the status quo. Of course, if you are a champion of the status quo, then they are equally important, but for you they would represent a threat. In either case, the implications are clear. Psychosocial hypotheses devised to explain the origin of cognitive sex differences have important ramifications for the ways we want society to change or remain the same as we approach the 21st century.

Nonconscious Ideology

Perhaps one of the reasons for the tendency to underestimate sex differentiated experiences, messages, and expectations is that these differences are so prevalent and so ingrained in American life that we are often blind to them. In fact, for most of us, it is hard to imagine a society in which they didn't exist. Bem and Bem (1976) have coined the term *nonconscious ideology* to describe this situation. We are simply unaware of the pervasiveness of sex differentiated practices. They have said that we are all like fish who are unaware that the water is wet. The clothes we wear, the way we furnish our rooms, the toys we were given as children, the hobbies we pursue, the salaries we receive at our jobs, the magazines we read, the household chores we perform, the language we use, and countless other examples all show differences between the sexes. Part of this nonconscious ideology is an unstated assumption that the male is norm and any departures from a male pattern of results are deviant.

In 1988, a much publicized study showing that aspirin helps to prevent heart attacks made media headlines (Roan, 1990). This finding was heralded for its potential for extending life. But, there was one big problem with this ballyhooed research—all of the 22,071 research participants were men. We simply do not know whether aspirin will work the same way in women because there were no women in the clinical trials. This is only one example of an expensive medical study with health implications for both women and men that excluded women. It reflects an underlying attitude that what is male is normative.

There are countless other examples of the way American and other Western societies have nonconsciously adopted sex differentiated practices. We expect to see little girls in the advertisements for Barbie dolls and little boys depicted on boxes that contain train sets and, therefore, never stop to consider the powerful messages they convey about sex appropriate interests and behavior. I remember receiving a prize for serving as president of my high school's honor society. I was delighted with the bracelet I was given. I knew all of the previous honor society presidents were male, and all of them had received a six-volume set of books by Winston Churchill. Yet, it had never occurred to me that the choice of this particular gift was an excellent example of sex differences in socialization practices. It wasn't until many years later that I was struck with the irony of the gift. Like most other people, I was simply unaware of the numerous subtle and not so subtle practices in our sex differentiated society.

The Words We Use.   Consider, for example, the simple matter of the grammatically correct use of the pronoun "he" to mean he or she (or she or he). Somewhere in junior or senior high school, we were all taught that the grammatically correct singular pronoun when sex is unknown is "he." Thus, it is grammatically correct to say, "Everyone should do his homework." There have been many objections to the use of "he" to mean "he or she." The use of "he" to refer to either sex has become known as the "generic he" to signify that its use is much like the use of generic labels for supermarket canned goods. One argument against changing from the generic he to either "s/he" or novel terms (e.g., te or E) is that the issue is trivial and of no real significance. Detractors have humorously labeled this debate as a case of "pronoun envy," a take off on Freud's theory of penis envy as a major determinant of sex differences. Research has shown, however, that the issue is far from trivial. MacKay (1983) has studied the use of the generic "he" to determine its psychological significance. He has estimated that the generic "he" is used over million times throughout an individual's lifetime. In addition, he found that people tend to think of a male whenever the pronoun "he" is used. It is clearly not a sex-neutral or generic term from a psychological perspective.

Consider this example of the subtle biasing effect that masculine pronouns can have:

> Because students are most familiar with the ways of the college professor, many choose academic careers which can range from the research scientist involved with man's search for knowledge to the psychologist trying to help solve his client's problems. . . . The average corporate businessman probably earns at least twice the salary of the college prof, yet he probably has half the education. (example taken from a study of gender-biased language by Murdock and Forsyth, 1985, p. 39)

There is now a considerable body of evidence that people tend to think of males, and not males and females, when they encounter terms like the *generic he*. Hamilton (1988) concluded from her study on the use of masculine generics that "use of the masculine generic pronoun per se increases male bias" (p. 785).

Do phrases like, "No woman is an island" or "Now is the time for all good women to come to the aid of their party" seem strange to you? One study on the use of the generic "he" found that high school women were less likely to respond to a job advertisement that used the pronoun "he" in its description than they were to respond to a similar ad that used the pronoun "she" (Bem & Bem, 1973). I remember once reading about the hardships encountered by early American pioneers and their wives. The nonconscious implication is that the women were not pioneers in the same sense that the men were.

If you still doubt that the English language conveys a strong male bias, try this: Ask several friends to provide the correct singular terms for (a) a married couple, (b) children, (c) siblings, (d) royalty, (e) the first humans named in the Bible, and (f) people who give parties. See how people give you these terms in the word order in which we expect to hear them—that is, the male term first: (a) husband and wife, (b) sons and daughters, (c) brother and sister, (d) king and queen, (e) Adam and Eve, (f) host and hostess. It must be more than coincidence that most people name the male title first.

Similarly, men are addressed as "Mr." throughout their adult lives, irrespective of their marital status; yet, women have traditionally been addressed in relation to the men they marry and carry either the title of "Miss" or "Mrs." There are still many people who object to the use of the marriage-irrelevant title of "Ms" for women. Smith (1985) noted that there are no feminine-oriented generics for terms like "bachelor's degree," "brotherhood," "mankind," "spokesman," and "workmanlike."

Socialization practices are also reflected in what and how much we say. For example, in an investigation of the nature of parents' speech to their toddler children, O'Brien and Nagel (1987) found that when children of both sexes play with dolls (a typical female toy), their parents provide more opportunities to learn and practice language than when they play with trucks and cars (typical male toys) and shape sorters (sex-neutral toys). These authors argue that young girls receive more language practice and encouragement than young boys because girls play with dolls much more often than boys do. Other evidence of sex differences in adults' conversations with children was reported by Wells (1986). Wells found that when adults talk to boys they encourage "a more free-ranging exploratory manipulation of the physical environment," whereas, in discussions with girls, adults emphasize domestic activities (p. 123).

Causal Statements and Psychosocial Research.   Critics of this sort of research are quick to point out that results like these cannot be used to explain causality because they are correlational in nature; that is, we cannot determine if children act in sex-differentiated ways because of the language we use, or if we use sex-differentiated language because children act in sex-differentiated ways. I discussed the limitations of correlational research in chapter 2, and it is instructive to reconsider correlational research in this context. Although it can be more difficult to establish causality with social variables because we cannot assign people at random to different social situations, it is not possible. We can look to other societies, as well as to variations with a particular society, to illuminate the relationship between social variables and sex differences. For example, we could compare children who live in the same neighborhood and attend the same school, but differ in the way their families encourage or discourage sex-role stereotypic behaviors. As you read about the psychosocial research that has been conducted on cognitive sex differences, be sure to keep these criticisms in mind and be as tough a critic as you undoubtedly were for the biological hypotheses.

SEX ROLES AND SEX ROLE STEREOTYPES

Girls' play involves dressing and grooming and acting out their future—going on a date, getting married—and boys' play involves competition and conflict.
—Glenn Bozarth (spokesperson for Mattel Inc. quoted in *New Women* 1990, p. 20)

A *stereotype* is "a relatively rigid and oversimplified conception of a group of people in which all individuals in the group are labeled with the so-called group

SALLY FORTH. Reprinted with special permission of Greg Howard and North America Syndicate. All rights reserved.

characteristics" (Wrightsman, 1977, p. 672). As a society, we have stereotypes about racial groups (e.g., "Blacks are musical"), nations (e.g., "The Scots are thrifty"), sports groups (e.g., "Football players are dumb"), people who wear eyeglasses, New Yorkers, redheads, obese people, cellists, Republicans, and so on. Any of these stereotypes can influence interactions, feelings, and expectations. Sex role stereotypes are those stereotypes that relate to differences between the sexes. For the purposes of this discussion, the term *sex role stereotypes* is used to encompass widely held assumptions about what females and males are like, as well as what they should be like. Sometimes authors make a distinction between these two components of the term *sex role stereotypes* (e.g., Eagly, 1987). Two questions concerning sex role stereotypes that have been raised are: Is there any evidence that they exist, and if so, can these stereotypes be used to understand sex differences in cognitive ability?

What are the stereotypes about women and men that exist in North America today? This question has been researched extensively by psychologists, sociologists, and others during the last several decades. In the numerous studies that have been conducted (Broverman et al., 1972; Intons-Peterson, 1988; Spence, Helmreich, & Stapp, 1974), two distinct clusters of traits have emerged: In general, (a) male stereotypic traits suggest competence and task orientation, a cluster of traits sometimes known as "instrumental," whereas (b) female stereotypic traits suggest warmth and expressiveness.

More recent studies of sex role stereotypes have gone beyond the notion that certain traits or characteristics are associated exclusively with being male or female. Deaux (1984), for example, examined the relative frequency with which traits are associated with either sex. As shown in Table 6.1, some characteristics are believed to be found more often in one sex or the other. Consider, for example, the role of "financial provider." According to Deaux's results, we expect about 83% of all males to be financial providers, whereas we expect only about 47% of females to assume this role. These data indicate that sex role stereotypes are alive and well in contemporary American society; however, instead of being attributed in an all-or-none fashion, most people acknowledge that there may be overlap between the sexes with regard to these characteristics.

A similar approach to understanding the attributes that constitute sex role stereotypes was taken by Intons-Peterson (1988). The purpose of her study was to compare sex role beliefs of Americans with those of the Swedish. In the process, she compiled a list of attributes that Americans believe to be true of females, males, and both sexes. These attributes are shown in the overlapping circles in Fig. 6.1. The attributes that are listed in the overlapping portion are those that are associated with both females and males, for example, "friendly" and "hard working." The attributes in the outer portions are associated with either females (e.g., "aware of feelings of others") or males (e.g., "stands up under pressure").

TABLE 6.1
Stereotypes of Males and Females Probability Judgments

Characteristic	Judgment[a]	
	Men	Women
Trait		
Independent	.78	.58
Competitive	.82	.64
Warm	.66	.77
Emotional	.56	.84
Role behaviors		
Financial provider	.83	.47
Takes initiative with opposite sex	.82	.54
Takes care of children	.50	.85
Cooks meals	.42	.85
Physical characteristics		
Muscular	.64	.36
Deep voice	.73	.30
Graceful	.45	.68
Small-boned	.39	.62

[a]Probability that the average person of either sex would possess a characteristic. Copyright (1985) by the American Psychological Association. Reprinted by permission of the author.

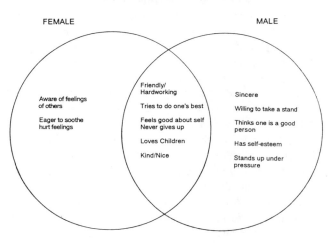

FIG. 6.1. Overlapping and distinct traits that are associated with the American Person Gender Schema. From Intons-Peterson (1988), p. 179. Reprinted with permission.

The Difference Between Sex Roles
and Sex Role Stereotypes

Gender is a biologically based social category.
—Hood, Draper, Crockett, and Petersen (1987, p. 65)

In a strict definitional sense, the term *sex role stereotype* refers both to those beliefs about what males and females are like and to those beliefs about what they should be like, whereas the term *sex roles* reflects actual differences between the sexes. Lueptow (1984) has operationalized the term *sex roles* as "any statistical difference between the sexes" (p. x). Although this may be a starting point for a definition, Lueptow's reliance on statistical differences would include sex differences in height, for example, as a sex role. A more useful definition would emphasize the fact that sex roles are a societal construction based on sex differences in psychosocial variables such as traits and dispositions. As an example of the difference between these two terms, consider beliefs about sex differences in social influence. A commonly held sex role stereotype is that females are more "conforming" or more easily influenced by social pressures than males; however, in Becker's (1986) review of the literature, she concluded that this is not true—that there is no statistically significant difference between the sexes in the tendency to conform to social pressures. This is an example in which the sex role stereotype does not agree with the finding that no sex differences exist in this area.

Repeatedly, the term *sex roles* has come under attack (Lopata & Thorne, 1978). Those opposed to the term have argued that because we do not use terms like *race roles* or *class roles,* why should researchers be so concerned with reifying (making a theoretical concept real or concrete by giving it a label) the concept of sex roles? It has also been argued that other roles in life, like that of student, or factory worker, or young adult, undergo changes as our life situations change; whereas, sex roles do not change cause they are tied to biological sex. It is also frequently argued that the term *gender roles* is more appropriate than *sex roles* because the term denotes societal rather than biological influences. Despite all of the rhetoric generated by this term, it is likely to remain in the psychological and sociological literature. One of the leading journals in the area of sex differences is entitled *Sex Roles,* and the term seems to have an intuitive meaning for people outside of academia. I believe that it is a useful term, even if it is used somewhat differently by different authors.

It is a widely held belief that sex role stereotypes, those beliefs about behaviors and dispositions that characterize males and females in our society, exert strong influences on male and female behavior. Eagly (1987) defined it this way: "Gender roles are defined as those shared expectations (about appropriate qualities and behaviors) that apply to individuals on the basis of their socially identified gender" (p. 12). These stereotypes seem to be narrower or to allow fewer options for males, leaving boys and men fewer choices and dispositional alternatives. Generally, it is far more deviant for a male to engage in traditionally female activities (e.g., homemaker, nurse, or secretary) than it is for females to enter the traditional man's world (medicine, physics, trucking, plumbing). The female sex role is a devalued role with less self-esteem and prestige than the male sex role (Intons-Peterson, 1988). Although young girls learn that they will be prized for their beauty, young men learn that they will be valued for their money and prestige. If you doubt that this is true, find a few friends and tell them that you saw a wealthy, old, pot-bellied man enter an expensive restaurant with a gorgeous young woman "on his arm." Ask them to guess the relationship between these two people. Most will respond in a way that is consistent with the notion that the man traded what is valuable for men (money and prestige) for what is valuable for women (beauty).

Accordingly, it should not be surprising to find that men outnumber women in the "hard" sciences, which are both high paying and prestigious. Mathematics, for example, is a masculine-typed academic subject. One possible explanation for the disparity in sex ratios among mathematically gifted youth is the unwillingness of girls to be identified with mathematics and/or their unwillingness to devote their time to the rigorous demands of mathematics—time that could be spent on "appropriate" female activities like curling their hair and painting their nails. A recent report in *Time* a popular magazine (Fall 1990), found that women use on the average, 17 to 21 grooming products every morning (e.g., shampoo, cream rinse, lipstick, mascara, face powder, blush, cologne, hand lotion, etc.) Is it any wonder that females are not achieving at the same rate as men?

Sherman (1983) summarized the effect of traditional sex role stereotypes on female intellectual development when she said: "Data indicate that intellectual excellence is still enmeshed in a pattern of sex-role expectations contrary to the feminine sex-role" (p. 342).

The impact of sex role stereotypes comes from pervasive life-long influences to conform to a pattern of behavior that is prescribed by sex. Sex differences in cognitive abilities mirror sex stereotypes about abilities, making it very difficult to determine the extent to which abilities differences and stereotype differences influence each other. The sex role literature is extensive. It contains numerous confirmations of the hypothesis that these stereotypes exert powerful influences on the way we think and behave. For example, in a recent poll of voters, female politicians were described as "hard working," "more caring," and "more ethical"; male politicians were described as "tougher" and "emotionally suited for politics" (Skelton, 1990, p. 1). It is difficult to know how these beliefs affect voting patterns, but there is ample evidence that racial and religious stereotypes have affected the outcome of numerous political campaigns. Few would doubt that sex role stereotypes have kept qualified candidates from office.

Consider, for example, a study that investigated the way sex role stereotypes influence memory (Halpern, 1985). High school students were asked to read a fairly bland story about 2 days in the life of a protagonist. For half the high school students, the main character was named Linda: for the other half, the main character was named David. It was hypothesized that errors in memory for stated events and inferences about the main character's goals and motives would be biased toward conformity with sex role stereotypes. In general, the results confirmed the hypothesis that sex role stereotypes influenced the way the students remembered information that was presented in the story. When these results were described to the students who participated in this study, they were surprised. Most of the students were unaware of the extent to which they maintained sex role stereotypes and of the possibility that these stereotypes were influencing how they think and remember. These results were confirmed in a study by Buczek (1986) in which he found that both professional counselors and college students recalled less information from female clients than from male clients. (For a more detailed discussion of the effect of stereotypes on memory and thought processes, see Halpern, 1989b.)

If you doubt whether sex role stereotypes still exist, consider a few of the questions taken from a questionnaire that was designed to show that sex role socialization is alive and well in contemporary society (Jonides & Rozin, 1981):

Would you be willing to kill a cockroach by slapping it with your hands?
a) yes   b) no
When you are depressed, does washing your hair make you feel better?
a) yes   b) no
Do you walk around freely in the nude in a locker room?   a) yes   b) no
Can you sew well enough to make clothes?   a) yes   b) no

Ask several male and female friends and see if you can detect a sex-related differences in the way your friends answer these questions. How does sex role socialization explain these differences?

Sex Role Identification as a Mediator in Intellectual Development

> *Many women in our present culture value mathematical ignorance as if it were a social grace.*
> —Osen (quoted in Burton, 1978, p. 35)

Although there are numerous conceptions of the way sex role stereotypes operate to influence behavior, a modal or typical model assumes that individuals identify with and conform to a particular sex role stereotype. Consider, for example, the fact that mathematical ability is often perceived to be part of the male sex role stereotype. As boys learn their sex roles, they identify with the notion that they should excel at mathematics. Girls, on the other hand, learn that mathematical ability is unfeminine and thus avoid advanced mathematics courses.

Several researchers have proposed more specific models of the way stereotypes influence behaviors (e.g., Deaux & Major, 1987). Let's consider in more
detail a model proposed by Eagly (1987). Eagley's model emphasizes the individual as a recipient of social pressures. Each individual reacts in ways that
conform to these pressures. Sex differences are a product of the "social rules that
regulate behavior in adult life" (p. 7). Eagly used this model to explain why
women are better at decoding nonverbal cues than men (a finding reported by
Hall & Halberstadt, 1986.) Because the female role includes nurturing, women
develop a greater sensitivity to nonverbal cues, and then, with practice and
attention, become better attuned to them. Thus, this sex difference is the result of
sex role stereotypes. Although Eagly acknowledged that there may be sex-
differentiated biological propensities, she maintains that sex role stereotypes are
far more important in the creation of sex differences.

Masculine and feminine stereotypes used to be viewed as separate and
orthogonal or independent concepts. During the early 1970s, however, several
psychologists (Bem, 1974; Constantinople, 1973; Spence, Helmreich, & Stapp,
1974) developed a multidimensional conception of the traits that constitute sex
role stereotypes and the term *androgynous* became a ubiquitous buzz word in the
literature. Individuals of either sex who reported both typical female and male
traits were labeled *androgynous*. Some researchers also adopted the term *undifferentiated* to refer to individuals who reported very few feminine or masculine traits. Unlike their androgynous peers who exhibited both masculine and
feminine traits, undifferentiated individuals seemed to exhibit very few of the
traits associated with either sex role.

This type of research introduced a third construct into the literature—*self-
concept*—which refers to individuals' beliefs about themselves. Thus, it is possible for someone to believe that men are and should be more aggressive than
women, a sex role stereotype; because empirical evidence suggests that differences actually exist with respect to aggression, this same belief is a sex role
difference; yet, any given woman may believe that she is more aggressive than
most men, or, any given man may believe that he is less aggressive than most
women, reflecting their self-concept. Thus, although most of us maintain sex
role stereotypes, we may or may not believe that we conform to them.

A deluge of research followed from the classification of self reports of sex-
typed behaviors and dispositions into masculine, feminine, androgynous, and
undifferentiated typological categories. It seems that these categories have been
related to almost every conceivable variable. Very often the assumption underlying the research was that "androgyny is good." Androgyny has been examined as
a mediating variable that affects success, career choice, psychosomatic problems, locus of control, self-esteem, and sexual behavior (Cook, 1985).

Given the immense popularity of sex role stereotypes and self concept, it
should not be surprising that they were also investigated as mediators of intellectual development. Using this framework, Mills (1981) tested the hypothesis that
mathematics and verbal skills achievement would be related to sex role identifi-

cation, or the extent to which someone identifies with the female or male sex role stereotype. She found a positive relationship between mathematical achievement and masculine traits for girls (i.e., the girls who had a more masculine self-identification performed better) and between verbal skills achievement and feminine traits for boys (i.e., the boys who had a more feminine self-identification performed better). Based on this study, she concluded that cross-sexed characteristics seemed associated with success in traditionally masculine (i.e., mathematics) and traditionally feminine (i.e., verbal) content areas. Other studies, however, have shown that the actual relationship between achievement and personality characteristics is quite complex. The extent to which an individual perceives a cognitive ability as sex typed may also be predictive of performance in that area (Nash, 1979).

There is a vast psychological literature that has addressed the possibility that cognitive sex differences exist as a result of conformity to sex role stereotypes. Signorella and Jamison (1986) summarized the literature in a meta-analytic review of the research. They concluded that there is no evidence that androgyny is associated with better cognitive performance. For spatial and mathematical tasks, they found limited support for the notion that girls who had higher masculine and lower feminine self concept scores tended to perform well on these masculine-sex-typed tasks. However, the proposed relationship was not found for boys on any of the cognitive tasks or for girls with verbal tasks. Thus, the idea that "individuals will perform better on cognitive tasks when the masculinity and femininity of their self concepts is consistent with the gender stereotyping of the tasks" (Signorella & Jamison, p. 207) has received minimal support. It seems likely that a web of other contributing variables will have to be unraveled before any conclusive statements about the relationship between sex role identification and academic area of achievement can be made.

Has the "Women's Movement" Changed Sex Role Stereotypes?

I have frequently been told by my students that "this sex role stereotype stuff is old hat." Much like the ads that proclaimed that females have come a long way, many people believe that sex roles have little relevance for today's young adults. Research, however, shows a very different picture. Lewin and Tragos (1987) compared the attitudes of adolescents toward sex role stereotyping in 1956 with those of adolescents in 1982. In 1956, the United States was in the midst of the post-war baby boom. Women were pressured to leave the jobs they held during the war so that the returning G.I.'s could find employment. The women, of course, were to get married, stay home, and have babies, in that order. If you were not alive in 1956, you can get a glimpse of what life was supposed to be like by watching "Leave it to Beaver" reruns or renting the move *Peggy Sue Got Married* (which, of course, is exactly what she was supposed to do). A superb documentary on women's lives and social pressures during and immediately following the war is entitled "Rosie the Riveter." Occasionally, it is shown on public television stations. Watch for it.

You are probably thinking that American sex role stereotypes have changed radically since the baby boom years. Well, if that is what you are thinking, you are wrong. Lewin and Tragos found very few differences between the attitudes expressed by adolescents in 1982 and those expressed by adolescents in 1956. They concluded that there is "only modest evidence of the impact of the feminist movement" (p. 131). The only difference was that girls in the 1982 survey expressed more satisfaction about being female than their earlier contemporaries. "Contrary to our prediction, sex role stereotyping was not significantly less in 1982 than in 1956" (p. 125).

Theoretical Models

How are appropriate sex role behaviors acquired? Several theories have been proposed to answer this question. Four major theories designed to explain the acquisition of appropriate sex role behaviors—Psychoanalytic Theory, Learning Theory, Social Modeling, and Cognitive Theories—are briefly described. Each theory begins with a different notion about the nature of the forces that cause humans to conform to sex role stereotypes.

Psychoanalytic Theory

Sigmund Freud proposed an influential theory around the turn of the century that encompassed developmental psychology, psychopathology, and personality. The foundation of Freud's Psychoanalytic Theory was built on the biological differences between the sexes, thereby representing a strong form of the belief that "biology is destiny." According to Freud, children come to identify with

Calvin and Hobbes   by Bill Watterson

CALVIN AND HOBBES copyright (1990), Universal Press Syndicate. Reprinted with permission. All rights reserved.

their same-sex parent, and through identification they imitate the appropriate sex role behaviors of their mothers or fathers. He maintained that all children at approximately 4 to 5 years of age enter a developmental period known as the "phallic stage," so named because of their preoccupation with their genitals. (Freud used the term *phallic stage* to refer to the development of both girls and boys even though the term phallic is derived from a Greek word meaning *penis*.) Children in the phallic stage go through a fairly involved sequence of primary alliances and jealousies that follows different paths depending on whether the child is a girl or a boy. It is during this developmental period that children resolve their early feelings of love and hate for their parents and ultimately identify with the same sex parent.

Let's consider first how this process proceeds for boys because it is somewhat less complicated than the process Freud attributed to girls. The impetus to identify with their same sex parent for boys is the *Oedipus complex,* named for a 5th century B.C. play by Sophocles called *Oedipus Rex.* In this play, Oedipus unknowingly commits the unspeakable crime of killing his father and later marrying his mother and fathering children with her. Freud believed that this represented a universal theme of all boys' sexual longing for their mother. During the phallic stage, the young boy's newly discovered erotic feelings are vaguely directed toward his mother (or mother substitute), because she has been the source of pleasure in the past. At the same time, he also begins to feel jealous of his father, a "rival" for his mother's love. This is also the time in his development when he learns that girls do not have a penis, leading him to conclude that it must have been cut off for some terrible reason. He then reasons that the same thing could happen to him because of his sexual desire for his mother and his jealousy of his father. All boys at this age must resolve the problem of "castration anxiety" (an unconscious fear of being castrated). Boys resolve this dilemma the only way possible; they repress their erotic feelings for the mother and identify with the father.

How do girls come to identify with their mothers according to Freudian theory? There is a roughly analogous version of the Oedipus complex known as the *Electra complex.* Electra was the heroine in a Greek tragedy who convinced her brother to kill their mother, also a supposedly universal theme. During the preschool years, girls discover that they do not have a penis and immediately develop "penis envy," an intense desire to have male genitals. For reasons never clearly explained, the girl concludes that she must have once had a penis and was castrated. She holds the mother responsible for this sad state of affairs when she realizes that the mother also lacks the prized organ. Girls then turn to their fathers, and, like their brothers, have to resolve feelings of hatred and jealousy. Because of fear of reprisal from jealous mothers, girls shift their identification back to their mothers and imitate female sex role behaviors.

Thus, for Freud, the key to sex role identification is the presence or absence of a penis during critical years of child development (approximately 4 to 6 years old) and the appropriate resolution of the Oedipus or Electra complex. Freudian theory is actually much more complex than this, but these are the basic assumptions underlying sex role identification. There are numerous problems with this aspect of Freudian theory. Most notably, research has shown that a large proportion of children in this age range don't have a conscious understanding about the anatomical differences between women and men (Katcher, 1955). Psychoanalytic Theory has also been criticized for its anti-female (penis-centered) orientation, especially for its assumption that children of both sexes immediately perceive the superiority of male genitals over female genitals. In addition, it implies that children who are raised in homes without a same-sexed parent will fail to develop sex role appropriate behaviors. Research with children in single parent families has shown this prediction to be false (Lynn, 1974).

Learning Theory

In some sense, all of the theories being described here can be characterized as "learning theories" because they are all concerned with understanding the way sex role stereotypes are learned. *Learning Theory,* however, has a very specific meaning in psychology. It refers to the theory that most learning is contingent upon the rewards and punishments that follow behavior. Although terms like "reward" and "punishment" have an intuitive meaning, they have a precise meaning in the jargon of Learning Theory. A *reward* is anything that will increase the probability of a particular behavior, and a *punishment* is anything that will decrease the probability of a particular behavior. Learning theorists explain the acquisition of sex roles by positing that children are rewarded when they evince appropriate sex role behaviors and attitudes and punished for behaviors and attitudes that do not conform to the sex appropriate roles. We are all familiar with sex role phrases like, "Boys don't cry" or "lady-like behavior." It's easy to imagine how rewards and punishments could function to reinforce sex role appropriate behavior.

Rewards and punishments can assume many different forms. A smile, a pat on the back, an award, or some candy could all functionally serve to increase desirable behavior. Similarly, a frown, scolding, physical punishment, or public humiliation could all serve to discourage or decrease the likelihood of some behavior. As children grow, they receive numerous rewards and punishments from parents and other socializing agents who want to influence their behaviors. Children and adults also receive rewards and punishments for certain intellectual activities. Mathematics, for example, is a highly sex-typed academic subject (Sherman, 1983). One way that children come to learn this is through differential rewards and punishments. Numerous studies have shown that boys are more likely than girls to receive encouragement to work through difficult mathematics problems, and girls receive less praise than boys for correct answers in mathematic classes (Stage & Karplus, 1981). It is also likely that a sex differentiated pattern of rewards and punishments could be used to explain sex differences in verbal and spatial ability, with girls encouraged to read more often than boys and boys encouraged to engage in spatial activities (blocks, erector sets, etc.) more often than girls. Thus, according to Learning Theory, through sex differentiated rewards and punishments children learn that mathematical and spatial activities are more appropriate for boys and that reading and other verbal activities are more appropriate for girls.

Social Modeling

Several prominent theorists have proposed that sex-typed behaviors are learned in several ways (Bandura & Walters, 1963; Mischel, 1966). They believe that while direct rewards and punishments can produce sex role learning, imitation learning or modeling may be the more important mechanism for producing sex role appropriate behaviors. Because of the importance they attach to imitation or modeling in social situations, this theory is sometimes called Social Learning or Social Modeling. In addition to receiving rewards and punishments for behaviors that are either consistent or inconsistent with sex roles, children are also told in numerous ways that they are either a girl or a boy. Children then begin to notice similarities among other girls and among other boys. A list of possible examples would be quite long: Girls may wear bows and barrettes in their hair, but boys may not. Girls may wear almost any color clothing, while boys may not wear pink clothes. Very few boys will own doll carriages, a common girl's toy. Combat dolls like G.I. Joe are appropriate for boys, but not for girls. There are also obvious differences among adult models. Women may wear high-heeled shoes, hose, make-up, nail polish, and dresses, whereas any man who wears these items is considered deviant.

According to Social Modeling Theory, children learn about sex role behaviors by observing between-sex differences. They then imitate the behaviors and attitudes of same sex models. Social modeling theory differs from learning theory in that it does not assume that rewards and punishments must be received in order to shape behavior. Sex role learning can occur from observing others and imitating them. Appropriate imitation is likely to be rewarded, as in the case of a young girl who dresses up in her mother's shoes and old dresses. Inappropriate imitation is likely to be punished, as in the case of a young boy who dresses up in his mother's shoes and old dresses. Thus, through a combination of observational learning, modeling, and rewards and punishments, boys and girls learn society's sex roles.

Social Modeling is not restricted to the acquisition of sex roles in childhood. As adults, we also observe how each sex should act, imitate appropriate models, and receive rewards and punishments for these actions. Social influences to conform to behaviors deemed appropriate by society are extremely strong, even for adults. Few women feel comfortable as the only female in all male mathematics course, and few men are comfortable in an all female nursing class. In this theoretical framework, it would be extremely important for women and men considering careers in these traditionally "sex-inappropriate" fields to have female mathematicians to serve as models for women and male nurses to serve as models for men.

Cognitive Theories

Cognitive Theories as a general class of theories that are based on the primary importance of children's and adults' knowledge of sex-differentiated behaviors. Kohlberg (1966) has proposed a cognitive development theory to explain the acquisition of sex-typed behavior by children. A more recent cognitive theory that explains sex role maintenance among adults is Gender Schema Theory, which was proposed by S. L. Bem (1981). Because each theory is designed for a different purpose, they are considered separately.

Cognitive Development Theory.   Kohlberg's Cognitive Development Theory begins with the notion that children's conceptions about the nature of the world change as they go through various developmental stages. Just as children's understanding of number concepts changes at different ages, so does their understanding of sex roles and sex appropriate behaviors. Around 3 years of age, children begin to label themselves as either a girl or a boy, and somewhere during the next 2 years they learn to label other people's sex. During this developmental period, they also develop "gender constancy," which is the idea that gender or sex is an immutable part of one's identity. Once the child has developed a notion of his or her own sex, the child models the behaviors of same sex models. In Serbin and Sprafkin's (1986) review of the literature in this area, they concluded that "it appears that learning about sex roles may be a universal phenomenon based on the early tendency to classify according to the gender dimension" (p. 1198).

In distinguishing the basic differences between Social Modeling or Social Learning Theory and Cognitive Development Theory, Kohlberg (1966) has said: "The social-learning syllogism is: 'I want rewards, I am rewarded for doing boy things, therefore I want to be a boy.' In contrast, a cognitive theory assumes this sequence: 'I am a boy, therefore I want to do boy things, therefore the opportunity to do boy things (and to gain approval for doing them) is rewarding" (p. 89). The basic difference between these two theories is that Social Modeling assumes that children conform to sex role stereotypes and acquire a sex role identity because they imitate sex role consistent behaviors, which are reinforced; whereas Cognitive Development Theory assumes that children first develop an awareness of sex categories, then they form a sexual identity as part of their self concept (I am a girl or I am a boy). After a sexual identity is formed, they perform sex role consistent behaviors, which get rewarded.

Gender Schema Theory.   S. L. Bem (1981) proposed that our knowledge about sex differences forms a "schema" or an organizing framework in which we process, interpret, and organize information. The term *schema* comes from cognitive psychology, the branch of psychology concerned with how we think, learn, and remember. The notion of a schema is very close to what we mean when we talk about stereotypes. It refers to the way we store information in memory and utilize that information. Hyde (1985) described it this way: "A schema is a general knowledge framework that a person has about a particular topic. A schema organizes and guides perception" (p. 56). Gender schemata (plural of schema) are "a set of ideas that define as appropriate for men and women particular skills, preferences, personalities and interpretations of events" (Goodnow, 1985, p. 19).

When we interact with people, we use our schemata first to understand and then to remember what transpired. For example, Koblinsky, Cruse, and Sugawawa (1978) showed that 10-year-old children remembered the masculine behaviors of boy characters and feminine behaviors of girl characters better than sex-reversed behaviors. A similar effect was found by Liben and Signorella (1980) using a picture recognition task with first and second grade children. Furthermore, children with the most rigidly defined sex role stereotypes showed the greatest recall and recognition memory for pictures that were consistent with stereotypes (Signorella & Liben, 1984) and showed a proclivity to distort information that was inconsistent with their schema into consistent information (G. D. Levy, 1989).

The organization and structuring of information is a normal cognitive process with important consequences for how we think and remember (Halpern, 1985; Martin & Halverson, 1981). The propensity to interpret and remember information that is consistent with our schemata serves to perpetuate these schemata (Stangar & Ruble, 1987). Gender schema theory addresses the issue of why gender (as opposed to other categories) is such an important organizer of information even at a young age. Thus, once these cognitive categories are established, they will resist change because information that is inconsistent will tend to be either forgotten or changed. In this way, our stereotypes or gender schemata bias the way we interpret behavior.

Theory Comparisons

Each of the theories devised to explain the acquisition and maintenance of sex role stereotypes assumes a different perspective on the issue. Psychoanalytic Theory views the adoption of sex-typed behaviors by young children as a necessary consequence of biological differences. Girls and boys will identify with the same-sex parent because of the need to resolve the Oedipus and Electra complexes. Learning Theory and Social Modeling Theory view sex differentiated rewards and punishments and modeling as primarily responsible for the adoption of sex role stereotypes by children. By contrast, cognitive theories posit that the way we develop and store information about sex role appropriate and inappropriate behaviors guides the way we interpret and remember information. It is difficult to determine which theory is "best" because there are areas of overlap among them. Nor do they necessarily represent mutually exclusive categories. It is likely that rewards and punishments, imitation of same-sex models, and gender schemata all operate in the establishment and maintenance of sex role stereotypes. As you might probably guess, Psychoanalytic Theory has been most heavily criticized because of its "penis-centered" orientation. An alternative explanation is that the male role is preferred not because males have a penis, but because males have greater power and greater freedom in our society.

A brief summary of the salient points in the four theories of sex role stereotypes is presented in Table 6.2.

SEX-LINKED SOCIALIZATION PRACTICES

A common theme among the theories of sex role acquisition is that girls and boys receive rewards and punishments for sex role appropriate and inappropriate behaviors. Let's take a closer look at the nature of these rewards and punishments

TABLE 6.2
A Brief Summarization of Four Theories of Sex-Typed Behavior

Freudian Theory

    Development of penis envy in girls --> eventual identification with the mother --> conforming to female behavior

    Development of castration anxiety in boys -->identification with the father --> conformity to male behavior

Learning Theory

    Girls and boys receive rewards for sex appropriate behavior and punishments for sex inappropriate behavior --> exhibit sex appropriate behavior

Social modeling

    Boys and girls observe male and female behavior --> imitation of same sex models --> receive rewards for sex appropriate behavior and punishment for sex inappropriate behavior --> exhibit sex appropriate behavior

Cognitive Theories

Cognitive Development

    Girls and boys develop a sexual identity --> imitation of same sex models --> receive rewards for sex appropriate behavior and punishment for sex inappropriate behavior --> exhibit sex appropriate behavior

Gender Schema Theory

    Boys and girls development cognitive categories for sex differentiated behaviors and dispositions --> interpret and remember information according to these categories --> exhibit behavior consistent with cognitive categories and other ways that sex role expectancies are communicated and learned. It is clear that the socialization practices we receive vary with age; therefore, a developmental perspective is assumed in examining this issue. For the purposes of this topic, the life span is broken up into three broad stages—childhood, adolescence, and adulthood and old age. The most salient aspects of sex role socialization practices in each of these broad stages is considered.

Childhood Experiences

> *The infant departments of retail stores are small worlds divided into colors of pink and blue. Perhaps it is not surprising that the infants for whom we purchase pink or blue booties, rattles, and diaper bags, grow into children who apply gender schemata to organize the world around them into male and female categories.*
> —Liben and Bigler (1987, p. 89)

Childhood is the time in life when socializing forces exert their greatest impact. Although almost any person or institution with which children come into contact can be considered socializing agents, we briefly examine three major forces in a child's life—parents, television and other media, and teachers and schools.

Parents

Without a doubt, parents play a major role in shaping their children's lives. As the primary socializing agents of the young, especially the very young, there are countless ways that parents could inculcate sex-typed behavior. Numerous studies have shown that parents respond differently to boy and girl babies, probably from birth (Rubin, Provenzano, & Luria, 1974). Stewart (1976), for example, found that within the first 6 weeks of life, male infants are handled more than female infants, and female infants receive more vocalizations. It is very possible that these early differences in home experiences provide the basis for later cognitive differences.

J. H. Block (1973, 1978) has found considerable differences in parenting practices as a function of a child's sex. She has found that, in general, the parents of boys are more concerned with task oriented achievement for their child than the parents of girls. She also found that boys' parents reported that they were more concerned with punishment, negative sanctions, and sex typing than the parents of girls. In general, fathers are more concerned with sex role stereotyping than mothers, and fathers are particularly concerned that their sons conform to traditional notions of masculinity.

Other sex-differentiated rearing practices were assessed in a sample of 160 pairs of Israeli parents (Ninio, 1987). In this study, the parents of 9-month-old babies were asked to estimate the age at which their infant would begin to acquire certain skills. Items included the age at which infants start to talk, when you should buy children their first picture book, and when you should expect a child to first be jealous of siblings. The researcher found that overall, fathers gave later age estimates than mothers, especially when the infant was a female and when the parents had a low level of education. Ninio used these data to suggest that parents have implicit theories of cognitive development that are affected by the child's sex with fathers more likely to expect later development from girl babies than mothers are.

What is the result of sex differentiated child rearing? Children as young as 2 years old express sex-stereotypic ideas and make sex-appropriate dispositional attributes (Kuhn, Nash, & Brucken, 1978). By age 3, children can ascribe sex-appropriate attributes to other children and adults (Gettys & Cann, 1981; Haugh, Hoffman, & Cowan, 1980). It seems that by the time children are able to express themselves verbally, they are able to report an awareness of sex role stereotypes.

There is direct evidence that children are influenced by their parents' sex role stereotypes. G. D. Levy (1989) found that girls with mothers who worked outside of the home (and presumably had less restrictive sex role stereotypes, on the average, than mothers who remained in the home) had greater sex role flexibility. It is interesting to note that Levy also found that mothers' work status (in or out of the home) did not predict the sex role stereotypes of their sons. Parents also spend different amounts of time with their children, depending on the child's sex. In general, mothers are the more involved parent, but fathers are more involved with their sons' play than with their daughters' (Burns & Homel, 1989), especially when the play is "rough and tumble," which fathers rate as more appropriate for boys than for girls (Pellegrini, 1987).

One major way in which parents influence the social and cognitive growth of their children is in the toys they select for them. Etaugh (1983) noted big differences in the kinds of toys purchased for girls and boys. Between the ages of 1 and 6, girls receive significantly more dolls and doll houses, and boys receive more building toys. Boys, of course, receive many more (toy) guns (Lewis, 1986). By age 2 to 3, children know which toys are deemed appropriate for their sex and tend to play with "sex-appropriate" toys. For older children, parents provide more science-related activities for their sons than for their daughters, including microscopes, puzzles, and chemistry sets. Graham and Birns (1979) reported that girls are less likely than boys to have mathematical toys and games and individual instruction in mathematics.

During childhood, girls and boys have different hobbies and different out-of-school activities. In a recent study of Australian youth, Burns and Homel (1989) computed the percentage of boys in the 9–11 age range that participated in selected activities. Their data are presented in Table 6.3. Results similar to these have been reported many times. For example, in a sample of British youth, Johnson (1987) found that significantly more boys claimed to make models, take things apart, and play with electrical toys. Significantly more girls claimed to cook, sew, and collect flowers.

TABLE 6.3
Percentage of Australian Boys and Girls that Engaged in Selected Activities

	Boys	Girls
making a model	79	33
building something out of wood	81	33
fixing a bicycle	71	23
ironing	53	86
baking	28	57

Data from Burns and Homel (1989).

Television and Other Media

> When it comes to stereotyped sex behavior, children more and more put
> on the cultural cloak that is provided by the society they are growing up
> in. They use the basic categories "male" and "female" as hooks on
> which to hang a great deal of cumulative information.
> —Maccoby (1990, p. 5)

Many people are amazed to learn that by age 4, most children have spent
between 2,000 and 3,000 hours watching television (Stewart, 1976). What are
they learning about males and females during all of these hours? With only a few
exceptions (e.g., "Sesame Street"), media depictions of females and males
parallel commonly held sex role stereotypes (Deaux, 1985). Overwhelmingly,
men and boys are shown as active, hard-working, goal-oriented individuals,
whereas women and girls are depicted as housewives and future housewives.
Numerous studies have noted that men on television are characterized as "dominant, aggressive, autonomous and active while female characters are passive and
defiant" (Calvert & Huston, 1987, p. 78). In an analysis of 300 television
commercials, Hoyenga and Hoyenga (1979) reported that over 90% of the following activities or occupations were portrayed by females: caring for babies and
infants, living in a nursing home, cleaning house, washing clothes and dishes,
shopping, cooking and serving food. Compare these with the following activities
and occupations that were portrayed by males over 90% of the time: farmer,
engaging in sports, driving a vehicle, working in an office (not secretary), being
a soldier, and working in a service station.

Television images of the lives of females and males differ dramatically. Wom-
en appear in a narrower range of roles, and they are significantly more often
depicted on the receiving end of violent attacks. Another message that is con-
veyed is that marriage and parenthood are of greater significance in females'
lives than in males' lives. Furthermore, researchers have found that children

who are heavy viewers of television maintain stronger sex role stereotypes than children who view less television.   It is tempting to conclude that television viewing *caused* the stereotypes to intensify, but we must remember that it is also possible that the children with the strongest stereotypes chose to watch more television. We can conclude that heavy television watching and strong sex role stereotypes are associated for children, but we cannot conclude that one caused the other.

There have been some positive changes in the television portrayal of men and women over the last 15 years, but many discrepancies still exist. In an examination of the way female and male depictions have changed, Bretl and Cantor (1988) reported that men and women now appear equally often in prime time commercials, but women are still more likely to be seen in domestic settings and advertising cleaning products. Approximately 90% of all narrators are male, a value that has not changed during the past 15 years. Similarly, Signorielli (1989) found that "sex-role images, over the past 10–15 years, have been quite stable, traditional, conventional, and supportive of the status quo" (p. 341).

Social Modeling theory would predict that children are learning about sex roles by observing the activities and occupations of the female and male characters they are viewing on television. The prediction that children will be more likely to imitate same sex models than other sex models has been difficult to demonstrate in the laboratory, possibly because of some of the constraints imposed by the nature of laboratory investigations. A typical laboratory study of this phenomenon might consist of exposing children to male and female models who engage in different sorts of activities. The researchers then observe the girls and boys to see if they are more likely to exhibit the activities of the same sex model than they are to exhibit the activities of the other sex model. It is likely, however, that observational learning followed by imitation of a same sex model occurs more frequently in real life where the child may have frequent contact with a model and a wider range of opportunities to demonstrate imitation.

Perry and Bussey (1979) have provided evidence in support of Social Modeling theory. They hypothesized that children learn sex-typed behavior by observing differences in the *frequencies* of sex-typed activities by female and male models. In a test of their hypothesis, they provided children with several male and female models. They found that children were more likely to imitate behaviors of same-sex models than they were to imitate behaviors of other-sex models. Perry and Bussey concluded that, "children are most likely to imitate persons whom they perceive to be good examples of their [own] sex role" (p. 1708). If, as Perry and Bussey suggest, repeated observations of the frequency of sex-typed behavior is the mechanism by which social modeling operates, then television should provide an optimal situation for such learning. Given the immense number of hours children and adults spend watching television, it is clear that television is a major socializing agent in modern American society. The sex-stereotyped characterizations it depicts serve to reinforce sex role stereotypes.

Teachers and Schools

> *It would be preposterously naive to suggest that a B.A. degree can be made as attractive to girls as a marriage license.*
> —Grayson Kirk (former president of Columbia University)

Schools are the only institution in our society charged with the exclusive responsibility of educating our children. It is there that the intellectual abilities of all girls and boys should be nurtured so that every individual can develop to his or her full potential. Sadker and Sadker (1985) set out to find any evidence that cognitive abilities are being differentially developed for girls and boys in our schools. In a 3 year study of 100 fourth-, sixth-, and eighth-grade classes in four states and the District of Columbia, they found ample evidence of sex biases. At all grade levels in all subjects, boys dominated classroom discussions. Teachers paid more attention to the boys and praised them more often. "While girls sit patiently with their hands raised, boys literally grab teacher attention. They are eight times more likely than girls to call out answers" (p. 56). They reported that boys also received more dynamic and informative feedback to their classroom comments than the girls did. Other studies have come up with similar findings: "Boys receive more of the teacher's attention, teachers interact with boys, particularly high achieving boys, more than with girls, and boys are more active in providing answers, particularly unsolicited answers, than are girls (Kimball, 1989, p. 201). Sex differentiated treatment in the classroom could be directly responsible for or contributing to sex differences in mathematics and science achievement. If girls are taught that they will receive fewer rewards for scholastic success than boys will, learning theory suggests that they will seek success in other areas in which rewards are more probable.

All of the teachers Sadker and Sadker observed reported that they treated boys and girls equally, yet observations conducted in their classrooms showed that their beliefs about their actions were not accurate. Recall that earlier in this chapter I discussed a study in which high school students showed the influence of sex role stereotypes in a memory task for a dull story. When the students were told these results, they also denied that they were influenced by sex role stereotypes. Thus, although students and teachers are denying that they are influenced by sex role stereotypes, all of the data suggest that they are not even aware of the pervasive and intransigent nature of sex role stereotypes.

Sex role messages pervade the school experience. Meece (1987) has identified teachers as "the hidden carriers of society's messages" (p. 58). According to Meece, teachers are still reinforcing stereotypes with job assignments (boys are more often classroom helpers) and division of labor. In a study of over 300 teachers in Israel, investigators found that boys were more frequently named by teachers as discipline problems, as outstanding in mathematics and general academic excellence, and as the students that they think about after school. The same teachers named girls as more eminent in Hebrew and in social skills (BenTsvi-Mayer, Hertz-Lazarowitz, & Safir, 1989).

Conformity to school regulations is also more important for girls than boys. In Grades 6 through 10, girls ranked "getting good grades" as their primary aspiration at school (Butcher, 1986). Recall that girls do, in fact, get higher grades than boys in school (Cordes, 1986). Even at the college level, females continue to maintain overall higher grade point averages than males (with the mean differences estimated at .17 on a 4.0 scale).

Although schools can no longer require students to take separate courses in drafting and home economics, in fact, most of these classes are still segregated by sex. Despite egalitarian rhetoric (at least in some school districts), some curriculum choices are not real. Although I am certain that every reader has his or her own personal examples, I cannot help but recall what happened when my daughter registered for eighth grade (in a Vancouver public school). She was told that she could pick either drafting or home economics, but if she chose drafting she would be the only girl in the class and she might find some "resistance" from the boys and their teacher. (Similarly, there were no boys in home economics.) The question is not whether it is better to take drafting or home economics, because both are valuable, but whether one's biological sex should be the determinant. Why doesn't everyone need to know about cooking, nutrition, food storage, and how machines work? (If you were wondering about my daughter's choice, get real. There are very few eighth graders who would risk peer status by doing anything as deviant as taking a sex role inappropriate course.)

It seems that all of the major socializing agents of childhood act in ways that encourage sex differentiated cognitive development. It also seems that few of us are aware of the multitudinous pressures to conform to traditional sex roles and of the diverse ways these pressures are communicated to children.

Adolescence

The pre-adolescent peer group tends to reject a girl who appears to be too smart or too successful.
—Noble (1987, p. 371)

Adolescence covers that time in the life span when boys and girls begin to develop secondary sex characteristics and ends when physical maturity is achieved. Considering the variety of individual differences in the timing of these developmental milestones, it can be roughly operationalized as beginning as early as age 10 and extending to as late as age 18, recognizing, of course, that a few individuals begin puberty before age 10, and a few continue physical maturity after age 18. Adolescence has already been identified in earlier chapters as a critical period in the development of cognitive sex differences. Although sex differences in verbal and spatial ability are found only on selected ability tests (e.g., mental rotation, Water Level [favoring boys], and some tests of language proficiency [favoring girls]), during childhood, other differences are more consistently found during adolescence. It is sometime during adolescence that boys begin to take the lead in standardized tests of mathematics (usually mathematical problem solving) and girls lose their lead in mathematical computation. Several biological hypotheses have been proposed that link the biological events of puberty to the emergence of cognitive sex differences during this time of life. However, along with the tremendous biological changes that occur during these years, there are also numerous and powerful psychosocial changes that occur during the preteen and teen years. Researchers who favor the nurture side of the nature–nurture controversy believe that the etiology of the cognitive sex differences is firmly rooted in the psychosocial forces that dominate the adolescent years.

Body Type and Developing Sexuality

Although biological definitions of puberty usually cite the development of adult patterns of body hair (the word "puberty" is derived from a Latin word meaning fine downy hair), psychosocial definitions of adolescence are more likely to stress romantic interest and concern with one's changing body. There are profound psychological consequences of the biology of adolescence.

The biological events that symbolize the ability to reproduce—menarche for girls and ejaculation for boys—have intense psychological significance. For each sex, these biological events signify that for the first time, the individual, along with a partner, can create life. Friendships with members of the other sex and preadolescent romances assume a new potential meaning when young adults develop sexually.

The biological changes associated with physical maturation have tremendous psychosocial significance. There is ample evidence to believe that girls and boys who attain puberty at an early age and develop adult-like body types before most of their peers are treated differently from their later maturing friends. As described in the preceding chapter, one biological theory to explain cognitive sex differences is that early maturers don't develop spatial skills as well or as fully as later maturing adolescents, possibly because of the effect of sex hormones on brain organization. It is also possible, however, that early maturers differ from late maturers for psychosocial reasons. Early maturing boys are more muscular and taller than later maturing ones; therefore, they experience greater peer group prestige (Hamburg & Lunde, 1966). There are numerous secondary gains from their physical stature. Their height gives them a competitive edge in sports such as basketball, volleyball, long jump, and soccer. The early growth of body hair allows them to cultivate a moustache while still in junior high school, and their developing biceps are likely to receive positive comments.

Puberty rate differences are even more pronounced for girls, who soon learn that their "hourglass" figures and growing breasts make them desirable dates and mates. They undoubtedly receive more attention from males, especially older males, than their less shapely girlfriends. It would seem that early maturers would be less concerned with academic pursuits than late maturers who still rely on good grades in school and teachers' praise as a major source of reward. Mazur and Robertson (1972) revealed the feelings of an anonymous girl who had experienced early puberty: "Sure, after I bloomed I always dressed so people could see how big my breasts were. After all, a pair of 48s can make a girl feel like a real person. Everybody pays attention" (p. 115).

It seems that early and late maturers have different social environments and receive different rewards. A psychosocial explanation of the sex-related cognitive differences that emerge during puberty would suggest that it is these different life experiences that result from the hormonal events that trigger maturation and not hormonal events per se that underlie cognitive differences.

In one of the few examinations of commonly held stereotypes about early and late-maturing girls and boys, Faust (1983) asked college students to describe individuals in these four categories. Early maturing girls were described as "attracted to the opposite sex, egocentric, absolutely boy crazy, and theatrical." By comparison, late-maturing girls were described as "afraid of the opposite sex, unassuming, friends of both boys and girls, and exhibiting normal behavior." Early maturing boys were described as "liking football, sexy and outgoing, macho, slow learner, and a typical jock." Late-maturing boys were described as "would rather read, fast learner, unmacho, and popular only with own friends." It seems that many people would agree with the research showing that early maturers have poorer intellectual skills than later maturers.

In a study of the relationship among age at puberty, intellectual abilities, and masculinity and femininity, Newcombe, Bandura, and Taylor (1983) tested 85 girls, aged 11. Spatial ability was positively correlated with a later age at maturity and with "masculine" interests. Girls with a younger age at puberty had higher scores on the Feminine Scale of the California Psychological Inventory. More recently, Butcher (1989) reported that adolescent girls with high self-esteem were more likely to participate in sports and had greater masculine sex role orientations than adolescent girls with less self-esteem. She analyzed her data to see if there were significant changes in sex role orientation, self-esteem, or sports participation as a function of age at menarche. If menarche served as a clear indicator of "womanhood" to developing adolescents, then differences on these measures would be expected. She found that there was no relationship between age at menarche and any of these variables. It seems that the biological onset of adulthood has little impact on the performance of cognitive tasks for adolescent girls.

Gender Intensification Hypothesis

The term *gender* is often used to refer to the psychological aspects associated with biological sex (Deaux, 1985). The term usually encompasses what I have been calling *sex role stereotypes*. *Adolescence* has been identified as the time when boys and girls, but especially girls, respond to environmental pressures to conform to appropriate sex role behavior (Hill & Lynch, 1983). The psychological aspects of being female or male are intensified, hence the term *gender intensification*. Adherence to traditional sex role stereotypes seems particularly important when boys and girls begin to interact in ways that are more characteristic of young women and men.

Adolescence is a transitional period in life during which children undergo a metamorphosis from which they emerge as adults. Peer interactions are especially important, and there are strict sanctions against sex role inappropriate behavior. The need to be "just like everyone else" is strong. Strict conformance to sex role stereotypes would also require boys and girls to conform to sex-typed cognitive activities (e.g., avoiding mathematics and science coursework for girls and avoiding poetry and literature for boys).

Several researchers have examined the relationship between conformity to traditional sex roles and intellectual development. Nash (1975) measured spatial visualization ability, sex role concepts, and sex role preferences among 11- and 14-year-old girls and boys. In accord with the usual research findings, she found that sex differences in spatial visualization ability did not emerge until age 14. (Recall that sex differences in some of the other components of spatial ability are found in early childhood.) However, the most interesting part of this study was the relationship between sex role preferences and spatial visualization ability. For males, viewing oneself as masculine was related to better spatial performance. For females, a preference for the male sex was positively related to spatial performance. Thus, for both sexes, good spatial ability was associated with either an identification with or a preference for the male sex role. Good spatial ability is usually considered to be a masculine trait, and it was those girls and boys who positively viewed masculine traits that scored well on Nash's test of spatial ability. Nash also found that more girls than boys would prefer to be a member of the other sex and were more likely to feel that it would be better to be the other sex.

One puzzling and distressing finding in the literature on adolescence is "adolescent intellectual decline" for girls. P. B. Campbell (1976) discussed replicated findings that a substantial proportion of adolescent girls show decrements in their IQ scores, whereas adolescent boys show a reverse trend toward increasing IQ scores. Although the magnitude of the actual losses and gains tends to be small, the sex differentiated pattern is consistently found. In Campbell's study of high school seniors, males gained an average of 1.62 IQ points, and females lost an average of 1.33 IQ points relative to their scores in seventh grade. She hypothesized that girls who declined in IQ would conform to feminine sex role stereotypes more than the girls whose IQs didn't decline because the feminine sex role stereotype is incompatible with academic or intellectual achievement. Her hypothesis was confirmed. Campbell concluded: "The girl decliners tended to express responses that were more typically stereotypic than did the total sample of girls" (p. 634). The sex role message for adolescent girls is clear: It isn't feminine to be smart.

Data that show this female-specific decline are puzzling. In a recent analysis of the achievement test scores of a large sample of children in a California school district, Peil (1990) found that females scored significantly higher than males on every subtest of the Metropolitan Achievement Test in fourth grade. (The Metropolitan Achievement Test provides scores on several verbal and mathematical skills such as word recognition, reading comprehension, computation, and mathematical problem solving.) In fifth grade, some of the female advantage turned into no significant between-sex differences, and in sixth grade, males scored significantly higher on some of the mathematics subtests. When we look at SAT scores for 12th graders, males are now scoring slightly higher on the verbal portion and much higher on the mathematics portion. This general pattern of decline for females, but not for males has been reported by other investigators (Marshall & Smith, 1987).

These results are most relevant to our interpretation of the report from Johns Hopkins University on the Study of Mathematically Precocious Youth (Benbow & Stanley, 1980, 1981, 1983). As reported in chapter 3, a national search for mathematically precocious youth identified more males than females, with large sex ratios among the most highly gifted group. If adolescent girls learn that it is unfeminine to succeed at mathematics, then it is likely that a large proportion of mathematically gifted girls either declined to participate in the search or never pursued advanced mathematics courses. Tomizuka and Tobias (1981) noted that such statistics are unfair because it may be difficult to identify the most gifted girls in such a talent search because of the social ostracism they would surely face for such inappropriate behavior during a time in life when sex role adherence is of particular importance.

Evidence of adolescent intellectual decline is seen most dramatically among the elite group of adolescents who are identified as "gifted." At least half of all elementary school children who are identified as gifted/talented/highly capable are female, but by junior high school less than one fourth of this elite group are female (Noble, 1987). It is difficult to imagine that there is any biological system that operates such that exceptionally able females become average over a short time period. Sex role stereotyping pressures, which intensify during adolescence, are a much more likely cause for this distressing phenomenon. As a society, we simply cannot afford to lose so many exceptionally talented minds.

There is ample evidence that somewhere between late elementary school and Grade 12, sex-typed attitudes play a major role in the lives of children. Furthermore, there are not many signs that times are changing. A recent survey reported that adolescents maintain sex-stereotyped beliefs about which occupations are appropriate for females and males (Gorrell & Shaw, 1988).

Video Games, Sports, and Other Adolescent Activities

American female and male adolescents have always engaged in sex differentiated activities ranging from hunting and gathering in early civilizations to barn raising and quilting bees in Colonial America. Even recent attempts at legislation to end sex segregation in groups such as Boy and Girl Scouts and their adolescent counterparts, Explorer and Junior Scouts, and little league and Babe Ruth league, have, for the most part, failed. Either the courts have ruled that sex segregation is legal, as in the case of scouting, or the lifting of sex restrictions has not in fact changed much, as in the case of adolescent baseball leagues, which typically enroll very few girls. Even in instances in which there is no formal sex segregation, boys and girls often self-segregate. One modern day example of this is billiards and video games that tend to attract a much higher percentage of boys than girls. (The next time you pass or enter a pool hall or arcade, count the number of males and females. I have been doing this for years, and am still surprised at how very sex-segregated these public facilities are.)

Both billiards and video games seem to require spatial skill. It seems likely that repeated practice at these activities would lead to improvement in some spatial skills. Greenfield and Lauber (1985) believe that the visual analysis involved in these leisure time spatial activities transfers to academic disciplines, such as the sciences, which require spatial ability. McClurg and Chaille (1987) studied the effects of computer games on spatial cognition. Their subjects were boys and girls in the fifth, seventh, and ninth grades. Overall, all subjects (regardless of sex or grade) showed gains on a mental rotation test after they played two spatial-type computer games. Because numerous surveys have shown that boys play more video games than girls, this is another way in which spatial skills are differentially developed in boys.

The computer explosion has changed our lives in many ways. Computer knowledge is already an essential skill for countless occupations, and is likely to become increasingly important in the next decade. Are the sexes participating equally in technologically rich fields? As we have already seen, there are large discrepancies in the use of "entertainment software." Much of the software that is written for children's entertainment has the potential to develop eye and hand coordination and to make the user more comfortable with computers. If you haven't played a computer game in a while, stop in an arcade, and after counting the males and females, look at the nature of the games. A majority involve acts of aggression such as "bombing" an assortment of objects and killing enemies. (The enemies are easy to spot—they are usually uglier than the other beings.) Boys seem to prefer the aggressive nature of these games far more than girls do. Not only are boys more likely to use computers in play, they are also more likely to use them in learning environments (Linn, 1985). When boys and girls both use computers, they also tend to use them for different purposes. In California high schools, females comprise 86% of all students in word-processing classes and only 37% of all students in programming classes. Enrollments in computer camps are equally lopsided, with females comprising only 30% of all students who enroll (Linn, 1985).

Adolescent boys also engage in more organized sports than adolescent girls. Football, a virtually exclusively male sport, requires considerable spatial analysis, especially if it includes carefully planned "plays" for passing. There are some spatial activities that girls are more likely to engage in than boys. Embroidery, especially embroidery without a preprinted pattern would seem to be an excellent spatial skill, as would sewing without a pattern. However, these are activities that probably attract few girls, especially in relation to the number of boys who participate in traditionally male activities that contain spatial components. Reading is a somewhat sex-typed female activity. In fact, some toy stores keep their books in the section that is labeled "girls' toys." We really do not know what the majority of girls are doing while adolescent boys are engaged in sports. It seems likely that adolescent girls probably do read more than adolescent boys and probably watch more daytime television (e.g., soap operas), but these are untested "hunches."

Typically, girls are required to perform more housework chores. It is difficult to imagine how these chores could improve intellectual growth. For example, the type of mathematics used in recipes is arithmetic conversions, and isn't likely to require any mathematical skills beyond addition, subtraction, and fractions. In general, typical adolescent activities seem to favor the development of cognitive skills for males over females.

ADULTHOOD AND OLD AGE

The average American woman spends 17 years raising children and 18 years helping aging parents.
—*Newsweek* (July 16, 1990, cover)

The bulk of our lives is spent as adults and later as older adults. There are numerous psychosocial factors that maintain the sex role stereotypic behaviors we learned in our youth. Below is a brief survey of some of the factors that have implications for cognitive functioning.

Sex-Related Power Differential

Even when both spouses work, wives perform a disproportionate share of child care and housework tasks, regardless of social class.
—Rodin and Ickovics (1990, p. 1023)

It is possible that psychologists who study cognitive differences are missing the most salient aspect of sex differences in human interactions. Meeker and Weitzel-O'Neill (1977) believe that many sex differences are merely an artifact of power and status differences. Men behave as they do because they hold substantially all of the real power in society, and women behave as they do because they are much less powerful than men. Men gain power and prestige through the status of their occupation and the size of their paycheck (R. E. Gould, 1974). Occupations that are typically male are more highly prized by society than occupations that are typically female. Even when a traditionally female and a traditionally male job require the same level of background or training (e.g., secretary and grounds-keeper), the male job will most often pay substantially more.

Most of society's powerful people are men. Virtually all government leaders, corporate officials, leading scientists, bankers, and stockbrokers are men. Society's power differential continues in most households. Even if men are no longer the sole breadwinner, in a vast majority of American households, they earn more than their wives. In most marriages, the husband not only earns more money, but he is also better educated, taller, and heavier than the wife. Thus, the power differential extends beyond money and prestige of occupation, it also includes the physical power associated with larger stature.

The occupations that require spatial and mathematical abilities frequently offer higher prestige, power, and higher salaries. Children learn that if they want to become physicians, pharmacists, engineers, computer analysts, accountants, scientists, or veterinarians, they will have to excel in mathematics and sciences. Because these are examples of the high paying prestigious occupations that are primarily filled by men, boys learn that success in the academic areas that are prerequisites for these occupations is necessary if they are to fulfill their adult sex role. Occupations that are traditionally female, such as teacher, secretary, and homemaker, do not require excellent mathematical or spatial skills. Good communication or verbal skills are needed in these occupations, which is exactly the academic area in which most females excel. Although there have been significant increases in the number of women in law, medicine, and business schools, other traditionally male areas have seen much less change. Female participation remains particularly low in chemistry, physics, mathematics, the building trades and engineering. The number of males entering traditional female domains is still relatively low (U.S. Bureau of the Census, 1989). If you are a young college student, you may be getting a false impression about sexual equality from your experiences in college. Are you surprised to learn that since 1970 approximately 4 million woman have entered the work force, and of these, 3.3 million are working as secretaries, nurses, bookkeepers, cashiers, and other female-dominated support occupations (e.g., social work) (Hacker, cited in Eccles, 1987)? The world of work is still segregated by sex for a large proportion of working adults (Bridges, 1989).

It is difficult to determine cause and effect when sex differences in occupations are considered. Females could dominate selected fields that require verbal ability because they are inherently better in verbal ability, or they could be better than males in verbal ability because they are educated for careers in these areas. The problem with this sort of explanation is that there are few differences between the sexes in verbal abilities for the majority of the population. (Recall that the largest differences are found for those with very low verbal abilities such as reading difficulties and stuttering and for the majority of the population only in fluency and ability to generate synonyms.) Similar problems arise when considering the relationship between male abilities and male occupational preferences. The only conclusion that can be reached is that many prestigious, high paying jobs require mathematical and spatial skills and that these jobs tend to be filled primarily by men. However, it is important to remember when considering the relationship among ability, occupation, and sex that more than ability is involved in determining who fills the high status occupations. Traditionally, other demographic indicators like race, socioeconomic status, religion, and country of origin, independent of ability, have determined who will succeed in high status positions. The fact that females have superior performance on some *tests* of verbal ability (e.g., fluency), has not translated into occupational success in high verbal fields like academia or journalism that are associated with high prestige and/or high salaries. This demonstrates the importance of psychosocial variables in determining occupational success. Even high status positions that primarily require verbal ability, such as lawyer and politician, are overwhelmingly male. Furthermore, it is difficult to think of any important occupation that does not require verbal ability because the ability to communicate is essential in all endeavors.

Performance Evaluations

One possible explanation for cognitive sex differences is that they don't really exist. We are misled into believing that they exist because we live in a sex-biased society that evaluates female and male performance and products differently. There is some evidence that a performance or product is evaluated differently, depending on whether the evaluator believes that it was created by a man or a woman (Goldberg, 1968; Pheterson, Kiesler, & Goldberg, 1971). More recent evidence suggests that people prefer articles that are written by males (Paludi & Bauer, 1983; Paludi & Strayer, 1985). In a meta-analytic review of the research literature on sex biases in evaluation, the authors concluded that average differences in the rating of male and female accomplishments is "negligible" (Swim, Borgida, Maruyama, & Meyers, 1989). They determined that people still use stereotypes, but the stereotypes are more complex than simple female–male distinctions. Subtypes of stereotypes are more important in evaluations (e.g., businesswoman and housewife stereotypes).

   Although the meta-analytic review of the literature pertaining to performance evaluations suggested that the effects are negligible, once again it seems that large effects are sometimes found. In Etaugh's (1989) review of evaluation bias, she found that ". . . males of low competence are evaluated more poorly than females of low competence. In the middle range of average competence, which includes most people, antifemale bias is the rule" (p. 125). Thus, overall results can appear as negligible when males are evaluated more harshly when their level of competence is below average and females are evaluated more harshly when their level of competence is average. What about evaluations for above average competence? Etaugh (1989) summarized the literature this way:

> . . . some studies have found that women who are portrayed as being highly successful in traditionally male occupations are judged more competent than males in the same occupation. This has been called the "talking platypus phenomenon": i.e., it makes little difference what the platypus says; the amazing thing is that it can talk at all. But even when the competence of a successful woman is recognized, the explanations offered for her success may differ markedly from those offered to explain a man's success. His successful performance generally is attributable to the stable, internal attribute of skill, while the same performance is attributed to such unstable or external factors as luck, effort, or ease of task. (pp. 124–125)

It may be more likely that our stereotypes lead us to evaluate fine art or literature or architecture in differentiated ways because standards are more subjective in these areas, but it is more difficult to apply the notion of sex-differentiated evaluation criteria to standardized tests of mathematics and spatial ability. Some have argued that if a test reveals consistent sex differences, then the test should be declared invalid, and a new test should be found. This line of reasoning begins with the assumption that sex differences cannot truly exist; therefore, the fault must lie in the test. Although it is always possible that any between-sex differences were due to some bias in the test itself (e.g., test uses examples that are unfamiliar to one sex), the standardized tests of spatial, mathematical, and verbal ability that have been used in a majority of the studies reviewed in this book are unlikely to contain many of these biases. The largest between-sex differences is found on the SAT-M, a multiple choice test that is machine graded. The Educational Testing Service has come under extreme criticism because of the male advantage on this test. In response to the criticism, every test item that is answered correctly more often by either sex is examined for bias. There is no obvious bias in the content of the questions. (For example, they are as likely to be about cooking as sports, and no knowledge of the content area is needed to answer the question) (Educational Testing Service, 1987). Thus, although sex differentiated performance evaluations can account for some of the sex differences in success rates in certain occupations, it cannot account for the sex differences found with many standardized ability tests.

Because so many lives are affected by SAT scores, the controversy concerning their use and the possibility of sex bias against women is a topic of considerable concern. Recall from chapter 3 that although women tend to score lower than men on the SATs, women get higher grades in college. Because of this, the SATs are clearly going to underestimate women's success in college and overestimate men's success in college. Furthermore, the issue of bias is far from resolved. In a review of the SATs by the American Association of University Women (1988), they found that "an analysis of 24 passages from the SAT's reading comprehension sections contained 34 references to famous men, but only one reference to a famous woman—Margaret Mead—and that was in a passage criticizing her work" (p. 2). Thus, many scholars still maintain that the SATs are biased against women.

Achievement Motivation

Another possible explanation for the cognitive sex differences that are typically found is that they do not represent ability differences. Instead, it is possible that they are indicators of motivational differences. It is possible, for example, that women and men are equally able to learn higher level mathematical concepts, but for some reason, men are more motivated to put in the hard work needed to learn the concepts and/or more motivated to demonstrate their knowledge. Horner (1969) examined the possibility of sex differences in academic motivation. She asked college students to complete the following story which concerned a protagonist named either Anne or John: "At the end of first-term finals, Anne [John] finds herself [himself] at the top of her [his] medical school class." She found that college students wrote about many more negative consequences of academic success for the female protagonist than for the male protagonist. Examples of some of the negative consequences that followed Anne's success were: "Everyone hates and envies Anne" and "Anne feels unhappy and unfeminine." It seems that the female protagonist had become unsexed by success. These results led Horner to hypothesize that, in addition to the usual motivational tendencies that are found in both men and women, women possess a fear of success or a motive to avoid success because success often has negative consequences for women.

Although Horner's research on fear of success captured media headlines, it has not held up in replications. Like most psychological constructs, success motivation is more complex than a simple approach–avoid continuum. It seems that we also need to be concerned with "success at what?" Later research showed that there was little negative imagery when Anne was successful in traditional female occupations like nursing. In addition, males have also been found to be concerned with negative consequences of success. More recent research suggests that if fear of success is a valid motivational tendency, then it exists about equally in men and women. It seems that although many women may want to become more than just a "sex object," many men want to become more than just a "success object." Thus, the well-publicized fear of success motivation cannot be used to understand cognitive sex differences. (See Spence & Helmreich, 1983 and Fogel & Paludi, 1984, for reviews of the literature.)

More recent examinations of achievement motivation have considered the multidimensional nature of this construct. Spence and Helmreich (1978, 1983) examined sex differences in achievement concerns in the areas of work (the desire to work hard and do a good job), mastery (the preference for challenging tasks and high performance standards), and competition (the enjoyment of inter-personal competition and the desire to do better than others). They found that, in general, women are more concerned with work achievement, and men are more concerned with achievement in competitive and mastery situations. Similar sex differences in competition are sometimes found with children (Halpern & Kagan, 1984). If males are more aggressive, more competitive, and more concerned with mastery throughout the life span, they might be expected to excel in the more competitive aspects of school and work. It is possible that a "competitive edge" or motivational achievement factor is underlying some of the cognitive sex differences. If you read the want-ads, you will find that many of the job adver-tisements use masculine-aggressive language. The ads often claim that the job needs to be filled by "a strong deal-closer," "an aggressive negotiator," or a "dominant personality." Sometimes the ads sound more like a job description for a soldier than a salesperson. Because achievement is a major component of the male sex role stereotype, it should not be surprising to find that males are more achievement oriented, at least in competitive and mastery situations.

Family Life

As much as women want to be good scientists or engineers, they want first and foremost to be womanly companions of men and to be mothers.
—Bruno Bettleheim (1965)

The overwhelming majority of adults marry and/or become parents. It is also true that despite recent social changes, women and men perform different roles and functions in most American homes. Although a majority of mothers now work outside of the home, most of these mothers still retain primary responsibil-ity for child care and housework (Allgeier, 1983). The result is severe strain and fatigue for women who want to maintain serious, demanding professional careers and a balanced family life. Recently, the Public Broadcasting Service aired a series exploring the lives of creative people. The diverse list of creative women they included all had one thing in common—none had children. This was, of course, not true for the creative men, most of whom had children. This result was replicated with a less stellar group. In a phone survey of working women "a larger than expected proportion of women with managerial positions are divorced or separated, and as the level of commitment and preparation required for a job rises, there is an increase in the proportion of childless women and a decrease in the proportion with three or more children under the age 18" (Valdez & Gutek, 1986, p. 157).

Although many people regard children as an important asset in their lives and would gladly trade other forms of success for parenthood, one conclusion is that children require mothers to prioritize their time and effort in ways that are not required of many fathers. It does seem that traditional family life mitigates against academic and other professional success for women, although the number of women who have successfully combined motherhood, marriage, and demanding occupations is growing.

Family life commitments can explain sex differences in demanding occupations that require years of preparation such as physicist, mathematician, and engineering. They can also explain the cognitive sex differences that arise during puberty if we assume that teens direct their energies and select their coursework to prepare for their anticipated adult life roles. Marriage and family are viewed by employers as an asset for a man's career and a hindrance for a woman's career. Surveys have shown the obvious: When mothers work outside the home they are much more likely to be called at work to care for a sick child than a father who works outside the home (Valdez & Gutek, 1986). It is not surprising to find that women's work is concentrated in low paying, deadend jobs (E. E. Diamond, 1986).

There was a recent uproar in the business community when Schwartz (1989) suggested that corporations give working mothers the option of a career track that allows more time for family and other home commitments. Her rationale for this suggestion is that the superwoman myth is just that. It is not physically possible to work the 60- to 80-hour corporate week (which is norm in some law firms, corporate offices, and medical internship programs) and still have time and energy for the demanding job of parenting. Presumably, men would also be given this option, but in reality, child care remains overwhelmingly (sometimes quite literally) the responsibility of the mother, and if such career options were available, more women would be involved than men. Is this a good idea? On the pro side, it would allow women to keep working, but at less than full speed (which in some occupations might mean 40 to 45 hours a week) if they choose to do so. Women could also opt to remain on the career track. It seems to take into account some harsh realities and offer help for women who are dragging from work to preschool to the pediatrician to the play group to piano lessons to PTA meetings, etc. On the con side, it would institutionalize a lower career track for women and make all mothers "suspect" of job neglect. This concept has been disparagingly nicknamed the "Mommy Track"—a separate, less career-oriented track for mothers.

When we consider old age, it is accurate to say that the future is female. Women live an average of approximately 7 years longer than men. If you are not yet a "golden ager," then you will find it informative to visit a community that caters to older people such as a "retirement village," an "elders' day center" or a nursing home. The participants are overwhelmingly females who are cared for primarily by their daughters (Beck, 1990). This fact has lead to the naming of yet another special track for women—the "Daughter Track." Women at midlife have been described as "a sandwich" because they are wedged between child-care responsibilities and parent-care responsibilities. Perhaps the answer to questions like "Why are there so few outstanding female mathematicians and research scientists?" can be found in the caregiver role in which so many women engage.

The topic of psychosocial hypotheses is continued in the next chapter, in which I take a different perspective on the impact of psychosocial variables. I consider the way in which socialization practices could lead to differential performance in cognitive activities.

CHAPTER SUMMARY

Psychosocial explanations of cognitive sex differences are important because of their implications for change. If sex differences in cognitive abilities can be attributed to psychosocial variables, then these changes can be reduced or eliminated with appropriate societal changes. One of the difficulties in identifying the relevant psychosocial variables is the pervasiveness of sex role stereotypes in our society. The result has been a nonconscious ideology in which we are blind to many of the sex differentiated attributes and expectations that have become ingrained in contemporary society.

Children develop an awareness of and conformity to sex roles stereotypes at a very young age. Freudian, Social Modeling, Learning, and Cognitive theories have been proposed to explain the acquisition and maintenance of sex stereotypic behavior patterns. Sex-linked socialization practices that vary over the life span were examined in an attempt to understand the myriad of sex role stereotypic influences that are part of every male's and female's life. One reason for the low participation rate of women in demanding fields is the caregiver role that women assume.

7 Psychosocial Hypotheses Part II: A Differential Abilities Perspective

Contents

7

In the preceding chapter, I considered the way psychosocial pressures to conform to sex role stereotypic behavior could operate to create or exacerbate cognitive sex differences throughout the life span. An alternate approach to the question of how psychosocial variables affect cognition is to consider spatial, mathematical, and verbal abilities separately. This is the perspective that is considered in this chapter.

SPATIAL ABILITIES

Much of the literature leads one to expect poorer spatial test performance from the aged, females, and left-handers. . . . Test data seem to corroborate all of these relationships.
—Sonnenfeld (1985, p. 109)

Spatial abilities are probably the most difficult of the three sex-related cognitive ability differences to describe or understand. As defined in chapter 3, they consist of at least four component abilities—spatial visualization, spatial perception, mental rotation, and spatiotemporal judgment (perception of objects moving in space). It is often measured with tests that require mentally rotating a figure in space (for mental rotation), or finding a smaller figure embedded within the borders of a larger figure, or indicating the water level of a tipped glass, or estimating when a moving object will hit a target. As reviewed earlier, almost all measures of spatial perception, mental rotation, and spatiotemporal judgment show consistent and sometimes substantial sex differences, with males performing more accurately and/or more rapidly than females. Let's consider how psychosocial variables could be underlying these sex differences.

Sex Role Conformity

It does not seem obvious that either sex should have the advantage when it comes to knowing that the water level remains horizontal in a tipped glass or in aligning a rod to the vertical position. However, if these results are related in a straightforward way to sex role stereotypes, then you would expect that those individuals who are the most feminine-sex-typed would have the poorest skills and those who are the most masculine-sex-typed would have the best skills. As discussed in chapter 7, this prediction was made by Nash (1979), who hypothesized that individuals will perform better on a cognitive task when their self-concepts match the gender stereotyping of the task. The underlying idea is that individuals value things that are like the "self." The cognitive and behavioral result is that individuals engage in activities that are consistent with their self-image and avoid activities that are inconsistent with their self-image. Thus, if we assume that spatial tasks are male stereotyped, then males and females with more masculine self-concepts would perform better on these tasks than their less male-stereotyped peers. There have been a large number of studies that have examined the possible congruence between self-concept and type of task at which one excels. In a meta-analytic review of the literature, Signorella and Jamison (1986) found partial confirmation. Recall from the last chapter that they determined that both high "masculine" scores and low "feminine" scores were associated with better performance of spatial and mathematics tests, but only for females. This result is interesting because it is contrary to the prediction that "androgynous" individuals (people with high feminine and high masculine subscores on sex role inventories) would have the intellectual advantage (e.g., Cook, 1985). Thus, at least to some extent, congruency between one's self concept and the way a cognitive task is sex role stereotyped is one determinant of how well an individual will perform. The underlying argument is that more males than females will conform to a masculine stereotype, and this is at least part of the reason why males tend to outperform females in tasks that are perceived of as masculine in nature—spatial and some advanced mathematical tasks.

Differential Life Experiences

Sex role stereotypes could also influence the development of spatial skills indirectly by providing each sex with different amounts and types of spatial experiences. This possibility was considered in the last chapter when video games and billiards were discussed as common adolescent activities among boys but not among girls. Boys' and girls' lives differ in many ways. For example, in an observation of preschool children, Adams and Bradford (1985) found that boys touched unfamiliar objects more often than girls did, and girls touched familiar objects more often than boys did. It is possible that early life exploration of the unfamiliar provides a head start in spatial skills learning.

Sex differences in life experiences are particularly striking among children 6 to 10 years old. Herman, Heins, and Cohen (1987) found that boys are allowed to travel a greater distance from home than girls. Boys are also much more likely to engage in sports and activities that involve throwing a ball or other object (Graber & Petersen, in press). According to this line of reasoning, there must be some advantage in judging moving objects that is accrued from the hundreds of hours boys are spending on baseball diamonds, basketball courts, and football fields. Of course, there are girls who also engage in these activities, but overall, more boys are spending more time in ball sports than girls are. The association between participation in spatial activities and spatial abilities was also found in a sample of college students (Newcombe, Bandura, & Taylor, 1983).

If you are thinking critically (and I hope you are), you will not be too quick to conclude from these findings that boys become better at spatial skills *because* they participate in more sports. Although this seems to be a possibility, it is also possible that more boys engage in throwing sports because they are better at spatial skills or for a reason that is unrelated to cognition such as boys' tendency to have greater upper body strength than girls. The same criticism can be made about a study that found that girls who play with traditional boys' toys tend to perform better on spatial tasks (Serbin, cited in Adler, 1989a). It is possible that these girls are able to develop their spatial abilities by playing with traditional boys's toys; it is also possible that the girls who chose boys' toys are the ones with better spatial abilities. What we can conclude from studies like these is that there is an association between participation in spatial activities and tests of spatial abilities.

In a meta-analytic review of the literature that linked spatial activity participation with spatial ability, Baenninger and Newcombe (1989) concluded that there is a weak relationship and that the magnitude of the effect is the same for females as for males. Thus, according to these authors, both sexes benefit about equally from participation in spatial activities.

It does seem that geographical knowledge is a very different sort of skill from mental rotation or visual perception, yet it is also included in the literature on sex differences in spatial abilities. In five different experiments with over 1,800 college students, Beatty and Troster (1987) found that males more accurately located places on maps of the United States than females. These sex differences could not be attributed to education, travel history, or desire to travel. The authors of this study suggested that males may be more likely to accept responsibility for planning routes to unfamiliar places and that this differential experience could be responsible for the differences in "map knowledge." It is interesting to note that cognitive psychologists who study people's memory for geographical locations have determined that geographical knowledge is stored in a spatial memory code, so there is a theoretical basis for linking geographical knowledge to spatial abilities (Kosslyn, Ball, & Reiser, 1978).

If different experiences are responsible for the sex differences in spatial abilities, then it should be possible to improve spatial abilities by providing appropriate training. Several psychologists have examined this possibility.

Spatial Skills Training

If I took a group of males and females and assigned them at random to different types of spatial activities and then found differences in their spatial abilities as a function of the kind of experiences they received, I would be able to make fairly strong causal statements. Notice how this experimental approach differs from merely looking at the sorts of tasks girls and boys typically engage in and relating participation in these activities to spatial abilities. By randomly assigning subjects to different conditions, we are able to make causal claims. For this reason, research that has provided different types and amounts of spatial training to subjects is particularly important.

In a direct test of the hypothesis that boys develop better spatial skills than girls *because* of their experiences with spatial activities, Sprafkin, Serbin, Denier and Connor (1983) gave 3½- to 4-year-old children special training with preschool toys that are typically preferred by boys—blocks, dominoes, tinker toys, and paper cut in geometric shapes. They believed that these typical "boys' toys" were important in the development of spatial ability. They found that the children who received the special training with these toys scored higher on a test of spatial ability than a control group of children who did not receive the special training. It seems clear that spatial ability can be taught, and that it can be taught to preschool children by increasing their exposure to typical male-preferred toys.

Support for the notion that differential experience underlies the spatial ability sex difference was obtained when spatial training was provided for first grade children. As discussed in chapter 3, the Embedded Figures Test is a spatial ability test that sometimes (but not reliably) yields sex differences. When Connor, Schackman, and Serbin (1978) tested first-grade children on a special children's version of the Embedded Figures Test, they found the usual sex difference, with the boys performing more accurately than the girls. They then provided both the girls and the boys with an "overlay training procedure" in which they used transparent overlays to highlight the way smaller figures were embedded within the boundaries of the larger figures. They found that after this training both girls and boys improved significantly. Most importantly, the sex differential disappeared after the training. They believe that the reason that the girls benefited more from the training than the boys is because the girls typically have less experience with spatial activities and therefore would improve more with specific instruction. These results provide a strong case for the importance of sex differentiated environmental factors in the development of spatial skills. They clearly demonstrate that spatial skills are trainable.

The finding that girls profit more from spatial training than boys has been partially replicated with other age groups of children. Vandenburg (1975) found that sixth-grade girls, but not sixth-grade boys, showed gains on a mental rotation task after receiving spatial training on building models with blocks. These results have been extended to eighth graders who also showed a significant increase in spatial ability following a 3-week training period that consisted of object manipulation exercises such as folding paper into geometric shapes (Brinkmann, 1966). There were no significant sex differences on the Spatial Relations Test for the eighth graders who participated in this program. Its seems reasonable to conclude from these studies that spatial skills can be learned and that the skills that are learned are transferable to a wide range of spatial tasks. Although earlier research showed that girls seemed to benefit more from spatial training than boys (presumably because the girls had not developed their ability as fully as boys), more recent literature reviews have concluded that both sexes seem to benefit equally from spatial skills training (Baenninger & Newcombe, 1989; Embretson, 1987; Koslow, 1987).

All of these studies point to one conclusion: *Spatial ability can be improved with appropriate training.*

If you recall the discussion on spatial abilities in chapter 3, you may remember that spatial skills decline more rapidly in old age than other cognitive abilities. We now have good evidence that the elderly can also benefit tremendously from spatial skills training. Willis and Schaie (1988) trained an elderly sample with a program that included concrete terms for various angles, manual rotation of figures and subject-generated names for abstract figures. The use of verbal labels in a spatial task allowed the elderly to use a preferred verbal mode of representation in a spatial task (e.g., Clarkson-Smith & Halpern, 1983). Willis and Schaie found that there were no significant sex differences in spatial tasks for the elderly who had participated in the spatial skills training.

Despite the multiplicity of positive results that implicate environmental factors in the development of spatial skills, there are still some nagging inconsistencies that remain unexplained. The principle that water remains horizontal when a glass is tipped seems particularly difficult for girls to comprehend (or perhaps to demonstrate), and the large sex differences found on the Water Level Test cannot be explained by psychosocial factors. Thomas et al. (1973) reported very little success in teaching this principle to girls. In addition, even the strong results supporting the trainability of spatial skills do not rule out the possibility of a biological–environmental interaction. It still remains possible, although unproven, that boys learn spatial principles more easily or readily than girls. It also seems reasonable to conclude that we should be providing all children with those toys that are typically labeled "boys' toys." There is enough evidence to suggest that experience with these toys may be useful in the development of spatial skills. We may be short-changing the intellectual development of girls by providing them with only traditional sex stereotyped toys.

Another important implication of this research is the finding that spatial skills are trainable. Very few schools incorporate spatial skill training into their curriculum. One way to be certain that all individuals develop their spatial abilities to their fullest capacity is to routinely provide such training to all students from their preschool through their high school years. Empirical results have shown that both girls and boys would benefit from such instruction.

MATHEMATICAL ABILITY

Ask yourself how you would respond to a "math freak" adolescent son and a "math freak" adolescent daughter.
—Braine (1988, p. 186)

Sex differences in mathematics achievement are well documented and have been described in the previous chapters. In the years since the first edition of this book was published, one thing we have learned is that general statements such as "males are better than females in mathematics" are simply wrong. Recall that girls outperform boys in computation in elementary school and that boys score significantly higher on some tests of mathematical reasoning beginning around late childhood/early adolescence. Despite the fact that girls receive higher grades than boys in all subjects, including mathematics, they score an average of 50 points lower than boys on the SAT-M. There are numerous psychosocial explanations that have been devised to explain mathematical sex differences. This class of theories places the "blame" squarely on socialization practices and the adherence to sex role stereotypes in contemporary American society.

Socialization Processes

Study after study has documented sex differences in the extent to which children are encouraged to pursue careers in mathematics, in mathematics role models, and in subtle pressures to eschew serious academic pursuits. Female mathematicians report that they were discouraged by others in their efforts to become mathematicians far more often than their male counterparts (Luchins & Luchins, 1981). Professor Martha Smith, a mathematician, described the negative stereotypes associated with being a female mathematician this way: "Many people on hearing the words 'female mathematician' conjure up an image of a six-foot, gray-haired tweed suited oxford clad woman. . . . This image, of course, doesn't attract the young woman who is continually being bombarded with messages, direct and indirect, to be beautiful, 'feminine' and catch a man" (quoted in Ernest, 1976, p. 14). Our stereotypes exert strong social pressures. Few women would choose to identify with this stereotype, even if they were mathematically talented. An artist's rendition of this stereotypic image of a female mathematician is depicted in Fig. 7.1.

FIG. 7.1. Artist's conception of the stereotypical "woman mathematician" as described by Professor Martha Smith: "Many people on hearing the words 'female mathematician' conjure up an image of a six-foot, gray-haired, tweed suited oxford clad woman. . . . This image, of course, doesn't attract the young woman who is continually being bombarded with messages, direct and indirect, to be beautiful, 'feminine' and catch a man." From Ernest (1976), p. 14.

Hilton and Berglund (1974) designed a Background and Experience Questionnaire to assess sex-related environmental differences in mathematics and science. Science interests and experience are often included in these studies because of the close relationship between science and mathematics as well as the corresponding sex differential in science achievement. It is interesting to note that although there are large differences in female and male participation rates in the physical sciences, there are no biological hypotheses for science achievement. Success in science course work requires verbal, spatial, and mathematical abilities. There is no brain site that corresponds to science excellence and there is no science counterpart to dyslexia or dyscalculia—two types of evidence that are frequently used to support biologically based hypotheses of sex differences in verbal and mathematics abilities. Sex differences in science participation rates are relatively noncontroversial: they have a predominantly psychosocial origin.

Hilton and Berglund gave their Background and Experience questionnaire to boys and girls in Grades 7, 9, and 11. They found that boys read more science books, report greater interest in mathematics, consider mathematics more useful in earning a living, talk more about science, and have parents who favor their continuing their education beyond high school more than the girls. Although all of these differences were negligible at Grade 7, they increased with age so that by Grade 11 when career decisions are being made, sex differences were sizable.

Mathematics skills are extremely important in many occupations. Mathematics has been described as a "critical filter" that keeps women out of engineering, computer science, business, and accounting fields because only those individuals with a solid background in mathematics are able to enter these fields. The single best predictor of scores on mathematics achievement tests is the number of mathematics courses an individual has taken (Jones, 1984). Females take fewer mathematics courses than males (Elmore & Vasu, 1986; Sherman, 1982a&b; Yee & Eccles, 1988). High ability women drop out of mathematics and science courses at greater rates than men beginning when the courses first become optional in high school and continuing into graduate school. For those concerned about the low participation of females in mathematically related careers, the solution seems to be simple: Encourage more females to take more mathematics courses. One program designed to encourage women in mathematics focused on the development of self-confidence and the awareness of the importance of mathematics as a key to many career options for women (MacDonald, 1980). Also incorporated in this program were cooperative learning strategies and optional tutoring. Although this was a small-scale study, the women who participated obtained higher class scores, had fewer dropouts, reported better attitudes toward mathematics, and were more likely to continue their mathematics education than a control group of women who did not participate in the program.

Even among those who are exceptionally gifted in mathematics, females are less likely to pursue a career in mathematics than males. Benbow (1988) followed up the tens of thousands of young adolescents who had been identified as mathematically precocious. She found that in adulthood, 42% of the males had chosen careers in mathematics or the sciences compared to only 22% of the females. This is a sad and distressing statistic because the United States cannot maintain its role as a world leader in science and technology without increasing the number of talented individuals who pursue careers in these areas. Of course, the scarcity of females planning a career in a mathematics-related field is an international problem as well. As long as women stay away from fields in which we need educated professionals, the entire international community will suffer as third world achievement also depends on an adequate supply of competent mathematicians and scientists.

Models of Mathematical Achievement

The psychosocial variables that mitigate against female success in mathematics are numerous and interacting. Several multifaceted models have been proposed to explain the relationships among variables.

Sherman (1967), for example, believes that spatial ability is a key factor in understanding sex differences in mathematical ability. She found that scores on the Spatial Relations Test, a test of spatial visualization ability, were more important in predicting girls' decisions to continue in high school mathematics courses than they were for boys. Sherman suggests that by including spatial visualization training in school, the sex differential in both spatial and mathematics ability would be reduced or eliminated. Other researchers have also found a relationship between spatial visualization ability and scores on mathematics tests (Elmore & Vasu, 1980). This suggestion has a logical appeal because mathematical areas such as topology, calculus, and geometry seem to have strong spatial components.

Sex differences in mathematics is an area that is ripe for expectancy effects. In one survey of teachers, 63% reported that they believed that boys were better than girls in mathematical ability, with the rest reporting no sex difference (Ernest, 1976). Harris and Rosenthal (1985) reviewed 135 studies on expectancy effects. They found that:

> Teachers who hold positive expectations for a given student will tend to display a warmer socioemotional climate, express a more positive use of feedback, provide more input in terms of the amount and difficulty of the material that is taught, and increase the amount of student output by providing more response opportunities and interacting more frequently with the student. (p. 377)

Simply put, teachers behave differently when they expect students to succeed than when they don't.

Although, in general, mothers help their children more with all homework (Ernest, 1976), fathers are seven times more likely to be consulted for help with mathematics homework than mothers are (Sherman, 1983). In a recent study of the factors that affect women's enrollment in nontraditional vocations, Houser and Garvey (1985) found that the amount of support, encouragement, and discouragement the women received from significant others in their lives was the most significant factor influencing these decisions. In general, females receive less support and encouragement and more discouragement to pursue mathematics coursework and related occupations than their male counterparts.

In a recent review article on her findings with precocious youth, Benbow (1988) listed many of the psychosocial hypotheses that have appeared in the literature to explain sex differences in mathematics. I summarize, embellish on, and borrow from her listing. Interested readers will want to consult Benbow's paper along with the many responses to it. There are approximately 500 references to related studies in mathematics that the author and commentators used to support their points and to refute those that they didn't agree with. I keep this section relatively brief because those of you who want to delve into the topic further can consult this excellent article with its related commentaries and rebuttal.

1. Females maintain more negative attitudes toward mathematics.   As with every area of research, the literature is not entirely consistent in reporting these findings, but the vast majority of times when differences are found they are in the predicted direction with females more negative than males. (See, e.g., Hyde, Fennema, Ryan, Frost, & Hopp, 1990).

2. Females perceive mathematics to be less important for career goals than males do.   Again, although there are some failures to confirm this hypothesis (e.g., Singer & Stake, 1986), when differences are found, they tend to support this contention. This is important because it relates directly to motivation. At least some of the time, most students will have to exert time and effort to comprehend advanced mathematical concepts. If females, in general, believe that mathematics is less useful, then they are likely to exert less effort to learn the concepts. This belief is sometimes seen in the popular media. I remember sitting in a movie theater watching the block buster "Peggy Sue Got Married." In this fantasy film, a young woman has the opportunity to return to high school with the knowledge of her adult life. In her mathematics class, she assures the teacher that she will never need to know the mathematics he wants her to learn. A spontaneous cheer went up from the movie audience, many of whom seemed to agree with her pronouncement about the uselessness of mathematics for women's lives.

3. Females have less confidence in their ability to learn mathematics.   This is an interesting hypothesis because, although females expect to receive lower course grades in mathematics than males do, females, in fact, receive the higher course grades even in advanced mathematics courses (Elmore & Vasu, 1986). Although females may be less confident, they are performing better in virtually all mathematics courses. Of course, this comparison may be unfair because there are fewer females than males in advanced mathematics courses, so they may represent a more select group of females. Females are also more likely to attribute success in mathematics to effort than to ability (Ryckman & Peckham, 1987).

4. Mathematics is a male-stereotyped cognitive domain.   In general, the disproportionate number of males in advanced mathematics courses suggests that this is true. If you doubt this, show a few friends Fig. 7.1 and ask them to guess the college major of the woman depicted. The stereotype that females who succeed in mathematics and the sciences are masculine can be vicious and demeaning. Again, I provide a personal example that brought this fact home to me in a much more vivid manner than any of the research that I have read. A male college student was showing me around UCLA's very large campus. We went to the portion of the campus that houses the engineering school, mathematics, and physical sciences departments. He told me that there is a derogatory name for the female students on that part of campus ("science dog"). The message was quite strong that being an attractive female and studying mathematics and the sciences are not compatible. This ugly moniker saddened and angered me. Name-calling designed specifically to denigrate females who study mathematics and the sciences provides strong support for the notion that mathematics is a male-stereotyped domain.

5. Females receive less encouragement and support for studying advanced mathematics.   In a recent survey of the parents of junior high school students,

Yee and Eccles (1988) found that parents believe that mathematics is more difficult for their daughters than for their sons. These beliefs would presumably translate into giving their daughters less support for studying advanced mathematics than their sons.

   6. *Females take fewer mathematics courses than males; therefore, they score lower on tests of mathematical reasoning ability.* This is a prediction that is difficult to disagree with, but it is not as straightforward as it may seem. It is true that fewer females are enrolled in advanced mathematics courses with the proportion decreasing as the level of the course increases. But there have been studies that have controlled for number of mathematics courses taken, and sex differences are still found favoring males (e.g., Meece et al., 1982).

   Even if some of these hypothesized reasons to explain sex differences in advanced mathematics are weak or even wrong, the effect of socialization on females and males comes from the totality of experiences and not any one of them in isolation. Several more complex models to explain mathematics sex differences have been proposed. Sherman (1982a), for example, has identified confidence in learning mathematics, perceived usefulness of mathematics, and attitudes of one's mother, father and teacher toward learning mathematics as important determinants of mathematics achievement. It seems intuitively obvious that these are important variables in understanding success in mathematics. Few people would persist in higher mathematics coursework if they believed that they did not have the ability to learn the material, if they felt that it was of little value, or if they were routinely discouraged by their parents and teachers.

Some Troubling Issues

Although the list of possible psychosocial influences that work in concert to discourage female participation in mathematics is extensive, there are some gaping holes in the reasoning. First, all of these theories suggest that males should uniformly score higher than females on tests of mathematical reasoning. As you know, females score higher than males on computation in the elementary

SALLY FORTH. Permission by Greg Howard and News America Syndicate.

school grades. Psychosocial hypotheses cannot easily explain why females score higher on *some* tests of mathematics.

Second, many authors (including me) have been perplexed by the robust finding that females obtain higher grades in mathematics than males (e.g., Kimball, 1989). It is clear that females learn mathematics at least as well, if not better, than males, but this does not translate into success in mathematical professions, and males are performing much better on the SAT-M even when females are at least as well prepared in terms of their coursework. It is clear that we need new and much more specific theories of how psychosocial variables work that could explain this disjointed pattern of results.

One suggestion is that boys have more autonomous learning styles, which means that they prefer more self-directed learning. According to this hypothesis, girls learn better when they are given directives. Therefore, males perform better than females when the test is not similar to the topics that are taught in school (as in standardized tests), and females perform better than males when they are tested on material that is similar to that taught in class (as in school exams) (Kimball, 1989). Although this is an interesting possibility, there are no independent confirmations that males and females have different learning styles.

An important part of the mathematics sex differences debate is which is the better measure of mathematical abilities. Is it grades, which reflect achievement on multiple tests over the course of a semester or a year, or is it single-session tests like the SAT-M? The SAT-M is not closely tied to any particular instruction; course grades are. It seems that this question is like many of the others posed in this book. The answer is not one or the other, but both are important depending on what you want to know about mathematical abilities.

VERBAL ABILITIES

In some ways, verbal abilities have become the stepchild of the cognitive sex differences literature. It is the one cognitive sex difference in which females have the advantage, and it is the least studied and discussed of the three ability differences. The tendency to neglect verbal abilities research is likely to continue in light of the conclusion by Hyde and Linn (1988) that "gender differences in verbal ability no longer exist" (p. 53). Recall from chapter 3 that they found small differences favoring females on anagrams and mixed and general tests of verbal ability, medium differences favoring females on speech production, and small differences favoring males on verbal analogies. Recall also that large sex differences are found on the low end of the verbal abilities distribution especially with regard to stuttering and reading disabilities. As discussed in chapter 3, Hines (1990) found extremely large differences favoring females on tests of associational fluency (generating synonyms) and word fluency.

Few would argue that verbal ability is less important than spatial or mathematical ability. In fact, it would seem that it is the most important of the abilities because virtually every human interaction relies on verbal or language skills. Of all of the ability differences, it is also the earliest to emerge. As reviewed earlier, sex-differentiated socialization practices begin at or before birth, with girl infants receiving more adult vocalizations than boy infants and parents making sex attributions that are consistent with commonly held stereotypes. It is also possible that when girls find mathematics and science courses closed to them, they then satisfy achievement needs in their language courses.

In a review of the cognitive sex differences literature, Bradshaw and Nettleton (1983) concluded that verbal abilities are more subject to environmental influences than spatial abilities. They based this conclusion on a review of ability studies in which correlations between parents and children, among siblings, and between identical and fraternal twins suggest that cultural and educational variables have a greater impact on verbal skills than spatial ones. Although this is an interesting possibility, correlational data can only provide weak support for this hypothesis and do not rule out the possibility of a biological–environmental interaction.

The Flip-Flop Nature of the Verbal Abilities Literature

Although females outscore males on some verbal ability tests, this advantage has not translated into exceptional occupational success. One area in which females have a clear ability advantage is in language fluency/speech production. If success depended solely on ability, then we would expect to find many more females in positions like politician, journalist, professor, and public relations than there are.

Recall from chapter 3 that a female advantage on the SAT-V has diminished over the years from a small female advantage to no differences to a small male advantage. I suspect that this result is due to the large number of analogies on the SAT-V, the one "verbal" area in which males excel. There are no biological hypotheses that can explain the change in SAT-V scores over 20 or so years. It is possible that the decline in female advantage on the SAT-V is indicative of a positive change for females because more females are taking the SATs and more females are enrolling in college than ever before.

The touchstone for a good psychosocial hypothesis is one that can explain the diverse pattern of results with verbal abilities. It may be that biological hypotheses are better for the large number of males at the low end of the disabilities distribution and psychosocial hypotheses are better for some of the other findings. After all, it is difficult to argue that we don't encourage boys to learn to read or speak fluently.

It seems that a useful approach is to look to the underlying cognitive processes. In chapter 3, I suggested that females may be more proficient in the rapid access and utilization of information held in memory (processes involved in comprehension) and males may be more proficient at representing and manipulating information in memory (processes involved in solving novel problems). It may be that we can devise more satisfactory theories by changing our conceptual framework than by trying to find one theory that can explain female superiority on some verbal tasks and male superiority on others.

It is interesting to note in this context that although there are many more males identified as mathematically precocious, there are no sex differences among youth who are identified as verbally precocious (Benbow, 1988). This is not the finding that I predicted in the earlier edition of this book. Perhaps we obtain these results because the SAT is used to identify the verbally precocious, and the SAT is heavily weighted with analogies (approximately one quarter of the questions) and males seem to perform better than females on analogies.

It is difficult to understand why sex differences in verbal ability have not been investigated to the same extent as the other cognitive sex differences. Perhaps because the pattern of results is complex (with males scoring higher on verbal analogies and females scoring higher on associational fluency and language production), it is easier to conclude that the differences are small or nonexistent.

The Bent Twig Hypothesis

One theory designed to explain female superiority in some language areas was proposed by Sherman (1967). It has come to be known as the "Bent Twig Hypothesis" in reference to an old saying that goes something like this, "As the twig is bent, so the tree shall grow." Sherman began with the assumption that girls talk at an earlier age than boys, although the evidence in support of this claim is somewhat mixed. Because of their early advantage with language, girls rely more on verbally and socially mediated approaches in their interactions with people and objects in their world. Boys, on the other hand, rely on their better developed musculature to interact with people and objects; thus, they move about more, a fact that could contribute to the development of their spatial skills. Each sex develops somewhat fixed patterns or preferences for interacting, with the result that early developmental differences guide later actions. In this way, a small initial difference in abilities between the sexes grows larger over time.

It is interesting to note that the Bent Twig Hypothesis does not explain the initial sex difference with respect to verbal ability. It could be due to early differential reinforcement patterns for infant vocalizations or due to biologically based readiness to produce language or some interaction of these two possibilities.

If, as Sherman suggested, girls tend to rely on verbal skills instead of utilizing spatial ones, then the finding that female's brains may be less lateralized, could in fact reflect strategy differences and not biological differences. In other words, the sex differences in lateralization that were discussed in the biological chapters could be an artifact of verbal strategy preferences among females and not reflective of "hard wired" neurological differences. Suppose, for example, that females use verbal strategies or modes of information processing when faced with the Embedded Figures Test. A verbal strategy would be less efficient than a spatial approach to this problem. Females would then be expected to perform less well than males who are relying on spatial modes of information processing when taking this test. If this hypothesis is true, then cognitive sex differences could be explained by the perseverative use of verbal strategies by females that leaves them at a disadvantage when performing spatial tasks.

SEX ROLES AND ACHIEVEMENT-RELATED DECISIONS

The superwomen are weary; . . . In the 80's American women learned that "having it all" meant doing it all. . . .
—Wallis (1989, p. 80)

The most comprehensive theoretical model designed to explain sex differences in academic achievement was proposed by Eccles (Parsons) et al. (1983) and, more recently by Eccles (1987). It is a variation of an expectancy × (times) value model. Models of this type are really models of motivation. The underlying idea is that individuals persist at tasks in which they *expect* success and avoid tasks in which they *expect* failure. Similarly, individuals persist at tasks when they *value* the goal and avoid tasks when they do not *value* the goal.

In this model, Eccles delineates the relationships among several important determinants of academic choices in general and career decisions. In her psychosocial model of achievement-related decisions, she posits a theoretical network composed of the following variables (which are described in ways that link them to the preceding discussion in this chapter): sex role stereotypes, beliefs and behaviors of parents and teachers, individual aptitude, previous experiences and the way the individual perceives these variables as well as the individual's goals and expectations of success. A copy of the model is shown in Fig. 7.2.

Take some time to look over the variables that are shown in Fig. 7.2 and the way they connect to each other. Consider for example, how women's long-term goals and "ideal self" differ from those of men's. Recall earlier discussions about the role that women play as primary caretaker for their children, their home, and later, for their aging parents. The ideal mother/daughter spends much time and effort caring for others and maintaining a clean orderly home. In this social context, it is easy to understand why we find fewer women in society's most demanding, prestigious and highly paid careers such as surgeon, high level politician (state and national level), research scientist, and chief corporate officer.

Eccles's model differs from most of the others in that it includes the issue of choice. Everyone makes choices all of the time; what this model attempts to do is

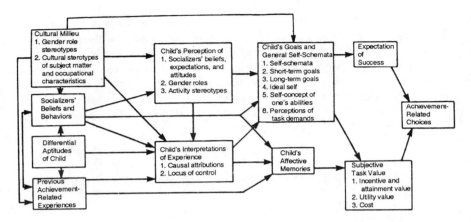

FIG. 7.2. Model devised to explain how an interdependent network of values and expectations influence academic and career choices. From Eccles (1987). Gender roles and women's achievement-related decisions. *Psychology of Women Quarterly, 11,* 135–172. Reprinted with permission.

delineate the variables that shape the choices we make. In this context, women and men (on the average) have different values, and in the context of one's own values, women and men would be expected to make different achievement-related choices.

As Eccles described, there is a complex web of psychosocial causative factors that all work against female excellence in achievement-related positions. Many researchers in this area have been highly critical of any claim that sex differences in cognitive performance or career choices can be traced to a biological etiology given the large number of psychosocial explanations that both logically and empirically have been used to explain the data (Fox, Tobin, & Brody, 1979; Sherman, 1979).

Psychosocial Mediating Variables

Sex role stereotypes and other pressures to behave in "womanly" or "manly" ways can have pervasive effects that operate indirectly on cognition. Sex differences are most often found and are largest when the dependent measure is response time. Let's consider exactly what happens in a testing situation like the SATs.

Speed-Accuracy Trade-Offs. The SATs are important in determining college admissions. Both the verbal and mathematics sections are taken under timed conditions. Suppose females, on the average, respond to timed pressures in a different way from males. Suppose further that there are no real differences in these cognitive abilities between the sexes (or the differences are too small to be consequential), but females take a more cautious approach to selecting answers. If there is not enough time to complete the tests, and females routinely take more time to select answers because of a bias to respond more slowly, then we would have a situation in which females score significantly lower than males.

This hypothetical scenario is not fiction. There are several indicators that at least part of the sex differences that are found in timed tests are due to differences in response styles. In a recent study (Linn, De Benedictis, Delucchi, Harris, & Stage, 1987) of sex differences on the National Assessment of Educational Progress in Science (NAEP), the researchers found consistent sex differences for children aged 13 to 17, with males answering about 5% more questions correctly than females. This corresponded to a $d = .27$. But when they went through the types of answers picked by females and males, they found that the females were more likely to use the "I don't know" alternative than the males were. It seems that females have less confidence in their science knowledge or ability.

In another study of sex differences in mode of responding, Goldstein, Haldane, and Mitchell (1990) found the usual male advantage on a mental rotation test, but when they analyzed their data using the ratio of correct responses to the number of items attempted, the male advantage on this test was eliminated. In a second test of the hypothesis that sex differences would be eliminated when time constraints were removed, they found no sex differences in untimed administrations of the mental rotation test. These results provide strong support for the idea that cautiousness or some other response bias that slows female response time is responsible for a large portion of the sex differences found in cognitive abilities (Gallagher, 1989). However, as you probably guessed by now, there is also evidence that sex differences cannot be explained by differences in speed of responding. There is a test of verbal abilities that is known as the Stroop test. In the Stroop test, the stimuli are color names (e.g., the words "green," "blue," "red") which are printed in different color ink. For example, the word "red" might be printed in blue ink and the word "blue" might be printed in yellow ink. The task for the subject is to name the ink color as quickly as possible while ignoring the word that the letters form. Although this may seem like a simple task, it is surprisingly difficult to ignore the printed word and name the ink color.

Nayak and Dash (1987) found that "girls are superior to boys in response speed" (p. 88) in the Stroop test. Thus, at least under some testing situation, girls respond faster than boys. If females are more cautious in responding, and therefore slower to respond, then we would expect this response bias in any timed task. The fact that girls were faster at responding to verbal stimuli suggests that a generalized tendency to respond cautiously cannot be the cause of all of the sex differences found in reaction times.

Of course, by now you should be able to recognize how this conclusion could be questioned. Recall that reaction time is one measure of intelligence or cognitive functioning. Psychologists who use reaction measures as an ability index are not going to accept untimed versions of the same test as a measure of intellectual prowess. Welford (1980) examined whether sex differences in reaction time were due to the actual time needed to move the hand to make the response (motor time) or the "premotor time"—the time between exposing the stimulus and the *initiation* of the response. Welford concluded that sex differences are due to differences in premotor time rather than musculature (movement) factors—that is, differences in thinking time, not movement time. "The longer mean time for women than men for completing the entire testing session could be explained in terms of longer premotor times of women" (Rammsayer & Lustnauer, 1989).

If you are thinking this controversy over response speed is confusing, you are right. On the one hand we have strong data that when tests are untimed, sex differences are reduced or eliminated. These results could be used to argue that there really are no sex differences in abilities, just in speed of responding. On the other hand, speed of responding is commonly used in cognitive psychology to measure ability. From this perspective, it would make no sense to give untimed versions of the same tests. There is no easy answer to this dilemma. People who tend to prefer psychosocial hypotheses will believe that Goldstein et al. have shown that sex differences in cognitive abilities are an artifact of response bias— females score lower on advanced tests of mathematics and spatial abilities because they are less confident of their abilities in these areas than males and therefore take longer to respond. People who prefer biological hypotheses will argue that Goldstein et al.'s data provide additional evidence for sex differences because they found that there are large sex differences in the amount of time needed to perform a cognitive task. It is important that you, as the reader, understand the controversies and difficulties that surround sex differences research and its interpretation.

The question of whether we should be using reaction times as an index of intelligence or cognitive abilities is important. Some psychologists have argued for the use of reaction times because they are relatively "culture free," that is they are less dependent on life experiences such as an enriched education than other measures so there is little advantage for the rich (e.g., Jensen, 1980). Psychologists study the relationship between speed of responding and accuracy of the responses by constructing "speed–accuracy curves" in which the speed of responding is plotted as a function of accuracy (e.g., proportion correct). Let's consider the rationale of speed–accuracy curves. Suppose that you responded very, very quickly to a series of questions. In an extreme example, suppose that you never read the questions, but picked answers at random. What would happen to your accuracy? It would be very low if responding were very, very fast. On the other hand, suppose that you were very slow and cautious about responding. Accuracy would be high, but speed would be slow. Thus, within limits, there is a reciprocal relationship between speed and accuracy. Lohman (1986) conducted an interesting study in which he examined speed–accuracy curves for different groups. He reported that subjects with low spatial ability produce different speed–accuracy curves than people with high spatial abilities. (He used the mental rotation paradigm in this example.) Furthermore, Lohman reported that the speed–accuracy curves for females were different for those of males, with the female speed–accuracy curves very similar to those found with females and males with low spatial abilities. Thus, he argues that the finding that females take longer to respond than males is good evidence that, on the average, females are poorer at this task than males are.

EXTRAPOLATING FROM EMPIRICAL TRENDS

Perhaps one of the greatest sources of support for proponents of psychosocial explanations of cognitive sex differences can be captured in a quote from a 1960s Bob Dylan song: "The times, they are a-changing." Sex differences with respect to cognitive abilities have not remained static over the years that psychologists and other investigators have been studying them. As discussed earlier in this book (chapter 2), the size of the sex differences is as important as the finding that there are sex differences. Rosenthal and Rubin concluded in 1982 that the effect size for studies of sex differences in cognitive abilities has been decreasing. As they aptly describe this state of affairs, ". . . in these studies, females appear to be gaining in cognitive skill relative to males rather faster than the gene can travel!" (p. 711). The only way that biological hypotheses can explain this finding would be to suppose that female and male biology has been rapidly changing over the last few decades, an assumption that flies in the face of everything that we know about biological and evolutionary trends.

Rosenthal and Rubin also note that one possible explanation for the decreasing effect size is that sampling differences have occurred over the years in which data on cognitive sex differences have been collected and, therefore, don't necessarily imply that sex differences are diminishing. The question of whether sex differences in cognitive abilities are decreasing is hotly debated (Feingold, 1988). Although some tests show decreases, others do not. In Signorella and Jamison's (1986) review of the mental rotation literature, they found no evidence that the size of the sex effect is changing.

Much of the research is conducted with college students. Colleges have been undergoing changes in their sexual composition, with more young females pursuing college educations, and more older women returning to college to complete a college career that was interrupted by marriage and family obligations. Thus, college women may be more representative of all adult women now than they were 20 years ago (i.e., college women with a broad range of abilities are now attending college rather than only the gifted portion of the range of abilities). Even with these differences in sampling, the fact remains that the most recent studies show substantial changes in cognitive performance by women relative to men (e.g., loss in SAT-V scores), a finding that cannot be explained with biological explanations.

CHAPTER SUMMARY

The replicated finding that spatial ability can be trained lends strong support for psychosocial hypotheses that attempt to explain spatial ability sex differences by appealing to environmental variables. This position would be even stronger if there were clear-cut evidence that females benefit more than males from such instruction; however, the data with respect to this second issue suggest that males and females benefit about equally from spatial training. Psychosocial explanations of sex differences in mathematics are based on the belief that mathematics is a male sex-typed academic domain. The problem with psychosocial hypotheses of mathematics is that females score higher than males on some tests of mathematics (e.g., computation). We have no psychosocial hypotheses that can predict female superiority on some mathematics tests.

Sex differences in verbal abilities have received the least experimental attention. The leading theoretical model in the area of verbal abilities builds on sex differentiated propensities to interact in either verbal or nonverbal ways. Psychosocial hypotheses of verbal abilities differences suffer from the problem that they are unable to explain why males score higher on some verbal tests (e.g., verbal analogies). They also cannot explain the high incidence of stuttering and dyslexia among males.

A host of psychosocial variables has been used to explain sex differences in academic and career achievement. A complex interacting web of expectations, modeling influences, and perceived usefulness provides a strong theoretical model for interpreting the usual sex differences results. The finding that sex differences often diminish or disappear when tests are untimed has been used to argue that response bias variables like confidence underlie the findings of cognitive sex differences. The very same data have also been used to support the notion that sex differences are largely based on the reasoning that slow response times are indicative of lower levels of abilities.

The finding that effect sizes with respect to sex differences in cognitive abilities have not remained stable (e.g., in some cases increasing, as in the SAT-V, and in other cases decreasing) provides the strongest case for the importance of psychosocial variables. Biological changes cannot occur within a species over a few decades, but psychosocial variables can.

8 Using a Biopsychosocial Perspective to Understand Cognitive Sex Differences

Contents

8

Like first year medical students, we have dissected the body of knowledge that pertains to the immensely complex system we are trying to understand. But medical science could not proceed unless the students put the pieces together and see the connectiveness of all of the systems. Similarly, we need to put the biological and psychosocial theories together because, in reality, they are as connected as the mind and brain.

THE NEED FOR CROSS-CULTURAL RESEARCH

As presented in the preceding chapters, biological and psychosocial hypotheses provide two frameworks for studying sex differences in cognitive abilities. Within any single society or culture these two types of influences are inextricably entwined. In North American society, for example, males receive more spatial toys as children and more rewards for engaging in spatial activities. They also have the male chromosome configuration, a preponderance of male hormones, and other biological indices that define them as male. At birth, they are classified by the shape of their genitals, and, on the average, are somewhat more active than females. Because biological sex and psychosocial environment are confounded, it is impossible to ascertain the independent contribution of either of these variables. All of the methods that have been discussed, such as examining medical anomalies, correlating twin data, and providing specific educational experiences to selected groups of subjects can only suggest an approximation of the relative importance of each of the variables under investigation. Another technique for approximating the relative contribution of biological and psychosocial variables is to look to other cultures.

The underlying rationale of cross-cultural research in this area is that all females, everywhere in the world, share a similar biology, as do all males. Although there are obvious differences among people in their skin color, hair texture and curl, shape of eyes, etc., the biology of femaleness and maleness is the same everywhere. Except for medical anomalies, members of each sex have the same chromosome configuration for determining sex, internal reproductive organs, gonads (sex glands), genitals, and sex hormone balance. It also seems true that cognitive abilities are universal. In their seminal book, Cole and Scribner (1974) concluded: "We are unlikely to find cultural differences in basic component cognitive processes" (p. 193).

Societal and environmental milieu, however, differ from culture to culture. Consider, for example, the implications of cognitive sex differences research conducted in a society whose sex roles are very different from those of western cultures. Suppose that some hypothetical society existed in which sex role stereotypes were the reverse of those in North America, such that girls were encouraged to succeed in the mathematics and science areas and boys were encouraged to be nurturant and to utilize their verbal skills. If we were to find the same cognitive sex differences that we typically find in North American studies, then we would have strong support for the importance of sex-related biological variables in the determination of cognitive abilities. Conversely, if we were to find the reverse, or a different pattern of cognitive sex differences, or no differences at all, then the psychosocial variables would have received a strong endorsement. Thus, one of the major advantages of cross-cultural research is that it allows the possibility of, at least partly, unraveling biological and psychosocial contributions to cognitive sex differences.

Myopia USA

Unfortunately, high quality cross-cultural research that employed comparable measures in a wide variety of cultures is rare. Fairweather (1976) used the term *myopia U.S.A.* to describe the relative paucity of cross-cultural data designed to investigate the origins of cognitive sex differences. There are several reasons why researchers have been so nearsighted in their search for answers to sex differences and other psychological questions. One of the primary reasons for the paucity of research is that cross-cultural data are difficult and expensive to collect. Unlike anthropologists, who tend to examine cross-cultural issues, few psychologists have the necessary connections in other countries to arrange for data collection. They also lack the requisite language skills to converse with subjects and foreign researchers. Subtle differences among languages and nuances that are lost in literal translation can render a research instrument that is valid in one culture invalid or even ludicrous when administered in another culture. There are also numerous experimental controls that are necessary in cross-cultural research. For example, much of the early research designed to compare Mexican youth with American youth employed poor Mexicans and middle-class Americans as subjects. Not surprisingly, large cultural differences emerged; however, these so-called cultural differences were really created by differences in socioeconomic status.

The Politics of Cross-Cultural Interpretations

Americans are not alone in their myopia. The majority of our knowledge about cognitive sex differences comes from research conducted with subjects in western industrialized nations by researchers living in those nations. Very little sex differences research is conducted in Third World countries. Sex differences research is simply not a priority in underdeveloped countries struggling to provide enough food for their citizens and fighting for political survival.

There are also political ramifications to research of this sort. For example, the "emancipation of women" was one of the tenets of communism as defined by Marx and Engels. The Russian newspaper, *Pravda,* interpreted the failure of Americans to pass the Equal Rights Amendment as tantamount to endorsing sex discrimination. In fact, there are large numbers of women in the scientific community in the Soviet Union. Detractors are quick to point out, however, that the Soviet Union cannot claim to be a sex-egalitarian society because there are still very few women in positions of power in the government of the Soviet Union. Whatever your political persuasion, the fact that a high proportion of engineers and scientists in the Soviet Union are women shows that if women are encouraged by society, they can demonstrate the ability to succeed in what has been construed by western society as "traditional men's fields."

Cross-cultural research is complicated by the possibility that while biological indicators of sex are nonvariant, other concomitant variables could vary by sex between ethnic and racial groups. For example, it is likely that different ethnic groups mature at somewhat different rates. (Differences in the average age at puberty could be due to genetically programmed ethnic differences and/or environmental variables like nutrition, sanitation, and working conditions.) If maturation rate were an important determinant of cognitive sex differences, as some researchers believe, then between-group sex differences could be due to maturation rate differences and not sex per se.

Unfortunately, the hypothetical example of a culture that differs from our own only in terms of its sex roles has never been found. In early research, world renowned anthropologist Margaret Mead (1961) studied societies with radically different sex roles for women and men. Her findings used to be routinely included in classes on the psychology of sex differences, but soon after her death, her work was questioned by another noted anthropologist (Freeman, 1983) who believes that she misinterpreted the cultures she visited. He also believes that the finding of societies with radically different sex role stereotypes is too coincidental to be real. Unfortunately, these allegations were made after Mead's death so she was unable to respond to them. Thus, we are left with no strong data comparing societies with fundamental differences in sex role stereotypes. It seems that cross-cultural research, like all of the other research that has been reviewed, cannot provide us with "the definitive answer" about the etiology of cognitive sex differences, although it can provide support for or against any particular hypothesis.

Outcomes of Cross-Cultural Research

Williams and Best (1982) reported the results of an extensive cross-cultural project whose objective was "to identify the beliefs commonly held in many cultures about the psychological characteristics associated with men and women and to examine these sex-trait stereotypes for evidence of cross-national similarities and differences" (p. 13). They examined the sex role stereotypic beliefs of adults and children in 39 different countries selected from six different areas of the world (Africa, Asia, Europe, North America, South America, and Oceania). They found a surprisingly high degree of similarity in sex role stereotypes. Williams and Best coined the term "pancultural generality" to describe the finding that instrumental or goal-oriented traits tend to be associated with being male, and expressive or interpersonal traits tend to be associated with being female in all of the cultures they studied.

Not only sex role stereotypes, but sex roles or actual statistical differences in traits or activities between the sexes tend to hold up across western industrialized societies, and it is from these societies that most of the available psychological data are collected. Men and women do play different roles in isolated cultures with little contact with modern industrialized society and have done so in other societies in the past (Leacock, 1980). Despite Williams and Best's evidence for pancultural generality, it is not true that women have always been "housebound" or the primary caretakers of the young and old, while the men always wandered from home. Unfortunately, we do not know much about sex differences in cognitive abilities in societies with social structures very different from our own.

Western Industrialized Nations.   Perhaps not surprisingly, when we look at other countries with sex roles similar to those in the United States, we find congruence between their patterns of sex-differentiated cognitive abilities and the ones discussed in this book. *The London Times,* (1984) for example, reported on the low level of participation by girls in science and technology courses. There are over four times as many boys as girls studying college preparatory physics in high school in England. Research on schools in England have shown the same sex-differentiated pattern of classroom interactions that was revealed by Sadker and Sadker (1985) in their research on American schools conducted in four states and the Washington, DC area. Like their American counterparts, English boys are asked more questions by teachers, receive most of the teachers' attention, and, according to the report in *The London Times*, "monopolise science labora-tory equipment, consistently depriving girls of practical experience." It seems inevitable that classroom experiences reflect societal biases about what is appro-priate girl and boy behavior.

One country that offers the possibility of assessing societal influences on sex-related cognitive differences is Sweden. Sweden has a government policy that institutionalizes sexual equality, including a parental leave policy for fathers as well as mothers. In a comparison of sex role stereotypes between children, adolescents and adults in the United States and Sweden, Intons-Peterson (1988) found that there is less sex role stereotyping in Sweden. Have Sweden's more egalitarian attitudes manifested themselves by changing the sex-differentiated pattern of cognitive abilities? Stage (1988) examined this question by investigat-ing sex differences in the Swedish Scholastic Aptitude Test. This test has been used to select candidates for higher education in Sweden since 1977. Although it has a similar name to the SAT that is produced in New Jersey by the Educational Testing Service, it is a different test. The Swedish test provides six subscores: Vocabulary; Quantitative Reasoning; Reading Comprehension; Interpretation of Diagrams, Tables, and Maps; General Knowledge; and Study Ability. Stage reported that the largest sex differences favoring males are found on the tests of quantitative reasoning and interpretation of diagrams, tables and maps. Females have a slight advantage on the vocabulary subtest, with no differences on the other subtests. This pattern of results is highly reminiscent of the one found with the U.S. SATs.

Although results from the Swedish SATs suggest that sex role stereotypes may not play a substantial role in establishing and/or maintaining cognitive sex dif-ferences, critics will point out that it is not a fair test of the hypothesis. Swedish society is only *more* egalitarian in its sex role stereotypes than North American culture, but the stereotypes that exist in Sweden are similar to the ones that most North Americans are familiar with. A strong test of the contribution of sex role stereotypes to cognition requires that we examine societies that are much more different from our own.

The Israeli kibbutz is another culture that was founded on a basis of social and sexual equality (all property is jointly owned), and sex differences are "less pronounced" for children raised in the kibbutz than for Israeli children raised in the traditional family setting (Safir, 1986). But, as in Sweden, the sex role stereotyping is a matter of degree, not of kind. In Israel, every male is a future soldier, and there is greater emphasis on scholastic success for Israeli boys than for girls (in keeping with Jewish tradition). Safir examined cognitive sex dif-ferences in Israeli youth and concluded that when they are found, they tend to favor males on all cognitive measures.

A study of the cognitive achievement of White children in South Africa and their parents (Afrikaans) mirrors the Swedish and Israeli results (Visser, 1987). Both mothers and fathers reported that they regard mathematics as more important for their sons than for their daughters. Correspondingly, more White South African males persist in advanced mathematics courses in high school, more males are identified at the highest levels of mathematics achievement (the Math Olympiad), and males score significantly higher on tests of spatial abilities.

You are probably wondering about the Black South Africans—does the same pattern hold up? I could not find any research on cognitive sex differences among the Black majority of South Africa. This is not surprising because such research would not tell us much. Black children in South Africa receive less education than the White children, and they receive it in seriously overcrowded, substandard schools (Wright, 1990). Any sex differences would be lost amid the massive other influences on academic achievement—crushing poverty, discrimination, disease, and poor nutrition.

The Soviet Union.   The preponderance of males in math and science related courses and professions remains true for almost all industrialized societies except the Soviet Union. As stressed in several places throughout this book, sex differences in academic course selection and success in selected professions don't necessarily address the issue of ability because there are many factors that are unrelated to ability that could create sex differentials.

There has been very little research on cognitive sex differences in the Soviet Union, but what little there is suggests that the pattern of cognitive abilities in the Soviet Union is not very different from that of western industrialized nations. A Russian study (Kovac & Majerova, 1974), reported that among children aged 9 to 15 years old, males were superior to females on standardized tests of spatial memory. Thus, even though Russian women are participating in science and mathematics at a higher rate, adolescent girls in Russia, like those in North America, score lower than boys on spatial ability tests.

The Soviet Union provides an interesting backdrop for contrasting the effects of socialization on the way cognitive abilities develop. In the early part of this century, a large number of American immigrants came from the countries that, as of this writing, comprise the Soviet Union. During the years following World War II, American women were pressured to leave their war jobs, marry, and have children. The situation in the Soviet Union was very different. World War II claimed the lives of a substantial number of young males in the Soviet Union. While large numbers of American males returned home after the war, the Soviet Union was left with an entire generation of males that had been decimated by war. In 1990, I visited the Russian portion of the Soviet Union with the goal of understanding how the scarcity of an entire generation of males affected life in this immense war-pocked country.

The relative absence of old men in the Soviet Union is particularly striking. According to our official Intourist Soviet guide, in the years immediately after the war, the proportion of males in the population was approximately 35%. Thus, many women never married because of the demographics of post-war Russia.

Post-war Russia was left in rubble, and the reconstruction effort still continues. For this reason, women assumed many of the physically demanding jobs that were traditionally men's, such as plastering and building construction and reconstruction. Women also assumed the majority of the jobs in medicine. Unfortunately, the assumption of work in traditional men's fields by women did not lead to sexual equality. The status of physicians in the Soviet Union is much lower than in Western nations. And, as mentioned earlier, women are still underrepresented in high level Party and government positions. The role that women and men will play in the era of Glasnost is unknown, although all of the official Soviet information sources (e.g., researchers at the Soviet Academy of Sciences) assured me that women enjoy full and equal participation with men in all aspects of Soviet life.

More Isolated Third World Ethnic Groups.   Although we live in a large world, you would never know it by perusing the literature on cognitive sex differences. It is only by looking at a variety of cultures that we can understand how psychosocial factors interact with the biology of femaleness and maleness to create us as unique beings. One study that is frequently cited as an exception to the usual short-sightedness is a study by Berry (1966) that compared Canadian Eskimos from the Baffin Islands with the Temne tribe in Africa on a variety of spatial tasks. Overall, the Eskimos outperformed the Temne on every spatial test. Most interestingly from the perspective of the sex differences literature, there were no differences between females and males in the Eskimo sample; whereas among the Temne, the males scored higher on the spatial abilities tests than the females. One interpretation of these data is that for the Eskimos, the males and females tend to lead similar lives. For both sexes, traveling from home and hunting are important and frequent activities, and both of these activities should help to develop spatial skills. Among the Temne, traveling far from home is largely a male prerogative, and the sexes tend to be more segregated in their daily activities. Although these results seem to favor environmental explanations of differences in spatial abilities, proponents of the biological position would be quick to point out that there may be genetic differences among isolated groups that have a restricted gene pool.

Another study that is of particular interest in examining the nature/nurture controversy compared two different New Zealand ethnic groups, the Maori and Pakeha, on eight different cognitive tasks (Brooks, 1976). Brooks found that male children in one ethnic group performed better on two different spatial tests; whereas, female children in the other ethnic group performed better on the same two spatial tests. Brooks concluded that cultural differences through different patterns of socialization develop unique ability patterns for each sex. With respect to verbal abilities, the Pakeha seemed to have a clear-cut advantage. Brooks concluded from this finding that verbal ability is the most sensitive to cultural influences of the cognitive abilities. It is interesting to note that this is the same conclusion that was reported in previous chapters based on correlational research with twin and nontwin siblings.

Other reports from more isolated tribal groups are not easily interpreted. For example, it is difficult to know what to conclude from reports that, in rural Kenya, girls score higher academically in Grades 1, 2, and 3, and boys score higher academically in Grades 6, 7, and 8, with no differences during the transition years of fourth and fifth grade (Arap-Maritim, 1987) or the report that among the Mizo children in India, males get more items correct on the embedded figures test (Srivastava, 1989). The lives of females and males differ in every world society, with many of the psychosocial differences occurring at the same time that biological differences become most pronounced. Even if we were to find a world-wide cross-cultural advantage for males on some tests of spatial abilities (a conclusion that is favored by Harris, 1978), we still would not know whether females would score as high or higher if they were exposed to male life experiences.

The Devalued Female

One truth that seems to hold up across cultures is the relative devaluation of what is female. In a recent newspaper article on helping couples select the sex of a child they are about to conceive, a physician in this field warned, "If we had 1,000 women coming to us in the next year, and all were going to have their first baby, and if all could easily select the sex, there's a substantial chance that we'd have 800 boys," (Barry May, Chief of Obstetrics and Gynecology at the Women's Hospital in Laguna Hills, quoted in the *Los Angeles Times,* September 5, 1990, p. E2). This is a frightening thought as we quickly approach a time when sex selection techniques will be widely and easily available.

Equal access to education is still a widespread myth. Recent statistics that show that females in the United States now comprise 54% of all college enrollments (*The Chronicle of Higher Education Almanac* 1990), failed to note that the large female enrollment is still found primarily in education, nursing, and other helping professions. When we look to other cultures, we find the average ratio of males to females enrolled in school tends to favor males, with large disparities found in many countries (Dix, 1975 cited in Williams, 1977). Thus, what we may be interpreting as an ability difference may actually be due to unequal access to education that is systematically biased against females.

THE WINNING HYPOTHESIS IS . . .

Any reader who picked up this book in the hope of finding easy answers is certainly frustrated by now. One moment the data seem to favor one conclusion; yet upon reflection or the accumulation of contradictory data, each theory seems inadequate, subject to alternative explanations, or completely wrong. This state of affairs is not unique to cognitive sex differences. It seems to be the norm in all areas of psychology and in the other sciences that are trying to understand the what, when, where, why, and how of complex phenomena. In the search for understanding why the sexes differ in some abilities, we have amassed a considerable quantity of information, although we still have many questions without answers and answers for which we haven't yet formulated the questions.

If you have been keeping score in the nature–nurture controversy, then you have already realized that the hypotheses in support of these two positions have "won some and lost some." Let's consider the nature of the wins and losses on the cognitive sex differences scoreboard.

Data Psychosocial Hypotheses Cannot Explain

There are some data that seem to demand that we consider biological hypotheses. Let's summarize the evidence on the biological side of the scale:

1. The strongest data in support of biological or nature explanations is the finding that scores on tests of spatial abilities and verbal abilities depend on sex *and* whether an individual is right- or left-handed. Recall from chapter 4, that at least among subjects with high reasoning ability, left-handed males performed poorer on spatial abilities tests than right-handed males, but left-handed males had the advantage over right-handed males on tests of verbal abilities. The opposite pattern was found for females. Left-handed females were better on tests of spatial abilities than right-handed females, with the reverse pattern among females for verbal abilities. (See chapter 4 for a more complete description of the sex-by-handedness interaction.) The finding that cognitive abilities depend both upon one's preferred hand and sex has been replicated many times (e.g., Benbow's 1988 finding with gifted youth). This is an important finding because there are no theories that suggest that sex role stereotypes or any other sex-related environmental difference vary as a function of handedness. In other words, there is no reason to believe that right-handed girls are socialized differently from left-handed girls or that right-handed boys are socialized differently from left-handed boys. Handedness, used as an indicator of cerebral organization in these studies, strongly suggests that at least some of the sex differences in spatial and verbal abilities is due to sex differences in the way the brain is organized to perform spatial and verbal tasks. This conclusion is bolstered by studies cited in chapter 4 that also found a link between a family history of left-handedness (familial sinistrality) and sex differences in cognitive abilities. (E.g., See Coren, 1990, for a review and an extensive list of references.)

The sex-by-handedness interactions make a convincing case for the role of cerebral lateralization as a contributing factor in cognitive sex differences. When handedness is included as an index of laterality, environmental explanations are no longer adequate, and the causal links between sex differences in lateralization and sex differences in cognitive abilities become stronger. Of course, I do not believe that we have the final word on this theory, nor has it emerged as the undisputed "winner" in the Best Hypothesis Sweepstakes. Research in this area is proceeding at a rapid rate and today's favored theory can quickly become a theoretical dinosaur. It was only a few years ago that the now discredited theory of spatial ability as an X-linked genetic trait was enjoying similar success in its ability to explain sex differences in spatial abilities.

2. We also know that prenatal sex hormones affect brain structures that are not related to reproduction (e.g., Fitch et al., in press). There are sex differences in the neural structures that underlie cognition, most probably in the size of the corpus callosum and in the organization of cognitive abilities within each hemisphere.

3. It is also likely that, at least under extreme conditions for males, a minimal amount of androgens during puberty is needed for the development of spatial abilities (Hier & Crowley, 1982).

4. Biological variables are most probably responsible for the high percentage of males with severe reading disabilities and stuttering problems. There is no reason to believe that there are societal sanctions against the production of fluid speech or the ability of males to read.

5. Another type of data that seems relatively immune to psychosocial explanations concerns the male advantage on some tests of spatial abilities that have been described in several places throughout this book. Piaget's Water Level Test is particularly puzzling: In this test, subjects are required to draw in the water level in a tipped glass. The usual finding is that far fewer females draw a horizontal line to represent the water level than males (or alternatively, the line drawn by females tends to be farther from the horizontal than the line drawn by males). Females tend to draw their line parallel to the direction in which the glass is tipped. This is a robust result that has been replicated many times with samples ranging from elementary school-age children to college students. This task requires two component skills: (a) Subjects must know that water will always remain horizontal even when its container is tipped; and (b) subjects must be able to draw an approximately horizontal line. Some of the research in this area used grid-square paper so that subjects merely had to trace a horizontal line if they had the knowledge that water remains horizontal (Robert, 1990). It is difficult to understand how either of these two skills could depend on sex-related environmental differences. It does not seem likely that males have more or better experiences with a tipped glass of water. In fact, one could argue that females, the primary cooks and dishwashers in many homes, might have more related experience with tipped glasses of water and other liquids than males. Nor does it seem likely that females are less able to express this knowledge with an approximately horizontal line. The ability to draw an approximately horizontal line is a "low level skill." Even if boys play with spatial toys like Tinker Toys and Lincoln

Logs more often than girls and are encouraged to pursue spatial professions like architecture and engineering, it does not seem intuitively obvious that these experiences are needed in order to be able to approximate a horizontal line.

There is, of course, no simple or direct biological explanation for these results either. I do not believe that there is a genetic code or hormone for performance on the Water Level Test. Rather, it seems to be an example of a generalized sex-differentiated spatial ability that emerges earlier in the life span (during the elementary school years) than some of the other spatial abilities tested.

Related to this problem is the finding that males score considerably higher on novel tests of spatial abilities. By novel, I mean ones that are not closely related to the kinds of spatial activities that males are more likely than girls to engage in. The largest between-sex differences are found on tests that require subjects to mentally rotate a two-dimensional (i.e., drawn on paper) representation of a three-dimensional object in space. This is a novel task, and it is highly unlikely that anyone of either sex would have any direct experience with mental rotation. Environmental hypotheses are somewhat more plausible in explaining this result than they are in explaining sex-by-handedness interactions or the Water Level Test because it is possible that males develop some generalized spatial skills through experience with spatial activities that are transferable to novel spatial tasks. Even if this were true, the large size of the between-sex difference on this task remains troublesome for those who prefer environmental hypotheses. Although any sort of spatial experience could be helpful in preparing someone for any sort of spatial task, why are sex differences so much larger in this task than they are in other spatial tasks? There are still many unknowns in this area.

6. The early female advantage in language also seems to tilt toward the biological end of the continuum for an adequate explanation. In general, results that emerge very early in life are usually attributed to biological explanations because environmental intervention is less likely to be effective for very young infants. As noted, girls acquire several more advanced language concepts (e.g., passive voice) at an earlier age than males. Although girls may be spoken to and read to more often than boys, the female advantage in maturation is also involved.

7. The finding that cognitive abilities vary (slightly) over the menstrual cycle also suggests the involvement of biological variables (Hampson & Kimura, 1988). We have no psychosocial theories that can predict a reciprocal relationship among cognitive abilities as a function of the menstrual cycle.

Data Biological Hypotheses Cannot Explain

There have been drastic changes in the educational and professional aspirations and achievements of females and, to a lesser extent, males since the Women's Movement in the 1960s. Any data that indicate change over a period of decades require a psychosocial explanation because biology does not change quickly.

1. Large numbers of women have begun entering medical school with the result that enrollments in medical schools are now approximately one-third female. Virtually every school of engineering and architecture, two areas in which spatial abilities are the *sine qua non* for success, has experienced dramatic increases in the number of female students enrolling and graduating. There is every indication that this figure has not begun to level off. The increasing number of women entering and succeeding in traditional *male* occupations demonstrates that they clearly have the ability to learn the required skills. Biological explanations simply cannot explain these data. Brains, hormones, genes, maturation rates, genitals, gonads, or other between-sex biological differences have not changed over the last 3 decades. Female participation in the work force and professional aspirations have.

2. The success of psychosocial models in relating values and attitudes to academic and career choices falls heavily in the psychosocial camp (e.g., Eccles, 1987). Because the number of courses taken in an academic area is the best single predictor of ability test scores in that area, models that explain why females and males tend to enroll in different academic courses are extremely important in understanding the origins of cognitive sex differences. Few would doubt that anyone's decision to enroll in an academic course is influenced by her or his belief that the course is important, parental beliefs and pressures, expectations of success, and the other psychosocial variables identified in these models.

3. The finding that females get higher grades in school even in areas in which males excel, when tested with ability tests, shows that a large portion of the sex differences effect must be psychosocial in origin. It is clear that females benefit from instruction at least as much as boys, and probably more. Even if class grades are biased in ways that are more consistent with female sex role stereotypes, it is clear that girls can and do learn advanced mathematical concepts when they receive appropriate instruction.

4. Several studies have shown that spatial abilities are amenable to training and that when girls are given typical male spatial toys, they score at least as well as boys on tests of spatial abilities. We do not know if prolonged and widespread experience with spatial activities would eventually eradicate the sex differences found in some spatial tasks.

5. Although females have a higher dropout rate in science courses and science majors in college than males, there are no sex differences in the dropout rate for medical school (Bar-Haim & Wilkes, 1989). Thus, for at least some scientific professions, the female retention rate is comparable to the male retention rate, so we cannot conclude that females drop out of careers in the sciences for ability reasons.

6. The low percentage of women that excel in prestigious occupations requiring verbal fluency demonstrates that societal expectations and values are important components of success. A majority of lawyers, judges, journalists, authors,

and poets are male. If women are, in fact, innately superior in verbal fluency, or even if they are superior for environmental reasons, the only possible explanations for their traditionally low level of participation in these areas are psychosocial expectations, sex role pressures, male preemption, and discrimination. This statistic is changing as an increasing number of women pursue higher education in these areas and as female achievement becomes recognized and rewarded.

7. In the United States, more than two-thirds of the Bachelor's degrees and 80% of the doctorates in mathematics are earned by Asian and White males (Steen, 1987). If biological variables are involved in determining mathematical ability or any other ability, their effects are much too small to account for sex differences of this magnitude. Nor can they explain the scarcity of males from other ethnic groups in higher mathematics—the biology of maleness is the same for all males. The relative absence of men of color from the sciences and mathematics requires psychosocial explanations.

Data Neither Type of Hypotheses Can Explain

There are some data that pertain to cognitive sex differences that are troubling because we have no satisfactory explanations for them.

1. The national search for mathematically precocious youth has shown that a vast majority of the most gifted youngsters in mathematics are male. These data can be interpreted in many ways. On the one hand, there are no sex differences in the number or type of mathematics courses that are taken by these precocious youth, suggesting that mathematical giftedness may be biological in nature. (Recall that mathematics courses first become optional in high school.) On the other hand, these children probably received numerous psychosocial messages that mathematics is more appropriate for boys than girls.

2. As we have learned more about cognitive sex differences, it is clear that simple sweeping statements are not possible. Girls perform better on some mathematics tests (e.g., computation), and boys perform better on other types of mathematics tests (e.g., multistep numerical problems); similarly, girls perform better on some verbal tasks (e.g., fluency) and boys perform better on others (e.g., verbal analogies). There are no simple biological or psychosocial hypotheses that could predict or account for these results.

3. Neither type of theory can account for changes in cognitive abilities over time. Why have females lost their advantage on the SAT-V over the last 25 years, whereas the male advantage on the SAT-M has remained fairly constant? (I have argued that these results are due to the changing nature of the population that takes the SATs as well as changes in the test, but many psychologists have offered other explanations (Feingold, 1988; Halpern, 1989a.)

4. Cross-cultural data do not provide unambiguous support for any of the hypotheses considered. Much more high quality work with diverse populations is needed before we can look to cross-cultural comparisons for help in understanding cognitive sex differences.

5. The female advantage in school and in some ability/achievement tests that is present in the early years of school and then disappears in later grades is particularly troublesome because we have no adequate explanation for this phenomenon. This phenomenon was described earlier in this book as "adolescent intellectual decline." The events of adolescence combine in a way that is detrimental to female intellectual achievement.

6. Sex differences are most frequently found in timed tests. As explained at some length, these data could be amenable to psychosocial explanations (females may be more cautious in responding) or as evidence for sex-based biological differences in the responsiveness of the central nervous system.

7. We need research that is more sensitive to ethnic differences within a culture. The fact that there are more African-American females than African-American males enrolled in college and that there are relatively few African-American males in the sciences and mathematics cannot be explained by appealing to sex differentiated biological theories. What are the psychosocial factors that affect the cognitive development of various ethnic groups in North America and in other countries around the world?

A Continuum of Results

As described in the preceding two sections, each of the experimental results can be placed somewhere along a hypothetical continuum anchored at one end by biological explanations and anchored at the other end by psychosocial explanations. I have placed some of the cognitive sex differences results in either end of this continuum, as shown in Fig. 8.1.

I have drawn the scale in balance, but I am certain that each reacher will come to her or his own conclusion about which end of this hypothetical continuum carries the weight of the evidence. If I have provided a fair interpretation of these data, then I have probably angered everyone who has a predilection for one type of explanation over another.

As shown in Fig. 8.1, neither biological nor psychosocial hypotheses have emerged as a clear winner in their ability to account for all of the cognitive sex differences. There are no biological theories or psychosocial theories that can explain all of the data pertaining to sex-related cognitive differences. This is, of course, no surprise for anyone who has ever tried to unravel the multiple determinants of cognitive abilities. In a recent discussion about this topic with friends, they asked me to give them "the bottom line." They didn't expect me to conclude that cognitive sex differences were due to either biology or environment.

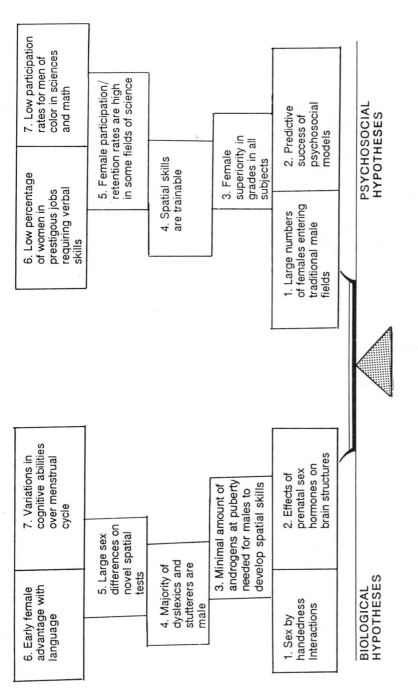

FIG. 8.1. Experimental results stacked at either end of a hypothetical continuum anchored at one end by biological explanations and at the other end by psychosocial explanations.

245

Instead they wanted to know how much of the differences were attributable to each of these positions. Unfortunately, I had to disappoint them because simple numerical answers cannot capture the nature of the multiple variables involved and their complex interactions.

My personal interpretation of the research findings is that explanations that are more biological in nature are needed to explain the high number of left-handed males with extremely low abilities (e.g., dyslexics and certain categories of retardation). I am less certain about how to classify the large number of left handers who have been identified in the extremely high ability tail of the abilities distribution. It may be that the extremely brilliant are as "deviant" as the retarded, but their deviancy is more valued by our society. For the vast majority of the population—that is, most of us in the middle range of abilities—I am convinced that psychosocial explanations are much more powerful than biological ones. Sex differences for the middle range of the abilities distribution tend to be smaller and more fragile than those at the extremes. Thus, the kind of answer that I am willing to accept as an explanation of cognitive sex differences will be one of degree, and it will differ for various portions of the abilities distribution and for type of test. It is important to note that this conclusion reflects my personal evaluation of the data.

Similarities are the Rule, Differences are the Exception

This may seem like a surprising statement given that the topic of this book is sex *differences* in cognitive abilities, but it is precisely because the focus is on differences that it is important to emphasize the vast number of between-sex cognitive similarities. There are only a few documented cognitive sex differences. Even in areas where the differences are large, there is much between-sex overlap in the abilities distributions. Keep in mind that some of the largest differences are found in reaction time tests in which a fraction of a second in response time is a large difference. Furthermore, even when sex differences are found, they are found on only *some* tests of the abilities being investigated.

A BIOPSYCHOSOCIAL PERSPECTIVE

In the search for factors that influence achievement levels, single explanations cannot adequately account for the observed performance differences.
—Sue and Okazaki (1990, p. 913)

The nature–nurture dichotomy has created a framework that has guided much of the research on cognitive sex differences. As noted in numerous places throughout this book, there are problems inherent in this dichotomy. A dichotomy requires an either/or answer, or, at best, a "more or less" type answer. Instead, the only answer we have been able to provide is "sometimes and under some conditions." That is, sometimes the data can be interpreted as requiring a primarily environmental answer; other times the data require a primarily biological answer. Simple answers have failed to capture the elusive nature of cognitive sex differences, which seem to depend on a multitude of variables such as experience, adherence to stereotypes, and biological differences within and between the sexes.

Ultimately, the answers we accept as explanations of cognitive sex differences will be much more complex than a single point along a biological–psychosocial continuum. We need a framework that incorporates both of these perspectives— a framework that has come to be called "biopsychosocial" (Petersen, 1980). Although laws of parsimony require researchers to accept the simplest explanation of a phenomenon, there is little likelihood that we will be able to respond to the many questions regarding cognitive sex differences with a simple answer. Like most researchers, I find beauty and elegance in simple answers—a single explanation for all of the differences. However, I do not believe that cognitive abilities are simply determined, nor do I believe that a single answer like, "it's all in the hormones" or "It's all because of mothers' attitudes" will ever emerge as the origin of all sex differences in cognitive abilities.

Whenever psychologists are faced with knotty problems like this one, they weave a nomological net, which is an interrelated network of variables designed to explain a phenomenon. Theories that incorporate the independent and joint effects of biology and environment are needed if we want to capture the nature of cognitive sex differences. Research is needed in which such measures as handedness, laterality, age at puberty, endorsement of sex role stereotypes, parents' endorsement of sex role stereotypes, and academic background and attitudes are considered simultaneously and in selected interactions. Multivariate approaches that examine the most likely biological and psychosocial variables within the same study will be more fruitful in untangling the web of possible variables that contribute to sex differences in cognitive abilities. This sort of design will allow direct comparisons of effect sizes for the variables investigated and their interactions. (Effect size data are important in understanding the magnitude of the underlying phenomena.)

The most important component of any biopsychosocial model is the reciprocal effects that biology, psychology, and socialization have on each other. A simple biopsychosocial model is shown in Fig. 8.2.

FIG. 8.2. A biopsychosocial model in which all of the elements have reciprocal effects on each other.

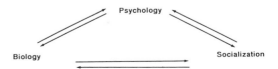

While most psychologists readily understand the way biology can affect psychological and social variables, it is important to remember that psychological and social variables affect biology. If, for example, boys are more active (as a result of prenatal hormones), they may tend to be more aggressive. Parents, teachers, and other socializing agents will reward/encourage and/or punish/discourage aggressive behavior. The developing individual will acquire a masculine self-concept. As the child engages in more active behaviors, he will develop stronger muscles and psychomotor skills, which in turn will increase his masculine self-concept and lead to additional rewards and punishments.

Several sophisticated models of biopsychosocial influences have been proposed. One possible model of the joint influences of biological and psychosocial variables is presented in Fig. 8.3. As shown in this figure, biological determinants of sex play a role in sex differentiation patterns of cerebral structures and organization and in determining sex-differentiated life experiences. Life experi-

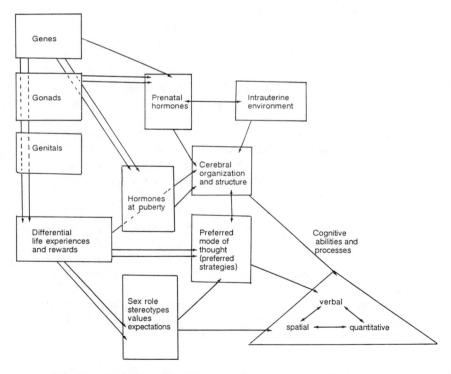

FIG. 8.3.   A biopsychosocial model of cognitive sex differences. The arrows linking these variables indicate the direction of an effect with double headed arrows representing the mutual effects of two variables on each other. Arrows drawn with single lines indicate weaker effects than arrows drawn with double lines.

ences in turn affect self-concept, including one's beliefs about her or his own abilities. Life experiences also change neural structures. Greenough, Black, and Wallace (1987) have used the term *experience-dependent* for neural pathways that are formed in response to experiences. Thus, different life experiences influence the formation and maintenance of neural pathways, and in this way, affect brain structures.

The entire network of variables determine actual cognitive abilities. The arrows linking these variables indicate the direction of an effect with double-headed arrows representing the mutual effects of two variables on each other. Arrows drawn with single lines represent weaker effects than arrows drawn with double lines.

Although most of the research into the questions of sex differences in cognitive abilities can be studied within the framework of the nature–nurture controversy, it is, in fact, an unresolvable controversy. Any given individual is a complete biological organism living in an environmental context. Females and males differ from each other in their biology in a number of salient ways; they also differ in their psychosocial environments. Given that these two types of differences are fully confounded, it is impossible to decide which of these differences is more important. This controversy can only be resolved by some future society in which the psychosocial environment does not vary as a function of biological sex. It is clear from the current research that biology is not destiny. Even if biological differences underlie some portion of the cognitive differences, there is ample evidence to conclude that under environmental conditions that encourage the total intellectual development of males and females, the size of the sex differential in cognitive abilities can be reduced, and possibly even eliminated.

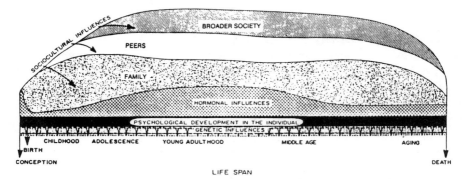

FIG. 8.4.   A hypothetical model for biopsychosocial development over the life span. From Petersen (1980). Biosocial processes in the development of sex related differences. In J. E. Parsons (Ed.), The psychology of sex differences and sex roles (pp. 31–55). Washington, D.C., Hemisphere. Reprinted with permission.

Another biopsychosocial model has been proposed by Petersen (1980). Petersen's model takes into account the relative contribution of hormonal influences, family, peers, and broader society. Petersen's model is depicted in Fig. 8.4.

As you can see in Fig. 8.4, hormones have the greatest impact during the prenatal and perinatal periods and through adolescence and middle age. By contrast, family influences are greatest during childhood. Other sociocultural influences—peers and broader society—assume importance late in childhood and have a fairly constant influence into old age.

NEW APPROACHES TO OLD PROBLEMS

Because the nature–nurture controversy has been found to be of limited usefulness, researchers need to construct new frameworks and new paradigms to answer old questions. For example, instead of arguing about the size of the sex difference in mathematical ability or whether it is better explained by biological or psychosocial explanations, researchers could be exploring the nature of the sex difference. Mayer (1985, in press) reported that mathematical ability can be broken down into component parts: (a) problem representation, which involves interpretation of the problem and some sort of mental representation of its salient features; and (b) problem solution, which involves manipulating the known information contained in the problem to derive the solution. These two parts of all mathematical problems can be investigated separately using methods currently available in cognitive psychology. Little is known about sex differences with respect to the component parts of mathematical ability. It would be useful to know if sex differences are found in one, both, or neither of these parts.

Along similar lines, spatial ability and verbal ability can be conceived of in a different manner. If sex differences occur in the speed of retrieving information from memory, then we can make sex-differentiated predications about research outcomes. For example, one way of investigating cognitive processes is with "interference paradigms." If I ask you to make spatial judgments (such as whether the "tail" is up or down in the following lower case letters—g, h, t, and j), this task will interfere more with a second spatial task (such as imagining a map) than it will with a verbal task (such as finding a synonym for a word). Suppose that males are, on the average, better at spatial tasks. Will they show less interference while simultaneously performing two spatial tasks than females will? If not, why not? Are there differences in the capacity of spatial memory or in the retrieval of spatial information or in the manipulation of spatial information? A more fine grained analysis of these cognitive mechanisms will help us to understand where sex differences occur and where they don't.

There is a host of similar questions that can be investigated in order to understand the whys and wherefores of the cognitive systems in which we are interested. One reason why so much of the literature has centered on three basic abilities—verbal, spatial, and quantitative—rather than the stages in information processing, is that much of the research has been conducted by researchers with expertise in the area of sex differences instead of by cognitive psychologists. The next generation of research will have to take a more detailed examination of cognitive processes. We need to begin with theories of verbal fluency, mathematical reasoning, and spatial abilities. What does it mean to have high spatial ability or excellent mathematical reasoning (Hunt, 1985), and how can we build on these theories?

Different Answers for Different Folks

In any case, a satisfactory explanation for sex differences in cognitive performance has not yet emerged.
—Signorella and Jamison (1986, p. 224)

Another new, or at least underutilized, approach to the question of cognitive sex differences is to determine how sampling differences affect results. We know that sex differences in mathematical ability are large for adolescents who are extremely gifted in mathematics and small for the remaining majority of adolescents (Benbow & Stanley, 1983). Similarly, the overwhelming majority of children learn to read and speak fluently, yet the majority of those who don't are male. We do not know if this finding is merely a statistical artifact of the way small mean differences affect differences in the tails of normally distributed distributions (as explained in chapter 2) or whether mathematical geniuses, dyslexics, and stutterers are predominantly male for an identifiable reason, either environmental, biological, or related to their interaction.

A majority of the cognitive sex differences research has used students as subjects. Because only a small percentage of adults attend college, we may have been biasing our conclusions by extrapolating to all females and males from research conducted on a select group. Perhaps spatial skills are particularly high among males who attend college. It is possible that if we were to sample males in occupations that do not require a college degree, for example, salesmen, gas station attendants, laborers, gardeners, and factory workers, we would not find them superior in spatial ability to a comparable group of females. Earlier in this chapter, I lamented about how little we know about populations that are culturally very different from our own. As a discipline, psychology also knows very little about the abilities of most adults—those people who never walk into research laboratories and never take standardized tests (e.g., high school dropouts—a group in which males and ethnic minorities are overrepresented—blue and pink collar workers such as waiters and waitresses, janitors, secretaries, taxi drivers, cooks, and homemakers).

Sampling differences also need to be considered when discussing environmental variables. All Americans do not have similar environments. Research conducted with poor Black, White, and Hispanic school children in large urban areas may not be applicable to wealthy children of any ethnicity in suburban areas or poor children in rural areas. Obviously, this caveat applies even more when researchers extrapolate their results as being applicable to all males and all females irrespective of their background or culture. The kind of answer that we get to questions about cognitive sex differences will depend on the people who serve as our subjects.

It is also possible that we could learn a great deal by studying females with outstanding spatial and mathematical skills and males with outstanding verbal skills. Do they differ from other members of their sex in systematic ways? For example, do outstanding women mathematicians all come from families that rejected traditional sex role stereotypes or were they exposed to high levels of androgens when they were fetuses? Very little research has been conducted on subjects at the low end of the ability spectrum. What about males and females who are low in spatial ability or any other ability? Are they uniformly dull in all cognitive areas or does an uneven pattern of abilities help to suggest a cause for a specific deficit?

Process-Oriented Theories

Another approach that is rarely used is to ask subjects directly about their mental processes. In one study where this technique was employed (Clarkson-Smith & Halpern, 1983), subjects who performed well on a mental rotation test reported that they used a mental rotation strategy, while those subjects who performed poorly were unable to describe the strategy they used. As reported earlier (chapter 3), we do not know why female performance is more variable in some visual spatial tasks and male performance is more variable in other sorts of visuospatial tasks. One way of investigating this question is to ask subjects what they are doing when they perform the task. It seems likely that we would find that subjects report strategy differences in how they approach these tasks.

Given that the old distinctions among verbal, mathematical, and spatial abilities are limited in their usefulness, a more process-oriented approach may prove useful in stimulating research. As I explained in chapter 3, the tasks at which females excel—verbal fluency, mixed verbal ability tests, and computation—all seem to require reliable and rapid access to and utilization of information stored in memory. By contrast, the tasks at which males seem to excel—mental rotation, mathematical problem solving, and making judgments about moving objects—all indicate a reliable visuospatial "sketchpad" that operates in working memory. The distinction between mental processes may prove to be a fertile direction for future research.

There is an endless list of research questions that can be generated. It remains the task of future research to find creative new ways of answering questions that may be as old as the human race.

INTO THE FUTURE

Unfortunately, there are no crystal balls to tell us about the changing nature of cognitive sex differences. No one believes that conclusions based on today's cognitive sex differences literature will remain unchanged even a few years from now. But where the changes will be and when they will occur is, of course, unknown. Predictions about future research results are always risky and sometimes humorous when viewed with the benefit of hindsight; yet I believe that we will continue to find that the magnitude of all of the sex differences will diminish. Future technology may, however, create new sex differences. We know, for example, that many more males than females are pursuing careers in computer related fields (*Chronicle of Higher Education,* 1985). The nature of the skills required for success in computer-related occupations varies with different jobs. Some computer jobs, like documentation analyst or writer, require high verbal ability. Others, like programming in "low-level languages" require mathematical ability, and still others, like computer graphic designer, require spatial ability. It would seem that almost everyone could find a niche in a computer field. Yet, computer science majors are predominantly male. If a major field of study becomes predominantly male or female, it seems likely that the skills stressed in that academic area will soon show sex differences.

Education for the 21st Century

Today's young people are tomorrow's citizens, and our future is in their hands. How can we best prepare them for life in the 21st century and ensure that every individual develops her or his unique abilities to their fullest? Here are some suggestions for educators, parents, and other concerned citizens:

1. Currently, we have reading and mathematics instruction in our schools with remedial programs for students with deficiencies in these areas. Given that we know that spatial skills are trainable, we should also be instituting spatial skills training for children from very young ages up through college. Remedial programs in spatial skills should also be offered for those with specific deficiencies in this area.

2. We also need to try various ways of presenting materials in all of the subject areas. Students should be taught how to solve problems using both verbal and spatial strategies, and when each strategy is more appropriate. Spatial aspects of mathematics should be carefully diagrammed with special attention paid to converting word problems to other abstract representations.

3. We also need to provide role models of both sexes in all aspects of the curriculum and in occupations. We need male teachers in typing and home economics as much as we need female teachers in mathematics and science. Counselors and advisors need to assess carefully their own sex biases and stereotypes to be sure that they don't automatically steer students into sex stereotyped fields.

4. Parents, the media, the corporate structure, and other aspects of society need to be educated too. The collective mentality of our society needs to change so that Lincoln Logs, building blocks, erector sets, and models to be assembled—all toys that relate to the development of spatial abilities—are no longer labeled "Boy's Toys," while baby dolls, play kitchens, pint-sized cleaning appliances, and vanity tables are labeled "Girl's Toys." We cannot pretend that our children can choose for themselves when they have very few real choices.

5. Programs that are designed for the gifted need to give careful consideration to the way the gifted are identified. The Talent Identification Program at Duke University uses a lower score on the SAT-M for girls than for boys because the SAT-M underestimates girls' ability to succeed in advanced courses. (Recall that females score lower on the SAT-M, but get higher grades in school in all courses.) In a recent ruling, a U.S. District Judge determined that using the SATs as the sole criterion for awarding New York State Scholarships discriminated against females (Landers, 1989). Criteria that include both SATs (on which males are more likely to excel) *and* grades (on which females are more likely to excel) provide a fairer basis for the award of college scholarships. All special needs programs should consciously consider if selection criteria are biased for or against any group. In a recent newspaper article, researchers reported that they found that more boys are classified as dyslexic because of sex differences in the way the criteria are applied (Kolata, 1990). If boys, on the average mature somewhat later than girls, then the average boy will learn to read somewhat later than the average girl. This does not make him dyslexic, only slower than a hypothetical average girl to become a proficient reader.

6. In a similar vein, cut-off scores for classifying young children as slow learners also need to be considered carefully so that we are not discriminating against boys. Boys mature later than girls and, for this reason, may need some additional time before they can read as fluently as girls (on the average). Of course, this does not mean that all boys are slower than all girls; differences are a matter of degree, and sometimes the degree is quite small.

7. It is important to encourage all able students, but particularly girls, to stick with math. As citizens and educators, we have an obligation to help all girls and boys realize that math counts. If we don't teach more able girls and minority children of both sexes not to leave school without math, then the United States will not be able to keep up with the rest of the world in research and development. We need to teach *all* children that math counts (Halpern, in press).

8. There is no evidence from the cognitive literature to support the notion of sex-segregated education. A good education will meet the needs of girls and boys. All children need to learn how to develop and use flexible cognitive strategies and multiple modes of representation. And all children need to learn the value of education. For most of the poor, it is the only legal route out of poverty.

9. The best single predictor of performance in any cognitive area is the number of courses taken. For this reason, all parents must become active advocates in the education of their children. Be certain that children are not steered into or away from any course of study because of stereotypes.

10. We must not fall prey to the dangers of self-fulfilling prophecies. The data presented in this text represent average differences based on large samples of males and females. No individual is average. There is considerable between-sex overlap in all cognitive abilities.

11. Finally, don't misuse or allow others to misuse research findings on cognitive sex differences. Even if there are some real differences, our cognitive abilities are flexible (Halpern, 1990). Many tasks can be performed with either spatial or verbal skills. Furthermore, there is no evidence that either sex is "smarter" or intellectually superior. Differences are not deficiencies.

Sex Differences, So What!

What are the applied and practical implications of cognitive sex differences? Consider the following applied problem: It seems safe to assume that most Americans and American allies would agree that the U.S. Air Force should have highly qualified officers. In order to assure that this is so, prospective officers take a test (U.S. Air Force Officers Qualifying Test) that measures their verbal, quantitative, and spatial ability. In general, results obtained with this test agree with the sex differences literature in these areas, with females scoring higher on verbal ability and males scoring higher on quantitative and spatial ability. Because spatial ability seems particularly important for air force officers, who often need to rely on aerial landmarks and spatial coordinates, it is likely that many women are disqualified on the basis of this test. In fact, 98% of all student aviators are male (Gordon & Leighty, 1988).

In an examination of the question of whether females can, on the average, become as qualified for air force officer duties as men, McCloy and Koonce (1982) trained women and men on standard simulated flight maneuvers. They found that men were faster at learning the flight tasks than the women were. But, as they pointed out, is this the right question? The more important question concerns the level of ability after training. Were the women as good as men? The dependent measure in this study was number of trials to criterion. In other words, the women required more training trials than the men did to learn a particular task. Perhaps the most important point is that the women apparently were as good as the men when they completed the training. These results are in accord with the general finding that spatial skills are trainable. If we rely on tests of abilities to decide who may enter training programs, we will miss able candidates who can learn to perform as well as their peers who scored higher on these tests prior to instruction.

We do not know why the women in this experiment required more trials to learn the same flight maneuvers as the men. It could be because of biological or psychosocial reasons, or both, or some other yet undiscovered difference between the sexes. While the etiology of cognitive sex differences is very important from a theoretical perspective, it is irrelevant in most applied settings. With appropriate training the sex differences disappeared in this study. We also do not know if the women who received this training will be able to transfer their new spatial ability to other novel spatial tasks as quickly as the men can. In other words, if they are faced with a new and different spatial task, will they now perform it as quickly as their male counterparts? This remains another important question for future research.

The example of the air force officers applies in other settings as well. Every teacher knows that some students will take longer to learn certain concepts than others. If one student takes a half hour to complete a homework assignment and another student takes 45 minutes, the difference is unimportant in most contexts. The important fact is that both students now know and understand something that they did not know before and, after training, both are able to perform tasks that require the use of the newly acquired knowledge.

It is important to keep in mind a point that has been reiterated throughout this book. The experimental results that have been reviewed concern average differences obtained from groups of men and women, and no one is average. The data reviewed in this text are largely irrelevant when making decisions about individuals. They should never be used to justify or predict anyone's success or failure. There is considerable between-sex overlap with respect to these abilities.

The literature on sex differences has been proliferating in recent years because the questions are of profound human interest. A firestorm of interest is ignited every time the media carry headlines like those associated with Benbow's finding that a majority of the intellectually precocious youth that she identified with the SATs are male or Hampson and Kimura's research showing a reciprocal relationship of cognitive abilities over the menstrual cycle. Both of these reports made front page news in the country's largest newspapers and were the subject of television and radio news programs. I hope that every reader of this text will understand the complexities, limitations and implications of research of this sort. The next time you read or hear about research findings in cognitive sex differences, you have all the rights and obligations of informed consumers. This knowledge should empower you.

References

Adams, R. P., & Bradford, M. R. (1985). Sex differences in preschool children's tactual exploration of novel and familiar objects with parents and strangers. *Journal of Genetic Psychology, 146,* 567–569.

Adkins-Regan, E. (1988). Sex hormones and sexual orientation in animals. *Psychobiology, 16,* 335–347.

Adler, T. (1989a, June). Early sex hormone exposure studied. *APA Monitor,* p. 9.

Adler, T. (1989b, November). Brain's language area is abnormal in disabled. *APA Monitor,* p. 7.

Adler, T. (1990, January). Differences explored in gays and straights. *APA Monitor,* p. 27.

Aiken, L. (1986–1987). Sex differences in mathematical ability: A review of the literature. *Educational Research Quarterly, 10,* 25–35.

Allgeier, E. R. (1983). Reproduction, roles and responsibilities. In E. R. Allgeier & N. B. McCormick (Eds.), *Changing boundaries: Gender roles and sexual behavior* (pp. 163–181). Palo Alto, CA: Mayfield Publishing.

American Association of University Women. (1988). *College admissions tests: Opportunities or roadblocks?* Washington, DC: Author.

American Psychiatric Association. (1987). *Diagnostic and statistical manual of mental disorders* (3rd ed., rev.). Washington, DC: Author.

Anderson, J. R. (1990). *Cognitive psychology and its implications* (3rd ed.). New York: Freeman.

Angier, N. (1990, July 20). Scientists find sex differentiation gene. *International Herald Tribune,* p. 3.

Annett, M. (1988). Comments on Lindsey: Laterality shift in homosexual men. *Neuropsychologia, 26,* 341–343.

Arap-Maritim, E. K. (1987). Developmental analysis of sex differences in class rank of primary-grade children. *Psychological Reports, 60,* 155–158.

Asaro, C. (1990, January 10). We need to know why women falter in math [Letter to the editor] *The Chronicle of Higher Education,* p. B4.

Backman, M. E. (1979). Patterns of mental abilities of adolescent males and females from different ethnic and socioeconomic backgrounds. In L. Willerman & R. G. Turner (Eds.), *Readings about individual and group differences* (pp. 261–265). San Francisco: W. H. Freeman.

Baenninger, M., & Newcombe, N. (1989). The role of experience in spatial test performance: A meta-analysis. *Sex Roles, 20* (5/6), 327–344.

Baker, M. A. (1987a). Sensory functioning. In M. A. Baker (Ed.), *Sex differences in human performance* (pp. 5–36). Chichester, England: Wiley.

Baker, M. A. (Ed.) (1987b). *Sex differences in human performance.* Chichester, England: Wiley.

Bandura, A., & Walters, R. H. (1963). *Social learning and personality development.* New York: Holt, Rinehart & Winston.

Bannatyne, A. (1976). *Language, reading, and learning disabilities: Psychology, neuropsychology, diagnosis, and remediation.* Springfield, IL: C. C. Thomas.

Bar-Haim, G., & Wilkes, J. M. (1989). A cognitive interpretation of the marginality and underrepresentation of women in science. *Journal of Higher Education, 60,* 371–387.

Baucom, D. H., & Welsh, G. S. (1978). In support of extreme groups design for studying masculinity-femininity and intelligence. *Intelligence, 2,* 6–10.

Baumeister, R. F. (1988). Should we stop studying sex differences altogether? *American Psychologist, 42,* 756–757.

Beatty, W. W., & Troster, A. I. (1987). Gender differences in geographical knowledge. *Sex Roles, 16* (11/12), 565–590.

Beck, A. (1990, July 16). The daughter track. *Newsweek,* pp. 48–54.

Becker, B. J. (1986). Influence again: An examination of reviews and studies of gender differences in social influence. In J. S. Hyade & M. C. Linn (Eds.), *The psychology of gender: Advances through meta-analysis* (pp. 178–209). Baltimore: Johns Hopkins University Press.

Becker, B. J., & Hedges, L. V. (1984). Meta-analysis of cognitive gender differences: A comment on an analysis by Rosenthal and Rubin. *Journal of Educational Psychology, 76,* 583–587.

Belenky, M. F., Clinchy, B. M., Goldberger, N. R., & Tarule, J. M. (1986). *Women's ways of knowing.* New York: Basic.

Bem, S. L. (1974). The measurement of psychological androgyny. *Journal of Consulting and Clinical Psychology, 42,* 155–162.

Bem, S. L. (1981). Gender schema theory: A cognitive account of sex-typing. *Psychological Review, 88,* 354–364.

Bem, S. L., & Bem, D. J. (1973). Does sex-biased job advertising "aid and abet" sex discrimination? *Journal of Applied Social Psychology, 3,* 6–18.

Bem, S. L., & Bem, D. J. (1976). Training the woman to know her place: The power of a nonconscious ideology. In S. Cox (Ed.), *Female psychology: The emerging self* (pp. 180–190). Chicago: Science Research Associates.

Benbow, C. P. (1988). Sex differences in mathematical reasoning ability in intellectually talented preadolescents: Their nature, effects, and possible causes. *Behavioral and Brain Sciences, 11,* 169–232.

Benbow, C. P. (1990). Gender difference: Searching for facts. *American Psychologist, 45,* 988.

Benbow, C. P., & Stanley, J. C. (1980). Sex differences in mathematical ability: Fact or artifact? *Science, 210,* 1262–1264.

Benbow, C. P., & Stanley, J. C. (1981). Mathematical ability: Is sex a factor? (Letters). *Science, 212,* 118–121.

Benbow, C. P., & Stanley, J. C. (1983). Sex differences in mathematical reasoning ability: More facts. *Science, 222,* 1029–1031.

Benbow, C. P., Stanley, J. C., Zonderman, A. B., & Kirk, M. K. (1983). Structure of intelligence of intellectually precocious children and of their parents. *Intelligence, 7,* 129–152.

Benderly, B. L. (1989, November). Don't believe everything you read. *Psychology Today,* pp. 67–69.

BenTsvi-Mayer, S., Hertz-Lazarowitz, R., & Safir, M. P. (1989). Teachers' selection of boys and girls as prominent pupils. *Sex Roles, 21,* 231–246.

Berenbaum, S. A., & Harshman, R. A. (1980). On testing group differences in cognition resulting from differences in lateral specialization: Reply to Fennell et al. *Brian and Language, 11,* 209–220.

Berrebi, A. S., Fitch, R. H., Ralphe, D. L., Denenberg, J. O., Freidrich, V. L., Jr., & Denenberg, V. H. (1988). Corpus callosum: Region specific effects of sex, early experience, and age. *Brain Research, 438,* 216–224.

Berry, J. W. (1966). Temne and Eskimo perceptual skills. *International Journal of Psychology, 1,* 207–229.

Bilous, F. R., & Krauss, R. M. (1988). Dominance and accommodation in the conversational behaviours of same- and mixed-gender dyads. *Language & Communication, 8,* 183–194.

Bleier, R. (1978). Bias in biological and human sciences: Some comments. *Signs, 5,* 159–162.

Bleier, R. (1984). *Science and gender: A critique of biology and its theories on women.* New York: Pergamon Press.

Block, J. H. (1973). Conceptions of sex roles: Some cross cultural and longitudinal perspectives. *American Psychologist, 28,* 512–526.

Block, J. H. (1976). Issues, problems, and pitfalls in assessing sex differences: A critical review of the psychology of sex differences. *Merrill Palmer Quarterly, 22,* 283–308.

Block, J. H. (1978). Another look at sex differentiation in the socialization behaviors of mothers and fathers. In J. A. Sherman & F. L. Denmark (Eds.), *The psychology of women: Future directions in research* (pp. 29–87). New York: Psychological Dimensions.

Block, R. A., Arnott, D. P., Quigley, B., & Lynch, W. C. (1989). Unilateral nostril breathing influences lateralized cognitive performance. *Brain and Cognition, 9,* 181–190.

Bock, R. D., & Kolakowski, D. (1973). Further evidence of sex-linked major-gene influence on human spatial visualizing ability. *American Journal of Human Genetics, 25,* 1–14.

Boles, D. B. (1980). X-linkage of spatial ability: A critical review. *Child Development, 51,* 625–635.

Bouchard, T. J., Jr., & McGee, M. G. (1977). Sex differences in human spatial ability: Not an x-linked recessive gene effect. *Social Biology, 24,* 332–335.

Bowers, C. A., & LaBarba, R. C. (1988). Sex differences in the lateralization of spatial abilities: A spatial component analysis of extreme group scores. *Brain and Cognition, 8,* 165–177.

Bradshaw, J. L., & Bradshaw, J. A. (1988). Reading mirror-reversed text: Sinistrals really are inferior. *Brain and Language, 33,* 189–192.

Bradshaw, J. L., & Nettleton, N. C. (1983). *Human cerebral asymmetry.* Englewood Cliffs, NJ: Prentice-Hall.

Braine, L. G. (1988). Sex differences in mathematics: Is there any news here? *Behavioral and Brain Sciences, 11,* 185–186.

Bretl, D. J., & Cantor, J. (1988). The portrayal of men and women in U.S. television commercials: A recent content analysis and trend over 15 years. *Sex Roles, 18,* 595, 609.

Bridges, J. S. (1989). Sex differences in occupational values. *Sex Roles, 20* (3/4) 205–211.

Brinkmann, E. H. (1966). Programmed instruction as a technique for improving spatial visualization. *Journal of Applied Psychology, 50,* 179–184.

Brooks, I. R. (1976). Cognitive ability assessment with two New Zealand ethnic groups. *Journal of Cross-Cultural Psychology, 7,* 347–356.

Broverman, D. M., Klaiber, E. L., Kobayashi, Y., & Vogel, W. (1968). Roles of activation and inhibition in sex differences in cognitive abilities. *Psychological Review, 75,* 23–50.

Broverman, I. K., Vogel, S. R., Broverman, D. M., Clarkson, F. E., & Rosenkrantz, P. S. (1972). Sex-role stereotypes: A current appraisal. *Journal of Social Issues, 28,* 59–78.

Brush, F. R., & Levine, S. (1989). Preface. In F. R. Brush & S. Levine (Eds.), *Psychoendocrinology* (pp. xiii–xiv). San Diego: Academic.

Bryden, M. P. (1977). Measuring handedness with questionnaires. *Neuropsychologia, 15,* 617–624.

Bryden, M. P. (1986). Dichotic listening performance, cognitive ability, and cerebral organization. *Canadian Journal of Psychology, 40,* 445–456.

Bryden, M. P. (1988). An overview of the dichotic listening procedure and its relation to cerebral organization. In K. Hugdahl (Ed.), *Handbook of dichotic listening* (pp. 1–43). Chichester, England: Wiley.

Bryden, M. P. (1989, March). *Sex differences in cerebral organization: Real or imagined*. Paper presented at the New York Neuropsychology Group, Tenth Annual Conference/New York Academy of Sciences.

Buczek, P. A. (1986). A promising measure of sex bias: The incidental memory task. *Psychology of Women Quarterly, 10*, 127–140.

Bumiller, E. (1990). *May you be the mother of a hundred sons*. New York: Random House.

Burnett, S. A., Lane, D. M., & Dratt, L. M. (1979). Spatial visualization and sex differences in quantitative ability. *Intelligence, 3*, 345–354.

Burnett, S. A., Lane, D. M., & Dratt, L. M. (1982). Spatial ability and handedness. *Intelligence, 6*, 57–68.

Burnham, D. (1977). Biology and gender: False theories about women and blacks. *Freedomways, 17*, 8–13.

Burns, A., & Homel, R. (1989). Gender division of tasks by parents and their children. *Psychology of Women Quarterly, 13*, 113–125.

Burton, G. M. (1978). Why Susie can't—or doesn't want to—add. In J. E. Jacobs (Ed.), *Perspectives on women and mathematics* (pp. 35–57). Columbus, OH: Eric Clearinghouse for Science, Mathematics and Environmental Education.

Butcher, J. (1986). Longitudinal analysis of adolescent girls' aspirations at school and perceptions of popularity. *Adolescence, 21*, 133–143.

Butcher, J. E. (1989). Adolescent girls' sex role development: Relationship with sports participation, self-esteem, and age at menarche. *Sex Roles, 20* (9/10), 575–593.

Butler, S. (1984). Sex differences in human cerebral function. In G. J. DeVries, J. De Bruin, H. Vylings, & M. Cormer. (Eds.), *Progress in brain research* (Vol. 61, pp. 443–454). Amsterdam: Elsevier Science.

Calvert, S. L., & Huston, A. C. (1987). Television and children's gender schemata. In L. S. Liben & M. L. Signorella (Eds.), *Children's gender schemata* (pp. 75–88). San Francisco: Jossey-Bass.

Campbell, N. (1987). *Biology*. New York: Benjamin Cumming.

Campbell, P. B. (1976). Adolescent intellectual decline. *Adolescence, 11*, 629–635.

Caplan, P. J., MacPherson, G. M., & Tobin, P. (1985). Do sex-related differences in spatial abilities exist? *American Psychologist, 40*, 786–799.

Carter, C. O. (1972). Sex-linkage and sex-limitation. In C. Ounsted & D. Taylor (Eds.), *Gender differences: Their ontogeny and significance* (pp. 1–12). Edinburgh: Churchill Livingstone.

Cattell, R. B. (1963). Theory of fluid and crystallized intelligence. *Journal of Educational Psychology, 54*, 1–22.

Christiansen, K., & Knussmann, R. (1987). Sex hormones and cognitive functioning in men. *Neuropsychobiology, 18*, 27–36.

The Chronicle of Higher Education (June 19, 1985). Study finds "gender gap" persists in high-tech jobs (p. 16).

The Chronicle of Higher Education Almanac (September 5, 1990). *The Nation*, p. 3.

Clarkson-Smith, L., & Halpern, D. F. (1983). Can age-related deficits in spatial memory be attenuated through the use of verbal coding? *Experimental Aging Research, 9*, 179–184.

Cohen, J. (1965). Some statistical issues in psychological research. In B. B. Woleman (Ed.), *Handbook of clinical psychology* (pp. 95–121). New York: McGraw-Hill.

Cohen, J. (1969). *Statistical power analysis for the behavioral sciences*. New York: Academic.

Cohen, J., & Cohen, P. (1983). *Applied multiple regression/correlational analysis for behavioral sciences*. Hillsdale, NJ: Lawrence Erlbaum Associates.

Cole, M., & Scribner, S. (1974). *Culture and thought: A psychological introduction*. New York: Wiley.

Connor, J. M., Schackman, M., & Serbin, L. A. (1978). Sex-related differences in response to practice on a visual-spatial test and generalization to a related test. *Child Development, 49,* 24–29.

Constantinople, A. (1973). Masculinity-femininity: An exception to a famous dictum? *Psychological Bulletin, 80,* 389–407.

Cook, E. P. (1985). *Psychological androgyny.* New York: Pergamon Press.

Corballis, M. C., & Beale, I. L. (1983). *The ambivalent mind: The neuropsychology of left and right.* Chicago: Nelson-Hall.

Corballis, M. C., & Sergent, J. (1989). Hemispheric specialization for mental rotation. *Cortex, 25,* 15–25.

Cordes, C. (1986, June). Test tilt: Boys outscore girls on both parts of SAT. *APA Monitor,* pp. 30–31.

Coren, S. (Ed.). (1990). *Left-handedness: Behavioral implications and anomalies.* Holland: Elsevier Science Publishers.

Coren, S., & Halpern, D. F. (1991). Left-handedness: A marker for decreased survival fitness. *Psychological Bulletin, 109,* 90–106.

Coren, S., & Ward, L. M. (1989). *Sensation and perception* (3rd ed.). San Diego: Harcourt Brace Jovanovich.

Crosson, C. W. (1984). Age and field independence among women. *Experimental Aging Research, 10,* 165–170.

Dalton, K. (1976). Prenatal progesterone and educational attainments. *British Journal of Psychiatry, 129,* 438–442.

Davis, R. B. (1986). The convergence of cognitive science and mathematics education. *Journal of Mathematical Behavior, 5,* 321–333.

Day, J. (1977). Right-hemisphere language processing in normal right-handers. *Journal of Experimental Psychology: Human Perception and Performance, 3,* 518–528.

Deaux, K. (1984). From individual differences to social categories: Analysis of a decade's research on gender. *American Psychologist, 39,* 105–116.

Deaux, K. (1985). Sex and gender. *Annual Reviews of Psychology, 36,* 49–81.

Deaux, K., & Major B. (1987). Putting gender into context: An interactive model of gender-related behavior. *Psychological Review, 94,* 369–389.

DeFries, J. C., Vandenberg, S. G., & McClearn, G. E. (1976). Genetics of specific cognitive abilities. *Annual Review of Genetics, 10,* 179–207.

de Groot, A. D. (1966). Perception and memory versus thought: Some old ideas and recent findings. In B. Kleinmuntz (Ed.), *Problem solving.* New York: Wiley.

De Lisi, R., Parameswaran, G., & McGillicuddy-DeLisi, A. (1989). Age and sex differences in representation of horizontality among children in India. *Perceptual and Motor Skills,* pp. 739–746.

Denenberg, V. H., Berrebi, A. S., & Fitch, R. H. (1988). A factor analysis of the rat's corpus callosum. *Brain Research, 497,* 271–279.

Deutsch, D. (1980). Handedness and memory for tonal pitch. In J. Herron (Ed.), *Neuropsychology of left-handedness.* New York: Academic Press.

Diamond, E. E. (1986). Theories of career development and the reality of women at work. In B. A. Gutek & L. Larwood (Eds.), *Women's career development* (pp. 15–27). Newbury Park: Sage.

Diamond, M. C. (1988). *Enriching heredity: The impact of the environment on the anatomy of the brain.* New York: Free Press.

Diamond, M. C., Johnson, R. E., & Ehlert, J. (1979). A comparison of cortical thickness in male and female rats—normal gonadectomized, young and adult. *Behavioral Neural Biology, 26,* 485–491.

Dimond, S. J., & Beaumont, J. G. (1974). Experimental studies of hemisphere function in the human brain. In S. J. Dimond & J. G. Beaumont (Eds.), *Hemisphere function in the human brain.* New York: Wiley.

Dodge, S. (1989, September 20). SAT, ACT scores remain steady or drop slightly. *The Chronicle of Higher Education*, pp. A37, A39.

Doering, C. H., Brodie, H. K. H., Fraemer, H., Becker, H., & Hamburg, O. (1974). Plasma testosterone levels and psychologic measures in men over a 2-month period. In R. C. Friedman & R. L. Vande Wiele (Eds.), *Sex differences in behavior: A conference*. New York: Wiley.

Dorries, K. M., Schmidt, H. J., Beauchamp, G. K., & Wysocki, C. J. (1989). Changes in sensitivity to the odor of androstenone during adolescence. *Developmental Psychobiology, 22*, 423–435.

Doyle, J., & Paludi, M. (1990). *Sex and gender* (2nd ed.). Dubuque, IA: Wm. C. Brown.

Dubas, J. S., Crockett, L. J., & Petersen, A. C. *A longitudinal investigation of sex differences in cognitive abilities during early adolescence.*

Eagly, A. H. (1987). *Sex differences in social behavior: A social-role interpretation*. Hillsdale, NJ: Lawrence Erlbaum Associates.

Eagly, A. H. (1990). On the advantages of reporting sex comparisons. *American Psychologist, 45*, 560–562.

Eaton, W. O., & Enns, L. R. (1986). Sex differences in human motor activity level. *Psychological Bulletin, 100*, 19–28.

Eccles (Parsons), J. et al. (1983). Expectancies, values, and academic behaviors. In J. T. Spence (Ed.), *Achievement and achievement motives: Psychological and sociological approaches* (pp. 75–146). San Francisco: W. H. Freeman.

Eccles, J. S. (1987). Gender roles and women's achievement-related decisions. *Psychology of Women Quarterly, 11*, 135–172.

Educational Testing Service. (1987). *Manual for information for test committee members*. Princeton, NJ: Author.

Ehrhardt, A. A., & Meyer-Bahlburg, H. F. L. (1979). Prenatal sex hormones and the developing brain: Effects on psychosexual differentiation and cognitive function. *Annual Review of Medicine 30*, 417–430.

Elias, M. F., & Kinsbourne, M. (1974). Age and sex differences in the processing of verbal and nonverbal stimuli. *Journal of Gerontology, 29*, 162–171.

Eliot, J., & Fralley, J. S. (1976). Sex differences in spatial abilities. *Young Children, 31*, 487–497.

Elliot, R. (1961). Interrelationship among measures of field dependence, ability, and personality traits. *Journal of Abnormal and Social Psychology, 63*, 27–36.

Elmore, P. B., & Vasu, E. S. (1980). Relationship between selected variables and statistics achievement: Building a theoretical model. *Journal of Educational Psychology, 72*, 457–467.

Elmore, P. B., & Vasu, E. S. (1986). A model of statistics achievement using spatial ability, feminist attitudes and mathematics-related variables as predictors. *Educational and Psychological Measurement, 46*, 215–222.

Embretson, S. E. (1987). Improving the measurement of spatial aptitude by dynamic testing. *Intelligence, 11*, 333–358.

Ernest, J. (1976). *Mathematics and sex*. Berkeley: University of California Press.

Etaugh, C. (1983). Introduction: The influences of environmental factors on sex differences in children's play. In M. B. Liss (Ed.), *Social and cognitive skills: Sex roles and children's play* (pp. 1–19). New York: Academic Press.

Etaugh, C. (1989). Evaluation bias. In H. Tierney (Ed.), *Women's studies encyclopedia* (pp. 124–125). New York: Greenwood.

Evans, S. H., & Anastasio, E. J. (1968). Misuse of analysis of covariance when treatment effect and covariate are confounded. *Psychological Bulletin, 69*, 225–234.

Fairweather, H. (1976). Sex differences in cognition. *Cognition, 4*, 231–280.

Faust, M. S. (1977). Somatic development of adolescent girls. *Monographs of the Society for Research in Child Development, 42*, 1–90.

Faust, M. S. (1983). Alternative constructions of adolescent growth. In J. Brooks-Gunn & A. C.

Petersen (Eds.), *Girls at puberty: Biological and psychosocial perspectives* (pp. 105–125). New York: Plenum Press.

Fausto-Sterling, A. (1985). *Myths of gender: Biological theories about woman and man.* New York: Basic.

Feingold, A. (1988). Cognitive gender differences are disappearing. *American Psychologist, 43,* 95–103.

Fennema, E., & Sherman, J. (1977). Sex-related differences in mathematics achievement, spatial visualization, and sociocultural factors. *Journal of Educational Research, 14,* 51–71.

Fennema, E., & Sherman, J. (1978). Sex-related differences in mathematics achievement and related factors: A further study. *Journal for Research in Mathematics Education, 9,* 189–203.

Fennema, E., & Tartre, L. A. (1985). The use of spatial visualization in mathematics by girls and boys. *Journal for Research in Mathematics Education, 16,* 184–206.

Fitch, R. H., Berrebi, A. S., Cowell, P. E., Schrott, L. M., & Denenberg, V. H. (in press). Corpus callosum: Effects of neonatal hormones on sexual dimorphism in the rat. *Brain Research.*

Fogel, R., & Paludi, M. A. (1984). Fear of success and failure or norms for achievement? *Sex Roles: A Journal of Research, 10,* 431–434.

Fox, L. H., Tobin, D., & Brody, L. (1979). Sex role socialization and achievement in mathematics. In M. A. Wittig & A. C. Petersen (Eds.), *Sex-related differences in cognitive functioning* (pp. 303–332). New York: Academic Press.

Freeman, D. (1983). *Margaret Mead and Samoa: The making and unmaking of an anthropological myth.* Boston: Harvard University Press.

Frisch, R. E. (1983). Fatness, puberty, and fertility: The effects of nutrition and physical training on menarche and ovulation. In J. Brooks-Gunn & A. C. Petersen (Eds.), *Girls at puberty: Biological and psychosocial perspectives* (pp. 29–50). New York: Plenum Press.

Gallagher, S. A. (1989). Predictors of SAT mathematics and scores of gifted male and gifted female adolescents. *Psychology of Women Quarterly, 13,* 191–203.

Gardner, H. (1983). *Frames of mind.* New York: Basic.

Gaulin, S. J. C., & Fitzgerald, R. W. (1989). Sexual selection for spatial learning ability. *Animal Behavior, 37,* 322–331.

Gaulin, S. J. C., Fitzgerald, R. W., & Wartell, M. S. (1990). Sex differences in spatial ability and activity in two vole species. *Journal of Comparative Psychology, 104,* 88–93.

Gaulin, S. J. C., & Wartell, M. S. (1990). Effects of experience and motivation on symmetrical-maze performance in the Prarie Vole. *Journal of Comparative Psychology, 104,* 183–189.

Gazzaniga, M. S. (1983). Right hemisphere language following brain bisection: A 20-year perspective. *American Psychologist, 88,* 525–537.

Geary, D. C. (1988, November). *Sex-dimorphic behavior patterns, maturational timing, and gender differences in spatial ability.* Paper presented at the 29th annual meeting of the Psychonomic Society, Chicago: IL.

Geary, D. C. (1989). A model for representing gender differences in the pattern of cognitive abilities. *American Psychologist, 102,* 1155–1156.

Gelman, D., Carey, J., Gelman, E., Malamud, P., Foote, D., Lubenow, G. C., & Contreras, J. (1981, May 18). Just how the sexes differ. *Newsweek,* pp. 77–83.

Gersh, E. S., & Gersh, I. (1981). *Biology of women.* Baltimore, MD: University Park Press.

Geschwind, N. (1974). The anatomical basis of hemisphere differentiation. In S. J. Dimond & J. G. Beaumont (Eds.), *Hemisphere function in the human brain.* New York: Wiley.

Geschwind, N. (1983). Biological associations of left-handedness. *Annals of Dyslexia, 33,* 29–40.

Geschwind, N. (1984). Cerebral dominance in biological perspective. *Neuropsychologia, 22,* 675–683.

Geschwind, N., & Behan, P. (1982). Left-handedness: Associations with immune disease, migraine, and developmental learning disorders. *Proceedings of the National Academy of Science, 79,* 5097–5100.

Geschwind, N., & Behan, P. (1984). Laterality, hormones and immunity. In N. Geschwind & A. M. Galaburda (Eds.), *Cerebral dominance: The biological foundations*. Cambridge, MA: Harvard University Press.

Geschwind, N., & Galaburda, A. M. (1987). *Cerebral lateralization: Biological mechanisms, associations, and pathology*. Cambridge, MA: MIT Press.

Gettys, L. D., & Cann, A. (1981). Children's perceptions of occupational sex stereotyping. *Sex Roles, 1,* 301–307.

Gilligan, C. (1982). *In a different voice: Psychological theory and women's development*. Cambridge, MA: Harvard University Press.

Gladue, B. A., Beatty, W. W., Larson, J., & Staton, R. D. (1990). Sexual orientations and spatial ability in men and women. *Psychobiology, 18,* 101–108.

Glaser, R. (1991). Expert knowledge and processes of thinking. In D. F. Halpern (Ed.), *Enhancing thinking skills in the sciences and mathematics*. Hillsdale, NJ: Lawrence Erlbaum Associates.

Goldberg, P. (1968, April). Are some women prejudiced against women? *Transaction,* pp. 28–30.

Goldstein, D., Haldane, D., & Mitchell, C. (1990). Sex differences in visual-spatial ability: The role of performance factors. *Memory & Cognition, 18,* 546–550.

Golub, S. (1976). The effect of premenstrual anxiety and depression on cognitive function. *Journal of Personality and Social Psychology, 34,* 99–104.

Goodnow, J. (1985). Topics, methods and models: Feminist challenges in Social Science. In J. Goodnow & C. Pateman (Eds.), *Women, social science and public policy*. Sydney: George Allen & Unwin.

Goolkasian, P. (1980). Cyclic changes in pain perception: An ROC analysis. *Perception and Psychophysics, 27,* 499–504.

Goolkasian, P. (1985). Phase and sex effects in pain perception: A critical review. *Psychology of Women Quarterly, 9,* 15–28.

Gordon, H. W. (1980). Cognitive asymmetry in dyslexic families. *Neuropsychologia, 18,* 645–656.

Gordon, H. W., & Leighty, R. (1988). Importance of specialized cognitive function in the selection of military pilots. *Journal of Applied Psychology, 73,* 38–45.

Gorrell, J., & Shaw, E. L. (1988). Upper elementary and high school students' attitudes toward gender-typed occupations. *Journal of Adolescent Research, 3,* 189–199.

Gorski, R. A. (1985). The 13th J. A. F. Stevenson Memorial Lecture: Sexual differentiation of the brain: Possible mechanism and implications. *Canadian Journal of Physiological Pharmacology, 63,* 577–594.

Gottfried, A. W., & Bathurst, K. (1983). Hand preferences across time is related to intelligence in young girls, not boys. *Science, 221,* 1074–1076.

Gould, J. S. (1978). Women's brains. *Natural History, 87,* 44–50.

Gould, R. E. (1974). Measuring masculinity by the size of a paycheck. In J. H. Pleck & J. Sawyer (Eds.), *Men and masculinity* (pp. 96–100). Englewood Cliffs, NJ: Prentice-Hall.

Goy, R. W., Bercovitch, F. B., & McBrair, M. C. (1988). Behavioral masculinization is independent of genital masculinization in prenatally androgenized female rhesus macaques. *Hormones and Behavior, 22,* 552–571.

Graber, J. A., & Petersen, A. C. (in press). Cognitive changes at adolescence: Biological perspectives. In K. Gibson & A. C. Petersen (Eds.), *The brain and behavioral development: Biosocial dimensions*. Hawthorn, NY: Aldine.

Graham, M. F., & Birns, B. (1979). Where are the women geniuses? Up the down escalator. In C. B. Kopp & M. Kirkpatrick (Eds.), *Becoming female: Perspectives on development* (pp. 291–312). New York: Plenum Press.

Greenfield, P., & Lauber, B. (1985, March). *Cognitive effects of video games*. Paper presented at the Claremont Conference on Applied Cognitive Psychology, Claremont, CA.

Greenough, W. T., Black, J. E., & Wallace, C. S. (1987). Experience and brain development. *Child Development, 58,* 539–559.

Guilford, J. P. (1967). *The nature of human intelligence*. New York: McGraw-Hill.

Gunter, N. C., & Gunter, B.G. (1990). Domestic division of labor among working couples. *Psychology of Women Quarterly, 14,* 355–370.

Hall, J. A. (1985). *Nonverbal sex differences: Communication accuracy and expressive style.* Baltimore: Johns Hopkins University Press.

Hall, J. A., & Halberstadt, A. G. (1986). Smiling and gazing. In J. S. Hyde & M. C. Linn (Eds.), *The psychology of gender: Advances through meta-analysis* (pp. 136–158). Baltimore: Johns Hopkins Press.

Halpern, D. F. (1984a). *Thought and knowledge: An introduction to critical thinking.* Hillsdale, NJ: Lawrence Erlbaum Associates.

Halpern, D. F. (1984b). Age differences in response time to verbal and symbolic traffic signs. *Experimental Aging Research, 10,* 201–204.

Halpern, D. F. (1985). The influence of sex-role stereotypes on prose recall. *Sex Roles, 12,* 363–375.

Halpern, D. F. (1986). A different response to the question "Do sex differences in spatial abilities exist?" *American Psychologist, 41,* 1014–1015.

Halpern, D. F. (1988). Sex differences in mathematical reasoning ability: Let me count the ways. *Behavioral and Brain Sciences, 11,* 191–192.

Halpern, D. F. (1989a). The disappearance of cognitive gender differences: What you see depends on where you look. *American Psychologist, 102,* 1156–1158.

Halpern, D. F. (1989b). *Thought and knowledge: An introduction to critical thinking* (2nd ed.). Hillsdale, NJ: Lawrence Erlbaum Associates.

Halpern, D. F. (Ed.). (1991). *Enhancing thinking skills in the sciences and mathematics.* Hillsdale, NJ: Lawrence Erlbaum Associates.

Halpern, D. F., & Coren, S. (1988). Do right-handers live longer? *Nature, 333,* 213.

Halpern, D. F., & Coren, S. (1990). Laterality and longevity: Is left-handedness associated with a younger age at death? In S. Coren (Ed.), *Left-handedness: Behavioral implications and anomalies* (pp. 509–545). Holland: Elsevier Science Publishers.

Halpern, D. F., & Coren, S. (1991). Laterality and life span. *New England Journal of Medicine, 324,* 998.

Halpern, D. F., & Kagan, S. (1984). Sex, age and cultural differences in individualism. *The Journal of Genetic Psychology, 145,* 23–25.

Hamburg, D. A., & Lunde, D. T. (1966). Sex hormones in the development of sex differences in human behavior. In E. E. Maccoby (Ed.), *The development of sex differences* (pp. 1–24). Stanford: Stanford University Press.

Hamilton, M. C. (1988). Using masculine generics: Does generic he increase male bias in the user's imagery? *Sex Roles, 19* (11/12), 785–799.

Hampson, E. (1990a). Estrogen-related variations in human spatial and articulatory-motor skills. *Psychoneuroendocrinology,* in press.

Hampson, E. (1990b). Variations in sex-related cognitive abilities across the menstrual cycle. *Brain and Cognition,* in press.

Hampson, E., & Kimura, D. (1988). Reciprocal effects of hormonal fluctuations on human motor and perceptual-spatial skills. *Behavioral Neuroscience, 102,* 456–495.

Hardyck, C., Goldman, R., & Petrinovich, L. (1975). Handedness and sex, race, and age. *Human Biology, 47,* 369–375.

Hardyck, C., Petrinovich, L. F., & Goldman, R. D. (1976). Left-handedness and cognitive deficit. *Cortex, 12,* 266–79.

Harris, D. R., Bisbee, C. T., & Evans, S. H. (1971). Further comments-misuse of analysis of covariance. *Psychological Bulletin, 75,* 220–222.

Harris, L. J. (1978). Sex differences in spatial ability: Possible environmental, genetic, and neurological factors. In M. Kinsbourne (Ed.), *Asymmetrical functions of the brain* (pp. 405–522). Cambridge, England: Cambridge University Press.

Harris, M. J., & Rosenthal, R. (1985). Mediation of interpersonal expectancy effects: 31 meta-analyses. *Psychological Bulletin, 97,* 363–386.

Harshman, R. A., & Hampson, E. (1987). Normal variation in human brain organization: Relation to handedness, sex, and cognitive abilities. In D. Ottoson (Ed.), *Duality and unity of the brain* (pp. 83–99). New York: Plenum.

Harshman, R. A., Hampson, E., & Berenbaum, S. A. (1983). Individual differences in cognitive abilities and brain organization: Part I. Sex and handedness differences in ability. *Canadian Journal of Psychology, 37,* 144–192.

Hassler, M., Birbaumer, N., & Feil, A. (1987). Musical talent and visual-spatial ability: Onset of puberty. *Psychology of Music, 15,* 141–151.

Haugh, S. S., Hoffman, C. D., & Cowan, G. (1980). The eye of the very young beholder: Sex typing of infants by younger children. *Child Development, 51,* 598–600.

Hays, W. L. (1963). *Statistics for psychologists.* New York: Holt, Rinehart & Winston.

Hays, W. L. (1981). *Statistics.* New York: Holt, Rinehart & Winston.

Healey, J. M., Waldstein, S., & Goodglass, H. (1985). Sex differences in the lateralization of language discrimination vs language production. *Neuropsychologia, 23,* 777–789.

Heister, G., Landis, T., Regard, M., & Schroeder-Heister, P. (1989). Shift of functional cerebral asymmetry during the menstrual cycle. *Neuropsychologia, 27,* 871–880.

Hendricks, B., Marvel, M. K., & Barrington, B. L. (1990). The dimensions of psychological research. *Teaching of Psychology, 17,* 76–82.

Herbst, L., & Petersen, A. C. (1980, August). *Timing of maturation, brain lateralization, and cognitive performance.* Paper presented at the Annual Meeting of the American Psychological Association, Montreal, Canada.

Herman, J. F., Heins, J. A., & Cohen, D. S. (1987). Children's spatial knowledge of their neighborhood environment. *Journal of Applied Developmental Psychology, 8,* 1–15.

Hertzog, C., & Carter, L. (1982). Sex differences in the structures of intelligence: A confirmatory factor analysis. *Intelligence, 6,* 287–303.

Hier, D. B., & Crowley, W. F., Jr. (1982). Spatial ability in androgen-deficient men. *The New England Journal of Medicine, 306,* 1202–1205.

Hill, J. P., & Lynch, M. E. (1983). The intensification of gender-related role expectations during early adolescence. In J. Brooks-Gunn & A. C. Petersen (Eds.), *Girls at puberty: Biological and psychosocial perspectives* (pp. 201–228). New York: Plenum Press.

Hills, J. R. (1957). Factor analyzed abilities and success in college mathematics. *Educational Psychological Measurement, 17,* 615–622.

Hilton, T. L., & Berglund, G. W. (1974). Sex differences in mathematics achievement—A longitudinal study. *The Journal of Educational Research, 67,* 231–237.

Hines, M. (1982). Prenatal gonadal hormones and sex differences in human behavior. *Psychological Bulletin, 92,* 56–80.

Hines, M. (1990). Gonadal hormones and human cognitive development. In J. Balthazart (Ed.), *Hormones, brain and behavior in vertebrates. 1. Sexual differentiation, neuroanatomical aspects, neurotransmitters and neuropeptides* (pp. 51–63). Basel: Karger.

Holding, C. S., & Holding, D. H. (1989). Acquisition of route network knowledge by males and females. *Journal of General Psychology, 116,* 29–41.

Holland, J. H., Holyoak, K. J., Nisbett, R. E., & Thagard, P. R. (1986). *Induction: Processes of inference, learning, and discovery.* Cambridge, MA: MIT Press.

Hood, K. D., Draper, P., Crockett, L. J., & Petersen, A. C. (1987). The ontogeny and phylogeny of sex differences in development: A biopsychosocial synthesis. In D. B. Carter (Ed.), *Current conceptions of sex roles and sex typing: Theory and research* (pp. 49–77). New York: Praeger.

Horgan, D. M. (1975). *Language development.* Unpublished doctoral dissertation. University of Michigan, Ann Arbor.

Horner, M. S. (1969). Fail: Bright women. *Psychology Today, 3,* 36–38, 62.

Houser, B. B., & Garvey, C. (1985). Factors that affect nontraditional vocational enrollment among women. *Psychology of Women Quarterly, 9,* 105–117.

Howell, D. C. (1987). *Statistical methods for psychology* (2nd ed.). Boston: Deuxbury.

Hoyenga, K. B., & Hoyenga, K. T. (1979). *The question of sex differences: Psychological, cultural, and biological issues.* Boston: Little, Brown and Company.

Humphreys, L. G. (1978). Research on individual differences requires correlational analysis, not ANOVA. *Intelligence, 2,* 1–5.

Hunt, E. (1985). Verbal ability. In R. J. Sternberg (Ed.), *Human abilities: An information processing approach* (pp. 31–58). New York: W. H. Freeman.

Hunt, E., Pellegrino, J. W., Frick, R. W., Farr, S. A., & Alderton, D. (1988). The ability to reason about movement in the visual field. *Intelligence, 12,* 77–100.

Hyde, J. S. (1981). How large are cognitive gender differences? *American Psychologist, 36,* 892–901.

Hyde, J. S. (1991). *Half the human experience: The psychology of women* (4th ed.). Lexington, MA: D. C. Heath.

Hyde, J. S. (1986). Gender differences in aggression. In J. S. Hyde & M. C. Linn (Eds.), *The psychology of gender: Advances through meta-analysis* (pp. 51–66). Baltimore: The Johns Hopkins University Press.

Hyde, J. S., Fennema, E., & Lamon, S. J. (1990). Gender differences in mathematics performance: A meta-analysis. *Psychological Bulletin, 107,* 139–155.

Hyde, J. S., Fennema, E., Ryan, M., Frost, L. A., & Hopp, C. (1990). Gender comparisons of mathematics attitudes and affect: A meta-analysis. *Psychology of Women Quarterly, 3,* 299–324.

Hyde, J. S., Geiringer, E. R., & Yen, W. M. (1975). On the empirical relation between spatial ability and sex differences in other aspects of cognitive performance. *Multivariate Behavioral Research, 10,* 289–309.

Hyde, J. S., & Linn, M. C. (Eds.). (1986). *The psychology of gender: Advances through meta-analysis.* Baltimore: The Johns Hopkins University Press.

Hyde, J. S., & Linn, M. C. (1988). Gender differences in verbal ability: A meta-analysis. *Psychological Bulletin, 104,* 53–69.

Hynd, G. W., & Semrud-Clikeman, M. (1990). Dyslexia and brain morphology. *Psychological Bulletin, 106,* 447–482.

Inglis, J., & Lawson, J. S. (1981). Sex differences in the effects of unilateral brain damage on intelligence. *Science, 212,* 693–695.

Intons-Peterson, M. G. (1988). *Gender concepts of Swedish and American youth.* Hillsdale, NJ: Lawrence Erlbaum Associates.

Jacklin, C. N. (1989). Female and male: Issues of gender. *American Psychologist, 44,* 127–133.

Jacklin, C. N., Wilcox, K. T., & Maccoby, E. E. (1988). Neonatal sex-steroid hormones and intellectual abilities of six year old boys and girls. *Developmental Psychobiology, 21,* 567–574.

Janowsky, J. S. (1989). Sexual dimorphism in the human brain: Dispelling the myths. *Developmental Medicine and Child Neurology, 31,* 257–263.

Janson-Smith, D. (1980). Sociobiology: So what? In the Brighton Women & Science Group, *Alice through the microscope* (pp. 62–86). London: Virago.

Jensen, A. R. (1980). Chronometric analysis of intelligence. *Journal of Social and Biological Structures, 3,* 103–122.

Johnson, C. D., & Gormly, J. (1972). Academic cheating: The contribution of sex, personality, and situational variables. *Developmental Psychology, 6,* 320–325.

Johnson, E. S., & Meade, A. C. (1987). Developmental patterns of spatial ability: An early sex difference. *Child Development, 58,* 725–740.

Johnson, O., & Harley, C. (1980). Handedness and sex differences in cognitive tests of brain laterality. *Cortex, 16,* 73–82.

Johnson, S. (1987). Early-developed sex differences in science and mathematics in the United Kingdom. *Journal of Early Adolescence, 7,* 21–33.

Jones, L. V. (1984). White-black achievement differences: The narrowing gap. *American Psychologist, 39,* 1207–1213.

Jonides, J., & Rozin, P. (1981). *Study guide for Gleitman's Basic Psychology.* New York: W. W. Norton.

Kail, R., Carter, P., & Pellegrino, J. (1979). The locus of sex differences in spatial ability. *Perception & Psychophysics, 26,* 182–186.

Kalichman, S. C. (1989). The effects of stimulus context on paper-and-pencil spatial task performance. *Journal of General Psychology, 116,* 133–139.

Katcher, A. (1955). The discrimination of sex differences by young children. *Journal of Genetic Psychology, 87,* 131–143.

Kee, D. W., & Cherry, B. (1990). Lateralized interference in finger tapping: Initial value differences do not affect the outcome. *Neuropsychologia, 28,* 313–316.

Kee, D. W., Gottfried, A. W., Bathurst, K., & Brown, K. W. (1987). Left-hemisphere language specialization: Consistency in hand preference and sex differences. *Child Development, 58,* 718–724.

Keeton, W. T. (1967). *Biological science.* New York: W. W. Norton.

Kenrick, D. T. (1988). Biology: Si, hard-wired ability: Maybe no. *Behavioral and Brain Sciences, 11,* 199–200.

Kerlinger, F. N. (1979). *Behavioral research: A conceptual approach.* New York: Holt, Rinehart and Winston.

Kimball, M. M. (1989). A new perspective on women's math achievement. *Psychological Bulletin, 105,* 198–214.

Kimmel, D. C., & Weiner, I. B. (1985). Adolescence: A developmental transition. Hillsdale, NJ: Lawrence Erlbaum associates.

Kimura, D. (1969). Spatial localization in left and right visual fields. *Canadian Journal of Psychology, 23,* 445–458.

Kimura, D. (1983). Sex differences in cerebral organization for speech and praxic functions. *Canadian Journal of Psychology, 37,* 19–35.

Kimura, D. (1985). Male brain, female brain: The hidden difference. *Psychology Today, 19,* 50–52, 54, 55–58.

Kimura, D. (1987). Are men's and women's brains really different? *Canadian Psychology, 28,* 133–147.

Kimura, D. (1989, November). How sex hormones boost—or cut—intellectual ability. *Psychology Today,* pp. 62–66.

Kimura, D., & Durnford, M. (1974). Normal studies on the function of right hemisphere in vision. In S. J. Dimond & J. G. Beaumont (Eds.), *Hemisphere function in the human brain.* New York: Wiley.

Kitterle, F. L., & Kaye, R. S. (1985). Hemispheric symmetry in contrast and oventation sensitivity. *Perception & Psychophysics, 37,* 391–396.

Koblinsky, S. G., Cruse, D. F., Sugawawa, A. I. (1978). Sex role stereotypes and children's memory for story content. *Child Development, 49,* 452–458.

Kogan, N. (1973). Creativity and cognitive style: A life-span perspective. In P. B. Baltes & K. W. Schale (Eds.), *Life-span developmental psychology: Personality and socialization.* New York: Academic Press.

Kohlberg, L. (1966). A cognitive-developmental analysis of children's sex-role concepts and attitudes. In E. E. Maccoby (Eds.), *The development of sex differences* (pp. 82–172). Stanford: Stanford University Press.

Kolata, G. (1990). Studies dispute views of dyslexia, finding girls as afflicted as boys. *New York Times,* pp. A1, B8.

Konner, M. (1988). She and he. In A. L. Hammond & P. G. Zimbardo (Eds.), *Readings on human behavior* (pp. 33–40). Glenview, IL: Scott, Foresman and Co.

Koslow, R. E. (1987). Sex-related differences and visual-spatial mental imagery as factors affecting symbolic motor skill acquisition. *Sex Roles, 17* (9/10),

Kosslyn, S. M., Ball, T. M., & Reiser, B. J. (1978). Visual images preserve metric spatial information: Evidence from studies of image scanning. *Journal of Experimental Psychology: Human Perception and Performance, 4,* 47–60.

Kovac, D., & Majerova, M. (1974). Figure reproduction from the aspect of development and interfunctional relationships. *Studia Psychologica, 16,* 149–152.

Kuhn, D., Nash, S. C., & Brucken, L. (1978). Sex role concepts of two- and three-year olds. *Child Development, 49,* 445–451.

LaHoste, G. J., Mormede, P., Rivet, J. M., & Le Moal, M. (1988). New evidence for distinct patterns of brain organization in rats differentiated on the basis of inherent laterality. *Brain Research, 474,* 296–308.

Lake, D. A., & Bryden, M. P. (1976). Handedness and sex differences in hemispheric asymmetry. *Brain and Language, 3,* 266–282.

Landauer, A. A. (1981). Sex differences in decision and movement time. *Perceptual & Motor Skills, 52,* 90.

Landers, S. (1989, June). NY ruling boosts state scholarship awards to women. *APA Monitor,* p. 27.

Lawson, J. S., Inglis, J., & Tittemore, J. A. (1987). Factorially defined verbal and performance IQs derived from the WISC–R: Patterns of cognitive ability in normal and learning disabled children. *Personality and Individual Differences, 8,* 331–341.

Leacock, E. (1980). Social behavior, biology and the double standard. In G. W. Barlow & J. Silverberg (Eds.), *Sociobiology: Beyond nature/nurture* (pp. 465–488). Boulder, CO: Westview Press.

Lehrke, R. G. (1974). *X-linked mental retardation and verbal disability.* New York: Intercontinental Medical Book Corporation.

Levy, G. D. (1989). Relations among aspects of children's social environments, gender schematization, gender role knowledge, and flexibility. *Sex Roles, 21,* (11/12), 803–823.

Levy, J. (1969). Possible basis for the evolution of lateral specialization of the human brain. *Nature, 224,* 614–615.

Levy, J. (1974). Psychobiological implications of bilateral asymmetry. In S. Dimond & J. G. Beaumont (Eds.), *Hemispheric function in the human brain.* London: Paul Elek.

Levy, J. (1976). Cerebral lateralization and spatial ability. *Behavior Genetics, 6,* 171–188.

Levy, J., & Gur, R. C. (1980). Individual differences in psycho-neurological organization. In J. Herron (Ed.), *Neuropsychology of left-handedness* (pp. 199–210). New York: Academic Press.

Levy, J., & Negylaki, T. (1972). A model for the genetics of handedness. *Genetics, 72,* 117–128.

Levy, J., & Reid, M. (1978). Variations in cerebral organization as a function of handedness, handposture in writing, and sex. *Journal of Experimental Psychology: General, 107,* 119–144.

Levy-Agresti, J., & Sperry, R. W. (1968). Differential perceptual capacities in major and minor hemispheres. *Proceedings of the National Academy of Science U.S.A., 61,* 1151.

Lewin, M., & Tragos, L. M. (1987). Has the feminist movement influenced adolescent sex role attitudes? A reassessment after a quarter century. *Sex Roles, 16* (3,4), 125–135.

Lewis, M. (1986). Early sex role behavior and school age adjustment. In J. M. Reinisch, L. A. Rosenblum, & S. A. Sanders (Eds.), *Masculinity/femininity: Basic perspectives* (pp. 202–239). New York: Oxford University Press.

Lewis, R. S., & Harris, L. J. (1990). Handedness, sex, and spatial ability. In S. Coren (Ed.), *Left-handedness: Behavioral implications and anomalies* (pp. 319–342). The Netherlands: Elsevier Science Publishers.

Liben, L. S., & Bigler, R. S. (1987). Reformulating children's gender schemata. *New Directions for Child Development, 38,* 89–105.

Liben, L. S., & Signorella, M. L. (1980). Gender-related schemata and constructive memory in children. *Child Development, 51,* 11–18.

Lindesay, J. (1987). Laterality shift and homosexual men. *Neuropsychologia, 25,* 965–969.

Linn, M. C. (1985). Gender equity in computer learning environments. *Computers and the Social Sciences, 1,* 19–27.

Linn, M. C., De Benedictis, T., Delucchi, K., Harris, A., & Stage, E. (1987). Gender differences in National Assessment of Educational Progress science items: What does "I don't know" really mean? *Journal of Research and Science Teaching, 24,* 267–278.

Linn, M. C., & Petersen, A. C. (1985). Emergence and characterization of sex differences in spatial ability: A meta-analysis. *Child Development, 56,* 1479–1498.

Linn, M. C., & Petersen, A. C. (1986). A meta-analysis of gender differences in spatial ability: Implications for mathematics and science achievement. In J. S. Hyde, & M. C. Linn, (Eds.), *The psychology of gender: Advances through meta-analysis* (pp. 67–101). Baltimore: The Johns Hopkins University Press.

Loehlin, J. C., Sharan, S., & Jacoby, R. (1978). In pursuit of the "spatial gene": A family study. *Behavior Genetics, 8,* 27–41.

Lohman, D. F. (1986). The effect of speed-accuracy tradeoff on sex differences in mental rotation. *Perception and Psychophysics, 39,* 427–436.

Lohman, D. F. (1988). Spatial abilities as traits, processes, and knowledge. In R. J. Steinberg (Ed.), *Advances in the psychology of human intelligence* (volume 4, pp. 181–248). Hillsdale, NJ: Lawrence Erlbaum Associates.

Lopata, H. Z., & Thorne, B. (1978). On the term "sex roles." *Signs, 3,* 718–721.

Los Angeles Times (1990, September 5). For many, picking a child's gender is a fertile field. p. E1–E2.

Lott, B. (1985). The potential enrichment of social–personality psychology through feminist research and vice versa. *American Psychologist, 40,* 155–164.

Luchins, E. H. (1979). Women and mathematics: Fact and fiction. *American Mathematical Monthly, 88,* 413–419.

Luchins, E. H., & Luchins, A. S. (1981). (Letters) Mathematical ability: Is sex a factor? *Science, 212,* 116–118.

Lueptow, L. B. (1984). *Adolescent sex roles and social change.* New York: Columbia University Press.

Lynn, D. (1974). *The father: This role in child development.* Monterey, CA: Brooks/Cole.

Lynn, R. (1987). The intelligence of the mongoloids: A psychometric, evolutionary, and neurological theory. *Personality and Individual Differences, 8,* 813–844.

Maccoby, E. (1990, July). Maccoby: Children are "ruthless stereotypers." *APS Observer, 3,* 5–7.

Maccoby, E. E. (1966). Sex differences in intellectual functioning. In E. E. Maccoby (Ed.), *The development of sex differences* (pp. 25–55). Stanford: Stanford University Press.

Maccoby, E. E., & Jacklin, C. N. (1974). *The psychology of sex differences.* Stanford: Stanford University Press.

MacDonald, C. T. (1980). Facilitating women's achievement in mathematics. In L. H. Fox, L. Brody, & D. Tobin (Eds.), *Women and the mathematical mystique* (pp. 115–137). Baltimore, MD: The Johns Hopkins University Press.

MacKay, D. G. (1983). Prescriptive grammar and the pronoun problem. In B. Thorne, C. Kramarae, & N. Henley (Eds.), *Language, gender, and society* (pp. 38–53). Rowley, MA: Newbury House.

MacLusky, N. J., & Naftolin, F. (1981). Sexual differentiation of the central nervous system. *Science, 211,* 1294–1303.

Marshall, S. P., & Smith, J. D. (1987). Sex differences in learning mathematics: A longitudinal study with item and error analyses. *Journal of Educational Psychology, 79,* 372–383.

Martin, C. L., & Halverson, C. F., Jr. (1981). A schematic processing model of sex typing and stereotyping in children. *Child Development, 52,* 1119–1134.

Martin, D. J., & Hoover, H. D. (1987). Sex differences in educational achievement: A longitudinal study. Special issue: Sex differences in early adolescents. *Journal of Early Adolescence, 7,* 65–83.

Matlin, M. W. (1987). *The psychology of women.* New York: Holt, Rinehart & Winston.

Mayer, R. (1985). Mathematical ability. In R. J. Sternberg (Ed.), *Human abilities: An information processing approach* (pp. 127–150). New York: W. H. Freeman.

Mayer, R. (1991). Teaching of thinking skills in the sciences and in mathematics. In D. F. Halpern (Ed.), *Enhancing thinking skills in the sciences and mathematics*. Hillsdale, NJ: Lawrence Erlbaum Associates.

Mazur, A., & Robertson, L. S. (1972). *Biology and social behavior*. New York: The Free Press.

McCardle, P., & Wilson, B. E. (1990). Hormonal influence on language development in physically advanced children. *Brain and Language, 38,* 410–423.

McCauley, E., Kay, T., Ito, J., & Treder, B. (1987). The Turner Syndrome: Cognitive deficits, affective discrimination, and behavior problems. *Child Development, 58,* 464–473.

McCloy, T. M., & Koonce, J. M. (1982). Sex as a moderator variable in the selection and training of persons for a skilled task. *Aviation, Space, and Environmental Medicine, 53,* 1170–1172.

McClurg, P. A., & Chaille, C. (1987). Computer games: Environments for developing spatial cognition? *Journal of Educational Computing Research, 3,* 95–111.

McEwen, B. S. (1981). Neural gonadal steroid actions. *Science, 211,* 1303–1311.

McGee, M. G. (1979). Human spatial abilities: Psychometric studies and environmental, genetic, hormonal, and neurological influences. *Psychological Bulletin, 86,* 889–918.

McGhee, M. (1976). Laterality, hand preference, and human spatial ability. *Perceptual Motor Skills, 42,* 781–782.

McGlone, J. (1980). Sex differences in human brain asymmetry: A critical survey. *The Behavioral and Brain Sciences, 3,* 215–227.

McGuiness, D. (1976). Sex differences in the organization of perception and cognition. In B. Lloyd & J. Archer (Eds.), *Exploring sex differences* (pp. 123–156). New York: Academic Press.

McHugh, M. C., Koeske, R. D., & Frieze, I. H. (1986). Issues to consider in conducting nonsexist research: A guide for researchers. *American Psychologist, 41,* 879–890.

McKeever, W. F. (1986). The influences of handedness, sex, familial sinistrality and androgyny on language laterality, verbal ability and spatial ability. *Cortex, 22,* 521–537.

McKeever, W. F., & Van Deventer, A. D. (1977). Visual and auditory language processing asymmetries: Influence of handedness, familial sinistrality, and sex. *Cortex, 13,* 225–241.

Mead, M. (1961). *Coming of age in Samoa; A psychological study of primitive youth for Western Civilization.* New York: Morrow.

Mebert, C. J., & Michel, G. F. (1980). Handedness in artists. In J. Herron (Ed.), *Neuropsychology of left-handedness.* New York: Academic.

Meece, J. L. (1987). The influence of school experiences on the development of gender schemata. In L. S. Liben & M. L. Signorella (Eds.), *Children's Gender Schemata* (pp. 57–73). New Directions for Child Development. No 38. San Francisco: Jossey-Bass.

Meece, J. L., Eccles-Parsons, J., Kaczala, C. M., Goff, S. B., & Futterman, R. (1982). Sex differences in math achievement: Toward a model of academic choice. *Psychological Bulletin, 91,* 324–448.

Meeker, B. F., & Weitzel-O'Neill, P. A. (1977). Sex roles and interpersonal behavior in task-oriented groups. *American Sociological Review, 42,* 91–104.

Meyer-Bahlburg, H. F. L., & Ehrhardt, A. A. (1977). Effects of prenatal hormone treatment on mental abilities. In R. Gemme & C. C. Wheeler (Eds.), *Progress in sexology* (pp. 85–92). New York: Plenum.

Mills, C. J. (1981). Sex roles, personality, and intellectual abilities in adolescents. *Journal of Youth and Adolescence, 10,* 85–112.

Mischel, W. (1966). A social-learning view of sex differences in behavior. In E. E. Maccoby (Ed.), *The development of sex differences* (pp. 56–81). Stanford: Stanford University Press.

Molfese, D. L. (1990). Auditory evoked responses recorded from 16-month-old human infants to words they did and did not know. *Brain and Language, 38,* 345–363.

Money, J. (1986). Lovemaps: Clinical concepts of sexual/erotic health and pathology, paraphilia, and gender transposition in childhood, adolescence, and maturity. New York: Irvington.

Money, J. (1987). Propaedutics of ducious G-I/R: Theoretical foundations for understanding dimorphic gender-identity/role. In J. M. Reinisch, L. A. Rosenblum, & S. A. Sanders (Eds.), *Masculinity/femininity: Basic perspectives* (pp. 13–34). New York: Oxford.

Money, J., & Ehrhardt, A. A. (1972). *Man & woman, boy & girl*. Baltimore, MD: The Johns Hopkins University Press.

Moore, T. (1967). Language and intelligence: A longitudinal study of the first eight years. *Human Development, 10*, 88–106.

Morrow, L., & Ratcliff, G. (1988). Neuropsychology of spatial cognition: Evidence from cerebral lesions. In J. Stiles-Davis, M. Kritchevsky, & U. Bellugi (Eds.), *Spatial cognition: Brain bases and development* (pp. 5–32). Hillsdale, NJ: Lawrence Erlbaum Associates.

Murdock, K. R., & Forsyth, D. R. (1985). Is gender-biased language sexist? A perceptual approach. *Psychology of Women Quarterly, 9*, 39–49.

Murphy, K. R. (1990). If the null hypothesis is impossible, why test it? *American Psychologist, 45*, 403–404.

Nagae, S. (1985). Handedness and sex differences in selective interference of verbal and spatial information. *Journal of Experimental Psychology: Human Perception and Performance, 11*, 346–354.

Nash, S. C. (1975). The relationship among sex-role stereotyping, sex-role preference, and the sex difference in spatial visualization. *Sex Roles, 1*, 15–32.

Nash, S. C. (1979). Sex role as a mediator of intellectual functioning. In M. A. Wittig & A. C. Petersen (Eds.), *Sex-related differences in cognitive functioning: Developmental issues* (pp. 263–302). New York: Academic Press.

National Educational Association. (1989). *The NEA 1989 almanac of higher education*. Washington, DC: Author.

Nayak, R., & Dash, A. S. (1987). Effects of grade, sex, nutritional status and time of testing on children's Stroop scores. *Psycho-Lingua, 17*, 87–93.

Neils, J. R., & Aram, D. M. (1986). Handedness and sex of children with developmental language disorders. *Brain and Language, 28*, 53–65.

Newcombe, N. S., & Baenninger, M. (1989). Biological change and cognitive ability in adolescence. In G. R. Adams, R. Montemayor, & T. P. Gullota (Eds.), *Biology of adolescent behavior and development* (pp. 168–191). Newbury Park, CA: Sage.

Newcombe, N., Bandura, M., & Taylor, D. G. (1983). Sex differences in spatial ability and spatial activities. *Sex Roles, 9*, 377–386.

Newcombe, N., & Dubas, J. S. (1987). Individual differences in cognitive ability: Are they related to timing of puberty? In R. M. Lerner & T. T. Foch (Eds.), *Biological-psychosocial interactions in early adolescence: A lifespan perspective* (pp. 249–302). Hillsdale, NJ: Lawrence Erlbaum Associates.

Newcombe, N., Dubas, J. S., & Baenninger, M. (1989). Associations of timing of puberty, spatial ability, and lateralization in adult women. *Child Development, 60*, 246–254.

Newsweek (July 16, 1990). The daughter track (pp. 48–54).

New Woman. (January, 1990). Stereotypes 'R' Us. p. 20.

Ninio, A. (1987). A comparison of mothers' and fathers' beliefs concerning the timetable of cognitive development in infancy. *Israel Social Science Research, 5*, 6–16.

Noble, K. D. (1987). The dilemma of the gifted woman. *Psychology of Women Quarterly, 11*, 367–378.

Nyborg, H. (1983). Spatial ability in men and women: Review and new theory. *Advances in Behaviour Research and Therapy, 5*, 89–140.

Nyborg, H. (1984). Performance and intelligence in hormonally different groups. In G. J. De Vries,

J. De Bruin, H. Uylings, & M. Cormer (Eds.), *Progress in Brain Research,* (61, pp. 491–508). Amsterdam: Elsevier Science Publishers.

Nyborg, H. (1988). Mathematics, sex hormones, and brain function. *Behavioral and Brain Sciences, 11,* 206–207.

Nyborg, H. (1990). Sex hormones, brain development, and spatio-perceptual strategies in Turner Syndrome. In D. B. Berch & B. G. Bender (Eds.), *Sex chromosome abnormalities and human behavior* (pp. 100-128). Washington, DC: American Association for the Advancement of Science.

O'Boyle, M. W., & Benbow, C. P. (1990). Handedness and its relationship to ability and talent. In S. Coren (Ed.), *Left-handedness: Behavioral implications and anomalies* (pp. 343–372). North Holland: Elsevier Science Publishers.

O'Brien, M., & Nagle, K. J. (1987). Parents' speech to toddlers: The effect of play context. *Journal of Child Language, 14,* 269–279.

O'Kelly, C. G. (1980). *Women and men in society.* New York: Van Nostrand.

Orwin, R. G., & Cordray, D. S. (1985). Effects of deficient reporting on meta-analysis: A conceptual framework and reanalysis. *Psychological Bulletin, 97,* 134–147.

Paludi, M. A., & Bauer, W. D. (1983). Goldberg revisited: What's in an author's name? *Sex Roles, 9,* 387–390.

Paludi, M. A., & Strayer, L. A. (1985). What's in an author's name? Differential evaluations of performance as a function of author's name. *Sex Roles, 12,* 353–361.

Patlak, M. (1990, March 19). Starting point. *Los Angeles Times,* p. B2.

Pearson, J. L., & Ferguson, L. R. (1989). Gender differences in patterns of spatial ability, environmental cognition, and math and English achievement in late adolescence. *Adolescence, 24,* 421–431.

Peil, C. L. (1990). *Literacy, school reform, and literature based reading programs.* Unpublished master's thesis. Submitted to the Faculty at California State University, San Bernardino.

Pellegrini, A. D. (1987). Rough-and-tumble play: Developmental and educational significance. *Educational Psychologist, 22,* 23–43.

Pennington, B. F., Smith, S. D., Kimberling, W. J., Green, P. A., & Haith, M. M. (1987). Left-handedness and immune disorders in familial dyslexics. *Archives of Neurology, 44,* 434–439.

Perry, D. G., & Bussey, K. (1979). The social learning theory of sex differences: Imitation is alive and well. *Journal of Personality and Social Psychology, 37,* 1699–1712.

Petersen, A. C. (1976). Physical androgyny and cognitive functioning in adolescence. *Developmental Psychology, 12,* 524–533.

Petersen, A. C. (1980). Biopsychosocial processes in the development of sex-related differences. In J. E. Parsons (Ed.), *The psychobiology of sex differences and sex roles* (pp. 31–55). Washington, D.C.: Hemisphere.

Petersen, A. C., & Crockett, L. (1985, August). Factors influencing sex differences in spatial ability across the lifespan. Symposium conducted at the Ninety-third Annual Convention of the American Psychological Association, Los Angeles, CA.

Petersen, A. C., & Crockett, L. J. (1987). Biological correlates of spatial ability and mathematical performance. In J. A. Sechzer & S. M. Pfafflin (Eds.), *Psychology and educational policy* (pp. 69–86). New York: The New York Academy of Sciences.

Petersen, A. C., & Hood, K. D. (1988). The role of experience in cognitive performance and brain development. In G. M. Vroman (Ed.), *Genes and gender: V women at work: Socialization toward inequality* (pp. 52–77). New York: The Gordian Press.

Pheterson, G. I., Kiesler, S. B., & Goldberg, P. A. (1971). Evaluation of the performance of women as a function of their sex, achievement, and personal history. *Journal of Personality and Social Psychology, 19,* 114–118.

Piaget, J., & Inhelder, B. (1956). *The child's conception of space.* London: Routledge Kegan Paul.

Piazza, D. M. (1980). The influence of sex and handedness in the hemispheric specialization of verbal and nonverbal tasks. *Neuropsychologia, 18,* 163–176.

Plake, B. S., Loyd, B. H., & Hoover, H. D. (1981). Sex differences in mathematics components of the Iowa Test of Basic Skills. *Psychology of Women Quarterly, 5,* 780–784.

Plomin, R. (1989). Environment and genes. *American Psychologist, 44,* 105–111.

Plomin, R. (1990). *Nature and nurture: An introduction to human behavioral genetics.* Pacific Grove, CA: Brooks/Cole.

Pontius, A. A. (1989). Color and spatial error in block design in stone-age Auca Indians: Ecological underuse of occipital-parietal system in men and of frontal lobes in women. *Brain and Cognition, 10,* 54–75.

Poole, C., & Stanley, G. (1972). A factorial and predictive study of spatial abilities. *Australian Journal of Psychology, 24,* 317–320.

Porac, C., & Coren, S. (1981). *Lateral preference and human behavior.* New York: Springer-Verlag.

Ramist, L., & Arbeiter, S. (1986). *Profiles, college-bound seniors, 1985.* New York: College Entrance Examination Board.

Rammsayer, T., & Lustnauer, S. (1989). Sex differences in time perception. *Perceptual and Motor Skills, 68,* 195–198.

Ray, W. J., Newcombe, N., Semon, J., & Cole, P. M. (1981). Spatial abilities, sex differences and EEG functioning. *Neuropsychologia, 19,* 719–722.

Rebok, G. W. (1987). *Life-span cognitive development.* New York: Holt, Rinehart & Winston.

Reinisch, J. (1981). Prenatal exposure to synthetic progestins increases potential for aggression in humans. *Science, 211,* 1171–1173.

Reinisch, J. M., Rosenblum, L. A., & Sanders, S. A. (1987). Masculinity/femininity: An introduction. In J. M. Reinisch, L. A. Rosenblum, & S. A. Sanders (Eds.), *Masculinity/femininity: Basic perspectives* (pp. 3–10). New York: Oxford University Press.

Resnick, S. M., Berenbaum, S. A., Gottesman, I. I., & Bouchard, T. J., Jr. (1986). Early hormonal influences of cognitive functioning in congenital adrenal hyperplasia. *Developmental Psychology, 22,* 191–198.

Richardson, J. T. (1976). How to measure laterality. *Neuropsychologia, 14,* 135–136.

Richardson, L., & Taylor, V. (Eds.). (1989). *Feminist frontiers II: Rethinking sex, gender, and society.* New York: McGraw-Hill

Ricketts, M. (1989). Epistemological values of feminists in psychology. *Psychology of Women Quarterly, 13,* 401–415.

Riefer, D. (1990). *Effect size statistics.* Unpublished manuscript. California State University Department of Psychology, San Bernardino.

Roan, S. (1990, August 3). Sex, ethnic bias in medical research raises questions. *Los Angeles Times,* pp. A1, A25.

Robert, M. (1990). Sex typing of the water-level task: There is more than meets the eye. *International Journal of Psychology, 25,* 475–490.

Robert, M. (1989, July). *Robustness of cognitive gender differences: The case of horizontality representations in the water-level task.* Paper presented at the Tenth Biennieal Meeting of the International Society for the Study of Behavioursl Development, Jyvaskyla, Finland.

Robert, M., & Chaperon, H. (1989). Cognitive and exemplary modelling of horizontality representation on the Piagetian water-level task. *International Journal of Behavioral Development, 12,* 453–472.

Robert, M., & Tanquay, M. (in press). Perception and representation of the Euclidean coordinates in mature and elderly men and women. *Experimental Aging Research.*

Rodin, J., & Ickovics, J. R. (1990). Women's health: Review and research agenda as we approach the 21st century. *American Psychologist, 45,* 1018–1034.

Rosenstein, L. D., & Bigler, E. D. (1987). No relationship between handedness and sexual preference. *Psychological Reports, 60,* 704–706.

Rosenthal, R. (1966). *Experimenter effects in behavioral research.* New York: Appleton-Century-Crofts.

Rosenthal, R., & Rubin, D. B. (1982). Further meta-analytic procedures for assessing cognitive gender differences. *Journal of Educational Psychology, 74,* 708–712.

Rosenthal, R., & Rubin, D. B. (1985). Statistical analysis: Summarizing evidence versus establishing facts. *Psychological Bulletin, 97,* 527–529.

Rossi, J. S. (1983). Ratios exaggerate gender differences in mathematical ability. *American Psychologist, 38,* 348.

Rovet, J., & Netley, C. (1979). Phenotypic vs. genotypic sex and cognitive abilities. *Behavior Genetics, 9,* 317–321.

Rozeboom, W. W. (1960). The fallacy of the null-hypothesis significance test. *Psychological Bulletin, 57,* 416–428.

Rubin, J., Provenzano, F., & Luria, Z. (1974). The eye of the beholder: Parents' views on sex of newborns. *American Journal of Orthopsychiatry, 44,* 512–519.

Rudel, R. G., Denckla, M. B., & Spalten, E. (1973). The functional asymmetry of Braille letter learning in normal sighted children. *Neurology, 24,* 733–738.

Ruse, M. (1987). Sociobiology and knowledge: Is evolutionary epistemology a viable option? In C. Crawford, M. Smith, & D. Krebs (Eds.), *Sociobiology and psychology: Ideas, issues and applications* (pp. 63–79). Hillsdale, NJ: Lawrence Erlbaum Associates.

Russett, C. E. (1989). *Sexual science: The Victorian constructions of womanhood.* Cambridge, MA: Harvard University Press.

Ryckman, D. B., & Peckham, P. (1987). Gender differences in attributions for success and failure situations across subject areas. *Journal of Educational Research, 81,* 120–125.

Sadker, M., & Sadker, D. (1985). Sexism in the schoolroom of the 80's. *Psychology Today, 19,* 54–57.

Safir, M. P. (1986). The effects of nature or of nurture on sex differences in intellectual functioning: Israeli findings. *Sex Roles, 14,* 581–590.

Sanders, B., & Soares, M. P. (1986). Sexual maturation and spatial ability in college students. *Developmental Psychology, 22,* 199–203.

Sanders, B., Soares, M. P., & D'Aquila, J. M. (1982). The sex difference on one test of spatial visualization: A nontrivial difference. *Child Development, 53,* 1106–1110.

Sanders, G., & Ross-Field, L. (1986). Sexual orientation and visual-spatial ability. *Brain and Cognition, 5,* 280–290.

Schaie, K. W. (1987). Aging and human performance. In M. W. Riley, J. D. Matarazzo, & A. Baum (Eds.), *Perspectives in behavioral medicine: The aging dimension* (pp. 29–37). Hillsdale, NJ: Lawrence Erlbaum Associates.

Schiff, W., & Oldak, R. (1990). Accuracy of judging time to arrival: Effects of modality, trajectory, and gender. *Journal of Experimental Psychology, Human Perception and Performance, 16,* 303–316.

Schwartz, F. N. (1989, Jan/Feb). Executives and organizations: Management women and the new facts of life. *Harvard Business Review,* p. 65.

Sells, L. W. (1980). The mathematics filter and the education of women and minorities. In L. H. Fox, & D. Tobin (Eds.), *Women and the mathematical mystique* (pp. 66–75). Baltimore, MD: The Johns Hopkins University Press.

Serbin, L. A., & Sprafkin, C. (1986). The salience of gender and the process of sex typing in three- to seven-year-old children. *Child Development, 57,* 1188–1199.

Seth-Smith, M., Ashton. R., & McFarland, K. (1989). A dual-task study of sex differences in language reception and production. *Cortex, 25,* 425–431.

Seward, J. P., & Seward, G. H. (1980). *Sex differences: Mental and temperamental.* Lexington, MA: D. C. Heath.

Shepard, R. N., & Metzler, J. (1971). Mental rotation of three dimensional objects. *Science, 171,* 701–703.

Sherman, J. A. (1967). Problems of sex differences in space perception and aspects of intellectual functioning. *Psychological Review, 74,* 290–299.

Sherman, J. A. (1977). Effects of biological factors on sex-related differences in mathematics achievement. In L. H. Fox, E. Fennema, & J. Sherman (Eds.), *Women and mathematics: Research perspectives for change* (pp. 137–206). Washington, D.C.: National Institute of Education.

Sherman, J. A. (1978). *Sex-related cognitive differences: An essay on theory and evidence.* Springfield, IL: Charles C. Thomas.

Sherman, J. A. (1979). Cognitive performance as a function of sex and handedness: An evaluation of the Levy hypothesis. *Psychology of Women Quarterly, 3,* 378–390.

Sherman, J. A. (1980). Mathematics, spatial visualization, and related factors: Changes in girls and boys grades 8–11. *Journal of Educational Psychology, 72,* 476–482.

Sherman, J. A. (1982a). Continuing in mathematics: A longitudinal study of the attitudes of high school girls. *Psychology of Women Quarterly, 72,* 132–140.

Sherman, J. A. (1982b). Mathematics the critical filter: A look at some residues. *Psychology of Women Quarterly, 6,* 428–444.

Sherman, J. A. (1983). Girls talk about mathematics and their future: A partial replication. *Psychology of Women Quarterly, 7,* 338–342.

Sherwin, B. B. (1988). Estrogen and/or androgen replacement therapy and cognitive functioning in surgically menopausal women. *Psychoneuroendocrinology 13,* 345–357.

Shields, S. A. (1975). Functionalism, Darwinism, and the psychology of women: A study in the social myth. *American Psychologist, 30,* 739–754.

Shields, S. A. (1980). Nineteenth-century evolutionary theory and male scientific bias. In G. W. Barlow & J. Silverberg (Eds.), *Sociobiology: Beyond nature/nurture* (pp. 489–502). Boulder, CO: Westview Press.

Shucard, D. W., Shucard, J. L., & Thomas, D. G. (1987). Sex differences in electrophysiological activity in infancy: Possible implications for language development. In S. U. Philips, S. Steele, & C. Tanz (Eds.), *Language, gender, and sex in comparative perspective* (pp. 278–295). Cambridge, England: Cambridge University Press.

Shuter-Dyson, R., & Gabriel, C. (1982). *The psychology of musical ability* (2nd ed.). London: Methuen.

Signorella, M., & Jamison, W. (1986). Masculinity, femininity, androgyny, and cognitive performance: A meta-analysis. *Psychological Bulletin, 100,* 207–228.

Signorella, M. L., & Liben, L. S. (1984). Recall and reconstruction of gender-related pictures: Effects of attitude, task difficulty, and age. *Child Development, 55,* 393–405.

Signorielli, N. (1989). Television and conceptions about sex roles: Maintaining conventionality and the status quo. *Sex Roles, 21,* Nos. 5/6.

Singer, G., & Montgomery, R. B. (1969). Comment on "role of activation and inhibition in sex differences in cognitive abilities." *Psychological Review, 76,* 325–327.

Singer, J. M., & Stake, J. E. (1986). Mathematics and self-esteem: Implications for women's career choice. *Psychology of Women Quarterly, 10,* 339–352.

Skelton, G. (1990, April 12). As women climb political ladder, sterotypes follow. *Los Angeles Times Los Angeles Times* (pp. A1, A24–A25).

Skinner, P. H., & Shelton, R. L. (1985). *Speech, language, and hearing: Normal processes and disorders* (2nd ed.). New York: Wiley.

Smith, J. (1987). Left-handedness: Its association with allergic disease. *Neuropsychologia, 25,* 665–674.

Smith, G. A., & McPhee, K. A. (1987). Performance on a coincidence timing task correlates with intelligence. *Intelligence, 11,* 161–167.

Smolak, L. (1986). *Infancy.* Englewood Cliffs, NJ: Prentice-Hall.

Smotherman, W. P., & Robinson, S. R. (1990). The prenatal origins of behavioral organization. *Psychological Science, 1,* 97–106.

Sonnenfeld, J. (1985). Tests of spatial skill: A validation problem. *Man-Environment Systems, 15,* 107–120.

Spence, J. T., & Helmreich, R. (1978). *Masculinity and femininity: Their psychological dimensions, correlates, and antecedents.* Austin: University of Texas Press.

Spence, J. T., & Helmreich, R. L. (1983). Achievement-related motives and behaviors. In J. T. Spence (Ed.), *Achievement and achievement motives: Psychological and sociological approaches* (pp. 7–74). San Francisco: W. H. Freeman.

Spence, J. T., Helmreich, R. L., & Stapp, J. (1974). The personal attributes questionnaire: A measure of sex role stereotypes and masculinity-femininity. *JSAS Catalog of Selected Documents in Psychology, 4,* 43.

Spiers, P. A. (1987). Acalcxlia revisited: Current issues. In G. Deloche & X. Seron (Eds.), *Mathematical disabilities: A cognitive neuropsychological perspective* (pp. 1–25). Hillsdale, NJ: Lawrence Erlbaum Associates.

Sprafkin, C., Serbin, L. A., Denier, C., & Connor, J. M. (1983). Sex-differentiated play: Cognitive consequences and early interventions. In M. B. Liss (Ed.), *Social and cognitive skills* (pp. 167–192). New York: Academic Press.

Springer, S. P., & Deutsch, G. (1989). *Left brain, right brain* (3rd ed.). New York: W. H. Freeman.

Srivastava, A. K. (1989). A study of field dependence-independence among Mizo children. *Psychological Studies, 34,* 55–58.

Stafford, R. E. (1961). Sex differences in spatial visualization as evidence of sex-linked inheritance. *Perceptual and Motor Skills, 13,* 428.

Stafford, R. E. (1963). An investigation of similarities in parent-child test scores for evidence of hereditary components. (RB-63-11). Princeton: Educational Testing Service.

Stafford, R. E. (1972). Hereditary and environmental components of quantitative reasoning. *Review of Educational Research, 42,* 183–201.

Stage, C. (1988). Gender differences in test results. *Scandinavian Journal of Educational Research, 32,* 101–111.

Stage, E. K., & Karplus, R. (1981). (Letters) Mathematical ability: Is sex a factor? *Science, 212,* 114.

Stangor, C., & Ruble, D. N. (1987). Development of gender role knowledge and gender constancy. *New Directions for Child Development, 38,* 5–22.

Stanley, J. (1990, January 10). We need to know why women falter in math [Letter to the editor]. *The Chronicle of Higher Education* p. B4.

Stanley, J. C., & Benbow, C. P. (1982). Huge sex ratios at upper end. *American Psychologist, 37,* 972.

Steen, L. (1987). Mathematics education: A predictor of scientific competitiveness. *Science, 237,* 251–251; 302.

Sternberg, R. J. (1985). *Beyond IQ: A triarchic theory of human intelligence.* New York: Cambridge University Press.

Stewart, V. (1976). Spatial influences on sex differences in behavior. In M. S. Teitelbaum (Ed.), *Sex differences: Social and biological perspectives* (pp. 138–174). Garden City, NY: Anchor Books.

Stones, I., Beckmann, M., & Stephens, L. (1982). Sex-related differences in mathematical competencies of pre-calculus college students. *School Science and Mathematics, 82,* 295–299.

Sue, S., & Okazaki, S. (1990). Asian-American educational achievements: A phenomenon in search of an explanation. *American Psychologist, 45,* 913–920.

Sutaria, S. D. (1985). *Specific learning disabilities: Nature and needs.* Springfield, IL: Charles C. Thomas.

Swim, J., Borgida, E., Maruyama, G., & Myers, D. G. (1989). Joan McKay versus John McKay: Do gender stereotypes bias evaluations? *Psychological Bulletin, 105,* 409–429.

Tanner, J. M. (1962). *Growth at adolescence.* Oxford: Blackwell Scientific.

Teng, E. L. (1981). Dichotic ear difference is a poor index for the functional symmetry between the cerebral hemispheres. *Neuropsychologia, 19,* 235–240.

Thomas, H. (1983). Familial correlational analyses, sex differences, and the X-linked gene hypothesis. *Psychological Bulletin, 93,* 427–440.

Thomas, H., Jamison, W., & Hummel, D. D. (1973). Observation is insufficient for discovering that the surface of still water is invariantly horizontal. *Science, 181,* 173–174.

Thurstone, L. L., & Thurstone, T. G. (1941). *Factorial studies of intelligence.* Chicago: University of Chicago Press.

Tiger, L. (1970, October). Male dominance? Yes, Alas. A sexist ploy? No. *The New York Times Magazine,* pp. 35–37, 124–127, 132–138.

Tiger, L. (1988). Sex differences in mathematics: Why the fuss? *Behavioral and Brain Sciences, 11,* 212.

Time (Fall, 1990). Special issue: Women: The road ahead. New York: Time Inc. Magazine Co.

Tinkcom, M., Obrzut, J. E., & Poston, C. S. (1983). Spatial lateralization: The relationship among sex, handedness and familial sinistrality. *Neuropsychologia, 21,* 683–686.

Tomizuka, C., & Tobias, S. (1981). (Letters) Mathematical ability: Is sex a factor? *Science, 212,* 114.

Unger, R. K. (1979). *Female and male: Psychological perspectives.* New York: Harper & Row.

Unger, R. K. (Ed.). (1989). *Representations: Social construction of gender.* Amityville, NY: Baywood.

U.S. Bureau of the Census. (1989). *Statistical abstract of the United States 1989* (109th ed.). Washington, DC: U.S. Government Printing Office.

Valdez, R. L., & Gutek, B. A. (1986). Family roles a help or a hindrance for working women? In B. A. Gutek & L. Larwood (Eds.), *Women's career development* (pp. 157–169). Newbury Park, CA: Sage.

Valentine, S. Z., & Brodsky, S. L. (1989). Personal construct theory and stimulus sex and subject sex differences. In R. K. Unger (Ed.), *Representations: Social constructions of gender* (pp. 112–125). Amityville, NY: Baywood.

Vandenberg, S. G. (1968). Primary mental abilities or general intelligence? Evidence from twin studies. In J. M. Thoday & A. S. Parkes (Eds.), *Genetic and environmental influences on behavior* (pp. 146–160). New York: Plenum.

Vandenberg, S. G. (1987). Sex differences in mental retardation and their implications for sex differences in ability. In J. M. Reinisch, L. A. Rosenblum, & S. A. Sanders (Eds.), *Masculinity/femininity: Basic perspectives* (pp. 157–171). New York: Oxford.

Vandenberg, S. G. (1975). Sources of variance in performance of spatial tests. In J. Eliot & N. J. Salkind (Eds.), *Children's spatial development.* Springfield, IL: Charles C. Thomas.

Vandenberg, S. G. (1969). A twin study of spatial ability. *Multivariate Behavioral Research, 4,* 273–294.

Vernon, P. A. (1987). New developments in reaction time research. In P. A. Vernon (Ed.), *Speed of information processing and intelligence* (pp. 1–20). Norwood, NJ: Ablex.

Visser, D. (1987). Sex differences in adolescent mathematics behavior. *South African Journal of Psychology, 17,* 137-144.

Voyer, D., & Bryden, M. P. (1990). Gender, level of spatial ability, and lateralization. *Brain and Cognition, 13,* 18–29.

Waber, D. P. (1976). Sex differences in cognition: A function of maturation rate? *Science, 192,* 572–574.

Waber, D. P. (1977). Sex differences in mental abilities, hemispheric lateralization, and rate of physical growth at adolescence. *Developmental Psychology, 13,* 29–38.

Wallis, C. (1989, December 4). Onward, women! *Time,* pp. 80–82, 85–86, 89.

Weisstein, N. (1972). Psychology constructs the female. In V. Gornick & B. K. Moran (Eds.), *Women in sexist society* (pp. 207–224). New York: New American Library.

Weisstein, N. (1982, November). Tired of arguing about biological inferiority? *Ms.,* pp. 41–46, 85.

Welford, A. T. (1980). Relationship between reaction time and fatigue, stress, age, and sex. In A. T. Welford (Ed.), *Reaction times* (pp. 321–354). London: Academic.

Wells, G. (1986). Variation in child language. In P. Fletcher & M. Garman (Eds.), *Language acquisition: Studies in first language development* (pp. 109–139). Cambridge, England: Cambridge University Press.

Wentzel, K. R. (1988). Gender differences in math and English achievement: A longitudinal study. *Sex Roles, 18* (11,12), 691–699.

Westkott, M. (1979). Feminist criticism of the social sciences. *Harvard Educational Review, 49,* 422–430.

Williams, J. E., & Best, D. L. (1982). *Measuring sex stereotypes. A thirty-nine nation study.* Beverly Hills, CA: Sage Publications.

Williams, J. H. (1977). *Psychology of women: Behavior in a biosocial context.* New York: W. W. Norton.

Williams, J. H. (1983). *Psychology of women: Behavior in a biosocial context* (2nd Ed.). New York: W. W. Norton.

Willis, S. L., & Schaie, K. W. (1988). *Sex Roles, 18* (3/4), 189–203.

Winograd, E., & Simon, E. V. (1980). Visual memory and imagery in the aged. In L. W. Poon, J. L. Fozard, L. S. Cermak, D. Arenberg, & L. W. Thompson (Eds.), *New directions in memory and aging: Proceedings of the George A. Talland Memorial Conference* (pp. 485–506). Hillsdale, NJ: Lawrence Erlbaum Associates.

Witelson, S. I. (1976). Sex and the single hemisphere: Specialization of the right hemisphere for spatial processing. *Science, 193,* 425–427.

Witelson, S. F. (1985). The brain connection: The corpus callosum is larger in left handers. *Science, 229,* 665–668.

Witelson, S. F. (1988). Neuroanatomical sex differences: of consequence for cognition? *Behavioral and Brain Sciences, 11,* 215–217.

Witelson, S. F. (1989). Hand and sex differences in the isthmus and genu of the human corpus callosum. *Brain, 112,* 799–835.

Witelson, S. F., & Kigar, D. L. (1988). Anatomical development of the human corpus callosum: A review with reference to sex and cognition. In D. L. Molfese & S. J. Segalowitz (Eds.), *Brain lateralization in children: Developmental implications* (pp. 35–58). New York: Guilford.

Witkin, H. A. (1950). Individual differences in case of perception of embedded figures. *Journal of Personality, 19,* 1–15.

Witkin, H. A., Dyk, R. B., Faterson, H. F., Goodenough, D. G., & Karp, S. A. (1962). *Psychological differentiation.* New York: Wiley.

Witkin, H. A., Lewis, H. B., Hertzman, M., Machover, K., Meissner, P. B., & Wapner, S. (1954). *Personality through perception.* New York: Harper & Row.

Wittig, M. A. (1985). Metatheoretical dilemmas in the psychology of gender. *American Psychologist, 40,* 800–811.

Wittig, M. A., & Allen, M. J. (1984). Measurement of adult performance on Piaget's water horizontality task. *Intelligence, 8,* 305–313.

Wolf, M., & Gow, D. (1985–1986). A longitudinal investigation of gender differences in language and reading development. *First Language, 6,* 81–110.

Wright, R. (1990, August 19). Black scars, white fears. *Los Angeles Time Magazine,* 10–16, 34–35, 39.

Wrightsman, L. S. (1977). *Social psychology* (2nd ed.), Monterey, CA: Brooks/Cole.

Yee, D. K., & Eccles, J. S. (1988). Parent perceptions and attributions for children's math achievement. *Sex Roles, 19,* (5/6), 317–333.

Yen, W. M. (1975). Independence of hand preference and sex-linked genetic effects of spatial performance. *Perceptual Motor Skills, 41,* 311–318.

Yeo, R. A., & Cohen, D. B. (1983). Familiar sinistrality and sex differences in cognitive abilities. *Cortex, 19,* 125–130.

Author Index

Subject Index

A

Abilities
  age of subjects in samples and, 38-39
  Use of term, 19
  see also Cognitive abilities, Mathematical abilities, Quantitative abilities; Spatial abilities; Verbal abilities; Visual-spatial abilities
Ability tests, 10-11
Acalculia, 167
Achievement motivation, 207-208, 225
Achievement tests, 11, 60
Activity level, effect size indicators in, 54
Adolescence
  aggression in, 62
  body type as variable in, 168
  career choices in, 218
  intellectual development and decline during, 200-201
  peer interactions in, 198, 200
  sex hormones during, 129, 168
  sex role stereotypes in, 197-203
  sexual orientation and, 134
  see also Puberty
Adulthood
  sensory system changes in, 63
  sex hormones in, 126-132
  sex role stereotypes in, 203-210
African-Americans
  brain structue of, 140, 141
  visual-spatial abilities and, 72

see also Race
Age
  cognitive sex differences and, 62
  generational differences in studies and, 55, 56
  hormone fluctuations and, 110
  interaction of variables with, 54
  maturation rate hypothesis and, 120-126
  mental rotation task and, 72, 122
  quantitative abilities and, 80, 81
  sampling issues in research and, 38, 39
  sensory system changes and, 63
  sex differences in brain responses and, 5
  verbal abilities and, 66, 67, 72
  visual-spatial abilities and, 71-73
Aggressive behavior
  achievement and, 208
  age and level of, 62
  cognitive abilities and, 64
  distributions for, 61
  effect size indicators for, 53
  games and, 202
  measurement of, 62
  prenatal sex hormones and, 114, 115, 168
  sex differences in, 64
American Association of University Women, 207
American College Tests (ACT), 92
American Psychiatric Association, 3
Androgenital syndrome (AGS), 115, 116